To My Dear Son
Sam
Merry Christmas 1999

Love, Dad

THE ULTIMATE
CLASSIC CAR
BOOK

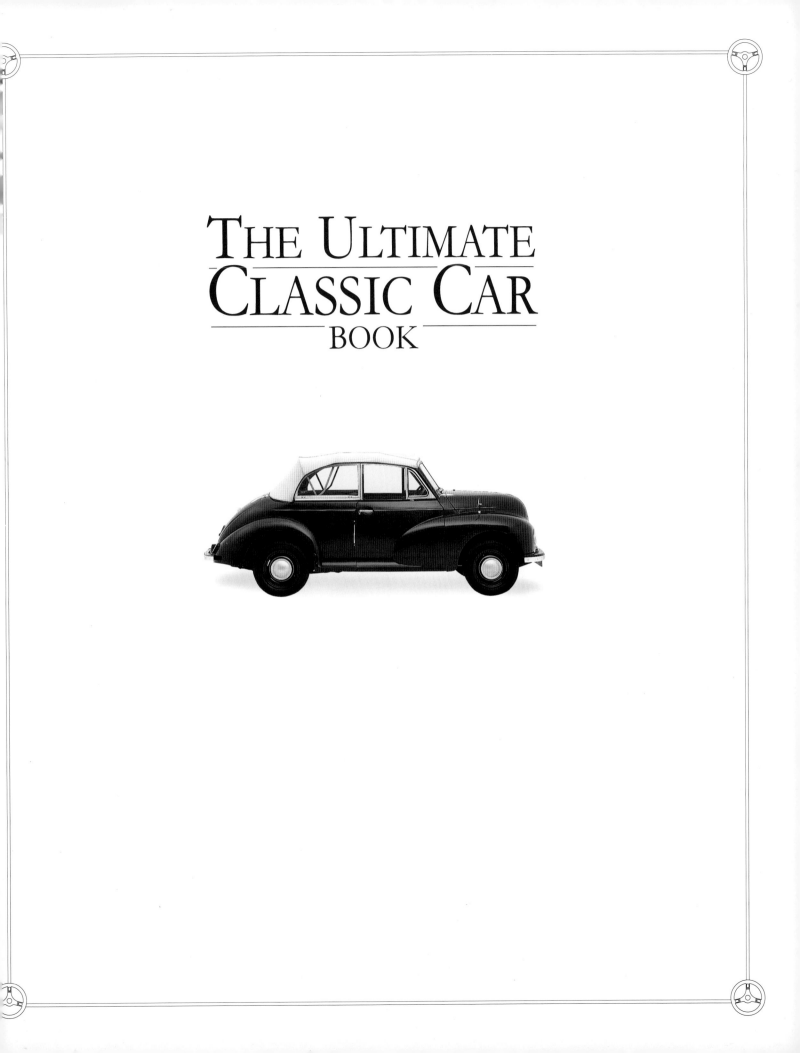

THE ULTIMATE CLASSIC CAR BOOK

Quentin Willson
with *David Selby*

DORLING KINDERSLEY
LONDON • NEW YORK • SYDNEY

A DORLING KINDERSLEY BOOK

PROJECT EDITOR
PHIL HUNT

ART EDITOR
KEVIN RYAN

US EDITOR
JOHN HEILIG

PHOTOGRAPHY
ANDY CRAWFORD, MATTHEW WARD

DESIGNERS
WENDY BARTLET, LUISE ROBERTS

MANAGING EDITOR
KRYSTYNA MAYER

MANAGING ART EDITOR
DEREK COOMBES

DTP DESIGNER
CRESSIDA JOYCE

PRODUCTION CONTROLLER
ADRIAN GATHERCOLE

●

First American Edition, 1995
2 4 6 8 10 9 7 5 3 1

Published in the United States by
Dorling Kindersley Publishing, Inc.,
95 Madison Avenue,
New York, New York 10016

First published in Great Britain in 1995
by Dorling Kindersley Limited,
9 Henrietta Street, London WC2E 8PS

Library of Congress Cataloguing-in-Publication Data

Willson, Quentin.
The ultimate classic car book / by Quentin Willson. – 1st American ed.
p.   cm.
Includes index.

1. Automobiles – Pictorial works. 2. Antique and classic cars –
Collectors and collecting. I. Title.
TL7.A1W48 1995
629.222'022'2–dc20   95–11903
                                                CIP

Color reproduced by Colourscan, Singapore
Printed and bound in Hong Kong by Dai Nippon

●

NOTE ON SPECIFICATION BOXES
Every effort has been made to ensure that the information
supplied in the specification boxes is accurate. As a rule,
engine capacity is measured in cubic inches (cid) for American cars and
cubic centimeters (cc) for all other cars. Power output is expressed as horsepower
(hp) for American cars and brake horsepower (bhp) for all other cars.
A.F.C. is an abbreviation for average fuel consumption.

CONTENTS

Author's Foreword

Between these covers you'll find ninety of what are loosely termed classic cars – a catholic collection of some of the most fascinating motoring confections spanning four decades. There's no particular order or hierarchy, no attempt at a definitive roll of honor. This is a selection of curious cars, products of another age that remind us of the way we were. The biggest problem I've had in compiling this book is deciding which cars should go in and which shouldn't. Not an easy job. Only a fool would argue that a Facel Vega HK500 is a better car than an Mk II Jaguar. It isn't. But the Facel, with its gloriously eccentric Gallic styling, is the more interesting of the two. And that's why it's here and the Jag isn't.

Degas once said that people should be full of those charming little idiosyncrasies without which there is no life. I think it's the same with cars. We prefer them to be interesting, diverting, beguiling even. Classic cars didn't exist before we invented them – a knee-jerk reaction to all that soulless modern metal that looks like it's been carved from a solid block of tungsten. In today's car, efficiency has supplanted aesthetics and technology has displaced charm. Our affair with old cars is purely emotional, fiercely partisan, terminally subjective, and completely without logic or order. And that's why nobody can define exactly what a classic car is. We've been trying for twenty years and still no one has even come close. The best I can do is to say that a classic car makes you smile when you look at it, grin when you drive it, and feel warm approval for the era it evokes. Old cars are awfully good fun.

Quentin Willson

Why Classic?

CLASSIC CARS are simply nostalgia triggers. They're a reminder of how we used to be. Of all the material symbols in society that define our worth and position, the automobile is the most powerful. It's tangible, mobile, and a currency everybody understands. Many of us have an uneasiness with modernity that makes us retrospective creatures. We're drawn back to those decades of change and excitement – hence our love affair with all things of the '50s and '60s. From tall, round-shouldered Frigidaires, neon diner signs, and flamboyant Wurlitzer jukeboxes to sunglasses, clothes, and music, they all appeal to us as talismans of what we remember as golden years.

VEHICLES FOR NOSTALGIA
Classic cars like this AC Ace are not simply quaint mechanical objects, but social monuments that remind us of the way we were.

Part of our Past

And what better transport of delight than the period automobile? The act of buying an old car demonstrates a subliminal desire to revisit our youth. We may say we've bought a beautiful inanimate object in need of restoration, rejuvenation, and preservation, but one of the prime motivations is

surely a need to re-create fond memories. We grew up with old cars, went on vacation in them, were taken to and from school in them, saw them in movies and on TV, and idolized our role models who drove them. They're as much a part of our consciousness as Elvis Presley, miniskirts, Kennedy, Lee Harvey Oswald, Korea, Vietnam, Woodstock, and Jimi Hendrix. It's not surprising that '60s classics are proving the most popular of all. We take one look at an Edsel or a Chevy Impala and realize that the world will never be the same again. Apart from being able to drive them every day (and keep up with modern traffic) they were the cars many of us promised ourselves as children, nose stuck to the showroom window thinking, "some day, some way."

Decades of Change

And we're doing it again with the '80s, another decade of upheaval. Cars like the Mk I Golf GTi, Saab Turbo, Audi Quattro, Jaguar XJS, and Lancia Delta Integrale are already being hailed as emergent classics. We feel the growing urge to cherish them as social sculptures, monuments to a faded lifestyle. Previous generations initiated the preservation of buildings, music, paintings, and literature. As New Age technological sophisticates, we are now choosing to cherish fine examples of the manufactured objects that have become such a dominant feature of our twentieth century past – the automobile. Perhaps this love affair is all about a need for simplicity, a suppression of reality. Modern life can be unromantic, and modern automobiles are mostly clinical, complex things. Who with a soul could not be moved by the wholesome innocence of an MGA or a Bugeye Sprite? With their

1959 EDSEL

POSTWAR STYLING
Cars like the flamboyant Edsel are empirical proof that post-war America really was like Hollywood told us. Their baroque styling shows everything that was right, or indeed wrong, with the swansong years of the most powerful nation on earth.

quaint buttons and switches, dainty gauges, spoked wheels, and hectic styling, they exude an eccentric charm that has no modern-day equivalent.

THE RETRO LOOK
The modern Mazda MX-5 looks like the 1960s Lotus Elan; it trades heavily on our fascination for retro styling.

If you want to know exactly how deeply classic cars have penetrated the suburban psyche, look at a new movement evolving from the car designer's drawing board. For years, car manufacturers thought we wanted the last word in sanitized efficiency. They tried to banish every sensation of noise and movement, sought to purge the automobile of every tremor and vibration. Yet our worship of yesterday's technology, the fact that we actually like an engine that sounds like someone tearing sheets, that we want our instruments to look like instruments and not LCD computer readouts, means that really, if we're honest, we don't want perfection. We want our cars to have personality. When Mazda designed its MX-5 Miata sports car it spent months trying to reproduce the authentic rasping exhaust note of a '60s sports car. It wanted to re-create the past with modern engineering.

Consumer Durables

There's already a detectable movement away from the efficiency and order of modern metal. Most people, if they had the choice, would really prefer something more separate. Our punishment for buying all those blameless zero-defect cars is a plague of bland models with all the passion of a dishwasher. Our obsession with control has made cars look and feel like consumer durables, labor-saving devices to be parked a short step away from the microwave. Mass produced for mass appeal, they lack sexuality, emotion, and excitement. But some car manufacturers have

recognized the fashion for old cars for what it is – a consumer's cry of protest. They've realized that so much retrospective admiration has a point – people prefer cars to look like cars. Jaguar has made its new models look so much like its old ones, because it knows that the Sir William Lyons tradition of swooping curves and chrome grins is actually what people want, and to lose that stylistic blood line would turn its products into pale facsimiles.

The retro look, they say, is back. Witness the latest crop of sports cars with hooded headlights, rakish lines, white dials, and badges in flowing chrome script. Bristling with antique styling features, they're all part of a new wave of cars deliberately sculpted to tap into the vogue for nostalgia. And the classic effect has even touched the occasional mainstream car. Major manufacturers are considering it necessary to add occasional flourishes of Old World dignity with wood and leather interiors and chrome radiator grilles. For all its self-indulgent enthusiasm, the old car movement has had a greater effect than you might think and has influenced the way multinational car makers style their products. It has taken two decades, but now the car mandarins have heard the message. If a large body of people, faced with buying a shiny new sedan or an elderly Austin-Healey, choose the Healey, then it means that classic cars are here to stay.

CLASSIC GLAMOR
Jaguar boss Sir William Lyons hands over an XK120 to Clark Gable. With period visions like this dripping with '50s glamor, how could classic cars fail to capture the popular imagination?

The Classic Car Phenomenon

THIRTY YEARS AGO, the classic car hadn't been invented. There were "old cars," which were the province of the lunatic fringe, feted and adored by characters with twigs in their beards and oil under their fingernails. Before this, during the '50s, vintage and veteran cars had been quietly preened and polished by an insular group of car buffs. In England, clubs like the Vintage Sports Car Club and the Historic Sports Car Club laid down the ground rules. Pre-1919 cars were Edwardian, pre-1931 were Vintage, and a handful of models produced up to the beginning of World War II were loosely named Post-Vintage Thoroughbreds. The icons then were machines like the Bugatti Type 35, Eight Liter Bentley, Duesenberg, Auburn, and Hispano Suiza. These were the Chippendales and Sheratons of an arcane catalog of motorized antiques.

1960s Sports Cars

Then came the 1960s, when Britain invaded the rest of the world with a new secret weapon – the sports car. These were the heady days of the E-Type, MGB, Austin-Healey, and Triumph TR. Roads without speed limits opened up a whole new fantasy world of power, sexuality, and image. Mass production brought beauty and hard-charging performance to the ordinary driver. America came up with the

VETERAN VERSUS CLASSIC
Veteran and vintage cars have never had the mass appeal of '50s and '60s boomer classics. These dignified Edwardians are expensive, need constant tinkering, and can be a liability in modern traffic. More importantly, they are too old to be part of most people's childhood memories and are just museum pieces.

EYE OF THE BEHOLDER
This 1935 Lagonda Rapide might look a million dollars, but most old car fanciers get more excited over a '60s Jaguar E-Type.

THE EXPENSIVE VETERAN
The monstrous 1935 Auburn Supercharged Speedster is prewar American glitz at its finest. But it is really too valuable to use, will only do 100 mph (161 km/h), and requires big biceps to turn the steering wheel. You would need a small fortune to buy, insure, and maintain such a car.

"muscle car" – Mustangs, Corvettes, Chargers, 'Cudas and Firebirds. It was driving's most exciting decade, when a generation let its motoring imagination run riot. But one day the humorless legislators slapped on mandatory speed limits, and choked engine power outputs with sweeping emission regulations. The automobile, they insisted, was getting too big for its boots.

1970s Kitsch

Their legacy was the car-history of the 1970s, a decade of kitsch that spawned machines like the gawky Triumph TR7, the rubber-bumpered MGB, the emasculated Mustangs, the potbellied V-12 E-Type, the truncated Cadillac Seville, and the unlovely Rolls-Royce Camargue. Mainstream cars were even worse. Who will ever forget the Edsel, DeSoto,

Studebaker Lark, Chrysler 180, Datsun Skyline, Volkswagen K70, or AMC Pacer? They were truly awful cars, painted in violent hues, laden with safety devices, and strangled by emission pipery. In desperation, enthusiasts looked backward and found that there was a cornucopia of interesting secondhand vehicles that could be bought for a fraction of the price of new ones. XK Jaguars, MG TFs, Aston Martins, and '60s Maseratis and Ferraris could be bought for the price of a two-year-old Ford. $6,000 was all it took to buy a Ferrari Lusso, $7,000 bought a Dino 246, and forking out $10,000 meant you drove home a genuine AC Cobra.

Cars with Attitude

In October 1973 a British magazine appeared called *Classic Cars*, its alliterative title coining a badly needed generic term. From then on, these old cars with attitude became affectionately known as classics, giving a new name to a hobby that in just ten years would mushroom into a multibillion dollar industry. By 1982 interest in old cars had increased dramatically and the price of an E-Type had risen from $2,000 to around $10,000, Dinos sold for $20,000, and Ferrari Lusso ads were followed by the ominous phrase – Price on Application. Classic cars had become fashion accessories.

SIXTIES CLASSIC
This Ferrari Lusso is the most admired car on the page because it's neat, modern-looking, easy to drive, and summons up the glamorous '60s.

ANOTHER WORLD
This 1933 Duesenberg SJ Speedster is serious collector's stuff and so far removed from most people's sphere of reference that it has assumed the status, not to mention the price tag, of fine art. Cars like this have become the province of the very wealthy — mothballed in heated garages or exhibited as rarefied automotive antiques.

Greatness was suddenly thrust upon old cars. Demand for classics was so huge that values exploded. The real price rises began in 1983 when Ronald Reagan gave the American public tax cuts. Within months, Americans came to England, lavishing their newfound affluence on "collectible" cars, accelerating an unbelievable price spiral in the process. In England, interest rates had fallen, house values soared, and corporate profits were up. The taxman hadn't even dreamed about taxing the capital gain on classic cars, so opportunist speculators moved in. The smart money poured out of the world's stock markets into "investment cars," graphs of appreciation were plotted, and syndicates laid down old cars like fine wine.

In 1984, the first of many banner headlines proclaimed the highest price ever paid for a classic. Sotheby's sold the ex-Woolf Bernato "Blue Train" Speed Six Bentley for a jaw-dropping

MAGAZINE COVERAGE
Classic Cars, *the magazine that really started it all, first appeared in October 1973, and kick-started an automotive revolution – giving voice to a growing disenchantment with modern cars.*

ENGLISH TOURER
This 1934 Bentley 3-liter may be the quintessential prewar English touring car, but, given the choice of a weekend with the Bentley or the Ferrari Testarossa, which would you choose?

FERRARI TESTAROSSA
The Testarossa is exciting because it comes from an exciting decade – the 1980s. Many of the world's most admired classics reflect times of social change and upheaval.

$450,000 – awesome at the time but a fraction of the amounts that were to be bandied about in the next four years. Dealers, some of whom had quietly become large and very profitable corporations, crammed the pages of the classic car press with "gilt-edged investments" and "appreciating assets." Restoration firms and parts suppliers flourished, owners clubs grew, and historic racing boomed. Messing about with old cars had become big business.

Market Mayhem

By 1986, things started to go berserk. Prices went up by the month, propelled by a seemingly insatiable demand tearing away at a dwindling supply. Auction records were made and broken in the same month. An American Duesenberg sold for the magic sum of $1 million, becoming the new highest amount paid for a car at auction. Within eight months a Bugatti Royale sold for $6.5 million, changing hands again only three months later for a staggering $8.1 million. The press fanned the flames with more hype and headlines, and in 1987 the sale of a Bugatti Royale Kellner took the market's breath away by selling at Christie's for an absurd $9.4 million. With the vintage greats out of reach for all but multimillionaires, other lesser cars were suddenly catapulted to stardom. Investors cast around for other sources of capital gain, and word spread that Ferraris had what it took, so up went their value. The Daytona that might have sold for $8,000 in 1973 had an asking price of $325,000 by 1988. GTOs and 250 Testarossas hit the $1.6 million mark and rumors were rife of a 330 P4 selling privately for

over $8 million. Even the modern Ferrari Testarossa – a brand new car with a list price of $134,000 – was being advertised at $340,000. Then the value of Aston Martins exploded with DB5s and DB6s soaring from $20,400 in 1987 to a peak of $120,000 by 1989. The domino effect dragged up Maserati values, which in turn invigorated E-Type prices, and so it went on. By the peak in 1989, the once $2,000 3.8 E-Type was homing in on $67,000.

As the supply of cheap classics in England evaporated, the classic car trade turned to America, South Africa, and New Zealand as a rich vein of rust-free '60s sports cars. Thousands of left-hand drive MGs, TRs, and Jaguars filtered onto the world's markets – some of them not so rust-free. The small ads were crammed with cars advertised by owners and dealers out to turn a profit. Classic car auctions were held every week and more and more classic car magazines lined the newsstands. But suddenly the market started to creak. In 1989, there was a worldwide recession. Interest rates rose, and borrowing money became expensive. There was a retail slowdown, cash was tight and the old car market spluttered and stopped. Demand died almost overnight and cars weren't selling.

BUGATTI LEGEND
Bugatti is still one of the world's most evocative and romantic car badges, but unfortunately accessible only to the privileged few.

CAR AUCTIONS
The first classic car auctions, like this one held in England by Sotheby's in 1982, were rather charming, ingenuous affairs. These days, old car sales are hi-tech, with satellite link-ups, multinational bidders, and glossy four-color magazines.

Prices fell, slowly at first, but by 1990, grass roots enthusiasts who had jumped on the bandwagon too late unloaded their cars in desperation to the highest bidder. Distress sales were common and prices hit the floor. The value of an Aston Martin DB6 that had pole-vaulted to $120,000 plunged to $42,000. The $68,000 E-Type Roadster swallow-dived to $34,000, and the Ferrari F40 that was hyped to nearly $1.6 million in '88 languished unsold with a price tag of $340,000. In the late '80s, speculators jammed Jaguar's phone

lines, desperate to put down deposits on the new XJ220 at a whopping $685,000. They were sure it would double in value overnight, that it was the king of classics. They couldn't have been more wrong. When they took delivery – and many tried not to – it was too late. The market had crashed like a milk bottle falling on a stone doorstep. XJ220s wouldn't even return their list price, let alone make a profit. One desperate owner put a low mileage example through an English auction house only to watch it struggle to make $250,000 for a net loss of $435,000. For a while, classic cars had fired the world's imagination as recreational money-makers. Prices had been inflated by market stimulation and, if we're honest, by pure greed. Owners of classics had seen similar cars advertised at crazier and crazier prices and priced theirs accordingly. The less scrupulous auctioneers had invented nonexistent high bids to further boost values and dealers had done what they always do – slapped on a couple of thousand more for profit.

The Emperor's New Clothes

Was it all just sound and fury signifying nothing, a momentary derangement of the mass imagination, or were classic cars really "investments" that would have gone on increasing in value but for a badly timed recession? Certainly there was an awful lot of trash talk spiked with naive enthusiasm and dubious authority. Here the classic press must shoulder some of the blame for deifying old cars indiscriminately. What started as an innocent and enthusiastic hobby went totally out of control. No enthusiast would deny that a Ferrari Daytona is worthy of

JAGUAR E-TYPE
The most romantic E-Type, the 3.8 Roadster, is probably one of the most lusted-after classics of all. Its appeal functions on many levels, but primarily as a direct link to the swinging '60s. Most of today's E-Type buyers vividly remember its launch day in March 1961, just as they recall the day JFK was assassinated.

preservation, but a Datsun Bluebird ? Surely not. Toward the end of the boom the earnest amateurs and dilettante buyers arrived and proceeded to hail some of the most appalling pieces of scrap ever to disgrace asphalt as desirable properties. Cars that should have been allowed to go the way of all flesh were often just cosmetically resurrected and unloaded on adoring fools as collectors' items.

A Good Return?

As for the notion that an old car is a "good investment," there must be scores of old car buyers who now regret the day that they were taken in by the idea. Some cars have indeed appreciated above the rate of inflation and shown their owners handsome gains. But they're usually the rare, very expensive, and highly desirable models rather than the less substantial mass-produced machines, which represent the bulk of the market. You could have bought a Jaguar 3.8 E-Type for $2,000 back in 1970. Today that car, in superlative condition, is worth around $40,000.

A considerable profit you might say – but don't forget inflation. Remember that $2,000 had quite a bit of purchasing power in 1970. Then consider that you'd have to add the cost of storing, insuring, and keeping the thing immaculate for 25 years, and that's only if it never turned a wheel. Enjoy your investment and drive it around and you'll have to throw in fuel, oil, tires, body restoration, servicing, and more, by which time your paper profit turns into an actual loss. Shrewd and strict accounting says that you'd have been better sticking your money in a bank for 25 years and forgetting all about the Jag.

It is a sad but inescapable fact of life that to popularize is to debase. The concept of the classic car was adulterated beyond recognition by greed, ignorance, and misrepresentation. Profit overtook pleasure, misty-eyed idealists were duped into handing over handsome amounts for indifferent cars, and, as with all mass markets, the lure of easy money attracted the less than upright. Chassis numbers were doctored, origin was falsified, and authenticity manufactured. Too many people jumped on the boat and it began to take on water. Glossy ads appeared from finance companies, banks, insurers, auctioneers, and car brokers, all hungry for a piece of the action. They spoiled an innocent pastime by creating a bull market that wasn't mature enough to support itself.

The Wheel Turns Full Circle

Those knowledgeable car buffs who stood back and shook their heads now breathe a deep sigh of relief. The market mayhem is over and most old cars are no longer being talked of as investments or designer accessories. The cautious and learned enthusiast, who drew the world's attention to classic cars in the first place, has supplanted the opportunist speculator and now represents the only market force. Prices are down to affordable levels and cars are once more being bought for enjoyment. The classic car boom was undoubtedly a bad thing for everybody, but out of it has come some good. Many cars were lavishly restored and saved for posterity, we've all learned a lasting lesson, and the huge losses suffered must serve as an awful warning that such anarchy should never happen again.

THOSE WERE THE DAYS
'50s and '60s sports cars radiate nostalgic messages. This Triumph TR2 sales brochure evokes laurel wreaths, checkered flags, and bravado – a glamorous, innocent world when men were men, cars were cars, and the girl in the passenger seat always wore a headscarf and pearls.

How to Buy a Classic Car

ONLY THE BRAVE SAY they can accurately and honestly evaluate a classic car. The old car market got the jitters because there was no established, thorough guide to the delicate business of accurate evaluation. The pricing structure that exists is based on opinion and exaggeration. Traditional methods of collating historical auction prices, along with publicly advertised prices, all too often ignore the vital factor of condition. It isn't enough to take an auction figure and accept that price as a benchmark for similar models. And you can't base values on advertised prices where descriptions of condition are imprecise and prices optimistic. The classic car in question will have been subjected to many years of wear and deterioration. Age alone doesn't give it any value – it's the condition in which it has survived the ravages of time that really matters. So no two cars can ever be assumed to be in the same condition and command the same price.

Buyer Beware

All used cars are by definition flawed and defy accurate evaluation. Modern cars are priced with the help of data from daily auctions, leasing companies, franchised dealers, used car dealers, and fleet operators. Even with so much regular information available, values of modern cars are still unpredictable. So what hope is there for classic car values? The used car is a unique product – only a third is actually visible. The rest lies behind a cosmetic skin, hidden from view unless dismantled. This is why documentation like service history, number of previous owners, and accuracy of mileage are vital to help make an informed guess about a car's previous existence. With old cars, the job is ten times more difficult. Most classics have had many owners and many restorations and have covered hundreds of thousands of miles. Buyers have been conditioned to accept that documentation is not always necessary or available because it's been lost or obscured in the mists of time. Without documentary help you're left to judge a car's mechanical and bodily state by eye. Unless you're very experienced or psychic, you can make expensive mistakes.

Only recently have old cars caught the public's imagination, so the market is young and foolish. Demand propelled by emotion accelerated values, ignoring more down-to-earth considerations. The desire to own, at any price, sometimes obscures reason. Buyers entered the market without questioning the intrinsic value and condition of the cars they were buying. Only now has it become clear that the prices they paid were based, in most cases, on nothing more than hot air.

For enthusiasts to buy and enjoy old cars, the pivot on which the market hinges, they must be affordable and realistically priced. The market is loaded with bad cars dressed up as good, whether restored at exorbitant cost or not, which places a considerable premium on well kept, genuine, and properly documented examples.

Classic Caveats

Honest, well-maintained, and unrestored cars are worth more than recent restorations. And don't ignore mileage or take it on trust. Find a car that has documentary evidence. Ignore statements like "mileage believed genuine." Make sure the mileage is warranted in writing. Recognize the value of

CHASSIS CHECK
This DeLorean chassis plate can help establish the exact date of manufacture and the name of the first owner. Avoid cars with missing chassis plates.

MANUFACTURED BY
DELOREAN MOTOR CARS LTD.
MONTH AND YEAR
OF MANUFACTURE   OCT. 81
GROSS VEHICLE WEIGHT RATING 3180 LBS
GROSS AXLE WEIGHT RATING FRONT 1244 LBS
                              REAR 1936 LBS
THIS VEHICLE CONFORMS TO ALL
APPLICABLE FEDERAL MOTOR VEHICLE
SAFETY AND BUMPER STANDARDS IN
EFFECT ON THE DATE OF MANUFACTURE
SHOWN ABOVE.
V.I.N. SCEDT2GT1BD004579
PASSENGER CAR.   105196

previous servicing bills and invoices. Choose a classic with a history file. Remember that originality is all. Carefully evaluate cars with color changes, nonstandard plastic instead of leather, or replacement engines. Watch out for chassis and engine numbers that don't match, and go for a car with as few owners as possible.

Be fussy about detail. Don't tolerate anything that looks like it's just been spruced up. While you may not be bothered about originality and sources, the next person who buys your car almost certainly will. Don't assume all classic car sellers and dealers are nice people. Rough cars and rough people sometimes go together, classic or not. If you're in any doubt about mechanical and bodily condition, have your potential purchase inspected by a qualified independent examiner.

The Desirability Factor

Old car values rely on desirability, which depends on their image and how much nostalgia they evoke. Some cars, even though identical in body shape, can be miles apart in value. A '68 Jaguar 240 is the least valuable and desirable Jaguar Mk II. Why? The 240 has the smallest engine of the range and cheaper trim. 240s had slimline bumpers and plastic upholstery, which aren't as nostalgic as the broad-bladed bumpers and leather seats of the pre-'67 models.

Why is a 2 + 2 E-Type worth considerably less than a Series I 3.8 E ? The 2 + 2 was designed as a four-seater and looks ungainly with a higher roof line and steeper windshield. It's slower, too. The earliest 3.8s are romantic because they were the lightest, fastest, and purest E-Types of them all, so they're the most sought after. The same is true of Series II E-Types.

PANHARD PL17
Garish mock tiger skin door inserts might offend the untrained eye, but they are completely original and exactly the way they left the factory – making this PL17 a prince among Panhards. Unusual period weirdness is highly desirable.

These had open headlights and bulky rear light clusters spoiling the smooth lines. Sounds silly – it's still an E-Type – but a mint Series II will always be worth less than a mint Series I. Why is a Bugeye Sprite worth more than a Mk II Sprite? Even though the later car has more creature comforts, is faster, and has a trunk that opens, the Bugeye is the most loved. Nostalgia wins again. The Bugeye looks saucy and is the oldest and purest Sprite, so it has become a cult car.

And so it goes, illogically and irrationally. It's not always age that's the deciding factor either. The last of the Jensen Interceptors, the Series III, is worth more than the first Series I models simply because the later car is faster, better built, and more refined. Unless you know which models have a fashionable image, and high market profile, you can easily overvalue a car. Some cars have added value because of special coachbuilt or limited edition bodywork. A Harrington Sunbeam Alpine is worth 30 percent more than a standard Alpine because of its rarity. Rolls-Royces and Bentleys are other examples. Hand-built and specialist coachwork conversions such as Hooper, James Young, and Mulliner Park Ward are more coveted and therefore more valuable than standard steel cars.

CLASSIC WITHIN A CLASSIC
Not every Jaguar Mk II is worth a mint. This one, a 240, might have wire wheels, but it also has slimline bumpers and plastic upholstery. Pre-'67 Mk IIs had much more nostalgic broad-bladed bumpers and leather trim, and are worth more. The market prefers its old cars as traditional as possible.

Factory-listed options can enhance an old car's value, whereas nonoriginal aftermarket accessories can actually detract from the value. Power steering on Bentley S-Series and Rolls-Royce Silver Clouds is considered essential to their value. Cars without it should be penalized by as much as 20 percent. An automatic transmission on an MGB or a Sunbeam Alpine, although a factory option, reduces the car's value because it spoils the sporting character and performance. Wire wheels are a period accessory and highly sought after. On an MGC they're essential, even though they are an option. On a '70s Mercedes 350 SL, leather interior and air conditioning will boost the car's value by 30 percent. But things like modern fender mirrors, spotlights, glass sunroofs and nonstandard aluminum wheels ruin a car's originality and its period attraction.

Classic Car Auctions

Over the last few years the classic car auction has dominated the old car market as the most convenient way of buying a classic. Auctions, whether for old or modern cars, are dangerous places. You can't drive the car, have it inspected on ramps or speak to the seller. Sometimes you can't even hear the engine running. So the risk of buying something that is not what it seems is huge. Many believe that the classic car auction is the best place to

CAUTION REQUIRED
Classic car auctions are dangerous and expensive places where you cannot inspect or test-drive properly. Emotion and money make unhappy bedfellows and it's easy to get carried away in the heat of the moment.

buy old cars – in fact it's the worst. Buying anything in a competitive and emotional environment without the time or opportunity to make a rational decision is courting disaster. Add to this such dubious practices as unrealistic reserves, invented bids, and a system that conceals the seller from the buyer, and you begin to question the popularity of auctions. Often it's much wiser and cheaper to buy privately or from a dealer, where you have the time to ask questions, make a thorough inspection, and drive the car at operating temperature. It's no coincidence that some of the highest prices achieved for classic cars have been at auction. The most important thing to remember is that unless the car is sold with a warranty, which is rarely the case, your rights at auction are few.

The Bottom Line

Buying a classic requires a steady hand. Reason, not emotion, must be your constant companion. Go at it blind, giddy with dewy-eyed sentimentality, and you'll regret the day you ever went near an old car. Practice a little temporary detachment, negotiate ruthlessly, and you'll buy a winner. And there's no better feeling than being a successful player in that sepia-tinted fantasy we call classic cars. They're a unique, innocent, and disarming form of amusement – fashionable, separate, and involving. Old cars have class.

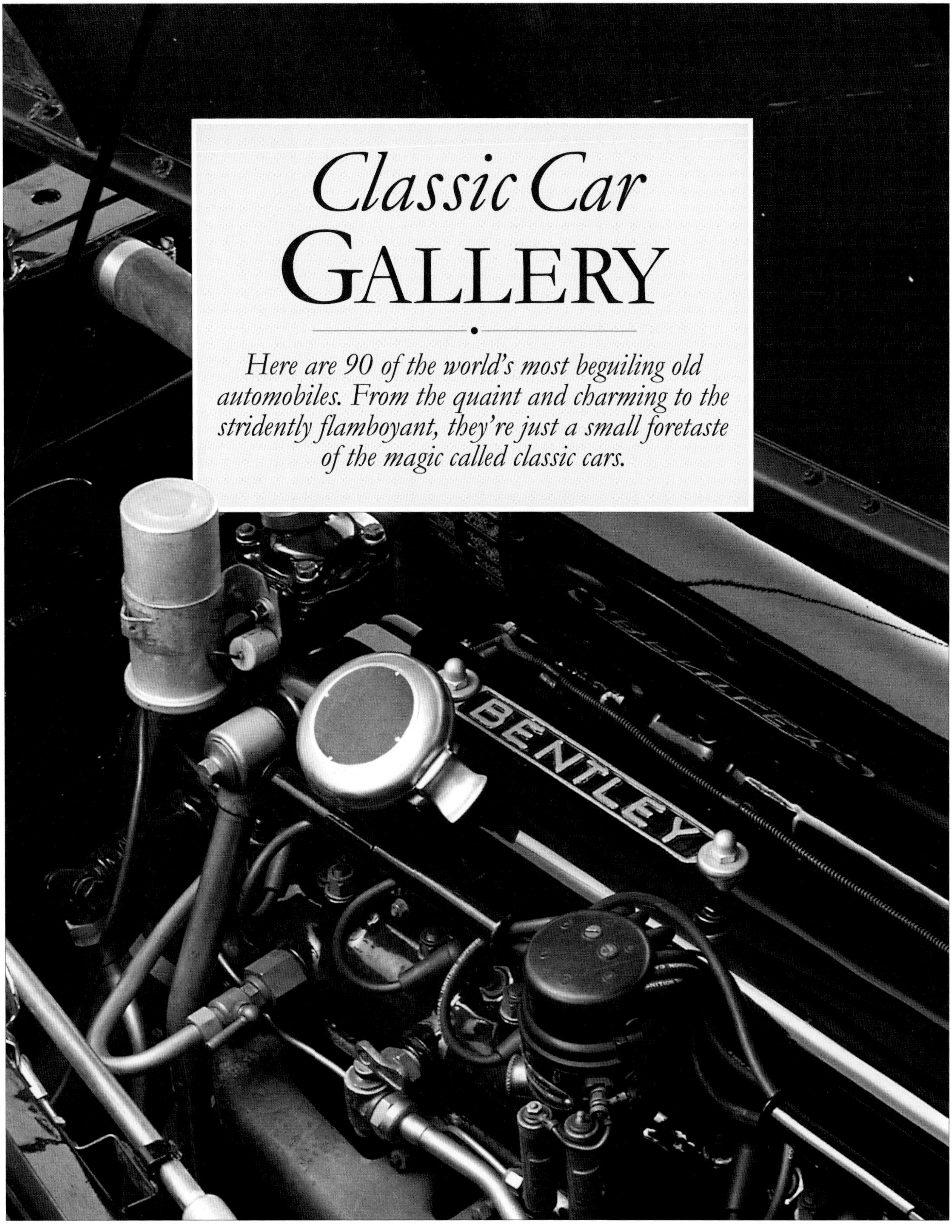

Classic Car GALLERY

—•—

Here are 90 of the world's most beguiling old automobiles. From the quaint and charming to the stridently flamboyant, they're just a small foretaste of the magic called classic cars.

AC *Ace-Bristol*

AGONIZINGLY PRETTY, the AC Ace catapulted the homespun Thames Ditton company into the automobile limelight, instantly earning it a reputation of a maker of svelte sports cars for the tweedy English middle classes. Timelessly elegant, swift, poised, and mechanically uncomplicated, the Ace went on to form the platform for the legendary AC Cobra *(see pages 24–25)*. Clothed in a light aluminum body and powered by a choice of AC's own delicate UMB 2.0 unit, the hardier 2.0 Bristol 100D2 engine, or the lusty 2.6 Ford Zephyr unit, the Ace drove as well as it looked.

Its shape has guaranteed the Ace a place in automobile annals. Chaste, uncluttered, and simple, it makes a Ferrari look top-heavy and clumsy. Purists argue that the Bristol-powered version is the real thoroughbred Ace, closest to its original inspiration, the Bristol-powered Tojeiro prototype of 1953.

ENGINE
Shared by the BMW 328, the hemi-head 125 bhp 2.0 Bristol engine was offered as a performance conversion for the Ace. With triple Solex carburetors, pushrod overhead valve gear, a light aluminum head, and cast iron crankcase, the Ace was a club racer's dream.

STEERING WHEEL SHARED WITH THE AUSTIN-HEALEY (SEE PAGES 36–39) AND THE DAIMLER SP DART (SEE PAGES 78–81)

INTERIOR
In pure British tradition, the Ace's cockpit was stark, with gauges and switches haphazardly scattered across the dash.

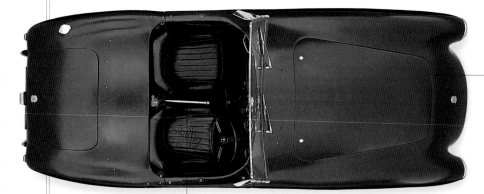

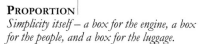

HANDLING
Production cars used Bishop cam-and-gear steering, which gave a turning circle of 36 ft (11 m), and required just two deft turns of the steering wheel lock-to-lock.

PROPORTION
Simplicity itself – a box for the engine, a box for the people, and a box for the luggage.

OTHER MODELS

Founded in 1902, AC was one of the longest established English car makers, nicknamed "the Savile Row of motordom."

AC ACECA
A coupe version of the Ace, the Aceca was sold until mid-1955.

COOLING
The Ace's wide, toothy grin fed air into the large radiator that was shared by the two-liter sedan.

REAR VIEW
Later Aces had a revised rear deck, with square taillights and a bigger trunk.

FOOT WARMER
For diehards who always drove with the hood down, the tonneau cover kept your feet warm while your face froze.

AC ACE-BRISTOL

The handsomest British roadster of its day, and as lovely as an Alfa Romeo Giulietta Sprint, the Ace had an Italianate simplicity. Proof of the dictum that less is more, the Ace's gently sweeping profile is a triumph of form over function. Known as *Superleggera* construction, a network of steel tubes was covered by aluminum panels, based on the outline of the 1949 Ferrari 122. Engines were placed well back and gave an 18 percent rearward bias to the weight distribution.

SIDESCREENS
Folding plastic sidescreens helped to prevent turbulence in the cockpit at speed.

OWNER DRIVING
An Ace-Bristol recorded an average of 97 mph (156 km/h) over 2,350 miles (3,781 km) at the 1957 Le Mans 24 Hours (a record for a Bristol-engined car).

HOOD CATCHES
Forward-hinged hood was locked by two chrome catches, opened by a small T-shaped key.

SPECIFICATIONS

MODEL AC Ace-Bristol (1956–61)
PRODUCTION 463
BODY STYLE Two-door, two-seater sports roadster.
CONSTRUCTION Space-frame chassis, light aluminum body.
ENGINE Six-cylinder pushrod 1971CC.
POWER OUTPUT 105 bhp at 5000 rpm (optional high performance tune 125 hp at 5750 rpm).
TRANSMISSION Four-speed manual Bristol gearbox (optional overdrive).
SUSPENSION Independent front and rear with transverse leaf spring and lower wishbones.
BRAKES Front and rear drums. Front discs from 1957.
MAXIMUM SPEED 117 mph (188 km/h)
0–60 MPH (0–96 KM/H) 9.1 sec
0–100 MPH (0–161 KM/H) 27.2 sec
A.F.C. 21.6 mpg

BRAKES
Front disc brakes, an option in 1957, were later standardized.

AC *Cobra 427*

AN UNLIKELY ALLIANCE BETWEEN AC Cars, a traditional British car maker, and Carroll Shelby, a charismatic Texan racer, produced the legendary AC Cobra. AC's sports car, the Ace *(see pages 20–21),* was turned into the Cobra by fitting a series of American Ford V-8s into the car, starting with 4.2-liter and 4.7-liter Mustang engines. In 1965 Shelby, always a man to take things to the limit, squeezed in a thunderous 7-liter Ford engine, in an attempt to realize his dream of winning Le Mans. Although the 427 was not fast enough to win and failed to sell in any quantity, it was soon known as one of the most aggressive and romantic cars ever built.

GTM 777F once held the record as The World's Fastest Accelerating Production Car. In 1967 it was driven by British journalist John Bolster to record such Olympian figures as an all-out maximum of 165 mph (265 km/h) and a 0–60 time of an unbelievable 4.2 seconds.

(see pages 20–21)

OTHER MODELS

AC Cars Limited began in 1922 and earned itself a reputation as a maker of good-looking, hand-built, luxury sports cars.

AC COBRA 289
Early Cobras had 260 engines. Later cars were fitted with Mustang 289 V-8s.

SPEEDY APPEAL
Even the "baby" 4.7 Cobras were good for 138 mph (222 km/h) and could squeal up to 60 mph (96 km/h) in under six seconds.

BODYWORK
The body was handrolled aluminum wrapped around a tubular steel frame, which proved to be very light yet extremely strong.

INTERIOR
The interior was kept stark and basic, with traditional 1960s British sports car features of black-on-white gauges, small bucket seats, and wood-rim steering wheel. 427 owners were not interested in creature comforts, only raw power, great brakes, and wonderful suspension.

TIRES
Cobra tires were always Goodyear since Shelby was a long-time dealer.

RADIATOR HEADER TANK KEPT THINGS COOL, HELPED BY TWIN ELECTRIC FANS

UNDER THE AIR CLEANER ARE TWO LARGE FOUR-BARREL CARBURETORS

ENGINE
The mighty 7-liter 427 block had years of NASCAR (National Association of Stock Car Automobile Racing) racing success and easily punched out power for hours. The street version output ranged from 300 to 425 bhp. Competition and semicompetition versions with tuned engines could exceed 500 bhp.

AC COBRA 427

The 427 looked fast standing still. Gone was the lithe beauty of the original Ace 289, replaced by bulbous front and rear arches, fat 7½-in (19-cm) wheels, and tires wide enough to roll a ball field. The chassis was virtually all new and three times stronger than the 289's, with computer-designed anti-dive and anti-squat characteristics. Amazingly, the 289's original Salisbury differential proved more than capable of handling the 427's massive wall of torque.

WHEELS
Initially pin-drive Halibrand magnesium alloy but changed for Starburst wheels (designed by Shelby employee Pete Brock) when supplies dried up.

COOLING
Fender vents helped reduce brake and engine temperatures.

SIDESCREENS
Small plastic side screens helped cut down cockpit-fender buffeting at speed.

FRAME
The windshield frame was handmade and polished.

BUMPERS
Bumpers were token chromed tubes with the emphasis on weight-saving. Racers took them off completely.

EXHAUSTS
Racing Cobras usually had side exhausts, which increased power and noise.

SPECIFICATIONS

MODEL 1965 AC Cobra 427 (1965–68)
PRODUCTION 316
BODY STYLE Light aluminum, two-door, two-seater, open sports.
CONSTRUCTION Separate tubular steel chassis with aluminum panels.
ENGINE V-8 6989cc
POWER OUTPUT 425 bhp at 6000 rpm.
TRANSMISSION Four-speed all-synchromesh.
SUSPENSION Four-wheel independent with coil springs.
BRAKES Four-wheel disc.
MAXIMUM SPEED 165 mph (265 km/h)
0–60 MPH (0–96 KM/H) 4.2 sec
0–100 MPH (0–161 KM/H) 10.3 sec
A.F.C. 15 mpg

AC 428

THE AC 428 NEEDS a new word of its very own – "brutiful" perhaps – for while its brute strength derives from its Cobra ancestor, the 428 has a sculpted, stately beauty. This refined bruiser was born of a thoroughbred crossbreed of British engineering, American power, and Italian design. The convertible 428 was first seen at the London Motor Show in October 1965; the first hardtop car – the so-called fastback – was ready in time for the Geneva Motor Show in March 1966.

But production was beset by problems from the start; first cars were not offered for sale until 1967, and as late as March 1969, only 50 had been built. Part of the problem was that the 428 was priced between the more expensive Italian Ferraris and Maseratis and the cheaper British Astons and Jensens. Small-scale production continued into the 1970s, but its days were numbered and it was finally done in by the fuel crisis of October 1973; the last 428 – the 80th – was built soon afterward and sold during 1974. But if you own one of them you have a rare thing – a refined muscle car, a macho GT with manners and breeding.

BADGING
The letters AC derive from Autocarrier, the company's name until it became known as AC Cars Ltd. in 1922.

SUSPENSION
Front suspension uses unequal-length wishbones with combined coilspring and telescopic-shock units.

ENGINE
Using the same 427 cubic inch (6998cc) V-8 engine as the Cobra, the car was known initially as the AC 427. In 1967, it gained the Ford Galaxie engine and an extra cubic inch. Both four-speed manual and three-speed automatic transmissions were available.

UNDER-HOOD HEAT MEANT THAT ON LONG, FAST RUNS THE ENGINE OIL COULD LITERALLY BOIL

TOP COVER
Early convertibles had a detachable metal tonneau to cover the top when folded, but this was soon abandoned.

SITTING COMFORTABLY
Interiors are lavishly furnished, with top-quality leather seats and extensive use of chrome-plated fittings.

DASHBOARD
Switches may be scattered around like confetti, but the instruments are grouped just in front of the driver. The speedometer *(far left)* reads to an optimistic 180 mph (290 km/h), the tachometer *(far right)* to 8000 rpm.

SUBTLE FILLER
The 18-gallon (82-liter) fuel tank is filled through a flap on the rear deck.

MAKING AN IMPACT
Slim, wraparound, chrome-plated bumpers accentuate the 428's length, but provide minimal impact protection.

BODY BEAUTIFUL
Like any Italian or Italian-bodied car of the period, the 428 suffers from corrosion due to poor quality steel.

WEATHER BEATER
While the top has rather large rear quarter panels which can make the cockpit feel rather claustrophobic, the plastic rear window is generously proportioned.

SUSPENSION
Salisbury final drive, with limited slip differential, is bolted to the tubular chassis. Short external shafts drive the rear wheels.

AIR VENTS
In an effort to combat engine overheating, later cars have air vents behind the front wheels.

PARTS BIN
The 428 features parts from other manufacturers; rear lights came from Fiat.

SPECIFICATIONS

MODEL AC 428 (1966–73)
PRODUCTION 80 (51 convertibles, 29 fastbacks)
BODY STYLES Two-seat convertible or two-seat fastback coupe.
CONSTRUCTION Tubular steel backbone chassis/separate all steel body.
ENGINE Ford V-8, 6997cc or 7016cc.
POWER OUTPUT 345 bhp at 4600 rpm
TRANSMISSION Ford four-speed manual or three-speed automatic; Salisbury rear axle with limited slip differential.
SUSPENSION Double wishbones and combined coil spring/telescopic shock units front and rear.
BRAKES Power-assisted Girling discs front and rear.
MAXIMUM SPEED 139.3 mph (224 km/h) (auto)
0–60 MPH (0–96 KM/H) 5.9 sec (auto)
0–100 MPH (0–161 KM/H) 14.5 sec
A.F.C. 12–15 mpg

AC 428

Styled by Pietro Frua in Turin, the AC 428 was available in both convertible and fastback form. It was based on an AC Cobra 427 chassis, virtually standard apart from a 6 in (15 cm) increase in wheelbase. The design contains subtle reminders of a number of contemporary cars, not least of which is the Maserati Mistral – which is hardly surprising really, since the Mistral was also designed by Frua.

THIN SKINNED
Early cars had aluminum doors and hood; later cars were all steel.

LIFTING THE LID
Like the Cobra, the 428's vast hood is hinged at the front.

DESIGN CREDIT
Frua is credited with a discreet "Creazione Frua" badge behind each front fender vent.

ALL LACED UP
Standard wheels were substantial wire-spoked affairs, secured by a three-eared nut.

ALFA ROMEO *1300 Junior Spider*

DRIVEN BY DUSTIN HOFFMAN to the strains of Simon and Garfunkel in the film *The Graduate*, the Alfa Spider has become one of the most accessible cult Italian cars. This is hardly surprising when you consider the little Alfa's considerable virtues: a wonderfully responsive all-aluminum, twin-cam engine, accurate steering, sensitive brakes, a finely balanced chassis, and matinee idol looks. It has been called "the poor man's Ferrari."

First launched at the Geneva Motor Show in 1966, Alfa held a worldwide competition to find a name for its new baby. After considering 140,000 entries, with suggestions like Lollobrigida, Bardot, Nuvolari, and even Stalin, they settled on Duetto, which neatly summed up the car's "two's-company-three's-a-crowd" image. Despite having the same price tag as the much faster and more glamorous Jaguar E-Type *(see pages 140–143)*, the Spider sold over 100,000 units during its remarkable 26-year production run. Alfa purists favor the pre-1970 "boat-tailed" cars, with the 1600 Duetto and 1750 model among the most collectible. Because of their large production numbers and relatively expensive maintenance costs, not to mention a serious propensity for body decay, prices of Spiders are invitingly low, running at similar levels to MGBs, Triumph TR6s, and Bugeye Sprites.

(see pages 140–143)

OTHER MODELS

The Spider has to be one of Alfa's great postwar cars. Next to the Alfasud, GTV, and Giulia, it is perhaps one of its most romantic concoctions.

ALFA ROMEO GIULIETTA
The Spider's ancestor was the comely little Giulietta, available in convertible, two-door coupe, or four-door Berlina versions.

ALFA ROMEO MONTREAL
For six years the Montreal was the jewel in Alfa's crown. A race-bred 2.5 V-8 gave a top speed of 140 mph (225 km/h).

REAR VIEW
The "boat-tail" rear was shared by all Spiders up to 1970, replaced by a squared-off Kamm tail. "Duetto" correctly refers to 1600 Spiders only.

LOGO
The Spider was designed by Battista Pininfarina, founder of the Turin-based design house.

HOOD
The Spider's hood is beautifully effective. It can be raised with only one arm without leaving the driver's seat.

TRUNK
Spiders have huge trunks by sports car standards, with the spare wheel tucked neatly away under the trunk floor.

BODYWORK
The Spider's bodywork corrodes alarmingly quickly. Poor-quality steel, scant rustproofing, and inadequate drainage make rust a serious enemy.

ENGINE
Some of the mid-'70s Spiders imported to the US were overly restricted – the catalyzed 1750 could only manage 99 mph (159 km/h).

DASHBOARD

The dashboard was painted metal up to 1970. All Spiders had the Italian "apelike" (long arms, short legs) driving position. Minor controls were on fingertip stalks, while the wipers had an ingenious foot button on the floor.

FLOOR MATS
Spiders came from the factory with austere rubber mats, now much prized by enthusiasts as they do not absorb water.

ALFA ROMEO 1300 JUNIOR SPIDER

One of Pininfarina's last designs, the Spider's rounded front and rear and deep-channelled scallop running along the sides attracted plenty of criticism. One British motoring magazine dubbed it "compact and rather ugly." The 1300 Junior was the baby of the Spider family, introduced in 1968 to take advantage of Italian tax laws.

STYLISH GRILLE

This hides a twin-cam energy-efficient engine with hemispherical combustion chambers.

SPECIFICATIONS

MODEL Alfa Romeo 1300 Junior Spider (1968–78)
PRODUCTION 7,237
BODY STYLE All steel.
CONSTRUCTION All steel monocoque body.
ENGINE All-aluminum twin-cam 1290cc.
POWER OUTPUT 89 bhp at 6000 rpm.
TRANSMISSION Five-speed.
SUSPENSION *Front:* independent; *Rear:* live axle with coil springs.
BRAKES All disc.
MAXIMUM SPEED 106 mph (170 km/h)
0–60 MPH (0–96 KM/H) 11.2 sec
0–100 MPH (0–161 KM/H) 21.3 sec
A.F.C. 29 mpg

HEADLIGHTS
Plastic headlight covers look good and raise the top speed slightly. They were banned in the United States and never fitted to 1300 Juniors.

NOSE SECTION
Disappearing nose is very vulnerable to parking dents. Many a Spider's snout contains more filler than it should.

ASTON MARTIN *DB4*

THE DEBUT OF THE DB4 in 1958 heralded the beginning of the Aston Martin glory years, ushering in the breed of classic six-cylinder DB Astons that propelled Aston Martin onto the world stage. Earlier postwar Astons were fine sporting enthusiasts' road cars, but with the DB4 Astons acquired a new grace, sophistication, and refinement that was, for many, the ultimate flowering of the grand tourer theme. Clothed in an Italian body by Carrozzeria Touring of Milan, it possessed a graceful yet powerful elegance. Under the aluminum shell was Tadek Marek's twin-cam straight-six engine, which evolved from Aston's racing program.

In short, the DB4 looked superb and went like the wind. The DB5, which followed, will always be remembered as the James Bond Aston. The final expression of the theme came with the bigger DB6. The cars were glorious, but the company was in trouble. David Brown, the millionaire industrialist owner of Aston Martin and the DB of the model name, had a dream. But, in the early '70s, with losses of $1.5 million a year, he bailed out of the company, leaving a legacy of machines that are still talked about with reverence as the David Brown Astons.

OTHER MODELS

Aston Martin's first postwar car was the short-lived DB1, a curious whale-shaped device replaced by the more shapely DB2 in 1950.

ASTON MARTIN DB2/4
With its WO Bentley engine, the DB2 evolved into the DB2/4, an occasional four-seater sports model.

UNHINGED
First-generation DB4s have a rear-hinged hood.

GAS FLAP
The single gas-tank is out of sight behind a discreet flap on the left-hand rear pillar.

SUSPENSION
Front suspension is double wishbones with coil springs and telescopic shocks.

1037 TE

LUXURIOUS LEATHER
While rear seats in the hardtop offer limited space, just look at the richness and quality of the leather.

ENGINE
While looking very much like the contemporary Jaguar XK twin-cam straight-six, Tadek Marek's design is more powerful and more complicated. Triple SU carburetors show this to be a Vantage engine with an extra 20 bhp.

IT'S IN THE MIRROR
The dipping rear-view mirror is also found in many Jaguars of the period.

DASHBOARD
The dash is an unergonomic triumph of form over function; gauges are scattered all over an instrument panel deliberately similar to the car's grinning radiator grille.

SPECIFICATIONS
MODEL Aston Martin DB4 (1958–63)
PRODUCTION 1,040 (hardtop); 70 (convertible); 95 hardtop DB4 GTs.
BODY STYLES Hardtop coupe or convertible.
CONSTRUCTION Pressed-steel and tubular inner chassis frame, with aluminum-alloy outer panels.
ENGINE In-line six 3670cc/3749cc.
POWER OUTPUT 240 bhp at 5500 rpm.
TRANSMISSION Four-speed manual (with optional overdrive).
SUSPENSION *Front:* independent by wishbones, coil springs and telescopic shocks. *Rear:* live axle located by trailing arms and Watt linkage with coil springs and lever-arm shocks.
BRAKES Discs front and rear.
MAXIMUM SPEED 140+ mph (225+ km/h)
0–60 MPH (0–96 KM/H) 8 sec
0–100 MPH (0–161 KM/H) 20.1 sec
A.F.C. 14–22 mpg

BRITISH LIGHTWEIGHT
Superleggera, Italian for "super-lightweight," refers to the technique of body construction: aluminum panels rolled over a framework of steel tubes.

ASTON MARTIN DB4
There is no doubt that the DB4 has serious attitude. Its lines may be Italian, but it has none of the dainty delicacy of some contemporary Ferraris and Maseratis; the Aston's spirit is truly British. Its stance is solid and powerful, but not brutish – more British Boxer than lumbering Bulldog, aggressive yet refined – and is an ideal blueprint for a James Bond car.

ASTON SMILE
The vertical bars in this car's radiator grille show it to be a so-called Series 4 DB4, built between September, 1961 and October, 1962.

1037 TE

ASTON MARTIN *V8*

A NEAR TWO-TON GOLIATH powered by an outrageous hand-made 5.3-liter engine, the DBS V8 was meant to be Aston's bread winner for the 1970s. Based on the six-cylinder DBS of 1967, the V8 did not appear until April 1970. With a thundering 160 mph (257 km/h) top speed, Aston's new bulldog instantly earned a place on every millionaire's shopping list. The trouble was that it drove into a worldwide recession – in 1975 the Newport Pagnell factory produced just 19 cars.

Aston's bank managers were worried, but the company pulled through. The DBS became the Aston Martin V8 in 1972 and continued on until 1989, giving birth to the legendary 400 bhp Vantage and gorgeous Volante Convertible. Excessive, expensive, impractical, and impossibly thirsty, the DBS V8 and AM V8 are wonderful relics from a time when environmentalism was just a word in the dictionary.

OTHER MODELS

The DBS was sold alongside the DB6, here in convertible Volante form. David Brown Astons were the staple vehicle of well-heeled British aristocrats.

ASTON MARTIN DB6 VOLANTE
Cars with incredible presence, Astons were good enough for James Bond, King Hussein of Jordan, Peter Sellers, and even the Prince of Wales – who still owns a DB6 Volante he bought new.

RACING ENGINE
The aluminum V-8 was first seen in Lola sports-racing cars. The massive air-cleaner box covers a quartet of twin-choke Weber carburetors.

CLASSY INTERIOR
Over the years the DBS was skillfully updated, without losing its traditional ambience. Features included leather and wood trim, air conditioning, electric windows, and state-of-the-art Blaupunkt radio cassette. Nearly all V8s were ordered with Chrysler Torqueflite automatic.

ASTON LINES
Smooth tapering cockpit line is an Aston hallmark echoed in the current DB7.

SPOILER
Discreet rear spoiler is part of the gently sweeping fender line.

SUSPENSION
Rear suspension was semi-independent De Dion tube with double trailing links, Watts linkage, coil springs, and lever arm shocks.

TIRES
Tires were massive 7-in (18-cm) Avon Turbospeeds.

REAR VIEW
Prodigious rear overhang makes the rear aspect look cluttered.

TWIN PIPES
Hand-made bumpers cover huge twin exhausts – a gentle reminder of this Aston's epic V-8 grunt.

ASTON MARTIN V8

DBS was one of the first Astons with a chassis and departed from the traditional Superleggera tubular superstructure of the DB4, 5, and 6. Like Ferraris and Maseratis, Aston prices were ballyhooed up to stratospheric levels in the 1980s. The best examples changed hands for $100,000 plus. But now sobriety has returned to the market; you can buy a decent V-8 for the price of a new Nissan.

WHEELS
To handle 300-plus bhp, V8s wore cast aluminum wheels instead of wires.

BODYWORK
V8 aluminum body was hand-smoothed and lovingly finished.

SPECIFICATIONS

MODEL Aston Martin V8 (1972–89)
PRODUCTION (including Volante and Vantage) 2,842
BODY STYLE Four-seater coupe.
CONSTRUCTION Aluminum body, steel platform chassis.
ENGINE Twin OHC 5340cc V-8.
POWER OUTPUT Never released but approx. 345 bhp (Vantage 400 bhp).
TRANSMISSION Three-speed automatic or five-speed manual.
SUSPENSION Independent front, De Dion rear.
BRAKES Four-wheel disc.
MAXIMUM SPEED 161 mph (259 km/h); Vantage 173 mph (278 km/h)
0–60 MPH (0–96 KM/H) 6.2 sec (Vantage 5.4 sec)
0–100 MPH (0–161 KM/H) 14.2 sec (Vantage 13 sec)
A.F.C. 13 mpg

BOND CAR
The 1984 AM V8 Volante from the film *The Living Daylights*, with James Bond actor Timothy Dalton. In 1964 a DB4 was the first Aston to star alongside James Bond, in the film *Goldfinger*.

HOOD BULGE
Massive hood power bulge is to clear four carburetors.

SPOILER
Chin spoiler and undertray help reduce front-end lift at speed.

FRONT END
Shapely "cliff-hanger" nose was always a DBS trademark.

AUDI *Quattro Sport*

THE MOST EXPENSIVE AND EXCLUSIVE Audi ever sold was the $100,000, 155 mph (250 km/h) Quattro Sport. With a short wheelbase, all-aluminum 300 bhp engine, and a body made of aluminum reinforced fiberglass and Kevlar, it has all the charisma, and nearly all the performance, of a Ferrari GTO.

The Quattro changed the way we think about four-wheel drive. Before 1980, four-wheel drive systems had foundered through high cost, weight, and lousy road behavior. Everybody thought that if you bolted a four-wheel drive system onto a performance coupe it would have ugly handling, transmission whine, and an insatiable appetite for fuel. Audi's engineers proved that the accepted wisdom was cockeyed and, by 1982, they were World Champions. Four-wheel drive cars are now part of most large carmakers' model ranges and, along with airbags and anti-lock brakes, have played their bit toward safer driving. We must thank the car that started it all, the Audi Quattro – a technical trailblazer.

INTERIOR
The interior looks like it may accommodate four people, but in practice it is a two-seater only, unless a rear passenger is willing to travel in the lotus position! Ride is harder than in normal Quattros, but steering is quicker.

DASHBOARD
While the dashboard layout is nothing special, everything is typically Germanic – clear, tidy, and easy to use. The only touch of luxury in the Quattro is half-leather trim.

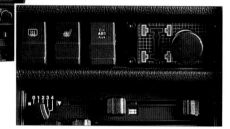

FOUR-WHEEL SWITCH
Center Torsen differential gives a 50/50 front-to-rear split. Rear differential lock disengages as soon as the car passes 15 mph (24 km/h).

BOX WHEELARCHES ARE A QUATTRO HALLMARK, ESSENTIAL TO COVER FAT 9JX15 WHEELS

INTER-AXLE QUATTRO DIFFERENTIAL WAS BORROWED FROM THE VW POLO

TURBO LAG WAS A BIG PROBLEM ON EARLY QUATTROS; FROM 20–60 MPH IN TOP GEAR IT WAS SLOWER THAN A 900CC VW POLO

POWER OUTPUT IS A MONSTER 304 BHP AT 6500 RPM – 0 TO 60 IN FOUR-AND-A-BIT SECONDS IS VERY QUICK

ENGINE
The five-cylinder 2133cc aluminum engine is 50 lb (22.7 kg) lighter than the stock item, with twin overhead cams, four valves per cylinder, a giant KKK-K27 turbocharger and Bosch LH-Jetronic injection.

BAUER LABELING
Some body parts were made by German coachbuilder Bauer, who was also responsible for the early BMW 3-Series Convertible.

LONGER NOSE AND HOOD BULGE COVER INTERCOOLER FOR THE TURBO UNIT

REAR VIEW WAS LIMITED

SPECIFICATIONS

MODEL Audi Quattro Sport (1983–87)
PRODUCTION 220 (all LHD)
BODY STYLE Two-seater, two-door coupe.
CONSTRUCTION Monocoque body from Kevlar, aluminum, fiberglass, and steel.
ENGINE 2133cc five-cylinder turbocharged.
POWER OUTPUT 304 bhp at 6500 rpm.
TRANSMISSION Five-speed manual, four-wheel drive.
SUSPENSION Independent all around.
BRAKES Four-wheel vented discs with switchable ABS.
MAXIMUM SPEED 155 mph (250 km/h)
0–60 MPH (0–96 KM/H) 4.8 sec
0–100 MPH (0–161 KM/H) 13.9 sec
A.F.C. 17 mpg

LIMITED EDITION
Of the 1,700 Audis produced each day in the mid-1980s, only 3 were Quattros, and of a year's output only a tiny amount were Sport Quattros.

DUE TO BOXY STYLING, QUATTRO AERODYNAMICS WERE POOR AT 0.43Cd

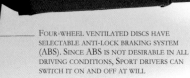

FOUR-WHEEL VENTILATED DISCS HAVE SELECTABLE ANTI-LOCK BRAKING SYSTEM (ABS). SINCE ABS IS NOT DESIRABLE IN ALL DRIVING CONDITIONS, SPORT DRIVERS CAN SWITCH IT ON AND OFF AT WILL

QUATTRO RALLY SUCCESS

In its day the Audi Quattro Sport had the latest four-wheel drive technology, married to the reliability and durability of Prussian engineering perfection.

THE SPORT'S capabilities make it not just a fast car, but a superfast supercar, more than able to rub noses with the best from Maranello and Stuttgart. Despite its passing resemblance to the more prosaic Audi GT Coupe, the Quattro Sport is one of the quickest, most surefooted cars in the world.

In 1984 Stig Blomqvist took Audi to the rank of world champion, with wins in Greece, New Zealand, and Argentina. But it was at the Ivory Coast event, the Sport's first true outing, that he showed just how competitive this incredible machine could be, trouncing all opposition in

his wake. In competition trim, Audi's remarkable turbocharged engine was developing 400 bhp. By 1987, Audi was admitting to an Olympian 509 bhp at 8,000 rpm for the fearsome S1 Sport that took Walter Rohrl to victory at Pikes Peak. To meet Group B homologation requirements, only 220 examples of the Sport were built, all left-hand drive,

AUDI SPORT IN RALLY ACTION

and only a few were destined for sale to some very lucky private owners.

In its first full competition season in 1985, the Sport took the laurels on the San Remo rally, as well as second place on the Monte Carlo, Swedish, and Acropolis rallies. The San Remo was to be the last Group B Quattro win in the World Rally Championship because the competition had come to

AUDI
Quattro Sport

DARKENED REAR LIGHTS WERE INCLUDED ACROSS THE QUATTRO LINE IN 1984

HOT PROPERTY
From any angle the Sport is testosterone on wheels, with a bold and aggressive stance.

Stig Blomqvist in icy conditions, 1985

Audi Sport, 1983 East Africa Safari Rally

grips with the Quattro phenomenon and was producing a growing number of four-wheel drive supercars, custom built for rallying events. Ultra-quick projectiles like the Metro 6R4, Ford RS 2000, Peugeot 205 T16, and Lancia

Delta S4 began to chew away at the Quattro's tail feathers. The reason for the Sport's short life was that all Group B supercars were outlawed after a number of terrible accidents. Audi withdrew from competition following the ill-fated 1986 Portugal

Rally that rewrote the rule book. From 1987 onward, the World Rally Championship would be contested by Group A cars in stock showroom specification, rendering the foreshortened Sport obsolete at a stroke. Gone but certainly not forgotten, the Quattro Sport is now a much admired collector's item, valued as high as three times its original price.

ROOF SECTIONS ARE OF ALUMINUM-BONDED FIBERGLASS

HAND-CRAFTED
Body shells were welded together at Ingolstadt, Germany, in small batches by a team of just 22 craftsmen.

AUSTIN-HEALEY *Sprite* MK1

SOME AUTOMOTIVE THEORISTS believe all the best car designs have a recognizable face. If that is the case, few cars have a cuter face than this little fellow, with that ear-to-ear grinning grille and those wide-open, slightly astonished, eyes. Of course, it is those trademark bulging peepers that prompted the nickname "Bugeye," by which everyone now recognizes this engaging little character. It is a compliment of kinds that the recent retro fad has offered similar designs, like the Suzuki Cappucino and Honda Beat, in an attempt to recapture some of the charm of the original. But these modern charm-bracelet trinkets lack one thing – real character. So much of the Bugeye's character was born of necessity. The Donald Healey Motor Company and Austin had already teamed up with the Austin-Healey 100. In 1958, its little brother, the Sprite, was born, a spartan little sports car designed down to a price and based on the engine and running gear of the Austin A35 sedan, with a bit of Morris Minor, too. Yet the Bugeye really was a sports car and had a sweet raspberry exhaust note to prove it.

INTERIOR
The Bugeye fits like a glove. Everything is within reach – speedometer on the right, tach on the left, and a well-placed stubby gear lever.

THE BUG'S EYES
Gerry Coker's original design incorporated retracting headlights like the later Lotus Elan, but extra cost ruled these out; the protruding headlight pods created a car with a character all of its own.

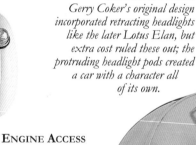

ENGINE ACCESS
Front-hinged hood gives great engine access and makes the Bugeye a delight for DIY tinkerers.

ENGINE
The Austin-Morris A-series engine was a little gem. It first appeared in the Austin A35 sedan and went on to power several generations of Mini *(see pages 40–41).* In the Bugeye it was modified internally with extra strong valve springs and equipped with twin SU carburetors to give a peppy 50 bhp gross (43 bhp net).

DUAL LIGHTS
Sidelights double as turn signals.

BUMPERS
The Bugeye was a budget sports car built down to a price. Bumpers with overrider were a sensible and popular extra that would set you back $10–15 in 1958.

WHEELS
*Drilled steel disc
wheels with AH
on plain hub.*

AUSTIN-HEALEY SPRITE MK1

At just under 11 ft 5 in (3.5 m), the Bugeye is not quite as
small as it seems. Its pert looks were only part of the car's
cult appeal, for with its firm, even harsh, ride it had a
traditional British sports car feel. A nimble performer,
you could hustle it along a winding road, cornering
flat and clicking through the gears on the gear lever.

CLEAN LINES
*The design has a classic simplicity, free
of needless chrome embellishment; there
is no external door handle to
interrupt the flowing flanks.*

SPECIFICATIONS

MODEL Austin-Healey Sprite Mk1
(1958–61)
PRODUCTION 38,999
BODY STYLE Two-seater roadster.
CONSTRUCTION Unibody/chassis.
ENGINE BMC A-Series 948cc, four-
cylinder, overhead valve.
POWER OUTPUT 43 bhp at 5200 rpm.
TRANSMISSION Four-speed manual,
synchromesh on top three ratios.
SUSPENSION *Front:* Independent, coil
springs and wishbones. *Rear:* Quarter-
elliptic leaf springs, rigid axle.
BRAKES Hydraulic, drums all around.
MAXIMUM SPEED 84 mph (135 km/h)
0–60 MPH (0–96 KM/H) 20.5 sec
A.F.C. 35–45 mpg

ROUND RUMP
*It is not so much a
trunk, as it does not
open; more a luggage
locker with access behind
the rear seats.*

HOOD
*The complex
one-piece hood
is made up of
four main
panels.*

LOW DOWN
*The Bugeye's low
stance aids flat
cornering.
Ground
clearance is
better than it
looks, just under
5 in (12.7 cm).*

COMPETITION
With its tunable A-series
engine, the Bugeye is still a
popular club racer. Sprites also
put up spirited performances
at Le Mans and Sebring.
Special-bodied Sebring
Sprites are rare and prized.

AUSTIN-HEALEY *3000*

THE HEALEY HUNDRED was a sensation at the 1952 Earl's Court Motor Show. Austin's Leonard Lord had already contracted to supply the engines, but when he noticed the sports car's impact, he decided he wanted to build it, too. It was transformed overnight into the Austin-Healey 100, with a new badge designed in the wee small hours. Donald Healey had spotted a gap in the American sports car market between the Jaguar XK120 *(see pages 134–35)* and the cheap and cheerful MG T series *(see pages 172–73)*. His hunch was right, for about 80 percent of all production went Stateside. Over the years this rugged bruiser became increasingly civilized. In 1956, it received a six-cylinder engine in place of the four, but in 1959 the 3000 was born. It became increasingly refined – with front disc brakes, then windup windows – and ever faster. Our featured car is the last of the generation, a 3000 MkIII. Although it edges into grand tourer territory, it is also the fastest of all Big Healeys and is still a true sports car.

ENGINE
Under the hood of the biggest of the so-called Big Healeys is the 2912cc straight six that was designated as the 3000. This is the most powerful of the big bangers, pumping out a hefty 150 bhp.

COUNTRY CLUB STYLE
Period advertisement emphasizes Austin-Healey's fine pedigree as a surefooted thoroughbred sports car.

WINDSHIELD
In 1962, the 3000 acquired a wraparound windshield and windup windows, as the once raw sports car adopted trappings of sophistication.

WHEELS
Wire wheels were options on some models, standard on others.

HOOD SCOOP
All six-cylinder Healeys featured a hood scoop; the longer engine pushed the radiator forward, the scoop cleared the underhood protrusion to aid airflow.

THE HEALEY GRIN
From the traditional Healey diamond grille, the mouth of the Austin-Healey developed into a wide grin, initially with horizontal bars and finally with vertical slats.

STOP AND GO
As the Healey 3000 became beefier throughout the 1960s, modern radial tires helped keep it on course.

SPECIFICATIONS

MODEL Austin-Healey 3000 (1959–68)
PRODUCTION 42,926 (all 3000 models)
BODY STYLES Two-seater roadster, 2+2 roadster, 2+2 convertible.
CONSTRUCTION Separate chassis/body.
ENGINE 2912cc overhead-valve, straight-six.
POWER OUTPUT 3000 MkI: 124 bhp at 4600 rpm. 3000 MkII: 132 bhp at 4750 rpm. 3000 MkIII: 150 bhp at 5250 rpm.
TRANSMISSION Four-speed manual with overdrive.
SUSPENSION *Front:* Independent coil springs and wishbones, antiroll bar. *Rear:* Semielliptic leaf springs. Lever-arm shocks all around.
BRAKES Front discs; rear drums.
MAXIMUM SPEED 110–120 mph (177–193 km/h)
0–60 MPH (0–96 KM/H) 9.5–10.8 sec
A.F.C. 17–34 mpg

AUSTIN-HEALEY 3000 MkIII

The Austin-Healey put on weight over the years. It became gradually more refined, too, but stayed true to its original sports car spirit. The two major influences on its changing faces were the all-important needs of the American market and the impositions of Austin, both as parts supplier and as frugal keeper of purse strings. But from the start, the styling was always a major asset and what you see here in the 3000 MkIII is the eventual culmination of those combined styling forces.

MORE POWER
In 1959, the 2639cc six cylinder of the Healey 100/6 was bored out to 2912cc and rounded up to give the model name 3000.

COMFORTS
Updated weather equipment is an improvement on earlier efforts, which took two jugglers 10 minutes to erect.

REFINED REAR
The first prototype rear end treatment featured fins that were replaced by a classic round rump.

INTERIOR
Once spartan, the cockpit of the Austin-Healey became increasingly luxurious, with a polished veneer dash and even a lockable glove box to complement the fine leather and rich carpet. One thing remained traditional – engine heat meant the cockpit was always a hot place to be.

AUSTIN *Mini Cooper*

THE MINI COOPER was one of Britain's great sports car legends, an inspired concoction that became the definitive rally car of the 1960s and 1970s. In the 1964 Monte Carlo Rally, with Paddy Hopkirk at the wheel, the Cooper produced a giant-killing performance, trouncing 4.7-liter Ford Fairlanes and coming in first, followed in fourth place by yet another Cooper driven by Timo Makinen. After that it never looked back, winning the 1962 and 1964 Tulip Rallies, the 1963 Alpine Rally, and the 1965 and 1967 Monte Carlo, as well as notching up more than 25 other prestigious competition wins.

Because of its size, maneuverability, and front-wheel drive, the Cooper could dance around bigger, more unwieldy cars and scuttle off to victory. Even driven to the absolute limit, it would still corner as if it were on rails long after rear-wheel drive cars were sliding sideways. The hot Mini was a perfect blend of precise steering, terrific handling balance, and a feeling that you could get away with almost anything. The Mini Cooper was originally the brainchild of racing car builder John Cooper, who received $4.00 royalty on every car. However, the Mini's designer, Alec Issigonis, thought it should be a "people's car" rather than a performance machine and did not approve of a tuned Mini. Fortunately BMC (British Motor Corporation) did, and agreed to a trial run of just 1,000 cars. One of BMC's better decisions.

ENGINE
The 1071cc A-series engine would rev to 7200 rpm, producing 72 bhp. Crankshaft, connecting rods, valves, and rockers were all toughened. The Cooper also had a bigger oil pump and beefed-up gearbox.

INTERIOR
The Cooper has typical rally-car features: wood-rim Moto-Lita wheel, fire extinguisher, Halda trip meter, tachometer, stopwatches, and map light. Only the center speedometer, heater, and switches are standard equipment.

THE RALLY CAR
Sir Peter Moon and John Davenport leave the start ramp in the 1964 Isle of Man Manx Trophy Rally in 24 PK. But, while leading the pack on the penultimate stage of the rally at Druidale, 24 PK was rolled and needed a complete rebodying. Many factory-built Coopers led a hard life, often rebuilt and rebodied several times.

SPEEDY CORNERING
With a low center of gravity and a wheel at each extreme corner, the Mini had the perfect credentials for race-car-like handling.

SPOTLIGHT
Roof-mounted spotlight could be rotated from inside the car.

WINDSHIELD
Windshield was glass but all other windows were made out of plastic to save weight.

GRILLE
Front grille was quick-release to give access for emergency repairs.

BRAKES
Lockheed disc brakes and power assist provided the stopping power.

COOPER S
The Cooper S, built between 1963–67, had wider wheels, radial tires, different labeling, and a choice of 970 or 1071cc engines. The 970 S is the rarest of all Coopers, with only 964 made.

NUMBER PLATE
Competitions departments often changed number plates, bodyshells, and chassis numbers, making it hard to identify former factory-built Coopers.

AUSTIN MINI COOPER
24 PK wears the classic Mini rally uniform of straight-through exhaust, Minilite wheels, roll bar, twin fuel tanks, and lightweight stick-on number plates. British Motor Corporation had a proactive Competitions Department, preparing racing Minis with enthusiasm and precision. The Cooper's success in the 1960s is testament to the department's work.

SPECIFICATIONS
MODEL Austin Mini Cooper (1963–69)
PRODUCTION 145,000 (all models)
BODY STYLE Sedan.
CONSTRUCTION All steel two-door monocoque mounted on front and rear sub-frames.
ENGINE 4-cylinder 970cc/997cc/ 998cc/1071cc/1275cc.
POWER OUTPUT 65 bhp at 6500 rpm to 76 bhp at 5800 rpm.
TRANSMISSION Four-speed, no synchromesh on first.
SUSPENSION Independent front and rear suspension with rubber cones and wishbones (hydrolastic from late 1964).
BRAKES Lockheed front discs with rear drums.
MAXIMUM SPEED 100 mph (161 km/h)
0–60 MPH (0–96 KM/H) 12.9 sec
0–100 MPH (0–161 KM/H) 20 sec
A.F.C. 30 mpg

BENTLEY *R-Type Continental*

IN ITS DAY the Bentley Continental, launched in 1952, was the fastest production four-seater in the world and was acclaimed as "a modern magic carpet which annihilates distance." Some 43 years later, it is rightly considered one of the greatest cars of all time. Designed for the English country gentleman, it was understated, but had a lithe, sinewy beauty rarely seen in any other car of its era.

Rolls-Royce's plan was to create a fast touring car for wealthy customers, and to do that the company had to reduce both size and weight. Aluminum construction helped shed the weight, while wind tunnel testing created that slippery shape. Small fins at the back were not for decoration – they actually aided the car's directional stability. The result was a magnificent touring machine that could exceed 115 mph (185 km/h) and manage a 0–60 mph (96 km/h) time of just over 13 seconds. But such avant-garde development did not come cheap. In 1952, the R-Type Continental was the most expensive production car in the world at $18,000 – today's equivalent is about $750,000.

HALFWAY THROUGH THE CONTINENTAL'S PRODUCTION RUN, AUTOMATIC GEARBOXES WERE OFFERED AS AN OPTION AND ADDED TO NO LESS THAN 46 OF THE 208 CARS BUILT

DASHBOARD
Beautifully detailed dash mirrored the Continental's exterior elegance. The first R-Types had manual gearboxes with a right-hand floor-mounted lever, thus reflecting the car's sporting character.

PRODUCTION CARS HAD AN EVEN LOWER ROOFLINE THAN THE ORIGINAL PROTOTYPE

PROTOTYPE HAD SKIRTS COVERING THE REAR WHEELS TO AID AIR FLOW

BENTLEY S-SERIES CONVERTIBLE
The Bentley S-Series Convertible of the late 1950s and early 1960s may bear a passing family resemblance to the Continental, but it does not possess the same tense urgency of line.

THE CONTINENTAL'S AERODYNAMICS WERE DECADES AHEAD OF ITS TIME

BODY WEIGHT WAS KEPT TO A MINIMUM BECALUSE NO 1950S TIRES COULD COPE WITH SPEEDS OVER 120 MPH (193 KM/H)

GENTLY TAPERING
REAR FENDERS
FUNNEL AIR INTO
THE SLIPSTREAM

SMALL REAR
WINDOW WAS A
THROWBACK TO
PREWAR CARS

AERODYNAMIC TESTING

The Continental spent much time in the wind tunnel to reduce air drag during forward motion. Sweeping rear quarters directed the wind over the rear wheels.

ENGINE

Continentals used a 4-liter straight six engine of 4566cc— increased to 4887cc in May 1954, known as the big bore engine. Carburetion was by two SU HD8 units. Speeds ranged from 50 mph (80 km/h) in first to almost 120 mph (193 km/h) in top.

SPECIFICATIONS

MODEL Bentley R-Type Continental (1952–55)
PRODUCTION 208
BODY STYLE Two-door, four-seater touring sedan.
CONSTRUCTION Steel chassis, aluminum body.
ENGINE 4566/4887cc straight sixes.
POWER OUTPUT Never declared, described as "sufficient."
TRANSMISSION Four-speed synchromesh manual or auto optional.
SUSPENSION Independent front with wishbones and coil springs, live rear axle with leaf springs.
BRAKES *Front:* Disc; *Rear:* Drums.
MAXIMUM SPEED 115 mph (185 km/h)
0–60 MPH (0–96 KM/H) 13.5 sec
0–100 MPH (0–161 KM/H) 36.2 sec
A.F.C. 19.4 mpg

ALUMINUM CONSTRUCTION

The body, side window, and window frames were made from lightweight aluminum – courtesy of H.J. Mulliner & Co. Ltd. The prototype had heavy-duty aluminum bumpers; production cars had steel ones.

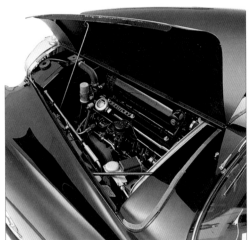

BENTLEY ORNAMENT

The Continental traded heavily on Bentley's prewar reputation for quick touring cars. Perhaps more than any other postwar Bentley, it remained loyal to that tradition of aristocratic speed.

DURING PROTOTYPE TESTING NORMAL SIX-PLY TIRES LASTED ONLY 20 MILES (32 KM)

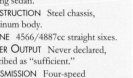

— A POSTWAR CLASSIC —

Designed by Rolls-Royce stylist John Blatchley, the Continental bears an uncanny resemblance to a Pininfarina R-Type prototype shown at the 1948 Paris Salon.

BLATCHLEY INSISTED that he arrived at the Continental's unmistakable shape using only the then-new principles of aerodynamics. He reduced the radiator height to help air distribution and gave the front windshield a steep angle, joining it to the sides of the body to allow the air to spill away. Such dramatic lines were claimed not to be a product of artistic endeavor, but of scientific research. Such was the lure, and indeed the cost, of the Continental that it was first introduced on an export-only basis – 100 of the total production of 208 went abroad. Only 108 were left in the hands of UK owners. This forced the British motoring magazine *Autocar* to remark: "such a car as the Continental is bound to be costly, and the British, who make it, cannot own it: but it goes abroad as proof that a nation where the creators are constantly subjected to the debasement of their own living standards can still keep alive the idea of perfection for others to enjoy." Nothing, it would seem, has changed.

Another car that possibly pre-empted the Continental's lines is the late 1940s Cadillac. There is the vaguest hint of plagiarism by Bentley. British motoring historian Andrew White declared "the 1949 Cadillac was certainly an inspiration for the 1952 Bentley Continental." And he might be

1953 BENTLEY R-TYPE
CONTINENTAL

BENTLEY R-Type Continental

TRUNK WAS CONSIDERED LARGE ENOUGH TO CARRY LUGGAGE FOR TOURING

REAR FLANKS ARE LIKE THE TENSE HAUNCHES OF A SPRINTER

REPATRIATED CONTINENTALS
During the Classic Car boom of the eighties, many Continentals were exported to America and Japan. British collectors, anxious to preserve their disappearing heritage, are now actively repatriating as many as possible. A full list of the whereabouts of every Continental made is now being compiled.

G B

UKL 109

right. Both had sweeping tails, dorsal fins, and lean, smooth lines. American historian Richard Langworth asserts that, "the Cadillac was one of the industry's all-time design greats. Indeed, the grandly praised Bentley Continental, which appeared in '52, had body styling not unlike that of the '49 Caddy."

But that is where the similarity ends. The Bentley handled, the Cadillac did not. America's luxury car was happy wallowing along Sunset Boulevard. The Continental was more at home on a hectic run from London to St. Tropez. It was a car that begged you to depress its accelerator pedal to the floor and reassured you with its immensely powerful brakes and commendable body control, always exuding the poise and grace of a well-

1947 CADILLAC "62" COUPE

mannered thoroughbred.

Collectors seem to agree that the Continental stands alone as the finest postwar Bentley and one of the world's all-time great cars. Proof that it is a far better car than the Cadillac can be found

in the current market values of each. The Cadillac is merely admired; the Bentley is revered, which is why you can buy ten 1949 Cadillacs for the price of a single R-Type Continental.

DOING THE CONTINENTAL

In 1952, with wartime austerity a fading memory, this was one of the flashiest and most rakish cars money could buy. Today, this exemplar of breeding and privilege stands as a resplendent memorial to the affluence and optimism of 1950s Britain.

DESPITE THE NEED TO KEEP WEIGHT DOWN, IT WAS UNTHINKABLE TO SKIMP ON THAT LAVISH INTERIOR

CLASSIC GOTHIC RADIATOR SHELL WAS CONSIDERED FAR MORE SPORTING THAN ROLLS-ROYCE'S DORIC EXAMPLE

FRONT FOG LIGHTS WERE KNOWN AS PASS LIGHTS FOR OVERTAKING

UKL 109

BENTLEY *Flying Spur*

ARGUABLY THE MOST BEAUTIFUL postwar Bentley, the Flying Spur was the first four-door Continental. Initially, Rolls-Royce would not allow coachbuilder H.J. Mulliner to use the name Continental, insisting it should only apply to two-door cars. After months of pressure from Mulliner, R-R relented and allowed the shapely coachbuilt car to be known as a true Continental. More than worthy of the hallowed name, the Flying Spur was launched in 1957, using the standard S1 chassis. In 1959, it inherited R-R's 220 bhp, oversquare, aluminum V-8. By July 1962, the body was given the quad headlight treatment and upgraded into what some consider to be the best of the breed – the S3 Flying Spur. Subtle, understated, and elegant, Flying Spurs are rare. In their day they were among the most admired and refined machines in the world.

ENGINE
Rolls-Royce's long-serving 6.2-liter V-8, still in use today, has aluminum cylinder heads, block, and pistons. The hydraulic tappets were originally supplied by Chrysler, but since this was not good for R-R's image, they insisted they be made back in England.

CAM AND ROLLER POWER STEERING PROVIDES 50 PERCENT ASSISTANCE AT HIGH SPEED, 80 PERCENT WHEN PARKING

INTERIOR
The Interior is pure gentleman's club, with carefully detailed switches, the finest leather and walnut, and West of England cloth for the headlining. The large, spindly steering wheel was power-assisted, standard equipment in 1962. All S3s were automatic, although a few manual S1 Continentals were built.

FRONTAL ASPECT
The four-headlight nose was shared with the standard Steel Bentley S3, although the radiator and hood line were lowered. The body is hand-rolled aluminum.

FPG 74

SUSPENSION
Rear suspension was by semielliptic leaf springs and radius arm and could be adjusted hydraulically between "firm" and "soft" settings.

BRAKES
Flying Spur has four-shoe drum brakes. Because Rolls-Royce brakes should never squeal, the company waited until 1965 to put disc brakes on its cars.

OPTIONAL UNIT
Optional air-conditioning unit hidden behind the front wheel.

SPECIFICATIONS
MODEL S3 Bentley Continental HJ Mulliner Flying Spur (1962–66)
PRODUCTION 291
BODY STYLE Four-door, five-seater.
CONSTRUCTION Aluminum body, separate steel cross-braced box section chassis.
ENGINE V-8, 6230cc.
POWER OUTPUT Never officially declared.
TRANSMISSION Four-speed automatic.
SUSPENSION *Front:* independent coil springs and wishbones.
Rear: semielliptic leaf springs.
BRAKES Four-wheel Girling drums.
MAXIMUM SPEED 115 mph (185 km/h)
0–60 MPH (0–96 KM/H) 10.8 sec
0–100 MPH (0–161 KM/H) 34.2 sec
A.F.C. 13.8 mpg

S2 FLYING SPUR
Beautifully proportioned, many believe the Flying Spur to be more handsome than other R-Rs or Bentleys of the period.

S3 BENTLEY CONTINENTAL H.J. MULLINER FLYING SPUR
Coachbuilder H.J. Mulliner would receive the chassis from Rolls Royce and clothe it with a hand-built body. Although customers would often have to wait up to 18 months for their cars to be completed, the finished product was considered the epitome of good taste and refinement.

WEIGHTY REAR
Rear view shows sheer bulk of the car, which weighed in at close to two tons. Yet the swooping roof line and tapering tail still manage to lend an air of performance.

TIRES
Tires were 8.20x15 Dunlop tubeless cross plys.

BMW *507*

INSTRUMENT PANEL
CONSISTS OF A CLOCK
FLANKED BY A BIG
SPEEDOMETER AND A
6500 RPM TACHOMETER

WHOEVER WOULD have thought that in the mid-'50s BMW would have unveiled something as voluptuously beautiful as the 507. The company had a fine pre-World War II heritage that culminated in the crisp 328, but it did not resume car manufacturing until 1952, with the curvy, but slightly plump, six cylinder 501 sedan. Then, at the Frankfurt show of late 1955, BMW hit us with the 507, designed by Count Albrecht Goertz. The 507 was a fantasy made real; not flashy, but dramatic and with poise and presence. BMW hoped the 507 would solve its precarious finances, winning sales in the lucrative American market. But the BMW's exotic looks and performance were more than matched by its high price. Production, which had been largely by hand, ended in March 1959 after just 252 – some say 253 – had been built. In fact, the 507 took BMW to the brink of financial oblivion, yet if that had been the last BMW it would have been a beautiful way to die.

INTERIOR
There are gimmicky horn pulls behind the steering wheel, but other features foretold later innovations; some cars had internally adjusting door mirrors.

RAKISH BODY
The 507's body is an all-aluminum affair atop a simple tubular steel chassis.

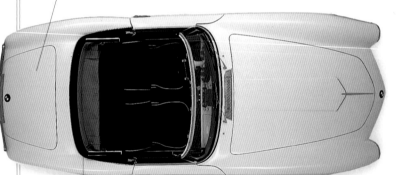

TOP
You rarely see a 507 with its top raised, but it is simple to erect and remarkably handsome.

REAR BUMPER
The 507 features minimal chrome. Rear bumpers have no bulky overriders.

PIPE MUSIC
The BMW has a brisk, wholesome bark and the unmistakable creamy wuffle of a V-8.

LUGGAGE
Inside, there is enough room for a reasonable amount of luggage.

WHEELS
Bolt-on steel wheels were fitted to many cars, but knock-off Rudge items like these remain the most sought-after option.

DOOR HANDLE
Like the bumpers, the door handles are surprisingly discreet if not particularly easy to use.

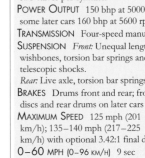

ROUNDELS
Eight BMW stylized propeller roundels, including those on wheel trims and wheel spinners, grace the 507, nine if you include the badge in the center of the steering wheel.

BRAKES
Most 507s were built with four-wheel Alfin drum brakes. Some later cars have more effective front disc brakes.

HANDLING
The 507 exhibited marked understeer; throttle response is so instant that the tail easily snaps out.

RADIATOR GRILLE
BMW's familiar kidney grilles become widely flared "nostrils."

TWIN ZENITH CARBURETORS ARE THE SAME AS THOSE OF CONTEMPORARY PORSCHES

SPECIFICATIONS

MODEL BMW 507 (1956–59)
PRODUCTION 252/3, most LHD
BODY STYLE Two seater roadster.
CONSTRUCTION Box section and tubular steel chassis; aluminum body.
ENGINE All-aluminum 3168cc V-8, two valves per cylinder.
POWER OUTPUT 150 bhp at 5000 rpm; some later cars 160 bhp at 5600 rpm.
TRANSMISSION Four-speed manual.
SUSPENSION *Front:* Unequal length wishbones, torsion bar springs and telescopic shocks.
Rear: Live axle, torsion bar springs.
BRAKES Drums front and rear; front discs and rear drums on later cars
MAXIMUM SPEED 125 mph (201 km/h); 135–140 mph (217–225 km/h) with optional 3.42:1 final drive.
0–60 MPH (0–96 KM/H) 9 sec
A.F.C. 18 mpg

BMW 507

Mounted on a tubular steel chassis cut down from sedans, Albrecht Goertz's aluminum body is reminiscent of the contemporary – and slightly cheaper – Mercedes-Benz 300SL roadster; from the front it resembles the later AC Aces and Cobra *(see pages 20–23)*. All 252 cars were built as convertibles; a detachable hardtop was available as an option.

ENGINE
The 3.2-liter all-aluminum engine was light and powerful and tuned 160 bhp versions, when mated to an optional 3.42 – 1 final-drive ratio, were good for 140 mph (225 km/h).

TOOL KIT
Like all modern BMWs, the 507 has a tool kit – now rarely complete – to carry out minor repairs and adjustments.

HOOD VENT
The ornate chrome plated grilles in the front fenders cover functional engine bay air vents.

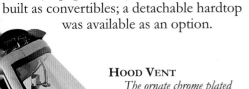

BMW 3.0 CSL

ONE LITTLE LETTER CAN MAKE so much difference. In this case it is the L at the end of the name tag that makes the BMW 3.0CSL so special. The BMW CS pillarless coupes of the late 1960s and early 1970s were elegant and good-looking green house tourers. But add that L and you have a legend. The letter actually stands for "Leightmetall," and when tacked to the rump of the BMW it amounts to war paint, far more intimidating than today's impotent GTi acronyms. The original CSL of 1974 had a 2985cc engine developing 180 bhp, no front bumper, and a mixture of aluminum and thinner-than-standard steel body-panels. In August 1972, a cylinder-bore increase took the CSL's capacity to 3003cc with 200 bhp, and allowed it into Group 2 for competition purposes. But it is the wild-winged, so-called "Batmobile" homologation special that really boils the blood of boy racers. An ultimate road car and great racer, rare, short-lived and high-priced, this charismatic, pared-down Beemer has absolutely classic credentials.

ROAD-GOING RACER
The Batmobile's aerodynamic aids had to be homologated by fitting to at least 500 road cars. They were considered so outrageous that most were supplied as kits for owners to fit – or not – at their discretion.

FLYING MACHINE
The highly effective fenders and spoilers of the so-called Batmobile (left) were developed to keep the 3.2-liter racing 3.0CSLs firmly on the track at high speed.

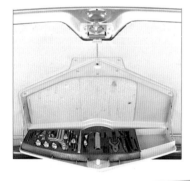

DO-IT-YOURSELF
Road-going cars were only slightly lighter than the CS and CSi; they even had BMW's trademark toolkit, neatly hinged from the underside of the aluminum trunk lid.

STEERING WHEEL IS STRAIGHT OUT OF THE CS/CSL

INTERIOR

British-spec CSLs, like this car, retained Scheel lightweight bucket seats, but had carpets, electric windows (front and rear), power steering, and a sliver of wood.

RACING TRIM
Optional air guide for rear end of roof.

KS·K 5405

CALLING CARD
The large script leaves no one in any doubt about what has just overtaken them.

KS·K 5405

BMW 3.0CSL

Mild rather than wild and winged, the CSL is certainly one of the best-looking cars of its generation. With its pillarless look, the cabin is light and airy, despite the black interior. But all that glass made it hot; air vents behind the BMW rear-pillar badge helped a little.

SPECIFICATIONS

MODEL BMW 3.0CSL (1971–74)
PRODUCTION 1,208 (all versions)
BODY STYLE Two-door pillarless coupe.
CONSTRUCTION Steel monocoque, steel and aluminum body.
ENGINE 2985cc, 3003cc, or 3153cc in-line six.
  POWER OUTPUT 200 bhp at 5500 rpm (3003cc).
  TRANSMISSION 4-speed manual.
  SUSPENSION *Front:* MacPherson struts and anti-roll bar. *Rear:* Semi-trailing arms, coil springs, and anti-roll bar.
  BRAKES Power assisted ventilated discs front and rear.
MAXIMUM SPEED 135 mph (217 km/h) (3003cc)
0–60 MPH 7.3 sec (3003cc)
0–100 MPH 21 sec (3003cc)
A.F.C. 22–25 mpg

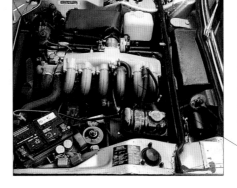

ENGINE

In genuine racing trim, the Batmobile's 3.2-liter straight-six engine gave nearly 400 bhp and, for 1976, nearly 500 bhp with turbocharging. But road cars like this British-spec 3003cc 3.0CSL gave around 200 bhp on fuel injection.

ORIGINAL 2985CC CAPACITY WAS INCREASED TO THIS 3003CC ENGINE FOR HOMOLOGATION PURPOSES

WHEELS
7-in (18-cm) light-aluminum wheels covered by delicate chrome-plated wheelarch extensions.

BUMPER TO BUMPER
German-market CSLs had no front bumper and a fiber-glass rear bumper; this car's metal items show it to be a British-spec model.

3.0 CSL

BMW M1

M1

THE M1 – A SIMPLE NAME, a simple concept. M stood for Motorsport GmbH, BMW's separate competition division. And the number one? Well, this was going to be a first, because this time BMW was not just going to develop capable racers from its competent sedans and coupes. It was going to build a high-profile, beat-all racer, with roadgoing versions basking in the reflected glory of on-track success.

The first prototype ran in 1977, with the M1 entering production in 1978. By the end of production in 1980, a mere 457 racing and roadgoing M1s had been built, making it one of the rarest and most desirable of modern BMWs. Although its racing career was only briefly distinguished, it is as one of the all-time ultimate road cars that the M1 stands out, for it is not just a 277 bhp, 160 mph (257 km/h) "autobahnstormer." It is one of the least demanding supercars to drive, a testament to its fine engineering, and is in many ways as remarkable as the gorgeous 328 of the 1930s.

SPECTACLE ON THE TRACK
BMW teamed up with the FOCA (Formula One Constructors' Association) to create the spectacular Procar series – M1-only races planned primarily as supporting events for Grand Prix meetings in 1979 and 1980.

INTERIOR
The all-black interior is somber, but fixtures are all made to a high standard; unlike those of many supercars, the heating and ventilation systems actually work. The driving position is good, with an adjustable steering wheel and well-placed pedals in the narrow footwells.

ENGINE
The M1's 3453cc straight six engine uses essentially the same cast-iron cylinder block as BMW's 635CSi coupe, but with a forged-aluminum crankshaft and slightly longer connecting rods. The cylinder head is an aluminum casting, with two chain-driven overhead cams operating four valves per cylinder.

LEFT-HAND DRIVE
All BMW M1s are left-hand drive.

AIR DAM
Unlike many of today's high-performance sedan cars, the M1 has only a vestigial lip-type front air dam.

HEADLIGHTS
*Retractable headlights are
backed up by grille-
mounted driving lights.*

SLATTED COVER
*Rearward visibility through the slatted,
heavily buttressed engine cover is restricted.*

BMW M1

The BMW M1 was not a strict in-house
BMW product, but one with widespread
international influences. From a concept
car created in 1972 by Frenchman Paul
Bracq, the final shape of the body was
created in Turin, Italy, by Giorgio
Giugiaro's ItalDesign.
Lamborghini also contributed
to the engineering. Yet
somehow it all comes
together in a unified shape
and, with the double kidney
grille, it is still unmistakably
a BMW.

REAR LIGHTS
*Large rear light clusters
are the same as those of
the BMW's 6-series coupe
and 7-series sedan models.*

GAS CAP
*Twin tanks are refilled via an orifice
behind each door. Remarkably, fuel
consumption can be as good as 30 mpg.*

MIRROR
*Big door mirrors —
essential for maneuvering the M1 —
are electrically adjustable.*

AIR VENT
*Strategically positioned
air vents keep the powerful
3.5-liter engine cool.*

SPECIFICATIONS

MODEL BMW M1 (1978–80)
PRODUCTION 457, all LHD
BODY STYLE Two seater
  mid-engined sports.
CONSTRUCTION Tubular steel space-
  frame with fiberglass body.
ENGINE Inline six, four valves per
  cylinder, dohc/3453cc.
POWER OUTPUT 277 bhp at 6500 rpm.
TRANSMISSION Combined ZF five-
  speed gearbox and limited
  slip differential.
SUSPENSION Coil springs, wishbones
  and Bilstein gas-pressure telescopic
  shocks front and rear.
BRAKES Power assisted ventilated discs
  all around.
MAXIMUM SPEED 162 mph (261 km/h)
0–60 MPH (0–96 KM/H) 5.4 sec
A.F.C. 24–30 mpg

WHEEL
*Slatted Campagnolo
wheels with five-bolts
are unique to the M1.*

BUICK *Roadmaster*

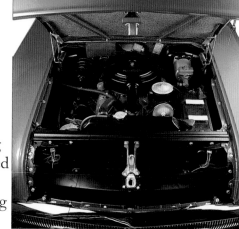

IN 1957 AMERICA WAS gearing up for the 1960s. Little Richard screamed his way to the top with "Lucille" and Elvis had nine hits in a row. Jack Kerouac penned his immortal novel *On the Road*, inspiring carloads of Americans to seek the adman's "Promised Land" along Eisenhower's new interstates. Fins and chrome were applied with a trowel and General Motors, whose styling had begun to lag behind the rest of Detroit's excesses, spent several hundred million dollars restyling its Buick model range. Despite celebrating the ninth million Buick built, 1957 sales were down 24 percent, ranking it fourth in the industry.

The Roadmaster of 1957 was low and mighty, a massive 17 ft 11 in (5.46 m) long and 6 ft (1.83 m) wide. Power was up to 300 hp, along with trendy dorsal fins, Sweepspear body moldings, and a trio of chrome chevrons on the rear fenders. Four Ventiports, a Buick trademark harking back to the original 1949 Roadmaster, still graced the sweeping front fenders. But America did not take to Buick's new look, especially some of the fashionable jet-age design motifs. The chrome bands separating the three-piece rear windows, for example, met with huge consumer resistance and were an option that could be deleted on the order form.

V-8 HAD 10:1 COMPRESSION RATIO, WHICH MEANT 100 OCTANE FUEL

FAST BUICK
The 5.9-liter V-8 pushed out 300 hp, making it one of the hottest Buicks; it was capable of 112 mph (180 km/h) and a zero-to-60 in ten seconds. Dynaflow transmission had variable pitch blades, which changed their angle like those of an airplane propeller.

FICKLE FASHION
Wraparound windshields first emerged in 1954 and by 1957 were standard.

AMERICAN CLASSIC
The 1951 Roadmaster Convertible had become an American icon, the shape of things to come, and one of the first of the great American land yachts with some "get-up-and-go."

GRATUITOUS ORNAMENTATION
The Roadmaster's flattened Ventiports were useless vanities, suggesting fire-breathing power.

GAS CAP
The Roadmaster's rear bumper was home to a new centered gas cap.

STYLING EXCESS
Vast chrome rear bumper made for a prodigious overhang, with massive Dagmar-like overriders, razor-sharp taillights and fluted underpanel – a stylistic nightmare.

FIN FASHION
The Roadmaster showed that by 1957 tail fin fashion was rising to ridiculous heights.

GM BADGE INDICATES THAT BUICKS WERE BUILT AT GM'S FACTORY IN FLINT, MICHIGAN

DASHBOARD
Roadmaster standard special equipment included a Red Liner speedometer, glovebox light, trip odometer, and a color-coordinated dash panel.

BUICK ROADMASTER

Aircraft design exerted a major influence on automotive styling in the 1950s and the '57 Roadmaster was no exception. With wraparound windshield, cockpitlike roof area, and turbine-style wheel covers, a nation of Walter Mittys could imagine themselves vapor-trailing through the stratosphere.

PRESTIGE
The Roadmaster was one of Buick's most luxurious models and wore its hood ornament with pride.

JET AGE
Giant chrome protuberances suggested jet-turbine power.

CABIN OR COCKPIT?
Rakish swooping roof line borrows heavily from bubble cockpits of jet fighters.

CADILLAC *Eldorado Convertible*

FOR 1950S AMERICA, cars did not come much more glamorous than the 1953 Eldorado. "A car apart – even from other Cadillacs," assured the advertising copy. The first Caddy to bear the Eldo name, it was seen as the ultimate and most desirable American luxury car, good enough even for Marilyn Monroe and Dwight Eisenhower. Conceived as a limited edition, the '53 brought avant-garde styling cues from Harley Earl's Motorama Exhibitions. Earl was General Motors' inspired chief designer, while the Motoramas were yearly futuristic car shows where his whims of steel took on form. At a hefty $7,750, nearly twice as much as the Cadillac Convertible and five times as much as a Chevrolet, the '53 was special. In 1954, Cadillac cut the price by 50 percent and soon Eldorados were leaving showrooms like heat-seeking missiles. Today collectors regard the '53 as the one that started it all – the first and most fabulous of the Eldorados.

ULTIMATE CRUISER
As Cadillac's finest flagship, the Eldorado had image by the bucketful. The 331cid V-8 engine was the most powerful yet, and the bodyline was ultrasleek.

WINDSHIELD
The standard Cadillac wraparound windshield was first seen on the '53.

CHROME STYLING
The missile-shaped protuberances on the bumpers were known as Dagmars after the lushly upholstered TV starlet of the day.

SPARE WHEEL
The trunk-mounted spare wheel was an after-market continental touring kit.

INTERIOR
Standard equipment on the Eldo convertible was Hydra-Matic transmission, hydraulic windows, leather and cloth upholstery, tinted glass, vanity and side mirrors, and a "search" radio.

FUTURISTIC EXHAUST
The twin exhausts emerge from the rear bumper – the beginnings of "jet-age" styling themes that would culminate in the outrageous 42-in (107-cm) fins on the 1959 Cadillac Coupe de Ville (see pages 58–61).

CADILLAC ELDORADO CONVERTIBLE
At the time the '53 was America's most powerful car, with a cast-iron V-8, four-barrel carburetor and wedge cylinder head. With the standard convertible weighing 300 lb (136 kg) less, the Eldorado was actually the slowest of the Cadillacs. But despite air conditioning boosting the car's weight to 4,800 lb (2,177 kg), top speed was still a brisk 116 mph (187 km/h).

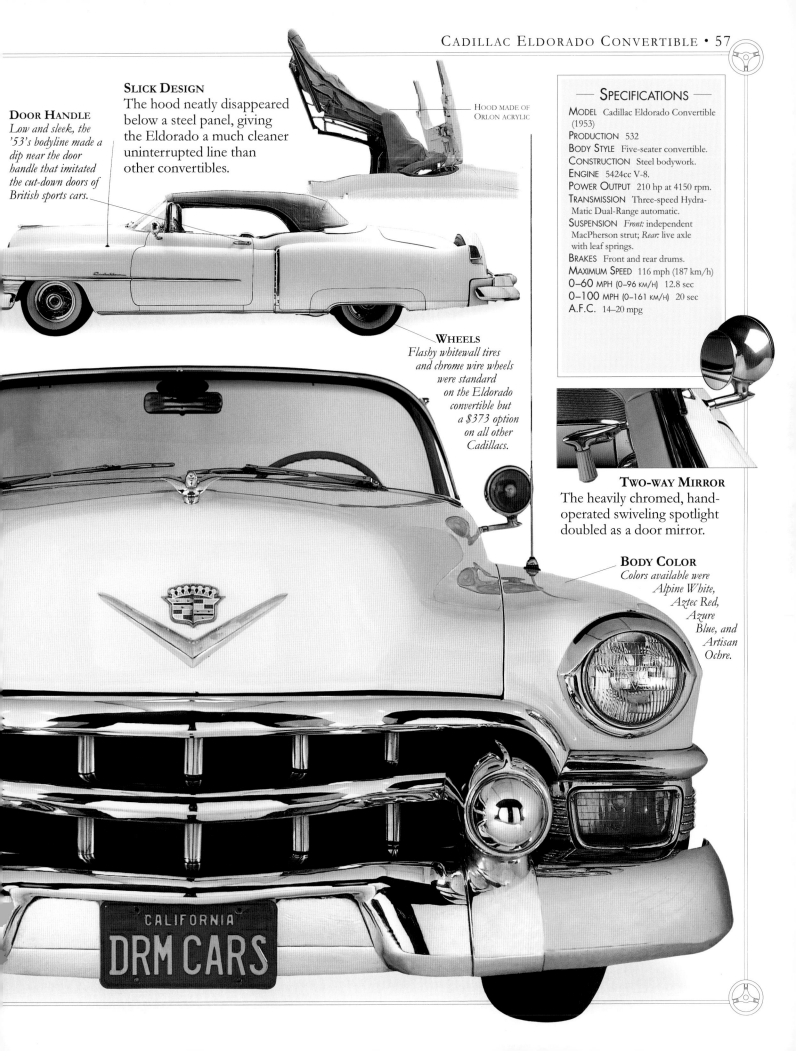

DOOR HANDLE
Low and sleek, the '53's bodyline made a dip near the door handle that imitated the cut-down doors of British sports cars.

SLICK DESIGN
The hood neatly disappeared below a steel panel, giving the Eldorado a much cleaner uninterrupted line than other convertibles.

HOOD MADE OF ORLON ACRYLIC

WHEELS
Flashy whitewall tires and chrome wire wheels were standard on the Eldorado convertible but a $373 option on all other Cadillacs.

SPECIFICATIONS

MODEL Cadillac Eldorado Convertible (1953)
PRODUCTION 532
BODY STYLE Five-seater convertible.
CONSTRUCTION Steel bodywork.
ENGINE 5424cc V-8.
POWER OUTPUT 210 hp at 4150 rpm.
TRANSMISSION Three-speed Hydra-Matic Dual-Range automatic.
SUSPENSION *Front:* independent MacPherson strut; *Rear:* live axle with leaf springs.
BRAKES Front and rear drums.
MAXIMUM SPEED 116 mph (187 km/h)
0–60 MPH (0–96 KM/H) 12.8 sec
0–100 MPH (0–161 KM/H) 20 sec
A.F.C. 14–20 mpg

TWO-WAY MIRROR
The heavily chromed, hand-operated swiveling spotlight doubled as a door mirror.

BODY COLOR
Colors available were Alpine White, Aztec Red, Azure Blue, and Artisan Ochre.

CALIFORNIA
DRM CARS

CADILLAC *Convertible*

NO CAR BETTER sums up America at its peak than the 1959 Cadillac – a rocket-styled starship for orbiting the galaxy of new freeways in the richest and most powerful country on earth. With 42-inch fins, the '59 Caddy marks the zenith of American car design. Two tons in weight, 20 ft (6.1 m) long, and 6 ft (1.83 m) wide, it oozed money, self-confidence, and unchallenged power. Under a hood almost the size of Texas nestled an engine almost as big as California, a 6.3-liter 390cid V-8 – welcome to the world of eight miles to the gallon. But while it might have looked like it was jet-powered, the '59 handled like the Exxon Valdés. That enormous girth meant you needed a nine-lane freeway to do a U-turn and two tons of metalwork gave it all the get-up-and-go of the Empire State Building.

But the '59 Caddy will always be remembered as a glorious monument to the final years of shameless American optimism. And for a brief, hysterical moment the '59 was the preeminent American car, the ultimate in crazed consumerism. It was not only a car, but a symbol of its time that says more about 1950s America than a trunk of history books. The '59 Caddy *was* the American dream.

— OTHER MODELS —

As well as the eight-seater Fleetwood limo, you could have a four-door sedan, convertible, or the cinematic Eldorado Biarritz convertible, which was the most valuable '59 Cadillac of all.

1959 COUPE DE VILLE
Anybody who was anybody in early 1960s America drove a '59 Caddy. It was the best American car money could buy, with the pillarless two-door Coupe de Ville its most popular incarnation.

STYLING
General Motors went crazy in 1959 and the Cadillac pushed car styling to a new peak of absurdity.

LOW PROFILE
The '59's outrageous fins are accentuated by its very low profile, 3 in (8 cm) lower than the '58 model's already modest elevation.

EGG-SHAPED RUBY TAILLIGHTS ARE PURE JET AGE

42-INCH FINS ARE THE HIGHEST OF ANY CAR IN THE WORLD

EXTRAVAGANT MOUNDS OF CHROME MIGHT LOOK LIKE TURBINES BUT CONCEAL BACKUP LIGHTS

WITH HOOD CLOSED, THE CADDY HAD AN UNINTERRUPTED, DARTLIKE PROFILE

SPECIFICATIONS

MODEL Cadillac Convertible (1959)
PRODUCTION 11,130
BODY STYLE Two-door, six-seater convertible.
CONSTRUCTION X-frame chassis, steel body.
ENGINE 6.3-liter 390cid V-8.
POWER OUTPUT 325/345 hp at 4800 rpm.
TRANSMISSION GM Hydra-Matic three-speed automatic.
SUSPENSION Coil springs all around with optional Freon-12 gas suspension.
BRAKES Four-wheel hydraulic power-assisted drums.
MAXIMUM SPEED 112 mph (180 km/h)
0–60 MPH (0–96 KM/H) 10.3 sec
0–100 MPH (0–161 KM/H) 2 3.1 sec
A.F.C. 8 mpg

INTERIOR EXTRAS

Along with power brakes and steering, automatic transmission, central locking, and tinted glass, you could specify automatic headlight dimmers, and electrically operated seats, windows, and trunk.

ELECTRIC WINDOW PANEL

Four electric window controls and remote control for the side mirrors live in a neat panel on the driver's door. Detailing can only be described as Baroque, with large helpings of chrome all around.

AUTRONIC EYE WAS A GIMMICK THAT SOON DISAPPEARED FROM THE BROCHURES

AUTRONIC EYE

For $55, you could specify the Autronic Eye, which dimmed your headlights automatically when it sensed the lights of an oncoming car.

CAR'S THE STAR

The '59 starred in many films. Here, in the aptly named movie *Pink Cadillac*, Clint Eastwood reclines on those dagger-sharp fins.

NOSE APPEAL

With a hood the size of an aircraft carrier, the '59 Caddy was perfect for a society where a car's importance was defined by the length of its nose.

ENGINE

The monster 6.3-liter V-8 engine had a cast-iron block, five main bearings, and hydraulic valve lifters, pushing out a not inconsiderable 325 hp at 4800 rpm.

CHROME DOOR QUARTERLIGHTS COULD BE SWIVELED FROM INSIDE THE CAR

STEEP, WRAP-AROUND WINDSHIELD COULD HAVE COME STRAIGHT OUT OF A FIGHTER PLANE

CHROME WAISTLINE STRIP GAVE BODY PANELS PROTECTION AGAINST JEALOUS CHEVROLETS

MASSIVE SLAB-SIDED DOORS GAVE EASY ENTRANCE AND EXIT

GLAMOROUS WHITE SIDEWALL TIRES WERE A CONVENIENCE OPTION AT $57

FIN DE SIECLE CADILLAC

Harley Earl, the man responsible for the '59, once said, "You can design a car so that every time you get into it, it's a relief – you have a little vacation for a while." His creations were not just a means of transportation but suggested an entire consumer culture and established a new set of national values.

AT THE END of the 1950s, the Russians had put the first Sputnik into orbit, Castro proclaimed a new government in Cuba, Khrushchev got cozy with China, and the gathering specter of nuclear war grew closer and closer. A year later, Kennedy would be elected to the White House and America would enter a new decade of stylistic, social, and political change that would alter the fabric of its culture and lifestyle forever.

But the '59 Cadillac really did belong to the 1950s. With tail fins that rose a full 3½ ft (1.07 m) off the ground, it is an artifact, a talisman of its times. It was not just a car, but a styling icon, wonderfully representative of the

1920S CIGARETTE CARD SHOWING A "CAR OF THE FUTURE"

end of an era – the last years of American world supremacy and an obsession with rockets and space travel.

Harley Earl, directly responsible for the design of 50 million vehicles, completely changed the face of America and the way Americans perceived themselves. No single individual has had such a profound impact on the shape of man-made objects as Earl, and nobody since has been guilty of so many design excesses. On top of the space-

ONE OF HARLEY EARL'S FUTURISTIC DESIGNS

CADILLAC
Convertible

SEATS SIT 4 IN (10 CM) LOWER THAN THE '57 MODEL

TRUNK IS CAVERNOUS AND CAN HOLD FIVE WHEELS AND TIRES

EXTENSIVE INTERIOR
The interior is vast, and a true six-seater, with acres of leg, knee, head, and elbow room. Bucket seats were an optional extra on the Biarritz – only 99 out of 1,320 had them.

AUG PENNSYLVANIA
XSU-385

PONTIAC FIREBIRD PROTOTYPE

vibration, and the general quality was not up to what the market had come to expect from the premier American carmaker. In fact, commentators thought the '59 was too strident and garish. So did Cadillac, which lopped 6 in (15.5 cm) off the fins the next model year. Yet it is those fins which give the car such status in the annals of excess and have guaranteed its collectibility as a glorious piece of American 1950s kitsch.

age theme, Earl grafted other images to his cars. Grilles had rows of chromium dentures, dashboards looked like flight decks with dozens of gratuitous switches, hoods sported phallic mascots, and bumpers sprouted enormous breast-shaped protrusions known as Dagmars. The grille was a subliminal form of threat display, while the sensuous bumpers were patently erotic. By the late 1950s, the American car was loaded with so many strange and sometimes contradictory symbols that the average American must have

felt as though he was in command of a four-wheeled, jet-powered bordello.

But the Caddy does not have a special place in the motoring history because it was an exceptional car. Far from it. '59s had a reputation as rust-raisers, front ends were notorious for

SKETCH OF JET-POWERED TWO-SEATER DRAWN UP BY FORD'S ADVANCE STYLING SECTION

THE '59 HAD A BIG THIRST, WITH A 21-GALLON FUEL TANK, 23-PINT (US) TRANSMISSION, 12-PINT CRANKCASE, AND 10-PINT RADIATOR CAPACITY

STEERING ASSISTANCE
The featherlight power steering required only three-and-a-half turns lock-to-lock. The '59 could be hustled around with great panache, but you needed a 24-ft (7.3 m) turning radius.

DOUBLE HEADLIGHTS WERE A STYLING ESSENTIAL ON ALL 1960s AMERICAN CARS

Z FINNS
XSU·385

CHEVROLET *Corvette Sting Ray*

THE CHEVROLET CORVETTE is America's native sports car. The "plastic fantastic," born in 1953, is still plastic, and still fantastic more than 40 years later. Along the way, in 1992, it recorded its millionth sale and it is still hanging in there. Admittedly it has mutated over the years, but it has stayed true to its roots on every important aspect. Other US sports car contenders, like the Ford Thunderbird *(see pages 116–17)*, soon abandoned any sporting pretensions, adding weight and middle-aged girth, but not the Corvette. All Corvette fanciers have their favorite eras: for some it is the purity of the very first generation from 1953; others favor the glamorous 1956–62 models; but for many the Corvette came of age in 1963 with the birth of the Sting Ray.

ENGINE CHOICES
Sting Rays came in three engine sizes – naturally all V-8s – with power options from 250 hp to more than twice that. This featured car is a 1966 Sting Ray with "small block" 327cid V-8 and Holley four-barrel carburetor.

HIDDEN LIGHTS
Twin, pop-up headlights were hidden behind electrically operated covers; more than a gimmick, they aided aerodynamic efficiency.

"DUAL COCKPIT"
The Batmobile-style interior, with twin-hooped dash, is carried over from earlier Corvettes, but updated in the Sting Ray. The deep-dished, wood-effect wheel comes close to the chest. Power steering was an option.

— **OTHER MODELS** —
Until 1963, all Corvettes were open roadsters, but with the arrival of the Sting Ray, a hardtop coupe was now also available.

1963 SPLIT-SCREEN COUPE
The distinctive two-piece back window was used for 1963 only; consequently, this "design failing" is now the most sought after of Sting Ray coupes.

19 MICHIGAN 71
RMG·319
GREAT LAKE STATE

SPECIFICATIONS

MODEL Chevrolet Corvette Sting Ray (1963–67)

PRODUCTION 118,964

BODY STYLES Two-door sports convertible or fastback coupe.

CONSTRUCTION Fiberglass body; X-braced pressed-steel box-section chassis.

ENGINE OHV V-8, 327cid, 396cid, 427cid.

POWER OUTPUT 250–375 hp (327cid), 390–560 hp (427cid).

TRANSMISSION Four-speed, all-synchromesh manual, optional three-speed manual, or Powerglide automatic.

SUSPENSION Independent all around. *Front:* Unequal-length wishbones with coil springs; *Rear:* Transverse leaf.

BRAKES Drums to 1965, then four-wheel discs.

MAXIMUM SPEED 152 mph (245 km/h, 427 cid).

0–60 MPH (0–96 KM/H) 5.4 sec, 427 cid

0–100 MPH (0–161 KM/H) 13.1 sec

A.F.C. 9–16 mpg

CHEVROLET CORVETTE STING RAY

The Sting Ray was a bold design breakthrough, giving concrete expression to many of the ideas of new GM styling chief Bill Mitchell. More than half of all production was in convertible roadsters, for which a hardtop was an option. From the rear, charismatic fastbacks could be a totally different car.

SIDE EXHAUST
Aluminum strip conceals side-mounted exhaust option; standard exhausts exited through bodywork below the rear bumper.

BRAKES
In 1965 the Sting Ray added four-wheel disc brakes in place of drums.

SEATING
Seats are low and flat, rather than figure-hugging, but the view over the hood is great.

FLAG WAVING
The checkered flag denotes sporting lineage, the other flag bears the GM corporate "Bow Tie" and a Fleur de Lis — lest we forget that Louis Chevrolet was French.

NAME TRIVIA
Corvettes from 1963 to 1967 were Sting Rays; the restyled 1968 model became Stingray, one word.

HOOD
You can tell this is a "small block" engine — the hood power bulge was widened to accommodate the "big block" unit.

TRUNK SPACE
Fuel tank and spare tire took up most of the available trunk space, but at least the trunk opened; it did not on the fastback.

CHEVROLET *Impala*

THE CHEVY IMPALA was an evergreen best-seller and America's favorite family sedan. Chevrolet's product planners figured that America's middle classes would be a boom market in the early 1960s – and they were right. The Impala notched up nearly half a million sales in 1960. The fins, chrome, and mock vents meant it was bumper-to-bumper glitz, all at a sticker price of under $3,000.

With a wide range of engine sizes, transmission types, and body styles to choose from, the Impala had it all. And those crossed racing flags were not just empty chrome rhetoric. Enlightened buyers could specify the special Turbo-thrust V-8, making the Impala a "hot one" with a respectable 0–60 mph canter of just over nine seconds. Even though the styling was toned down for the 1960 model year, the finny Impala remains a perfect embodiment of 1960s American exuberance.

ENGINE
From a 235cid six-cylinder all the way up to a hot 348cid V-8, the Impala could be specified with some serious iron under its hood.

CHEVROLET BADGE
1959 marked a watershed for Chevrolet, moving out of the budget market to seduce aspirational suburbia with new styling themes.

GLASS AREA
With the windows rolled down, the car is pillarless, with 90 percent all-around visibility.

DASHBOARD
Aeronautical styling motifs abound, with gauges enclosed in flight-deck-type modules. Lower dash and glove compartment were covered in anodized aluminum for that high-tech look. Radio and electric clock were options.

ORIGINAL '58 IMPALA
1958 was the first year of the Impala, the flagship of the Chevy fleet and a calculated attempt to catch Ford and Plymouth, which had restyled their products the previous year. Styling was close to Cadillac's, and the Impala's new look rendered Buick and Oldsmobile dated. Some 181,500 Impalas were sold in 1958 – 15 percent of Chevy's production.

LIGHT CLUSTER
Triple taillights and an aluminum rear panel were glorious pieces of gratuitous kitsch.

TURN SIGNALS
Clear white lights nestling under the front bumper were not parking lights, but turn signals.

WHEEL COVERS
Deluxe wheel covers and whitewalls helped cut a mild suburban dash.

LABELING
Only crazy stylists would stoop to putting labels on the rear doors.

TAILPIPE
Single rear chrome exhaust exits impudently from behind the rear wheel.

CHEVROLET IMPALA FOUR-DOOR HARDTOP

Low, flashy, and beguiling, the Impala looked fast just standing still. Styling was a riot of streaking chrome. Quarter panel missile ornaments thrust rearward, while a chromium-finned projectile darted across the rear door, a quaint reminder of 1960s American obsession with all things space age. And those gullwing rear fins pursue a perfect horizontal line along the waist of the car, ending in a rounded flare on the extreme tip of both front fenders. Front and back windshields could have been taken straight out of the cockpit of a Lockheed Lightning. Even the radio antenna was raked at a provocative angle.

GRILLE
The Impala's slatted frontal aspect is its least pleasing facet. Built on a budget, the Venetian blind grille is an eyesore.

FINS
Compared to the '59, the fins on the '60 Impala were tame. Conventional Chevrolet customers did not like the previous model's weird extravagance.

STYLING
Despite the '60 Impala's supposedly quieter styling, no self-respecting American could bear to be without those trendy quad headlights.

HANDLING
With upper and lower A arms and coil springs, the Impala cornered with cinematic tire squeal and plenty of body roll.

SPECIFICATIONS

MODEL Chevrolet Impala (1960)
PRODUCTION Approx. 500,000
BODY STYLE Six-seater, four-door hardtop.
CONSTRUCTION Separate chassis, steel body.
ENGINE Various – 235cid straight-six to 348cid V-8.
POWER OUTPUT 230 hp at 4800 rpm to 335 hp at 5800 rpm.
TRANSMISSION Three-speed manual, two-speed Powerglide, and three-speed Turboglide automatics.
SUSPENSION *Front:* Coil springs and wishbones.
Rear: Coil springs and live axle.
BRAKES Four-wheel drums.
MAXIMUM SPEED 90–135 mph (145–217 km/h)
0–60 MPH (0–96 KM/H) 9–13 sec
0–100 MPH (0–161 KM/H) 20–27 sec
A.F.C. 14–17 mpg

CHEVROLET *Camaro* RS *Convertible*

RUMORS THAT General Motors had at last come up with something to steal sales from Ford's massively successful Mustang *(see pages 120–23)* swept through the American auto industry in the spring of 1966. Code-named Panther, the Camaro was announced to newspaper reporters on June 29, 1966, reaching showrooms on September 21. The Pony Car building-block philosophy was simple: sell a basic machine and allow the customers to add their own extras.

The trouble was that the Camaro had an option list as arcane as a lawyer's library. From Strato-Ease headrests to Comfort-Tilt steering wheel, the Camaro buyer was faced with an embarrassment of riches. But it worked. Buyers ordered the Rally Sport equipment package for their stock Camaros and suddenly they were kings of the road. Go-faster body striping, hidden headlights, and matte black taillight bezels were all calculated to enhance the illusion of performance pedigree, especially if the buyer could not afford the real thing – the hot Camaro SS.

Z28 CAMARO
Trans Am racing spawned the Z28 Camaro, a thinly veiled street racer designed to take on the Shelby Mustang. Top speed was 124 mph (200 km/h) and 60 mph came up in just 6.7 seconds.

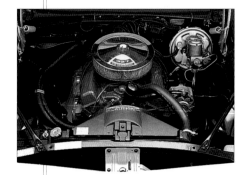

ENGINE
The basic V-8 power plant for Camaros was the trusty small block cast-iron 327cid lump, which, with a bit of tuning, evolved into the 350cid unit of the desirable SS models. Compression ratio was 8.8:1, and it produced 210 hp at 4600 rpm.

327 LABEL
Unlike Europe, where power was measured in cc, American horsepower was all about cubic inches.

INTERIOR
Standard Camaro interiors included color-keyed, all-vinyl trim, Strato-bucket front seats, and color-keyed carpeting. Strato-back bench seat was optional.

NOSE JOB
Lengthening the Camaro's wheelbase created a frontal overhang of 36.7 in (93 cm).

BRAKES
Disc brakes were a popular option and included special vented steel rally wheels.

camaro

327

rs

REAR LIGHTS
All-red taillight lenses with black bezels were an RS feature.

BACKUP LIGHTS
On the RS package, back-up lights were moved to the rear valance panel.

GAS CAP
Center-mounted fuel filler had RS emblem inscribed.

TOP
When the Camaro raised its roof, the purity of line was not disturbed.

INTERIOR
Dash was the usual for the era, with acres of plastic and mock woodgrain veneer. This model has the optional four-speed manual gearbox.

CHEVROLET CAMARO RS CONVERTIBLE

The market accepted the Camaro as a solid response to the Mustang. Its styling was cleaner, more European, and less boxy, and it drove better than the Ford. Even so, Camaro sales were considerably less than the Mustang.

RS PINSTRIPING
Stick-on pinstriping helped flatter the Camaro's curves.

POWER
The 327 V-8 was puny. Real grunt came from the 375 hp 396cid cooking SS version.

SPECIFICATIONS

MODEL Chevrolet Camaro RS Convertible (first generation, 1967–70)
PRODUCTION 1967 model year: 10,675 RS convertibles, 195,765 coupes, and 25,141 convertibles.
BODY STYLE Two-door, four-seater convertible.
CONSTRUCTION Steel monocoque.
ENGINE 327cid small block V-8.
POWER OUTPUT 275 hp at 4800 rpm.
TRANSMISSION Three- or four-speed manual, two- or three-speed automatic.
SUSPENSION Independent front, rear leaf springs.
BRAKES Drums with optional power-assisted front discs.
MAXIMUM SPEED 110 mph (177 km/h)
0–60 MPH (0–96 KM/H) 8.3 sec
0–100 MPH (0–161 KM/H) 25.1 sec
A.F.C. 18 mpg

CITROËN 2CV

RARELY HAS A CAR been so ridiculed as the Citroën 2CV. At its launch at the 1948 Paris Salon, journalists lashed into this defenseless runabout with vicious zeal. Everyone who was near Paris at the time claimed to be the originator of the quip, "Do you get a can opener with it?" They all missed the point, for this minimal car was not meant to be measured against other cars; its true rival was the farmer's horse and cart, which Citroën boss Pierre Boulanger hoped to replace with his *toute petite voiture* – or very small car. As the Deux Chevaux, it became much more than that and putt-putted into the history books, selling more than five million by the time of its eventual demise in 1990. As devotees of the 2CV say, "You either love them or you don't understand them."

TOUGH TWO-CYLINDER
The original 375cc air-cooled twin, as seen here, eventually grew to all of 602cc, but all versions are genuinely happy to rev flat out all day. They love it.

DOORS
You were lucky to get them; prototypes featured oilcloth door coverings.

CITROËN 2CV
In 1935, Pierre Boulanger conceived a car to woo farmers away from the horse and cart. It would weigh no more than 661 lb (300 kg), carry four people at 37 mph (60 km/h), and run cheaply, going 56 miles on a gallon of gas. The suspension should be supple enough to transport a basket of eggs across a plowed field without breaking a single shell. The car that appears "undesigned" was in fact carefully conceived.

BACK IN FASHION
The two-tone Dolly was a 1985 special edition that, due to strong demand from the fashion-conscious who wanted to be seen in a 2CV, became a standard production model.

SEATS
Minimal, but handy; lightweight, hammock-style seats lift out to accommodate more goods or provide picnic seating.

INSTRUCTIONS ON HOW TO START AND STOP THE 2CV

SOLE INSTRUMENT ON CONSOLE IS AN AMMETER; NO IGNITION KEY

TRUNK
Roll-up canvas trunk lid of the original saved both weight and cost; a metal trunk lid took over in 1957 on French cars.

BODY COLORS
Gray until late 1959, the 2CV later came in Glacier Blue; in 1960, adding green and yellow gave a kaleidoscope of choices.

DRIVER FEEDBACK
Who needs banks of aircraft-style instruments anyway? These days they call it driver feedback, but in a classic 2CV you can tell that you are moving because the scenery changes – albeit slowly. In fact there is a speedometer to help reinforce the notion, but in the 2CV's less-is-more idiom the speedometer cable also drives the windshield wipers.

SURPRISING HANDLING
The tenacious grip of the skinny tires is astonishing, providing an exceptional ride.

HEADLIGHTS
Prewar production prototypes had only one headlight.

SIMPLE CHASSIS
Although designers flirted with notions of a chassis-less car, cost dictated a more conventional sheet steel platform chassis.

SPECIFICATIONS

MODEL Citroën 2CV (1949–90)
PRODUCTION 5,114,966 (includes vans)
BODY STYLES Four-door convertible sedan, two-door van.
CONSTRUCTION Separate steel platform chassis, steel body.
ENGINE Air-cooled, horizontally opposed twin of 375cc, 425cc, 435cc, 602cc.
POWER OUTPUT 9, 12, 18, and 29 bhp, respectively.
TRANSMISSION Four-speed manual, front-wheel drive.
SUSPENSION Independent interconnected coil-sprung.
MAXIMUM SPEED 375cc, 43 mph (69 km/h); 425cc, 49 mph (79 km/h); 435cc, 53 mph (85 km/h); 602cc, 72 mph (116 km/h).
0–60 MPH (0–96 KM/H) 30 sec (602cc)
A.F.C. 45–55 mpg

ROLL-TOP REASON
The sober design purpose of the roll-top roof was to allow the transportation of tall, bulky objects.

AIR VENT
Fresh air was obtained by opening the vent on the firewall; a mesh strained out the insects and leaves.

DUAL TURN SIGNALS
A good example of the functional design ethos. Why put turn signals on the front and back, when you could give your car "ears" that could be seen front and rear?

BOLT ON
All the body panels simply unbolt, and even the body shell is held in place by only 16 bolts.

537-BV-43

SUSPENSION
The sophisticated independent suspension system together with that 2CV trademark, body roll, gave a soft ride.

CITROËN *Traction Avant*

LOVED BY POLITICIANS, poets, and painters alike, the Traction Avant marked a watershed for both Citroën and the world's motor industry. A design prodigy, it was the first mass-produced car to incorporate a monocoque bodyshell with front-wheel drive and torsion-bar springing, and began Citroën's love affair with the unconventional.

Conceived in just 18 months, the Traction Avant was costly for the French company. By 1934 Citroën had emptied the company coffers, laid off 8,000 workers, and, on the insistence of the French government, was taken over by Michelin, which gave the Traction Avant the backing it deserved. It ran for over 23 years, with more than three quarters of a million sedans, hardtop coupes, and convertibles sold. The world lavished unstinting praise on the Traction Avant, extolling its road-holding, hydraulic brakes, ride comfort, and cornering abilities. Citroën's audacious sedan was the most significant and successful production car of its time, eclipsed only by the passage of 20 years and another *voiture revolutionnaire*, the Citroën DS.

SUSPENSION ATTRACTION
In 1954, the six-cylinder Traction Avant was known as "Queen of the Road" because of its hydro-pneumatic suspension – a mixture of liquid and gas.

STYLISH DESIGN
The Art Deco door handle is typical of Citroën's obsession with form and function.

SIDE-OPENING HOOD WAS A PREWAR FEATURE

ENGINE REPAIRS MEANT REMOVING THE HOOD COMPLETELY

NEW COLORS
In 1953, buyers had the option of gray or blue. Until then all Traction Avants had been black.

FRONT SUSPENSION
All-independent suspension with torsion-bar springing, upper wishbones, radius arms, friction shocks, and worm-and-roller steering (later rack-and-pinion) gave crisp handling.

ENGINE
The Traction's Maurice Sainturat-designed engine was new. "Floating Power" came from a short-stroke four-cylinder unit, with a three-bearing crankshaft and pushrod overhead valves – producing seven French horsepower.

ENGINE, GEARBOX, RADIATOR, AND FRONT SUSPENSION WERE MOUNTED ON A DETACHABLE CRADLE FOR EASY MAINTENANCE

FRONT WHEEL
Front-wheel drive made for tenacious road holding.

REAR SUSPENSION
Rear suspension was through a trailing axle with twin transverse torsion bars, longitudinal radius arms, and hydraulic shocks.

WINDOW
Minimal rear visibility.

CITROËN TRACTION AVANT

With aerodynamic styling, unit steel body and sweeping fenders without running boards, the Traction Avant was a technical and aesthetic tour de force. Yet, despite lavish praise, it was this great grand routier that devoured André Citroën's wealth and pushed him to his death bed.

REVISED TRUNK
In 1952, Citroën dispensed with the earlier "bobtail" rear end and gave the Traction a "big trunk."

DASHBOARD
Three-speed gearbox was mounted ahead of the engine, with synchromesh on second and third. Drive reached the road by Cardin driveshafts and constant velocity joints at the axles. The dash-mounted gearshift *(right)* lived on in the DS of 1955 *(see pages 72–75).*

WHEEL
Michelin produced these Pilote wheels and tires for the Traction.

SPECIFICATIONS

MODEL Citroën Traction Avant (1934–55)
PRODUCTION 758,858 (including six-cylinder)
BODY STYLE Five-seater, four-door sedan.
CONSTRUCTION Steel front-wheel drive monocoque.
ENGINE 1911cc in-line four-cylinder.
POWER OUTPUT 46 bhp at 3200 rpm.
TRANSMISSION Three-speed manual.
SUSPENSION Independent front and rear.
BRAKES Hydraulic drums front and rear.
MAXIMUM SPEED 70 mph (113 km/h)
0–60 MPH (0–96 KM/H) 25 sec
A.F.C. 23 mpg

CITROËN *DS DECAPOTABLE*

IN 1955, WHEN CITROËN FIRST DROVE prototypes of its mold-breaking DS through Paris, the cars were pursued by crowds shouting "La DS, la DS, voilà la DS!" Few other cars before or since were so technically and stylistically audacious. At its launch, the DS created as much interest as the death of Stalin. Cushioned on a bed of hydraulic fluid, with a semiautomatic gearbox, self-leveling suspension, and detachable body panels, it instantly rendered half the world's cars out of date.

Parisian coachbuilder Henri Chapron produced 1365 convertible DSs using the chassis from the Safari Estate model. Initially Citroën refused to cooperate with Chapron but eventually sold the Decapotable models through its dealer network. At the time the flashy four-seater convertible was considered by many to be one of the most charismatic open-top cars on the market. Today, genuine Chapron cars command three to four times the price of their sedan counterparts.

ENGINE
The DS 21's rather sluggish 2145cc engine developed 109 bhp and was never highly praised, having its origins in the prewar Traction Avant *(see pages 70–71).*

SUSPENSION INACTIVE

AERODYNAMICS
The slippery, streamlined body penetrated the air with extreme aerodynamic efficiency. Body panels were detachable for easy repair and maintenance. Rear fenders could be removed for wheel changing in minutes, using just the car's jack. The novel suspension could be raised to clear rough terrain or navigate flooded roads.

THE DS WAS ACKNOWLEDGED TO HAVE THE FINEST RIDE QUALITY OF ANY CAR IN THE WORLD

SUSPENSION RISING

THE DS WAS NICKNAMED THE "SHARK" BECAUSE OF ITS PRODIGIOUS NOSE

SUSPENSION RAISED

MICHELIN DESIGNED UNIQUE X-TYPE RADIAL PLY TIRES SPECIALLY FOR THE DS

PAST OWNERS OF THE DS INCLUDE GENERAL DE GAULLE, BRIGITTE BARDOT, AND THE POET C. DAY-LEWIS

DESIGN CLASSIC
Smooth Bertone-designed lines have made the Citroën DS a cult design icon and the cerebral choice for doctors, architects, artists, and musicians.

GEAR LEVER
The four-speed semiautomatic gearbox had no clutch and changes were made by hydraulic servo motors; the driver lifted off the accelerator and moved the lever gently along the gate.

DASHBOARD
Bertone's asymetrical dashboard makes the interior look as futuristic as the rest of the car. The single-spoke steering wheel was a Citroën hallmark.

CUSTOMER CHOICE
Because the Decapotable was virtually handbuilt, customers could specify almost any stylistic or mechanical extra.

ADVERTISEMENT
Citroën's advertising made much of the car's futuristic looks; it was once displayed without wheels to enhance its rocket-ship styling. The London Design Museum once held a special DS exhibition.

THE INSIDE WAS AS INNOVATIVE AS THE OUTSIDE, WITH CLEVER USE OF CURVED GLASS AND COPIOUS LAYERS OF FOAM RUBBER, EVEN ON THE FLOORS

CITROEN KNEW THAT HEAVY FRONT-WHEEL DRIVE CARS NEEDED POWER-ASSISTED BRAKES AND STEERING, AND PATENTED THEIR HYDRAULIC SYSTEM AS EARLY AS 1940

THE DISAPPEARING NOSE WAS VERY VULNERABLE TO PARKING MANEUVERS; THIN RUBBER OVERRIDER-TYPE BUMPERS OFFERED SOME PROTECTION

CITROËN'S VISION OF THE FUTURE

Never before in the history of the automobile had a mass market machine achieved such an incredible quantum leap in performance, comfort, and styling.

THE DS'S LIST of innovations was remarkable. Fully independent gas suspension gave a magic-carpet ride, front-wheel drive gave unerring high-speed control and maneuverability, Michelin X-Radial tires contributed high levels of grip, and stopping power was provided by inboard disc brakes with dual circuits. Even gear-shifting and clutch action were aided by hydraulic power-assisted motors, and its sharp rack-and-pinion steering was assisted by high pressure hydraulic power. Add a body style that looked like something out of a Buck Rogers comic and you begin to marvel that all this occurred in 1955, when the novelty of electric razors had just worn off.

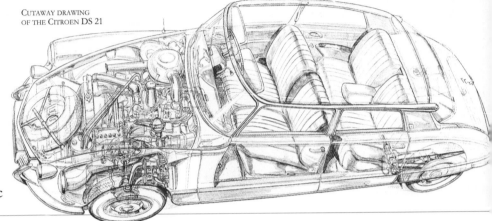

CUTAWAY DRAWING OF THE CITROEN DS 21

CITROËN *DS Decapotable*

HIGH PRAISE
The French philosopher Roland Barthes was captivated by the DS's design and compared its technical pre-eminence to the Gothic flourish of medieval cathedrals.

TURN SIGNALS
The Decapotable's trademark was angled chrome-plated turn signals perched on the rear fenders.

CITROEN'S DOUBLE CHEVRONS ARE MODELED ON HELICAL GEARS

ON ALL DSs THE REAR TRACK WAS NARROWER THAN THE FRONT

DS 21

2724 Y 33

Success came soon for the DS. On the first day of the 1955 Paris Motor Show, 749 orders were taken within 45 minutes, 12,000 within the first day and, by the end of the week, Citroën's prodigy had amassed 80,000 confirmed orders. But the French company had launched the DS too early, prompted by scoop pictures in the French magazine *L'Auto Journal* in 1953. Reliability was patchy – the suspension literally let itself down, Citroën dealers had no technical manuals to work from, and owners, whose expectations were understandably high, limped home crestfallen. In 1962, the image of the DS got a shot in the arm when terrorists attacked President General De Gaulle. Despite being sprayed with bullets and having two flat tires, the presidential DS was able to swerve and speed away to safety.

By the time the DS was deleted from the brochures in 1975, no less than 1½ million had been sold worldwide. For a brief period, the DS fell from grace. In the 1970s, it was eclipsed by the CX, and was seen as overly complicated and difficult to mend. But by the early 1980s, that shape began to recapture the imagination of car enthusiasts, who rightly hailed it as a style icon and a work of art. Championed as the Car of the Century, the DS was unique, a mechanical invention so brilliant that

CITROEN DS 21 PALLAS

it stood alone as an inspired vision of the future that owed nothing to conventional wisdom and everything to creative genius.

FRONT SHOT

Low, rakish, and space-age in appearance, the DS was so perfectly styled that it hardly altered shape in 20 years. A major change came in 1967 when the headlights and optional pod spot lights were faired in behind glass covers.

UNLIKE MANY CHAPRON CONVERTIBLES, THIS CAR IS NOT FITTED WITH A CHROME HOOD HANDLE

EARLY EXPOSED HEADLIGHTS MAY HAVE LOOKED GOOD BUT WERE VIRTUALLY USELESS ON LOW BEAM

2724 Y 33

CITROËN *SM*

CITROËN ⌃ SM

THE CITROËN SM makes about as much sense as the Concorde, but since when have great cars had anything to do with common sense? It is certainly a flight of fancy, an extravagant, technical *tour de force* that, as a 16-ft (4.9-m) long streamliner, offered little more than 2+2 seating.

The SM bristled with innovations – many of them established Citroën hallmarks – like swiveling headlights and self-leveling hydropneumatic suspension. It was a complex car – too complex, in fact. And of course there was that Maserati V-6 motor. Yet once again Citroën had created an enduringly futuristic car where other "tomorrow cars of today" were soon exposed as voguish fads.

THIS IS THE 2.7-LITER V-6; LATER A 3-LITER AUTO WAS OFFERED, MAINLY FOR THE US MARKET

ENGINE
SM stands for Serié Maserati, and here it is – the exquisite Maserati all-aluminum V-6 engine, weighing just 309 lb (140 kg) and only 12 in (31 cm) long, but producing at least 170 bhp. Capacity was initially kept below 2.8 liters to escape France's punitive vehicle taxation system.

PURELY FUNCTIONAL
This bulge in the tailgate above the rear number plate is for purely functional, aerodynamic reasons. It also suited the deeper license plates used in the US.

REAR CRAMP
Citroën's publicity material tried to hide the fact, but rear-seat legroom and headroom are barely sufficient for two large children.

SUPPORTING ROLE
Like that of most front-wheel-drive cars, the SM's rear suspension does little more than hold the body off the ground.

COMPOUND CURVES
The tinted rear window, with compound curves and heating elements, must have cost a fortune to produce.

ROLLING ALONG
Despite its size and weight the SM can be thrown around like a sports car. It rolls, as here, like a trawler in a heavy sea and, like all front-wheel-drivers, it understeers strongly, but resolutely refuses to let go.

US INFLUENCE
Only the SM's over-elaborate chromed rear "fins" betray the General Motors styling influence.

SKIRTS
Fender skirts were a throwback to an earlier age, but necessary to allow the removal of the rear wheel.

WHEELS
Lightweight wheels reinforced with carbonfiber were optionally available.

IT TOOK PRACTICE
TO DECIDE IN A
HURRY WHAT EACH
OF THE TINY
WARNING LIGHTS
ACTUALLY MEANT

DASHBOARD

The SM's controls owe more to style than ergonomics. The oval speedometer and tachometer are visible through the single-spoke steering wheel, and the perennially confusing cluster of warning lights *(above)* is to the right.

SPECIFICATIONS

MODEL Citroën SM, SM EFI, and SM Auto (1970–75)
PRODUCTION 12,920 (all types, all LHD)
BODY STYLE Two-door, 2+2 coupe.
CONSTRUCTION All-steel unibody, with steel body and aluminum hood.
ENGINE All-aluminum 90-degree V-6 of 2670cc (2974cc for SM Auto).
POWER OUTPUT SM: 170 bhp at 5500 rpm; 2974cc: 180 bhp at 5750 rpm.
TRANSMISSION Citroën five-speed manual or Borg-Warner three-speed automatic; front-wheel drive.
SUSPENSION Hydro-pneumatic springing; independent transverse arms front, independent trailing arms rear.
MAXIMUM SPEED 137 mph (220 km/h) (SM EFI)
0–60 MPH (0–96 KM/H) 8.3 sec (SM EFI)
0–100 MPH (0–161 KM/H) 26–30 sec
A.F.C. 15–17 mpg

HARD TO PLACE

Slim windshield pillars should have meant excellent visibility but, in practice, the left-hand-drive SM was sometimes difficult to place on the road.

HEADLIGHTS

The SM had an array of six headlights, with the inner light on each side swiveling with the steering.

WIND CHEATER
The tapering body is apparent in this overhead view.

BACK TO FRONT
The SM's engine is mounted behind the transmission, and thus well behind the front axle.

CITROËN SM

The SM's striking low-drag body was designed by ex-General Motors stylist Henri de Segur Lauve. The sleek nose and deep undertray, together with the noticeably tapered rear end, endow it with a drag coefficient of 0.27, still credible today.

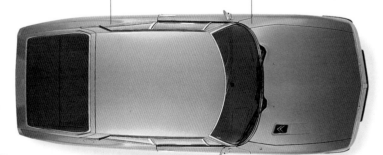

BRAKES
Inboard front disc brakes incorporate the handbrake mechanism.

DAIMLER *SP250 Dart*

AN ECCENTRIC HYBRID, the SP250 was the car that sank Daimler. By the late 1950s, the traditionalist Coventry-based company was in dire financial straits. Hoping to woo the car-crazy Americans, Daimler launched the Dart, with its odd pastiche of British and American styling themes, at the 1959 New York Auto Show.

Daimler had been making buses out of fiberglass and the Dart emerged with a quirky, rust-free plastic body. The girder chassis was a blatant copy of the Triumph TR2 *(see pages 208–09)* and, to keep the basic price down, necessities like heater, windshield wipers, and bumpers were made extra-cost options. Hardly a great car, the SP250 was a commercial failure. Projected sales of 7,500 units in the first three years dissolved into just 2,644, with only 1,200 going Stateside. Jaguar took over Daimler in 1960 and, by 1964, Sir William Lyons had axed the sportiest car Daimler had ever made.

TRADITIONAL INTERIOR
The cockpit was pure British tradition, with central gauges mounted on an aluminum plate, leather seats and dash, an occasional rear seat, fly-off handbrake, wind-up windows, and thick pile carpets.

TRUNK WAS HUGE DESPITE ACCOMMODATING FUEL TANK AND SPARE WHEEL

VESTIGIAL REAR SEAT COULD JUST ACCOMMODATE ONE CHILD OR A VERY TOLERANT ADULT

ENGINE
The turbine-smooth, Edward Turner-designed V-8 was the Dart's *tour de force*. If you were brave enough, it could reach 125 mph (201 km/h).

SPEED STRAIN
At speed the Dart was hard work; the chassis flexed, doors opened on bends, and the steering was very heavy.

FLUTED FENDERS LOOK GOOD AND GIVE THE BODY EXTRA RIGIDITY

EARLY CARS HAD TO HAVE A STEEL HOOP AROUND THE BULKHEAD TO STOP COWL SHAKE

FIBERGLASS BODY IS 1 IN (25 MM) THICK IN PLACES

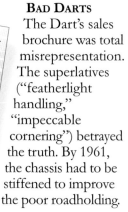

BAD DARTS
The Dart's sales brochure was total misrepresentation. The superlatives ("featherlight handling," "impeccable cornering") betrayed the truth. By 1961, the chassis had to be stiffened to improve the poor roadholding.

STEERING WHEEL
Heavy worm-and-peg steering made maneuvering in tight spaces a real chore. In the 1970s many Darts were converted to the rack-and-pinion type.

GAUGES FOR OIL PRESSURE, FUEL, AMPERAGE, AND ENGINE TEMPERATURE

PADDED LEATHER GLOVEBOX HAD A QUALITY CHROME LOCK

RACING DAIMLER
Quick enough in a straight line, corners were the Dart's Achilles heel and it never achieved any significant competitive success. This period shot shows a Dart pirouetting around Brands Hatch in 1962, complete with optional hardtop, bumpers, and badge bar.

AUTOMATIC OPTION
Borg-Warner was an option but slowed the car down considerably. British police forces who used the Dart still thought it fast enough.

REAR FENDER
Dart development had three phases: 1959–61 A-spec cars came with no creature comforts; April 1961 and later B-specs had standard bumpers, windshield wipers, and chassis modifications; while the last and most refined C-specs, produced from April 1963 to September 1964, boasted a heater and cigar lighter as standard.

DUNLOP RS5 TIRES WERE STANDARD; WIRE WHEELS WERE EXTRA-COST OPTIONS

PROVOCATIVE TWIN EXHAUSTS EMITTED A DEEP BURBLE, RISING TO A THUNDEROUS ACK-ACK AT SPEED

— THE DAIMLER MISFIT —

The Dart belongs here not because it is dynamically brilliant, but because it perfectly chronicles the influence of American styling on British cars of the period.

1950 DAIMLER MAJESTIC

SO PENETRATING was the genius of Harley Earl, General Motors' chief stylist and the man who gave shape to 50 million American cars, that almost every other contemporary carmaker jumped on the bandwagon. The fashion for fins even percolated down to a tiny company like Daimler and there is a sad irony in their fundamental incompatibility. Daimler had been churning out stuffy establishment sedans with all the aerodynamics of church pews. Cars like the Majestic and Conquest Century bore no family resemblance to the rakish Dart and, in trying to seduce the Americans, Daimler alienated the conservative British market as a result.

When it was launched, Dodge, who had registered the trademark Dart, forbid them to use it. And, if that was

CHRYSLER IMPERIAL CROWN SEDAN, WITH REAR FINS RESEMBLING THOSE OF THE LATER DAIMLER DART

not enough, enthusiasts sniggered at the Dart's unhappy styling, which, compared to the smooth MGA, Triumph TR3, and Sunbeam Alpine, looked downright clumsy. With a hefty initial price tag of $3,900, the Dart was not competitive either.

But the Dart's prime attraction was that light, compact, and powerful engine, Britain's only V-8 other than Rolls-Royce's Silver Cloud II unit. The British car magazine *Motor* called the

DAIMLER
SP250 Dart

CHROME-ON-BRASS REAR LIGHT FINISHERS WERE MONOGRAMMED WITH A DAINTY "D"

HOOD FURLED AWAY NEATLY BEHIND REAR SEAT AND WAS COVERED WITH A FABRIC HOOD BAG

QUALITY INSULATION
In the 1950s, few sports cars had windup windows. The Dart had beautifully finished chrome-surrounded glass which, when raised, kept cockpit buffeting to a minimum.

4068 WK

Daimler's engine, "quite exceptional in its torque output and turbine-like smoothness over an incredibly wide range of speeds. Other aspects of the car are quite overshadowed by the performance, and its chassis and coachwork are made to seem undistinguished by the engine which propels them." With aluminum heads and hemispherical combustion chambers, it was a gem of a unit which survived until 1969, providing sterling service as power for the Jaguar Mk II-bodied Daimler 250 sedan.

Underdeveloped and rushed into production, Dart sales were slow. In 1959, Jaguar produced and sold 22,000 cars, while Daimler managed only a few hundred Darts. Never enjoying any reflected glory from racing or celebrity

1961 DAIMLER SP250 DART POLICE CAR

ownership, the only unusual Dart buyers were the British Metropolitan Police, who ran a fleet of around 30 black automatics with brass bells on the front.

The Dart was a 1950s concept born too late to compete with the New Wave of monocoque sports cars headed by the stunning E-Type. It stands as a memorial to both the haphazard 1960s British motor industry and its self-destructive love affair with all things American.

DAIMLER CONQUEST CENTURY ROADSTER

FRONT VIEW

The guppy-style front could never be called handsome but, when 1960s drivers caught it in their rearview mirrors, they knew to move over. The drastic plastic Dart was seriously quick.

FIBERGLASS HOOD HAD A NASTY HABIT OF SPRINGING OPEN AT SPEED

DART HAS MANY DELICATE PERIOD DETAILS, LIKE TINY CHEVRON-SHAPED PARKING LIGHTS PERCHED NEATLY ON BOTH FRONT FENDERS

4068 WK

DATSUN *Fairlady 1600*

Fairlady

THE SIMILARITY between the Datsun Fairlady and the MGB *(see page 175)* is quite astonishing. The Datsun actually appeared first, at the 1961 Tokyo Motor Show, followed a year later by the MGB. Hardly a great car in its early 1500cc form, the Fairlady improved dramatically over the years, a foretaste of the Japanese car industry's culture of constant improvement. The later two-liter, twin-carb, five-speed variants of 1967 could reach 125 mph (200 km/h) and even raised eyebrows at American sports car club races.

Aimed at the American market, where it was known as the Datsun 1500, the Fairlady sold only 40,000 in nine years. But it showed Datsun how to make the legendary 240Z *(see pages 84–87)*, which went on to become one of the world's best selling sports cars.

EUROPEAN LINES
Higher and narrower than the MGB, the Fairlady had an unmistakable and deliberate European look. However, of the 7,000 1500cc models sold, half went to the United States.

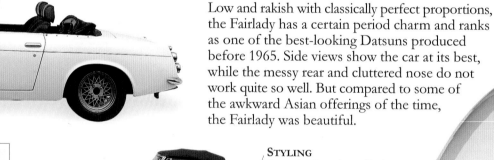

DATSUN FAIRLADY 1600
Low and rakish with classically perfect proportions, the Fairlady has a certain period charm and ranks as one of the best-looking Datsuns produced before 1965. Side views show the car at its best, while the messy rear and cluttered nose do not work quite so well. But compared to some of the awkward Asian offerings of the time, the Fairlady was beautiful.

— OTHER MODELS —

Over nine years Datsun refined the Fairlady until, by the late 1960s, it had evolved into quite a reliable machine.

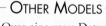

DATSUN 1500
Early cars had a less-than-willing 1500cc engine which lacked both mid-range heave and top-end power.

DATSUN 2000 ROADSTER
2000s pushed out 145 bhp and boasted a five-speed overdrive gearbox.

STYLING
Rear view has echoes of both the MGB and MG TC.

THIRD SEAT
Early Fairladies had a third seat set across the car behind the front bucket seats.

MUF 625F

DATSUN DASH

The cockpit was typical of the period, with acres of black plastic. Interestingly, no attempt was made to make the interior harmonize with the Fairlady's traditional exterior lines. Note how the square clock clashes with the circular instruments, plus a steering wheel that would not look out of place in a pickup truck.

SNUG INTERIOR IS DOMINATED BY FULL-LENGTH CENTER CONSOLE.

POINTS OF SALE
Although the Fairlady was aimed at a worldwide market – America in particular – it was never actually listed in Britain.

SPECIFICATIONS

MODEL Datsun Fairlady 1600 (1965–70)
PRODUCTION Approx 40,000
BODY STYLE Two-seater sports convertible.
CONSTRUCTION Steel body mounted on box-section chassis.
ENGINE 1595cc four-cylinder.
POWER OUTPUT 90 bhp at 6000 rpm.
TRANSMISSION Four-speed all-synchro.
SUSPENSION *Front:* independent; *Rear:* leaf springs.
BRAKES Front wheel discs, rear drums.
MAXIMUM SPEED 105 mph (169 km/h)
0–60 MPH (0–96 KM/H) 13.3 sec
0–100 MPH (0–161 KM/H) 25 sec
A.F.C. 25 mpg

ENGINE
The 1595cc 90 bhp power-plant was the mainstay of the Fairlady range until 1970. The simple four-cylinder engine had a cast-iron cylinder block and aluminum head, breathing through twin Hitachi carburetors made under license from SU in England. Later 1600s were uprated to 96 bhp with a five-bearing crankshaft.

BODY PANELS
In common with the MGB, the Fairlady also had bolt-on removable front fenders for easy repair.

FRONT SUSPENSION
Front suspension was independent, courtesy of telescopic shock absorbers, wishbones, and coil springs.

DATSUN

MUF 625F

DATSUN *240Z*

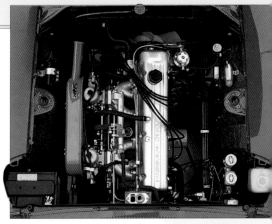

THROUGHOUT THE 1960s, Japanese car makers were teetering on the brink of a sports car breakthrough. Toyota's 2000 GT *(see page 207)* was a beauty, but with only 337 made, it was an exclusive curio. Honda was competing too, with the dainty S600 and S800. As for Datsun, the MGB-lookalike Fairladies were relatively popular in Japan and the United States, but virtually unknown elsewhere. The revolution came with the Datsun 240Z, which at a stroke established Japan on the world sports car stage.

The breakthrough had been in the cards for a while. The E-Type Jaguar *(see pages 140–43)* was not in its first flush of youth. At the lower level, the Austin-Healey 3000 *(see pages 38–39)* was on its last legs; neither was the MGB exactly factory fresh. There was a gaping hole, particularly in the US, and the Datsun 240Z filled it handsomely. It was even launched in the States in October 1969, a month before its official Japanese release, and on a rising tide of Japanese exports to the US it scored a massive hit. It had the looks, performance, handling, and equipment levels – a great value sporting package that outsold all rivals.

ENGINE
The six-cylinder twin-carburetor 2.4-liter engine, developed from the four-cylinder unit of the Bluebird sedan range, provided smooth, reliable power. Japanese buyers had the option of a tax-break 2-liter version, and there were 420 cars built for the Japanese market with a more powerful 24-valve twin-cam 2-liter unit.

Z IDENTITY
The model was launched in Japan as the Fairlady Z replacing the earlier Fairlady models; export versions were universally known as 240Z and were labeled accordingly.

RACK-AND-PINION STEERING WAS LIGHT AND PRECISE AND ADDED TO DRIVING ENJOYMENT

TRUNK-MOUNTED SPOILER WAS NOT STANDARD 240Z EQUIPMENT IN ALL MARKETS

REAR SIDE WINDOW WAS TINY, BUT WITH NO REAR PASSENGERS NOTHING BIGGER WAS NEEDED

INTERIOR
Cockpit layout was tailored to American tastes of the time, with hooded instruments and beefy controls. The vinyl-covered bucket seats offered generous rear luggage space, but the low seating position marred otherwise excellent visibility.

HANDLING
With independent suspension all around, the 240Z handled well, with a true sporting character to match its beefy good looks. One of the few criticisms was the rough ride.

TASTELESS PLASTIC WHEEL TRIM IS ORIGINAL EQUIPMENT

STYLING CUES

As with the recessed lights at the front, there is an echo of the E-Type Jaguar coupe at the rear, with a little Porsche 911, Mustang fastback, and Aston Martin DBS of 1969 thrown in.

240Z OFFERED EXCELLENT FUEL ECONOMY; YOU COULD GET 30 MPG FROM A 13-GALLON TANK

DESIGN

The lines of the 240Z were based on earlier styling exercises by Albrecht Goertz, master stylist of the BMW 507 *(see pages 48–49).*

BALANCE

This view shows that the engine was placed far forwards of the centerline, with the occupants well behind it; yet the Z was noted for its fine balance.

SPECIFICATIONS

MODEL Datsun 240Z (1969–73)
PRODUCTION 156,076
BODY STYLE Three-door, two-seater sports hatchback.
CONSTRUCTION Steel monocoque.
ENGINE Inline single overhead camshaft six, 2393cc.
POWER OUTPUT 151 bhp at 5600 rpm.
TRANSMISSION All-synchromesh four- or five-speed manual or automatic.
SUSPENSION *Front:* Independent by MacPherson struts, low links, coil springs, telescopic shocks.
Rear: Independent by MacPherson struts, lower wishbones, coil springs, telescopic shocks.
BRAKES Discs front/drums rear.
MAXIMUM SPEED 125 mph (210 km/h)
0–60 MPH (0–96 KM/H) 8.0 sec
A.F.C. 20–25 mpg

DATSUN LABEL

Cars were sold in some markets as Nissans, but were labeled as Datsuns in the US and the UK.

LARGE REAR WINDOW GAVE GOOD REAR VISION

BIG REAR HATCH GAVE MUCH BETTER LUGGAGE ACCESS THAN THE E-TYPE COUPE

STEEPLY RAKED WINDSHIELD AIDED AERODYNAMIC EFFICIENCY

THIN, RUST-PRONE BODY PANELS WERE ONE OF THE FEW THINGS THAT LET THE 240Z DOWN

HOOD WAS UNCLUTTERED BY UNNECESSARY LOUVERS; IT LATER BECAME FANCIER

DATSUN

JAPANESE SPORTING SUCCESS

When the Datsun 240Z's sleek and aggressive lines broke on the world stage late in 1969, it was a sporting breakthrough that once and for all transformed the image of Japanese automobiles.

AGAINST A RISING tide of postwar recovery and growing Japanese exports, the Datsun 240Z was somehow inevitable. The British sports car invasion of America was, if not quite in retreat, at least losing momentum, and Japanese cars were notching up ever increasing sales in the land of Uncle Sam. In fact, the impetus for the 240Z came from North American Nissan executives who spotted the gap and demanded a true sporting contender to fill it. The first Datsun Fairlady, the SP211 of 1959 (a 1960

model is illustrated), was a pretty car, but really little more than a sporting pretender; its successor, the remodeled,

1952 DATSUN SPORTS ROADSTER

bigger-engined Fairlady SP213 of 1962, was closer to the mark. But, in fact, as early as 1952, Datsun had given expression to its sporting ambitions with a quirky little Sports Roadster. About the only sporting aspect was its fold-flat screen. The 240Z, when it appeared, had an instant pedigree, for it was designed by none other than Albrecht Goertz, master stylist of the beautiful BMW 507 and the shortlived

DATSUN 240Z

DESIGNER ALBRECHT GOERTZ INSISTED THE 240Z SHOULD SEAT TWO 6 FT 3 IN (1.9 M) ADULTS

FIRST-OF-BREED
As with so many long-lived sports cars, the first-of-breed 240Z is seen as the best sporting package – lighter and nimbler than its successors.

SOPHISTICATED SUSPENSION WAS INDEPENDENT WITH MACPHERSON STRUTS ON ALL FOUR WHEELS

Toyota 2000GT. As if to underline its true sports car status, its evolution is an uncanny mirror of the E-Type Jaguar's, for sporting Datsun devotees generally opt for the purity of the original. The process of fattening up began with the 260Z of 1973–78. With a bigger

2565cc engine to cope with American emission laws, it was not quite as quick as the 240Z and weighed more. In 1974, a stretched 260Z 2+2 was offered. In 1978, the Z-series added more weight and girth with the immensely popular 280ZX.

As for the figures, they speak volumes. Add them all together and you have over a million. In fact, the 240Z alone sold twice as many as the E-Type total of 70,000 in less than half the time. To underline its sports car status, the 240Z

TIMO SALONEN'S 240RS, 1983 EAST AFRICA SAFARI RALLY

1960 DATSUN FAIRLADY SP2111

also accumulated a creditable cabinet of trophies. Its ruggedness earned it a 1–2 in the 1971 East African Safari Rally, and a repeat win in 1973. And in 1983, the 240 name was briefly revived with the Group B competition 240RS, again on the East African Safari.

ULTIMATE 240Z

If you wanted to cut a real swath in a 240Z, the ultimate Samurai performance option had what it takes. Modifications gave six-second 0–60 mph figures.

THE LATER 280ZX OFFERED A POPULAR TARGA OPTION

THE NAME DATSUN – LITERALLY SON OF DAT – FIRST APPEARED ON A SMALL DAT IN 1932

RECESSED FRONT HEADLIGHT TREATMENT IS VERY REMINISCENT OF THE E-TYPE JAGUAR

RHX 156L

DeLorean *DMC 12*

STARRING ROLE
The 1985 film *Back to the Future* used a DeLorean as a time machine to travel back to 1955; in reality the car was very orthodox.

"THE LONG-AWAITED transportation revolution has begun," bellowed the glossy brochures for John Zachary DeLorean's mold-breaking DMC 12. With a unique body of brushed stainless steel, gullwing doors, and an all-electric interior, the DMC was intended as a glimpse of the future. Today it is known as one of the car industry's greatest failures, on a par with Ford's Edsel *(see pages 114–15)*. Despite $130 million in government aid to establish a specially designed factory in West Belfast, DeLorean closed in 1982 with debts of $50 million. As for the hapless souls who bought the cars, they were faced with a litany of quality control problems, from doors that would not open, to windows that fell out. Even exposure in the film *Back to the Future* did not help the DeLorean's fortunes. Success depended on American sales and the company's forecasts were wildly optimistic. After the initial novelty died down, word spread that DeLoreans were dogs and sales completely evaporated.

GULLWINGS
The DeLorean's most celebrated party trick was gullwing doors that leaked and did not open or close properly.

ENGINE
The overhead cam, Volvo-sourced 2.8-liter V-6 engine used *Bosch K-Jetronic* fuel injection, developing 145 bhp. Standard spec was five-speed manual with optional three-speed automatic.

COMPLEX ELECTRONICS WERE DUE TO LAST-MINUTE COST-CUTTING MEASURES

INTERIOR
The leather-clad interior looked imposing, with electric windows, tilting telescopic steering column, double weather seals, air conditioning, and a seven-position climate control function.

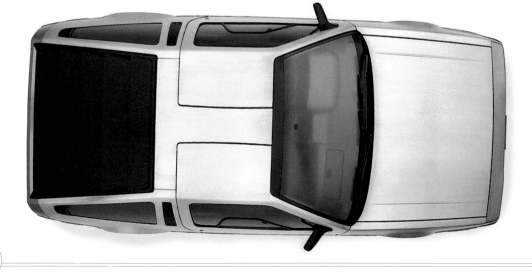

Light Front
With rear-engined layout, the weight distribution was split 35 percent front to 65 percent rear.

Wheels
Custom-made spoked alloys were larger at the back than the front.

DeLorean DMC 12

The DeLorean was targeted at "the bachelor who's made it!" and part of the design brief was that there had to be room behind the front seats for a full set of golf clubs. Designed by Giugiaro and overseen by Colin Chapman of Lotus fame, the gullwing doors and stainless-steel body were cynical marketing ploys which, as everybody involved in the prototype agreed, were more trouble than they were worth.

Disaster Doors
Overloaded doors were crammed with locks, glass, electric motors, mirrors, stereo speakers, and ventilation pipery. Held by a puny single gas strut, it was an act of the purest optimism to expect them to work properly.

1970s Styling
By the time of its launch in 1979, the DeLorean was old before its time. '70s styling motifs abound, like the slatted rear window and cubed rear lights.

Air Conditioning
With tiny windows and climate control that regularly failed, temperatures got very hot indeed.

Stainless-Steel Body
Brushed-stainless-steel was disliked by Colin Chapman but insisted upon by DeLorean himself. Soon owners found that it was impossible to clean.

Specifications

Model DeLorean DMC 12 (1979–82)
Production 6,500
Body Style Two-seater rear-engined sports coupe.
Construction Y-shaped chassis with stainless-steel body.
Engine 2850cc ohc V-6.
Power Output 145 bhp at 5500 rpm.
Transmission Five-speed manual (optional three-speed auto).
Suspension Independent with unequal length parallel arms and rear trailing arms.
Brakes Four-wheel discs.
Maximum Speed 125 mph (201 km/h)
0–60 mph (0–96 km/h) 9.6 sec
0–100 mph (0–161 km/h) 23.2 sec
A.F.C. 22 mpg

DE TOMASO *Pantera GT5*

AN UNCOMPLICATED SUPERCAR, the Pantera was a charming amalgam of Detroit grunt and Italian glam. Launched in 1971 and sold in North America by Ford's Lincoln-Mercury dealers, it was powered by a mid-mounted Ford 5.7-liter V-8 that could muster 159 mph (256 km/h) and belt to 60 mph in under six seconds. The formidable 350 bhp GT5 was built after Ford pulled out in 1974 and De Tomaso merged with Maserati.

With a propensity for the front lifting at speed, hopeless rear visibility, no headroom, awkward seats, and impossibly placed pedals, the Pantera is massively flawed; yet it is remarkably easy to drive. Handling is poised and accurate, plus there is the wall of power that catapults the car to 30 mph (48 km/h) in less time than it takes to pronounce its name.

ENGINE
The Pantera is really just a big power plant with a body attached. The monster V-8 lives in the middle, mated to a beautifully built aluminum-cased ZF transaxle, which was also used in the Ford GT40 *(see pages 124–27)* and cost more to make than the engine.

INTERIOR
The Pantera requires typical driving position – long arms and short legs. Switches and dials are strewn all over the place, but the glorious-sounding speakers are just inches from your ears.

PANTERA TRIVIA
Elvis Presley shot his Pantera when it wouldn't start.

LIMITED HEADROOM
Don't buy a Pantera if you are over 5 ft 10 in (178 cm) tall – there is no headroom.

De Tomaso Pantera GT5

Fat arches, aggressive GT5 graphics down the flanks, wheels 11 inches wide, and ground clearance you could not slide an envelope under make the Pantera look evil. Americans were not able to buy the real GT5 due to the car's lack of engine-emission controls and had to settle for just the GT5 badges.

SPECIFICATIONS

MODEL De Tomaso Pantera GT5 (1974–93)
PRODUCTION N/A
BODY STYLE Mid-engined two-seater coupe.
CONSTRUCTION Pressed steel chassis body unit.
ENGINE 5763cc V-8.
POWER OUTPUT 350 bhp at 6000 rpm.
TRANSMISSION Five-speed manual ZF Transaxle.
SUSPENSION All-around independent.
BRAKES All-around ventilated discs.
MAXIMUM SPEED 159 mph (256 km/h)
0–60 MPH (0–96 KM/H) 5.5 sec
0–100 MPH (0–161 KM/H) 13.5 sec
A.F.C. 15 mpg

WIDE NOSE
Top view shows just how wide the nose really is.

THE PANTERA AT SPEED
The huge fender helps rear down-force, but actually slows the Pantera down. At the General Motors Millbrook proving ground in England, a GT5 with the fender in place made 148 mph (238 km/h); without the fender it reached 151.7 mph (244 km/h).

WHEEL ARCH
Wheel arches strain outwards to cover 13-in (33 cm) rear tires.

RAISED TRUNK
Lift-up rear panel gives total engine accessibility for maintenance.

COOLING
Early Panteras would overheat, with the temperature creeping past 230 degrees F.

COCKPIT
With the engine so close to the interior, the cabin temperature could get very hot.

CONSTRUCTION
The underside is old-fashioned welded pressed steel monocoque.

TIRES
Giant Pirelli P7 345/45 rear tires belong on the track and give astonishing road traction.

AERODYNAMICS
With little weight up front, at over 120 mph (193 km/h) the nose would lift and the steering would lighten up alarmingly.

DODGE *Charger* R/T

COLLECTORS RANK THE 1968 Dodge Charger as one of the fastest and best-styled muscle cars of its era. This, the second generation of Charger, marked the pinnacle of the horsepower race between American car manufacturers in the late 1960s. Gasoline was then only 10 cents a gallon, Americans had more disposable income than ever before, and engine capacity was everything to the aspiring car buyer.

With its hugely powerful 7.2-liter capacity engine, the Charger 440 was, in reality, a thinly veiled road racer. The Rapid Transit (R/T) version was a high-performance factory option, which included heavy-duty suspension and brakes, dual exhausts, and wider tires. While idling, the engine produced such massive torque that it rocked the car body from side to side. Buyers took the second generation Charger to their hearts in a big way, with sales outstripping the earlier lackluster model by a factor of six.

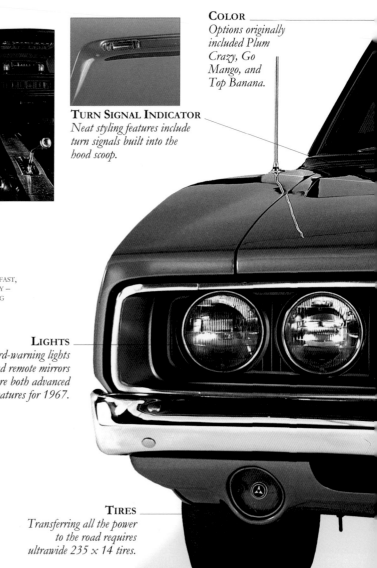

STAR OF THE SCREEN
A car with star quality, the Charger featured in the classic nine-minute chase sequence in the film, *Bullitt*. It also had major roles in the 1970s cult movie, *Vanishing Point*, and the American television series, *The Dukes of Hazzard*.

DASHBOARD
The standard R/T cockpit is functional to the point of being stark. There are definitely no distractions here – just a matte black dash with six gauges, a 150 mph (241 km/h) speedometer and, of course, *de rigueur* bucket seats. Factory options included cruise control and wood-grained steering wheel.

TURN SIGNAL INDICATOR
Neat styling features include turn signals built into the hood scoop.

COLOR
Options originally included Plum Crazy, Go Mango, and Top Banana.

ENGINE IS FAST, BUT THIRSTY – JUST 8.1 MPG

LIGHTS
Hazard-warning lights and remote mirrors are both advanced features for 1967.

ENGINE
The wall-to-wall engine found in the R/T Charger is Dodge's immensely powerful 440 Magnum – a 7.2-liter V-8. This versatile powerplant produced maximum torque at a lazy 3200 rpm – making it obscenely quick, yet as docile as a kitten in town traffic.

TIRES
Transferring all the power to the road requires ultrawide 235 x 14 tires.

SPECIFICATIONS

MODEL Dodge Charger (1967–70)
PRODUCTION 96,100
BODY STYLE Two-door, four-seater
CONSTRUCTION Steel monocoque body.
ENGINE V-8 7.2-liter.
POWER OUTPUT 375 hp at 3200 rpm.
TRANSMISSION Three-speed Torqueflite auto, or Hurst four-speed manual.
SUSPENSION *Front:* Heavy duty independent; *Rear:* Leaf-spring.
BRAKES Heavy duty, 11 in (280 mm) drums, with optional front discs.
MAXIMUM SPEED 150 mph (241 km/h)
0–60 MPH (0–96 KM/H) 6 sec
0–100 MPH (0–161 KM/H) 13.3 sec
A.F.C. 8.1 mpg

DODGE CHARGER R/T

The Charger was the creation of Dodge's chief of design, Bill Brownlie. Its clean, voluptuous lines gave this car one of the handsomest shapes of the day. It left you in no doubt as to what this car was all about: guts and purpose. The mean-looking nose, blacked-out grille, and low hood make this the type of car that, if seen in the rear view mirror, would make you move over, fast.

SECURITY
The chrome, quick-fill, racing-style gas cap is attached to the car by wire to stop souvenir-hunters.

REAR VIEW
"Buttress-backed" styling was America's version of a European 2+2 sports coupe.

HEADLIGHTS
These were hidden under electric flaps to give the Charger a sinister grin.

STEERING WHEEL
Its huge size allows the driver to apply plenty of his own torque to turn the car.

ENGINE
The potent engine has enough power to spin the rear wheels in every gear.

ANTIROLL BARS
Enormous antiroll bars 1 in (25 mm) in diameter guarantee that the Charger handles well, despite its size.

NEVADA
OCT481

FACEL VEGA *II*

WHEN SOMEONE LIKE PABLO PICASSO chooses a car, it is going to look good. In its day, the Facel II was a poem in steel and easily as beautiful as anything turned out by the Italian styling houses. Small wonder then that Facels were synonymous with the 1960s jet setters. Driven by Ringo Starr, Ava Gardner, Danny Kaye, Tony Curtis, François Truffaut, and Joan Fontaine, Facels were some of the most charismatic cars of the day. Even death gave them glamor; the novelist Albert Camus died while being driven in his publisher's FVS in January 1960.

In 1961, the HK 500 was redesigned and given cleaner lines, an extra 6 in (15 cm) in length, and dubbed the Facel II. At 3640 pounds, the II was lighter than the 500, could storm to 140 mph (225 km/h), and squeal from 0–100 mph (161 km/h) in 17 seconds. Costing more than the contemporary Aston Martin DB4 *(see pages 28–29)* and Maserati 3500, the Facel II was as immortal as a Duesenberg, Hispano Suiza, or Delahaye. We will never see its like again.

(see pages 28–29)

OTHER MODELS

Early Facels, such as the HK 500, had appalling drum brakes until 1960, when pressure from the press made Facel bolt on Dunlop disc brakes.

FACEL HK 500
The HK 500 was the most popular Facel, with 5.8-liter and 6.2-liter Chrysler V-8s married to three-speed Torqueflite or four-speed Pont-a-Mousson automatic gearboxes.

FABRIC, ROLL-BACK, FULL-LENGTH SUNROOF WAS AN AFTERMARKET ACCESSORY

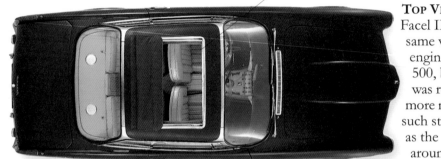

TOP VIEW
Facel II used the same wheelbase and engine as the HK 500, but the shape was refined to look more modern, losing such styling cliches as the dated wrap-around windshield.

SMOOTH LIGHTING
Brake lights are cut out of the rear fenders and help to enhance the Facel's seamless lines.

REAR VIEW
The enlarged rear window gave a much greater glass area than the HK 500 and almost 90 percent visibility, helped by slimmer pillars.

BUMPER IS NOT CHROME BUT RUST-RESISTANT STAINLESS STEEL

HOOD IS HUGE, BUT THEN SO IS THE ENGINE

FACEL WHEELS

Light aluminum, chromed knock-off disc wheels were the most common equipment on Facel IIs. Borrani-Rudge "record" wire wheels were also listed in the brochures, but rarely specified.

PANELS WERE HAND-FINISHED AND MATED TO EACH OTHER TO CREATE A ONE-PIECE LOOK

KNOCK-OFF WHEEL SPINNERS WERE REMOVED WITH A SOFT-HEADED HAMMER

⊢ SPECIFICATIONS ⊣

MODEL Facel Vega Facel II (1962–64)
PRODUCTION 184
BODY STYLES Two-door, four-seater Grand Tourer.
CONSTRUCTION Steel chassis, steel/light aluminum body.
ENGINE 6286cc cast-iron V-8.
POWER OUTPUT 390 bhp at 5400 rpm (manual) 355 bhp at 4800 rpm (auto).
TRANSMISSION Three-speed Torqueflite automatic or four-speed Pont-a-Mousson manual.
SUSPENSION Independent front coil springs, rear live axle leaf springs.
BRAKES Four-wheel Dunlop discs.
MAXIMUM SPEED 149 mph (240 km/h)
0–60 MPH (0–96 KM/H) 8.3 sec
0–100 MPH (0–161 KM/H) 17.0 sec
A.F.C. 15 mpg

DASH MIGHT HAVE LOOKED LIKE WOOD BUT WAS ACTUALLY PAINTED METAL

REAR SEATING

The leather rear seat might look inviting, but it is very occasional and folds down to make a luggage platform.

INTERIOR

Steering wheel points straight to the driver's heart. Note the unmistakable aircraft-type panel layout with center gauges and heater controls like hand throttles.

ENGINE

The Facel II was powered by a 6286cc castiron Chrysler V-8, which, when coupled to the rare and balky four-speed manual gearbox, pushed out 390 bhp.

MANUAL PONT-A-MOUSSON GEARBOX BEGAN LIFE IN A TRUCK

RAKISH BODY WAS ARTISTICALLY SIMILAR TO THE FACELLIA COUPE

THE FASCINATING FACEL

*The first products of the Facel stable were known as Vegas, a name
deliberately chosen for its American associations.*

MADE BETWEEN 1954 and 1955, an early Vega is a rare thing. Only about a dozen survive out of 46 built. In 1956, the Vega was renamed the FVS, this time powered by a 5.5-liter Chrysler V-8 that replaced the 4.6-liter DeSoto unit, but hampered by unpowered drum brakes. Despite the heart-stopping brake pedal, skittish front-end geometry, and suspension reliability glitches, some 357 FVSs were built, with over three quarters of the run going to America.

In terms of finish, image, and quality, Facel Vegas were among the most successful handmade supercars. Body joints were perfectly flush, doors closed like heavy vaults, brightwork was stainless steel, and even the roofline was fabricated from five seamlessly joined sections. Meticulous detailing and engineering panache earned Facel an image of wealthy arrogance, somewhere between a Bentley Continental and a Mercedes-Benz SL. But, more importantly, the HK 500 and Facel II were a unique amalgam of 1950s American and European styling motifs. Facels oozed self-confidence, with huge wraparound windshields, rocketship rear lights, and aircraft interiors, yet they were clothed in a softly curved

FRENCH ADVERTISMENT FOR THE FACEL VEGA EXCELLENCE

tapering body style – France's answer to Detroit's swank tanks.

The third generation FV was the HK 500, launched in 1959, with even more grunt, courtesy of the frenzied

FACEL
Vega II

DIMENSIONS
At 3,640 pounds (30 cwt), 15 ft (4.57 m) long, 6 ft (1.83 m) wide, and only 4 ft 3 in (1.3 m) high, the Facel II aped the girth and bulk of contemporary American iron.

HK 500s HAD A MIRROR ON
THE ROOF RAIL; IIs HAD IT
MOUNTED ON THE DASH

UNLIKE THE DASHBOARD,
THE WOOD-RIM WHEEL
WAS THE REAL THING

BADGE
The Facel II represents Facel creator Jean Daninos's last and greatest achievement few other cars of i era possessed the same cachet.

American horsepower race among GM, Ford, and Chrysler. As soon as one of them came up with another handful of cubic inches, the others did too, and engine sizes became progressively crazier. The first of the HK 500s had a 290 bhp 5.9-liter V-8, which, a year later, was swapped for the hairier 6.3-liter hemihead design, bringing the already commendable maximum speed to a wild 140 mph (225 km/h). Over 500 HKs were produced, the majority with the standard Torqueflite automatic, but some with the awkward Pont-a-Mousson four-speeder. Up to April, 1960, most 500s still had the fade-prone drum brakes of the FVS, later changed to Dunlop discs.

The Excellence, an Olympian 17-ft (5.18-m) long stretched Facel introduced in 1958, was a Quixotic tilt at the R-R Silver Cloud and Mercedes 300 market. Production ceased in 1964 with just 230 cars built and only 13 sold in Britain. Unloved for its great thirst and dropping pillarless doors, the Excellence is now significantly cheaper than any other big Facel. Facel IIs, on the other hand, are considered the most desirable of the breed, with sharper lines and even more power – 390 bhp. Introduced in late 1961, they came with wire wheels, disc brakes, automatic gearshift, and Selectaride shocks. By far the rarest Facel, with only 184 made, IIs are still fiercely admired by Facel fanciers.

The Facellia, a scaled-down HK 500, available as a convertible or coupe, bankrupted Facel. Pont-a-Mousson's first engine-building venture was a

THE FACEL VEGA IN WHICH ALBERT CAMUS DIED, 1960

disaster; the under-developed 1647cc dohc (double overhead camshaft) soon had a reputation as a piston-burner. Even ownership by such celebrities as Joan Collins could not prevent the Facellia's reputation for unreliability, hastening Facel's demise.

PRODIGIOUS HOOD BULGE CLEARED VAST OIL DRUM-LIKE AIR CLEANERS OVER DOUBLE CARBURETORS. DRIVEN FAST, THE FACEL II WOULD DRINK ONE GALLON OF FUEL EVERY TEN MILES

WINDSHIELD IS EVEN MORE STEEPLY RAKED THAN ON THE HK 500

IN THE 1950S, FACEL MADE MOTOR SCOOTERS, JET ENGINES, OFFICE FURNITURE, AND KITCHEN CABINETS

FRONT VIEW

The intimidating front is all grille, because the hot-running castiron V-8 engine needed all the cooling air it could get. HK 500 had four round headlights, but the Facel II's voguish stacked lights were shamelessly stolen from contemporary Mercedes sedans.

FERRARI 250 *GT SWB*

IN AN ERA WHEN FERRARI was turning out some lackluster road cars, the 250 GT SWB became a yardstick, the car against which all other GTs were judged and one of the finest Ferraris ever. Of the 167 made between 1959 and 1962, 74 were competition cars – their simplicity made them one of the most competitive sports racers of the 1950s. Built around a tubular chassis, the 3.0-liter V-12 engine lives at the front, along with a simple four-speed gearbox with Porsche internals. But it is that delectable Pininfarina-sculpted shape that is so special. Tense, urgent, but friendly, those smooth lines have none of the intimidating presence of a Testarossa or Daytona. The SWB stands alone as a perfect blend of form and function. It is one of the world's prettiest cars, and on the track one of the most successful. The SWB won races from Spa to Le Mans, Nassau to the Nürburgring. Which is exactly what Enzo Ferrari wanted. "They are cars," he said, "which the sporting client can use on the road during the week and race on Sundays." Happy days.

OTHER MODELS

The California Spyder was a boulevard racer aimed at the American market, suggested by the company's principal importer, Luigi Chinetti.

FERRARI CALIFORNIA SPYDER
SWB California Spyders owed much to the 250 GT, with the same type 539 chassis, and were built from May 1960 until February 1963.

HORSE RACING
In the middle 1960s, 250 GTs were cheap enough to be bought by amateurs who raced them at club events.

OVERHEAD VIEW
The car has perfect balance. Form is rounded and fluid and the first 11 SWBs were built in aluminum. Road cars had a steel body and aluminum hood and doors.

COCKPIT IS SNUG AND AIRY BUT FILLS WITH NOISE WHEN YOU TURN THE KEY

GENTLY TAPERING NOSE IS A MASTERPIECE OF THE PANEL BEATER'S ART

RARE LIGHTWEIGHT COMPETITION CARS SUFFERED FROM STRETCHING ALUMINUM

SWB SAT ON ELEGANT CHROME-PLATED BORRANI COMPETITION WIRE WHEELS

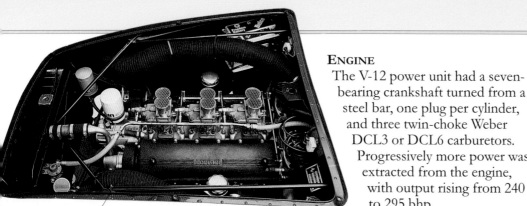

ENGINE
The V-12 power unit had a seven-bearing crankshaft turned from a steel bar, one plug per cylinder, and three twin-choke Weber DCL3 or DCL6 carburetors. Progressively more power was extracted from the engine, with output rising from 240 to 295 bhp.

INSTEAD OF AIR CLEANERS, COMPETITION CARS USED FILTERLESS AIR TRUMPETS

SPECIFICATIONS
MODEL Ferrari 250 GT SWB (1959–62)
PRODUCTION 167 (10 rhd)
BODY STYLE Two-seater GT coupe.
CONSTRUCTION Tubular chassis with all-aluminum or aluminum/steel body.
ENGINE 2953cc V-12.
POWER OUTPUT 280 bhp at 7000 rpm.
TRANSMISSION Four-speed manual.
SUSPENSION Independent front coil and wishbones, live rear axle with leaf springs.
BRAKES Four-wheel discs.
MAXIMUM SPEED 147 mph (237 km/h)
0–60 MPH (0–96 KM/H) 6.6 sec
0–100 MPH (0–161 KM/H) 16.2 sec
A.F.C. 12 mpg

250 DOMINATION
Stirling Hamil leads Ed Lowther's Corvette in a mid-1960s American club race. For many years the 250 GT dominated hillclimbs and track races at circuits all over the world. The SWB is a small car with wonderfully predictable handling.

SIMPLE INTERIOR
Despite the exotic exterior, the interior is a place of work. Functional dash is basic crackle black with no frills. Sun visors were notably absent.

COMPETITION VERSIONS HAD LIGHT, BUT EASILY SCRATCHED, PLEXIGLASS WINDOWS. ROAD CARS USED HEAVIER GLASS

EXPANSIVE REAR WINDOW SITS ABOVE ENORMOUS 26-GALLON (120-LITER) GAS TANK

TWIN EXHAUSTS
Two sets of aggressive drainpipe twin exhausts dominate the SWB's rump and declare its competition bloodline.

INTERIOR SEAT
Roll cage and harnesses are concessions to safety. Bucket seats look supportive, but were thinly padded.

AERODYNAMICS
In Pininfarina's wind tunnel with the radiator grille closed, a 250 GT achieved a drag coefficient of only 0.33, a figure that would shame many cars 20 years later.

FERRARI'S LEGEND RACER

Although the 250 GT SWB was based on Ferrari's first real mass produced car, the 250 Europa, it was anything but mainstream. More race than road car, it was soon feted as one of the finest sports cars of the time.

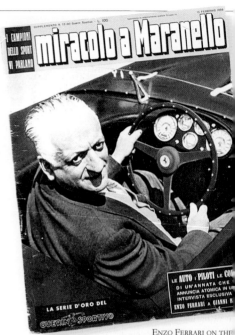

ENZO FERRARI ON THE FRONT OF ITALIAN MAGAZINE, MIRACOLO A MARANELLO, IN 1955

THERE WERE TWO versions of the SWB, the steel-bodied Lusso for the road, or the aluminum-bodied Competizione for the track, and it was on those tortuous tarmac chicanes that the SWB shone. Its most famous win in the UK was with Stirling Moss in the 1960–61 Tourist Trophy. Moss thought it was a "really comfortable grand touring car with good brakes, a super engine and crisp gearbox ... a very well mannered, well balanced car, especially good for Le Mans or any other circuit where one could give it its head."

Yet, despite its loose pretensions towards being a road machine, one walk around the SWB tells you that this is no aimless boulevardier. A racer stripped of all superfluous fat, there were front air scoops to cool the disc brakes, fender air extraction vents for underhood cooling, and reinforced points for racing-type quick-action jacks. Even the gas cap, an aluminum quick-fill variety, was *de rigueur* on all the best Le Mans racers. This was a road rocket in a Savile Row suit, an elegant projectile equally at home crunching up the gravel drive of an English country house or howling around a circuit locked in combat with the Aston Martin DB4GT.

FERRARI
250 GT SWB

RUDIMENTARY REAR WINDOW VENT WAS FOR COCKPIT COOLING

HUGE ALUMINUM GAS CAP WAS FOR FAST FUEL STOPS

DESIGN CREDITS
Soft, compact, and rounded, Pininfarina executed the design, while Scaglietti took care of the sheet metal. The result was one of the most charismatic cars ever produced.

REAR STOPLIGHT AND INDICATORS WERE USED ON MANY OTHER FERRARIS

GUT-WRENCHING THUDS BETRAY THE SWB'S HARD-SPRUNG LIVE AXLE

1960s' FERRARI PRODUCTION LINE

With a 4:1 final drive, it would accelerate from standstill to 100 mph (161 km/h) in a head-jerking 14 seconds. First gear was good for 61 mph (98 km/h), second 85 mph (137

km/h), and third saw the needle touching 155 mph (249 km/h), with one more gear to go, enough to give today's V-12s a very bad scare. In the 1961 Tourist Trophy at Goodwood, England, Moss won the four-hour race at an average speed of 87.73 mph (141.15 km/h). In the same year he recorded the seventh fastest lap at Le Mans at the time.

One of the first Ferraris with a well-constructed chassis, the 250 GT not only had a lightness and fluidity found in only a handful of the world's most precocious sports cars, but also a stunning beauty. The SWB was one of the final flowerings of that

great Grand Touring tradition – cars you could drive to the track, annihilate all competitors, and drive home again. It was a true gentleman's sports car.

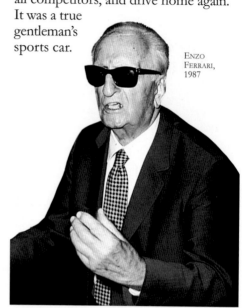

ENZO FERRARI, 1987

IMPOSING FRONT

The 250 GT is a polished gem, hugging the road in corners. Front combines beauty and threat with steely grin and squat wheel arch-filling attitude. Nothing is exaggerated for effect.

DRAMATIC SMALL HOOD VENT SUCKED AIR INTO THREE DOUBLE-CHOKE WEBER CARBURETORS

ROAD CARS HAD PRANCING HORSE BADGE IN GRILLE AND VESTIGIAL FRONT BUMPERS

SWEEPING BODY PANELS ARE ALMOST PRICELESS. EACH WAS HAND MADE, WITH SCANT REGARD FOR REPAIR OR REPLACEMENT

FERRARI *308 GTB*

ONE OF THE BEST-SELLING Ferraris ever, the 308 GTB started life with a fiberglass body designed by Pininfarina and built by Scaglietti. Power was courtesy of the 3.0-liter V-8 engine and five-speed gearbox inherited from the 308 GT4. With America the GTB's target market, Federal emission regulations made the GTB clean up its act, evolving into a refined and civilized machine with such high-tech goodies as four valves per cylinder and Bosch K-Jetronic fuel injection. Practical and tractable in traffic, it became the 1980s entry level Ferrari, supplanting the Porsche 911 *(see pages 194–95)* as the standard issue yuppiemobile. In the television detective series *Magnum P.I.*, Tom Sellick gave the 308 prime time exposure and turned it into an aspirational icon. Prices went crazy, but values have softened and a good low mileage 308 is one of the least traumatic and most cost-effective entries into the prancing horse club.

SPECIFICATIONS

MODEL Ferrari 308 GTB (1975–85)
PRODUCTION 712 (308 GTB fiberglass); 2,185 (308 GTB steel); 3,219 (GTS).
BODY STYLE Two-door, two-seater sports coupe.
CONSTRUCTION Fiberglass/steel.
ENGINE Midmounted transverse dohc 2926cc V-8.
POWER OUTPUT 255 bhp at 7600 rpm.
TRANSMISSION Five-speed manual.
SUSPENSION Independent double wishbones/coil springs all around.
BRAKES Ventilated discs all around.
MAXIMUM SPEED 154 mph (248 km/h)
0–60 MPH (0–96 KM/H) 7.3 sec
0–100 MPH (0–161 KM/H) 19.8 sec
A.F.C. 16 mpg

GTS ROOF
The GTB always had a metal roof; the chic GTS had a removable Targa top panel.

FERRARI 308 GTB
The handsome styling is a blend of Dino 246 *(see pages 108–09)* and 365 GT4. The Dino provided concave rear windows and conical air intakes, while the 365 brought double bodyshell appearance with a waistline groove.

ENGINE
The 2926cc V-8 has double overhead cams per bank and four carburetors.

VENTILATION
With the engine at the back, the wide slatted grille scooped up air for brake and interior ventilation.

AERODYNAMICS
Retractable flush-fitting popup headlights keep wind force down on the nose and front wheels.

FERRARI *275 GTB/4*

THE GTB/4 WAS A HYBRID made for two short years, 1966 to 1968. With just 350 built, a mere 27 in right-hand drive, it was not exactly one of Ferrari's money-makers. So named for its four camshafts, the GTB still ranks as the finest road car Ferrari produced before Fiat took control of the company.

With fully independent suspension, a musical five-speed gearbox, and a wonderfully fetching Pininfarina-designed and Scaglietti-built body, it was the last of the true Berlinettas. The forerunner of the Daytona *(see page 104)*, the GTB was built more for hard charging than posing. This was Ferrari's first-ever production four-cam V-12 engine and its first road-going prancing horse with an independent rear end. Nimble and compact, with exemplary neutral handling and stunning design, this is probably one of the most desirable Ferraris ever made.

RACE ENGINE
Type 226 engine was related to the 330 P2 prototypes of the 1965 racing season.

HIDDEN CAP
So as not to clutter the seamless lines, the gas cap was hidden from view inside the trunk.

CARBURETORS
A gentle hood bulge is required to clear the huge air cleaner atop six Webers.

INTERIOR
The interior is cramped, impractical, and trimmed in distinctly unluxurious vinyl.

SPECIFICATIONS

MODEL Ferrari 275 GTB/4 (1966–68)
PRODUCTION 350
BODY STYLE Two-seater front-engined coupe.
CONSTRUCTION Steel chassis, aluminum body.
ENGINE 3.3-liter twin overhead-cam dry sump V-12.
POWER OUTPUT 300 hp at 8000 rpm
TRANSMISSION Five-speed all synchromesh.
SUSPENSION All around independent.
BRAKES Four-wheel power-assisted discs.
MAXIMUM SPEED 160 mph (257 km/h)
0–60 MPH (0–96 KM/H) 5.5 sec
0–100 MPH (0–161 KM/H) 13 sec
A.F.C. 12 mpg

STYLING
Small trunk, small cockpit, and long nose are classic Pininfarina styling cues – an arresting amalgam of beauty and brawn.

FERRARI 275 GTB/4
Prettier than a Jaguar E-Type *(see pages 140–43)*, Aston Martin DB4 *(see pages 28–29)*, or Lamborghini Miura *(see pages 146–47)*, the GTB/4 has a chassis made up of a ladder frame built around two oval tube members.

FERRARI *Daytona*

KNOWN TO EVERY SCHOOLCHILD as the world's fastest car, the classically sculptured and outrageously quick Daytona was a supercar with a split personality. Under 120 mph (193 km/h), it felt like a truck with heavy inert controls and crashing suspension. But once the needle was heading for 140 mph (225 km/h), things started to sparkle. With a romantic flat-out maximum of 170 mph (280 km/h), it was the last of the great front-engined V-12 war horses.

Launched at the 1968 Paris Salon as the 365 GTB/4, the press immediately named it "Daytona" in honor of Ferrari's success at the 1967 24-hour race. Faster than the contemporary Lamborghini Miura (see page 146), De Tomaso Pantera (see pages 90–91), and Jaguar E-Type (see pages 140–43), the chisel-nosed Ferrari won laurels on the race track as well as in the hearts and pockets of wealthy enthusiasts all over the world.

─ SPECIFICATIONS ─

MODEL Ferrari 365 GTB/4 Daytona (1968–73)
PRODUCTION 1,426 (165 RHD)
BODY STYLE Two-seater fastback.
CONSTRUCTION Steel/aluminum/ fiberglass body, separate multitube chassis frame.
ENGINE V-12 4390cc.
POWER OUTPUT 352 bhp at 7500 rpm.
TRANSMISSION Five-speed all synchromesh.
SUSPENSION Independent front and rear.
BRAKES Four-wheel discs.
MAXIMUM SPEED 174 mph (280 km/h)
0–60 MPH (0–96 KM/H) 5.4 sec
0–100 MPH (0–161 KM/H) 12.8 sec
A.F.C. 14 mpg

INTERIOR
With hammock-type racing seats, a cornucopia of black-on-white instruments, and a provocatively angled, extra long gear shift, the cabin promises some serious excitement.

CLASH OF THE TITANS
On the track the Daytona did battle with the best and destroyed all competitors. With racing modifications, it not only handled but could muster 190 mph (306 km/h) on the straightaway.

FERRARI 365 GTB/4 DAYTONA
A poem in steel, few other cars could be considered in the same aesthetic league as the Daytona. Beneath the exterior is a skeleton of chrome-molybdenum tubes, giving rigidity and strength. Body panels were hand-hammered on wooden bucks, with no two being exactly the same.

HEADLIGHTS
American safety regulations dictated that the double retractable headlights could be raised in 3 seconds.

SUSPENSION
Double wishbone front suspension was strong enough for hell-raising speeds.

TOURING TRUNK
As a GT car, the Daytona has an accommodating trunk.

WIPERS
The windshield wipers disappear neatly behind the raised edge of the hood.

TOUGH TIRES
200 x 15 G70 Michelin XVRs were the only tires then available to cope with the top speed.

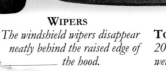

FERRARI *400 GT*

THE FIRST FERRARI ever offered with an automatic transmission, the 400 was aimed at the American market, and was meant to take the prancing horse into the boardrooms of Europe and the US. But the 400's automatic box was a most un-Ferrari-like device, a lazy three-speed GM Turbo-Hydramatic as used in Cadillac, Rolls-Royce, and Jaguar. It may have been the best automatic in the world, but it was a radical departure for Maranello, and met with only modest success.

The 400 was possibly the most discreet and refined Ferrari ever made. It looked awful in Racing Red – the color of 70 percent of Ferraris – so most were finished in dark metallics. The 400 became the 400i GT in 1973 and the 412 in 1985. It became an alternative for the 1980s executive bored with Daimler Double-Sixes and BMW 750s.

SPECIFICATIONS

MODEL Ferrari 400 GT (1976–79)
PRODUCTION 501
BODY STYLE Two-door, four-seater sports sedan.
CONSTRUCTION Steel/aluminum body, separate tubular chassis frame.
ENGINE 4390cc twin ohc V-12.
POWER OUTPUT 340 hp at 6800 rpm.
TRANSMISSION Five-speed manual or three-speed automatic.
SUSPENSION Independent double wishbones with coil springs, rear and front with hydro-pneumatic self-leveling.
BRAKES Four-wheel ventilated discs.
MAXIMUM SPEED 150 mph (241 km/h)
0–60 MPH (0–96 KM/H) 7.1 sec
0–100 MPH (0–161 KM/H) 18.7 sec
A.F.C. 12 mpg

DASHBOARD
The 400's cockpit was a study in luxury, with leather dash and real wood and the option of a second rear air conditioning unit to keep tired tycoons cool. Rear passengers could also benefit from a four-speaker sound system.

MIRROR
Driver's door mirror was remotely controlled from a switch in the interior.

INTERIOR
The 400 was a genuine 2+2, with ample accommodation for four.

WINDSHIELD
Massive glass area and thin pillars gave the 400 the best visibility of any Ferrari.

HEADLIGHTS
Four headlights were retracted into the bodywork by electric motors.

PININFARINA BADGE
The Turin-based Pininfarina company is perhaps the most famous name in automotive styling in the world.

TRUNK
Trunk line was raised to limit drag.

FERRARI 400 GT
Apart from the delicate chin spoiler and bolt-on aluminum wheels, the shape was pure 365 GT4 2+2. The rectangular design of the body was lightened by a plunging hood line and a waist length indentation running along the 400's flanks.

FERRARI *365 GT4 Berlinetta Boxer*

THE BERLINETTA BOXER was meant to be the jewel in Ferrari's crown – one of the fastest GT cars ever. Replacing the legendary V-12 Ferrari Daytona *(see page 104)*, the 365 BB was powered by a flat-twelve "Boxer" engine, so named for the image of the horizontally located pistons punching at their opposite numbers. First unveiled at the 1971 Turin Motor Show, the 4.4-liter 380 bhp Boxer was so complex that deliveries to buyers did not start until 1973. The problem was that Ferrari had suggested that the Boxer could top 185 mph (298 km/h), when it could only manage around 170 mph (274 km/h), slower than the Daytona. In 1976 Ferrari replaced the 365 with the 5-liter Boxer 512, yet of the two cars the 365 is faster and rarer, with only 387 built.

TESTING THE STALLION
A handful of prototypes were subjected to extensive testing. This one is recognizable by the roof-mounted antenna.
Factory cars had antennas in the windshield.

INTERIOR
An amalgam of racer and grand tourer, the Boxer's cabin was functional yet luxurious, with electric windows and air conditioning.

SWITCHES FOR THE POWER WINDOWS AND AIR CONDITIONING

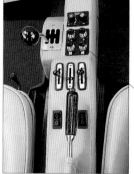

CENTER CONSOLE
The rear-mounted gearbox meant only a small transmission tunnel was needed.

LOWER BODYWORK
This was fiberglass, along with the wheelarch liners and bumpers.

WHEELS
Wheels were the same as on the Daytona – cast light aluminum, with Rudge knock-off hubs.

LOW-SLUNG POSITION
The Boxer engine layout was favored because it allowed the whole car to sit that much lower, giving better aerodynamics and a lower center of gravity.

SPECIFICATIONS

MODEL Ferrari 365 GT4 Berlinetta Boxer (1973–1976)
PRODUCTION 387 (58 rhd models)
BODY STYLE Two-seater sports.
CONSTRUCTION Tubular spaceframe chassis.
ENGINE Flat-12, 4.4 liter.
POWER OUTPUT 380 bhp at 7700 rpm.
TRANSMISSION Five-speed all synchromesh rear-mounted gearbox.
SUSPENSION Independent front and rear.
BRAKES Ventilated front and rear disc brakes.
MAXIMUM SPEED 172 mph (277 km/h)
0–60 MPH (0–96 KM/H) 6.5 sec
0–100 MPH (0–161 KM/H) 15 sec
A.F.C. 14 mpg

FERRARI 365 GT4 BERLINETTA BOXER

In the classic car boom of the mid-Eighties, Boxers changed hands for mad money. The 512 trebled in value before the crash, with the 365 doubling its price. Now both machines have fallen back to realistic levels.

CHASSIS
The Boxer's chassis was derived from the Dino (see pages 108–09), with a frame of steel tubes and doors, bellypan, and nose in aluminum.

COOLING VENT
Slatted hood cooling vent helped keep interior cabin temperatures down.

FERRARI ENGINE

A magnificent piece of foundry art, the flat-twelve has a crankshaft machined from a solid piece of chrome molybdenum steel. Cylinder heads were light aluminum, holding two camshafts each. Instead of timing chains, the 365 used toothed composite belts, an innovation in 1973.

HEART OF THE BEAST
The Boxer 4.4-liter engine could produce an Olympian 380 bhp at 7600 rpm. Note the twin oil filters, one for each bank of six cylinders.

ENGINE POSITION
The entire engine/drivetrain ensemble was positioned longitudinally behind the cockpit.

TIRES
The Boxer was shod with ultrawide Michelin XWX 215/70 tires.

FERRARI *Dino 246 GT*

PRETTY ENOUGH TO STOP a speeding train, the Dino came not from Enzo Ferrari's head, but from his heart. The Dino was a tribute to the great man's love for his son, Alfredino, who died of a kidney disease. Aimed at the Porsche 911 buyer *(see pages 194–95)*, the 246 Dino engine came with only half the number of cylinders usually found in a Ferrari. Instead of a V12 configuration, it boasted a 2.4-liter V-6 engine, yet it was nonetheless capable of a very Ferrari-like 150 mph (241 km/h).

    With sparkling performance, small girth, and midengined layout, it handled like a go-kart, and could be hustled around with enormous aplomb. Beautifully sculpted by Pininfarina, the 246 won worldwide acclaim as the high point of 1970s automotive styling. In its day, it was among the most fashionable cars money could buy. The rarest Dino is the GTS, with Targa detachable roof panel. The Dino's finest hour was when it was driven by Tony Curtis in the '70s ITC television series *The Persuaders*. One of the most accessible Ferraris, Dino prices went berserk in the '80s, but are now half that value.

INTERIOR
The dashboard is suede and strewn with switches, while the cramped-looking interior is actually an ergonomic triumph. Slotting the five-speed gearbox though its chrome gate flows like honey.

ENGINE
The transversely mounted 2418cc V-6 has four overhead cams and a four-bearing crankshaft; it breathes through three twin-choke Weber 40 DCF carburetors. The engine's distinctive throaty roar is a Ferrari legend.

AERODYNAMICS
Sweeping roofline is unmistakable from any angle. The Dino's sleek aerodynamic shape helps to give the car its impressively high top speed.

POSITIONING
The engine is positioned in the middle, while the spare wheel and battery are located in the front.

COCKPIT
Interior is cramped, but no one cared with a car that looked this good.

FERRARI 246 GT

Early Dinos were constructed from aluminum, later ones from steel, with the bodies built by Italian designer Scaglietti. Unfortunately, little attention was paid to rust protection. Vulnerable interior body joints and cavities were covered with only a very thin coat of paint and most surviving Dinos will have had at least one body rebuild by now.

WINDSHIELD
Windshields do not come much more steeply raked than this one.

STYLING
The sensuous curves are supplied by Ferrari. The Ferrari badge and prancing horse were added by a later owner.

COLOR
Metallic brown is a rare color – 75 percent of Dinos were red.

EXHAUSTS
Four exhausts mean the V-6 sounds almost as musical as a V-12.

SPECIFICATIONS

MODEL Ferrari Dino 246 GT (1969–74)
PRODUCTION 2,487
BODY STYLE Two-door midengine sports coupe.
CONSTRUCTION Steel body, tubular frame.
ENGINE Transverse V6/2.4 litre.
POWER OUTPUT 195 bhp at 5000 rpm.
TRANSMISSION Five-speed, all synchromesh.
SUSPENSION Independent front and rear.
BRAKES Ventilated discs all around.
MAXIMUM SPEED 148 mph (238 km/h)
0–60 MPH (0–96 KM/H) 7.1 sec
0–100 MPH (0–161 KM/H) 17.6 sec
A.F.C. 22 mpg

FERRARI *Testarossa*

THE TESTAROSSA was never one of Modena's best efforts. With its enormous girth and overstuffed appearance, it perfectly sums up the 1980s credo of excess. As soon as it appeared on the world's television screens in *Miami Vice*, the Testarossa, or Redhead, became a symbol of everything that was wrong with a decade of rampant materialism and greed.

The Testarossa fell from grace rather suddenly. Dilettante speculators bought it new at $400,000-odd and ballyhooed its values up to a million. By 1988, when this particular car was built, secondhand values were going down the slippery slope, and many an investor stood back in horror as his hedge against inflation shed three-quarters of its value overnight.

1958 FERRARI TESTA ROSSA
Ferrari bestowed on its new creation one of the grandest names from Maranello's glorious racing past – the 250 Testa Rossa, of which only 19 were built for retail customers. The distinctive bodywork by Scaglietti, with its sloping nose separated from the cutaway front wheel arches, was known as "pontoon-fendered."

INTERIOR
The cockpit was restrained and spartan, with a hand-stitched leather dash and little distracting ornamentation. For once a Ferrari's cockpit was accommodating, with electrically adjustable leather seats and air conditioning as standard.

ENGINE
The flat-12 mid-mounted engine was 4942cc, producing 390 bhp at 6500 rpm. With four valves per cylinder, coil ignition, and fuel injection, it was one of the very last flat-12 GTs.

STYLING
Striking radiator cooling ducts obviated the need to pass water from the front radiator to the midmounted engine, freeing the front luggage compartment.

WHEELS
Wheel rims were 8 in (20 cm) in the front and 10 in (25 cm) in the rear.

REAR VENTS

Borrowed from Grand Prix racing experience, these cheese-slicer cooling ducts are for the twin radiators, located forward of the rear wheels to keep heat away from the cockpit.

REAR END TREATMENT
Pininfarina's grille treatment was picked up on the rear end, giving stylistic continuity.

DOOR MIRRORS
Prominent door mirrors on both sides gave the Testarossa an extra 8 in (20 cm) in width.

ORIGINAL GRILLES
The Testarossa's distinctive side grilles are now among the most widely imitated styling features

REAR-VIEW MIRROR
The curious, periscopelike rear-view mirror was developed by Pininfarina and manufactured by Gilardina.

FERRARI TESTAROSSA

Design was determined with the help of Pininfarina's full-sized wind tunnel, but enthusiasts were initially cool about the Testarossa's size and shape. Wider than the Ferrari 512 BB, the Corvette *(see pages 62–63),* and the Countach *(see pages 148–49),* it measured a portly 6 ft (1.83 m) across. While this meant a bigger cockpit, the ultrawide door sills collected mud in wet weather and the headlights were inadequate for a 180 mph (290 km/h) road rocket.

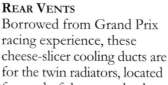

AERODYNAMICS
Front spoiler keeps the nose firmly attached to the asphalt, and channels cooling air to the front brakes.

FIAT *500D*

WHEN THE FIAT 500 NUOVA appeared in 1957, long-time Fiat designer Dante Giacosa defended his frugal flyweight by saying, "However small it might be, an automobile will always be more comfortable than a motor scooter." Today though, the diminutive scoot-about needs no defense, for time has justified Giacosa's faith – over four million 500s and derivatives were produced up to the demise of the Giardiniera estate in 1977. In some senses the Fiat was a mini before the British Mini *(see pages 40–41)*, for the baby Fiat not only appeared two years ahead of its British counterpart, but was also 3 in (7.6 cm) shorter. With its very small 479cc two-cylinder motor, the original 500 Nuova was rather frantic. 1960 saw it grow to maturity with the launch of the 500D, shown here, which was pushed along by its enlarged 499.5cc engine. Now, the baby Fiat could almost touch 60 mph (96 km/h) without being pushed over the edge of a cliff.

FIAT'S FIRST BABY
The lineage of the postwar baby Fiat descends from this little mite, the original 500, launched in 1936. To be precise, Fiat called it the 500A, the suffix referring to the airplane engine offices where it was drawn up. But the public instantly dubbed it *Topolino*, or little mouse.

MINIMAL MOTORING
The Fiat 500's interior is minimal but functional. There is no fuel gauge, just a light that comes on when three-quarters of a gallon remains – enough for another 40 miles (64 km).

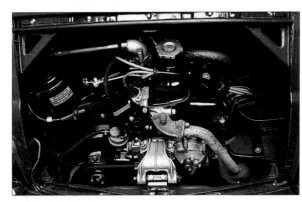

ENGINE
Rear-engined layout, already employed in the Fiat 600 of 1955, saved space by removing the need for a transmission tunnel. The use of an air-cooled engine and only two cylinders in the 500 was a completely new direction for Fiat, and gave an added space-saving bonus by doing away with a radiator. The 500 started with a 479cc engine; the 500D adopted the larger 499cc engine of the 500 Sport, which it replaced. All engines, though, were feisty devils of indefinite flat-out driving.

EARLY "SUICIDE" DOORS

You can tell this Fiat is pre-1965 because of the rear-hinged, so-called "suicide doors." After that the hinges moved to the front in line with more modern practice. The Giardiniera estate kept suicide doors until its demise in 1977.

BACK-TO-FRONT

Some rear-engined cars aped front-engined cousins with fake grilles and air intakes. Not the unpretentious Fiat.

SUNROOF

Some 500s had small fold-back sunroofs. On convertibles the fabric roof with plastic rear screen rolled right back.

FIAT 500D

This pert little package is big on charm. From any angle the baby Fiat seems to present a happy, smiling disposition. When it comes to parking it is a winner, although accommodation is a little tight. Two average-sized adults can fit up front; realistic back-seat permutations are two children, one adult sitting sideways, or a large shopping basket.

DRIVING THE 500

The baby Fiat was a fine little driver's car that earned press plaudits for its assured and nimble handling. Although top speed was limited and the gearbox was a little primitive, the car's poise meant you rarely needed to slow down on clear roads.

"HOOD"

This houses the fuel tank, battery, and spare wheel, with a little space left for a modest amount of luggage.

SPECIFICATIONS

MODEL Fiat 500D (1957–77)
PRODUCTION 4 million plus (all models)
BODY STYLES Sedan, convertible. Giardiniera estate.
CONSTRUCTION Unibody/chassis.
ENGINE Two-cylinder air-cooled 479cc or 499.5cc.
POWER OUTPUT 17.5 bhp at 4400 rpm (499.5cc)
TRANSMISSION Four-speed non-synchromesh.
SUSPENSION *Front:* Independent, transverse leaf, wishbones. *Rear:* Independent semitrailing arms, coil springs.
BRAKES Hydraulic drums.
MAXIMUM SPEED 59 mph (95 km/h)
0–40 MPH (0–64 KM/H) 32 sec
A.F.C. 53 mpg

FORD *Edsel*

THE POOR OLD EDSEL, consigned to the dustbin of history as the ultimate clunker. Everyone blames that unfortunate "horse-collar" frontal treatment, but that is only part of the story. Kinder critics say that its aim was true, but the target moved. Conceived when sales of low-end medium-priced cars were booming, the Edsel should have been a winner. Unfortunately, by the time it was officially launched on September 4, 1957, the US auto industry was in a slump, with sales particularly affected in the Edsel's market segment.

The Edsel was also a victim of its own hype. Throughout its conception, the marketing men had gone into overdrive. They forecast 200,000 sales in the first year and predicted they would have to build extra factories to cope with the demand for a car they claimed had cost $250 million to develop. The truth is that in its first year the Edsel set an all-time record for deliveries of a brand new medium-priced model. Yet it fell so short of the grandiose claims that it was almost instantly dubbed a failure. Today the Edsel is an emblem, a comforting reassurance for the little man that mighty corporations can get it wrong. And, of course, its comparative failure marks it as a prized collector's piece.

INTERIOR
Well over 80 percent of Edsel buyers cho automatic transmissions. Some 1958 mo featured these transmissions, operated pushbuttons in the steering wheel hub. is a 1959 automatic Corsair with padded dash. Less than half of all Edsels had power steering.

TELLTALE TAILLIGHTS
1958 Edsels had a higher rear light-cluster that one cruel critic likened to an ingrown toenail. The remodeled lights identify this as a 1959 model.

EDSEL MODELS
The Edsel launch lineup featured 18 models in four series, starting with the Ranger and moving up to the Pacer, Corsair, and top-of-the-line Citation. Station wagons were Ranger, Villager, and Bermuda.

EDSEL EXTREMES
The 1958 frontal treatment was more muted than the 1959, shown here with more chrome than a roadside diner.

HYPE HOPES
Edsel's launch was preceded by a massive marketing buildup. The official launch was in September 1957, but sales for the 1958 model year of 63,110 slumped to 44,891 for 1959, then 2,846 for 1960.

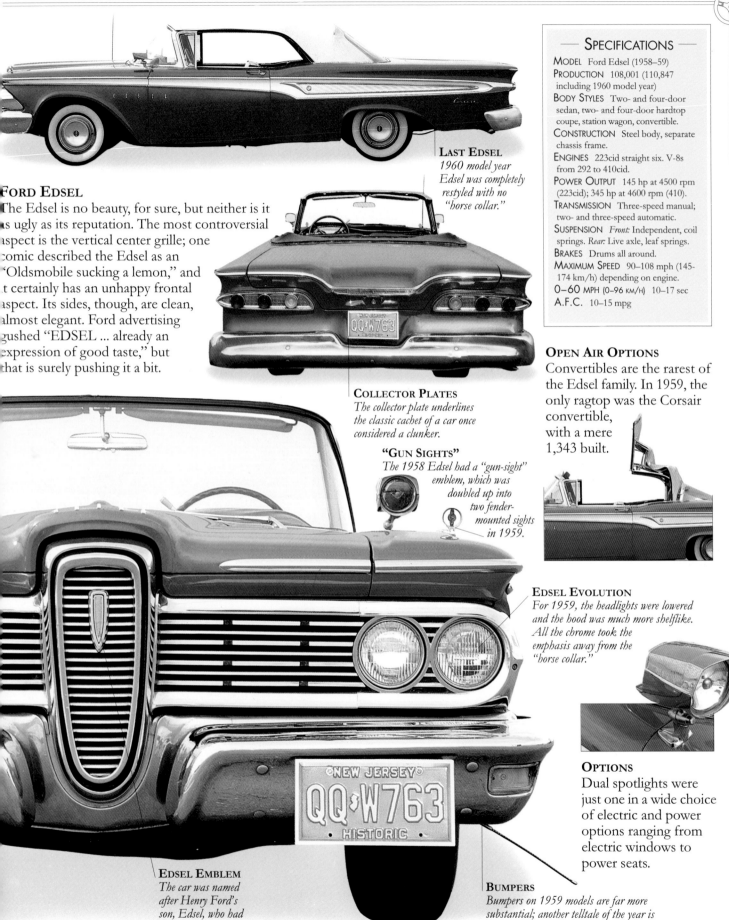

LAST EDSEL
1960 model year Edsel was completely restyled with no "horse collar."

FORD EDSEL

The Edsel is no beauty, for sure, but neither is it as ugly as its reputation. The most controversial aspect is the vertical center grille; one comic described the Edsel as an "Oldsmobile sucking a lemon," and it certainly has an unhappy frontal aspect. Its sides, though, are clean, almost elegant. Ford advertising gushed "EDSEL ... already an expression of good taste," but that is surely pushing it a bit.

COLLECTOR PLATES
The collector plate underlines the classic cachet of a car once considered a clunker.

"GUN SIGHTS"
The 1958 Edsel had a "gun-sight" emblem, which was doubled up into two fender-mounted sights in 1959.

SPECIFICATIONS

MODEL Ford Edsel (1958–59)
PRODUCTION 108,001 (110,847 including 1960 model year)
BODY STYLES Two- and four-door sedan, two- and four-door hardtop coupe, station wagon, convertible.
CONSTRUCTION Steel body, separate chassis frame.
ENGINES 223cid straight six. V-8s from 292 to 410cid.
POWER OUTPUT 145 hp at 4500 rpm (223cid); 345 hp at 4600 rpm (410).
TRANSMISSION Three-speed manual; two- and three-speed automatic.
SUSPENSION *Front:* Independent, coil springs. *Rear:* Live axle, leaf springs.
BRAKES Drums all around.
MAXIMUM SPEED 90–108 mph (145–174 km/h) depending on engine.
0–60 MPH (0–96 KM/H) 10–17 sec
A.F.C. 10–15 mpg

OPEN AIR OPTIONS
Convertibles are the rarest of the Edsel family. In 1959, the only ragtop was the Corsair convertible, with a mere 1,343 built.

EDSEL EVOLUTION
For 1959, the headlights were lowered and the hood was much more shelflike. All the chrome took the emphasis away from the "horse collar."

OPTIONS
Dual spotlights were just one in a wide choice of electric and power options ranging from electric windows to power seats.

EDSEL EMBLEM
The car was named after Henry Ford's son, Edsel, who had died in 1943.

BUMPERS
Bumpers on 1959 models are far more substantial; another telltale of the year is the lowered taillight.

FORD *Thunderbird*

LAUNCHED IN 1955 as a stylish, personal sports compact, the Thunderbird broke new ground in American car styling. Against the backdrop of overstyled and overchromed land yachts, Ford came up with an altogether more subtle creation which suggested youth, money, and success. An instant hit, the T-Bird was pitched against the first generation Chevrolet Corvette *(see pages 62–63)*. While the Chevy had an asthmatic straight-six engine, simple fiberglass body, and few creature comforts, the Thunderbird boasted a Mercury V-8, steel body, and wind-up windows. In the showrooms of 1955 the T-Bird annihilated the 'Vette, outselling it 24-to-1 and whetting America's appetite for sports cars. The two-seater Thunderbird of 1955–57 has become a design icon, a romantic piece of 1950s American ephemera that features in the lyrics of half a dozen cult songs and as many movies.

T-BIRD ENGINE
The Thunderbird's cast-iron V-8 breathed through a Holley carburetor and developed 200 hp with three-speed manual transmission and 202 hp with Ford-O-Matic automatic transmission.

HOOD
Fiberglass hardtop was standard, with a rayon convertible hood an extra-cost option at $290.

CARBURETOR SPACE
Hood bulge was for the beefy four-barrel carburetor.

FORD THUNDERBIRD
The Thunderbird was an extremely successful blend of luxury and prestige. The sporting overtones and snug two-seater shape were exactly right for the lifestyles of a new generation of baby boomers.

FORD STYLING
Thunderbird's rear lights, rear fender, and hooded headlights were all styling themes present in other Ford sedans.

RETRO SHAPE
To many, the long hood and short trunk recalled the Lincoln Continental of the early 1940s.

WINDSHIELD
By 1956 curved windshields were fitted to virtually everything.

LOW FRONT
Ground clearance was only 5½ in (14 cm).

JET EXHAUST
On the '55 and some '56 models exhausts were routed through the bumper overriders.

SPORTY LABELING
Although Ford's marketeers tried to sell the T-Bird as a sports car, it had a softer image, with comfort and convenience emphasized over raw speed and power.

BACK END
Rear fender treatment was more restrained than other contemporary American cars and has a definite European feel.

INTERIOR
Dashboard sports a tachometer and high-mount speedometer. 1956 models had softer springs and slower steering than the '55 models. Buyers preferred it that way.

SPECIFICATIONS

MODEL Ford Thunderbird (1955–56)
PRODUCTION 31,786
BODY STYLE Two-door two-seater.
CONSTRUCTION Steel ladder chassis.
ENGINE V-8/4785cc (292cid).
POWER OUTPUT 200 hp at 4400 rpm.
TRANSMISSION Three-speed manual with optional overdrive or automatic.
SUSPENSION *Front:* coil springs; *Rear:* leaf springs.
BRAKES Drums front and rear.
MAXIMUM SPEED 114 mph (183 km/h)
0–60 MPH (0–96 KM/H) 9.5 sec
0–100 MPH (0–161 KM/H) 21 sec
A.F.C. 18 mpg

SUSPENSION
Rear suspension was courtesy of old-fashioned leaf springs under a live rear axle.

FORD *Fairlane 500 Skyliner*

FORD REALLY RAISED the roof with this one, and eyebrows too, for a Ford Fairlane Skyliner pulling up at the curb was an engaging spectacle. All you had to do was flick a switch and watch the amazed faces of onlookers as your Skyliner performed its remarkable and unique retracting hardtop act. The "world's only hide-away retractable hardtop," as Ford billed it, was based on an earlier development project. That plan proved hopelessly grandiose and to redeem the $2 million development costs Ford created the remarkable Skyliner. Ford was pleased with its party trick and gushed in ads that the Skyliner was "just about the most revolutionary change in transportation since the Ford replaced the horse on the American road." Well, not quite. It was a technical tour de force certainly, but also an expensive gimmick whose novelty wore off in three short years. By the end of 1959 the retracting hardtop had disappeared.

LIFTING THE LID
This press ad from 1957 shows how the drama unfolds. To run the show it took 610 ft (186 m) of electrical wire, 10 power relays, 10 limit switches, four lock motors, three drive motors, and eight circuit breakers. Despite its complexity, the mechanism was surprisingly reliable.

ENGINE OPTIONS
All Skyliners were V-8-powered. Base models were 272cid for 1957, then 292cid. The most potent option was a 352cid unit pushing out 300 hp.

INTERIOR
As the top-of-the-line Fairlane, the glamorous Skyliner was luxuriously appointed, with color coordinated seats and dash, and power-assisted steering and brakes. This 1959 car has Cruise-O-Matic automatic transmission.

SEATING
Hood does not infringe on passenger space; the Skyliner, with benches front and rear, is a spacious six-seater.

FORD FAIRLANE 500 SKYLINER

Each of the three Skyliner model years has its own distinct identity. The original of 1957 had full-length side trim, kinked at the rear of the door to create hips; the full-width grille was a simple slatted affair. In 1958 the trim was revised; the hood received a fake air intake and twin headlights appeared (grille resembled the '58 Thunderbird, *see pages 116–17*). Further revisions followed in 1959 to create this, the final expression of the Skyliner theme.

JET STYLING
1950s rocket ship themes are expressed here by big red rear lights mimicking jet afterburners.

FIN TALE
To you and me they are fins, but Ford called them "high-canted fenders."

LUGGAGE LOCKERS
Retracting hardtop reduced luggage space to a small tub in the center of the trunk.

EXTRA LENGTH
At nearly 17.5 ft (5.3 m) the Skyliner is slightly longer than standard Fairlanes to accommodate the retracting hardtop; extra length is in the rear deck.

SPECIFICATIONS

MODEL Ford Fairlane Skyliner (1957–59)

PRODUCTION 48,394

BODY STYLE Retractable hardtop.

CONSTRUCTION Steel box-section chassis, steel body.

ENGINE Various overhead-valve V-8s. 272cid (1957); 292cid (1958–59). Options of 312, 332 and 352cid V-8s.

POWER OUTPUT 190 hp at 4500 rpm (272cid); 205 hp at 4500 rpm (292cid); 300 hp at 4600 rpm (352cid).

TRANSMISSION Three-speed manual with optional overdrive or Ford-O-Matic automatic.

SUSPENSION *Front:* independent, coil-springs; *Rear:* leaf springs with live axle.

BRAKES Drums all around.

MAXIMUM SPEED 96–100+ mph (154–161+ km/h)

0–60 MPH (0–96 KM/H) 10–18 sec

A.F.C. 14 mpg

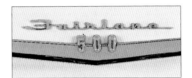

FAIRLANE ORIGINS
The car took its name from Henry Ford's mansion, Fair Lane. Up to 1958, the car was called Ford Fairlane 500 Skyliner; in 1959 it became the Ford Fairlane 500 Galaxie Skyliner.

FORD *Mustang*

THIS ONE HIT THE GROUND RUNNING – galloping in fact, for the Mustang rewrote the sales record books soon after it burst onto the market in April 1964. It really broke the mold, for it was from the Mustang that the term "pony car" was derived to describe a new breed of sporty "compacts." The concept of an inexpensive sports car for the masses is credited to dynamic young Ford vice president Lee Iacocca. In reality, the Mustang was more than classless, almost universal in appeal. Its extensive option list meant there was a flavor to suit every taste. There was a Mustang for mothers, sons, daughters, husbands, and even young-at-heart grandparents. Celebrities who could afford a ranch full of thoroughbred race horses and a garage full of Italian exotics were also proud to tool around in Mustangs. Why, this car's a democrat.

MASSIVE AIR CLEANER, HERE IN BODY COLOR, DOMINATES ENGINE BAY

302, 390, 427, AND 428CID OPTIONS WERE SOON ADDED TO THE STANDARD FORD 289 V-8

ENGINE CHOICES

Mustangs were offered with the option of V-8 (289cid pictured) or six-cylinder engines; eights outsold sixes two-to-one in 1964–68. Customers could thus buy the car just for its good looks and make do with 100 bhp – or they could order a highwayburner producing four times that much, and enjoy real sports car performance.

1965 MUSTANG WITH FORD CRUISE-O-MATIC THREE-SPEED AUTOMATIC

THE SPORTS WHEEL IS STANDARD 1965 EQUIPMENT; MUSTANG EMBLEM SERVES AS HORN

INTERIOR

The first Mustangs shared their instrument layout with more mundane Ford Falcons, but in a padded dash. The plastic interior is a little tacky, but at the price, no one was going to complain.

V-SIGN

V-8s advertised engine size and their V configuration. Less powerful sixes kept quiet about their lack of horsepower.

BOTH FRONT AND REAR USE OF CHROME IS RESTRAINED AND TASTEFUL

BANDED, TINTED WINDSHIELD WAS YET ANOTHER OPTION

FRONT DISCS WERE A NEW OPTION FOR 1965

PILLARLESS COUPE
Both front and rear side windows rolled completely out of sight to enhance the hardtop's looks and keep things cool.

SPECIFICATIONS

MODEL Ford Mustang (1964–68)
PRODUCTION 2,077,826
BODY STYLES Two-door, four-seat hardtop, fastback, convertible.
CONSTRUCTION Unibody chassis/body.
ENGINE Six-cylinder 170cid to 428cid.
POWER OUTPUT 195–250 hp at 4000–4800 rpm or 271 hp at 6000 rpm (289cid).
TRANSMISSION Three- or four-speed manual or three-speed automatic.
SUSPENSION Independent front with coil springs and wishbones; semielliptic leaf springs at rear.
BRAKES Drums; discs optional at front.
MAXIMUM SPEED 110–127 mph (177–204 km/h) (289cid)
0–60 MPH (0–96 KM/H) 6.1 sec (289)
0–100 MPH (0–161 KM/H) 19.7 sec
A.F.C. 13 mpg

RACE WINNER
Mustangs enjoyed success on both sides of the Atlantic. The big engine in a relatively small package meant they were more at home on many European tracks than previous American contenders.

FLANK EXPRESSION
Scalloped, simulated air scoop serves no function but is an enjoyable styling flourish.

POPULAR VINYL-COVERED ROOF OPTION ON THE HARDTOP SIMULATES THE CONVERTIBLE; IT LOOKS LEANER THAN HARDTOPS WITH BODY-COLORED ROOFS

STYLING
The Mustang's almost understated styling was a breath of fresh air compared with the extravagant size-is-everything excesses of the 1950s and early 1960s.

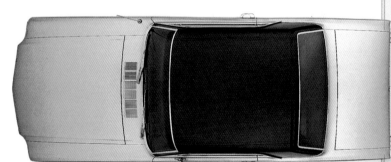

THREE TOPS
In April 1964, first Mustangs were hardtops or convertibles; a fastback coupe arrived in October. Three quarters of 1964–68 cars were hardtops; fastbacks and convertibles split the balance.

LONG DOORS HELPED ENTRY AND EXIT FOR REAR PASSENGERS

THE MUSTANG WAS SO SUCCESSFUL THAT A MICHIGAN BAKER ADVERTISED, "OUR HOTCAKES ARE SELLING LIKE MUSTANGS"

MYRIAD OPTIONS INCLUDED SMALLER WHEELS, WIDER TIRES, WIRE WHEEL COVERS, AND KNOCK-OFF STYLE HUBCAPS

—MUSTANG'S MASS APPEAL—

The Mustang galloped into the history books almost the moment it was unveiled to the public in April 1964. In one stroke it revived the freedom of spirit of the early sporting Thunderbirds and brought sports car motoring to the masses.

THE UNDISPUTED FATHER of the Mustang is Lee Iacocca, the engineer-turned-salesman whose meteoric career catapulted him to the position of vice president of the Ford Division by 1960. His concept, born of intuitive belief and market research, was for a "personal" Ford. In his early days as sales manager, people had pleaded with him to bring back the two-seater Thunderbird. The idea lodged and grew. The Mustang I prototype of 1962 was a V-4 mid-engined two-seater – pretty, but too exotic. No, Iacocca's Mustang would

have to be a practical four-seater.

The Mustang II show car debuted at the US Grand Prix in October 1963, and its rapturous reception gave the production Mustang the green light. Launched with a huge promotional blitz at the New York World's Fair of 1964, it caught the opposition sleeping and hit home with American car buyers. As part of the well orchestrated bally hoo, the first cars in showrooms were auctioned off to the highest bidders. One East Coast customer outbid 14 rivals and slept in the car overnight to

1967 FORD MUSTANG CATALOG

ensure that it was not sold from under him while his check cleared.

But there was more to the Mustang than mere hype. Sharing many components with the Ford Falcon to keep costs down, it was an honest

FORD
Mustang

IN 1965, MUSTANG BUYERS SPENT AN AVERAGE $1,000 ON OPTIONS ON TOP OF THE BASE PRICE OF $2,368

CIRCULAR MUSTANG MOTIF NEATLY CONCEALS GAS CAP

DRIVING
All Mustangs are different to drive, with 0–60 mph times ranging from six to a loping 15 seconds.

THIS IS IDENTIFIABL A FIRST SERIES MUSTANG; CONCAVE REAR END AND DIFFERENT LIGHT CAM IN 1967

CALIFORNIA
588 FNM

bargain. What's more, your Mustang could be as cheap or expensive as you liked. "The Mustang is designed to be designed by you," gushed an early sales brochure. From an entry price of $2,368, you could check the option boxes to turn your "personal" car into a hot-rod costing double that. Some 100,000 were sold in the first four months – Iacocca thought it would take a year.

LIMITED-EDITION PACE CAR MUSTANGS PRODUCED IN 1979

1966 SHELBY MUSTANG

1970 FORD MUSTANG MACH 1

In fact, it sold 417,471 in its first year, and the total topped a million in 1966. It was a winner on the track and its sporting image was boosted on the road with the Shelby GT350 Mustangs from 1965. By 1969, the Mustang was getting bigger and heavier, but the hot Boss and Mach 1 Mustangs preserved the performance image.

And maybe that was the beginning of the end, as the original pony became tethered by emissions regulations. Like the T-bird before it, the Mustang succumbed to middle age.

MUSTANG MYTHOLOGY
Cryptically, the horse on the Mustang grille runs opposite to the way race horses run on US tracks.

PUSHBUTTON RADIO AND ANTENNA WERE ALL PART OF THE OPTION LIST

STIFFER SUSPENSION AND HANDLING KITS COULD BE ORDERED AS AN OPTION

PERFECT FOR CALIFORNIA; SONNY AND CHER HAD A MATCHED PAIR OF "HIS AND HERS" MUSTANGS

FORD *GT40*

TO APPLY THE term "supercar" to the fabled Ford GT40 is to demean it; in the modern idiom Jaguar XJ220s, McLaren F1s and Bugatti EB110s are all the acme of supercar superlatives, but when did any one of them win Le Mans outright? The Ford GT40, though, was not only the ultimate road car but also the ultimate endurance racer of its era, a twin distinction no else can match. In fact, the GT40 was so good that arguments are still going on over its nationality, as both Britain and America are proud to claim the honors. Let us call it a joint design project between the American manufacturer and independent British talent, with a bit of Italian and German input as well.

What really matters is that it achieved what it was designed for, claiming the classic Le Mans 24-hour race four times in a row. And there is more to the GT40 than its Le Mans legend. You could, if you could afford it, drive around quite legally on public roads in this 200 mph (320 km/h) projectile. The cockpit might be cramped, but the impracticality of the package is part of the car's extravagance.

Ultimate supercar? No, it is better than that. Ultimate car? Maybe.

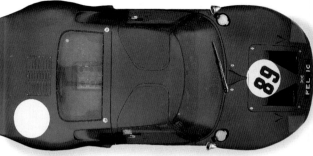

WIND CHEATER
The graceful and muscular shape was created in Ford's Dearborn design studios. Essential requirements included a mid-engined layout and aerodynamic efficiency.

INTERIOR
As befits a custom-made racer, the cockpit is designed for business rather than pleasure. Height and width of the door sills make entry and exit a chore, but once in place everything falls to hand. Racers had a side gear-change, road versions a central location.

SHORT NOSE
There is just enough room in this road car for the radiator, spare tire, and a bit of plumbing.

LIP ON TAIL HELPED HIGH-SPEED STABILITY

KNOCK-OFF HUBS FOR QUICK CHANGES; SIMPLE SIX-SPOKED WHEEL FROM 1967

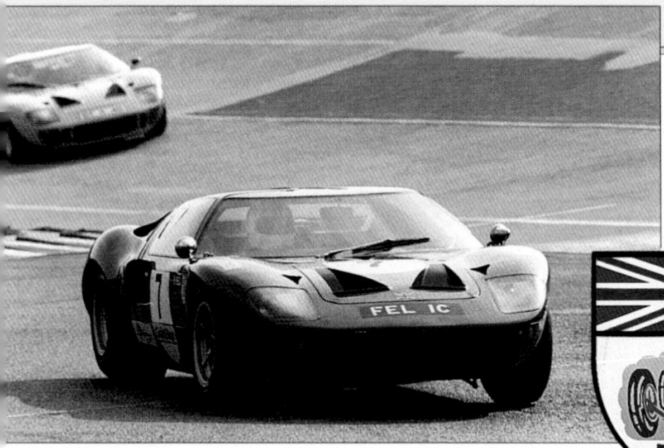
FEL IC

STILL WINNING
GT40s can still be seen in retrospective events such as the 1994 Tour de France rally, which our featured car won. The circuit is the Montlhéry track outside Paris, scene of many minor GT40 successes. The British-owned car proudly displays the British Racing Drivers' Club badge.

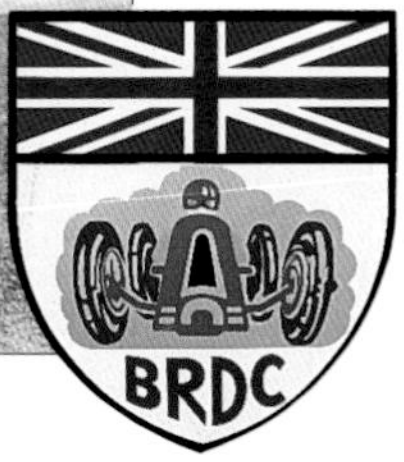
BRDC

— SPECIFICATIONS —

MODEL Ford GT40 MkI, II, III & IV (1964–68)
PRODUCTION 107
BODY STYLE Two-door, two-seat coupe.
CONSTRUCTION Sheet-steel monocoque (honeycomb MkIV), fiberglass body.
ENGINE Rear-mounted, Ford V-8, 4195cc (MkI), 4727cc (MksI & III), 6997cc (MksII & IV).
POWER OUTPUT From 350 hp at 7200 rpm (Mk1 4195cc) to 500 hp at 5000 rpm (Mk1V).
TRANSMISSION Transaxle and four- or five-speed ZF gearbox.
BRAKES Ventilated discs all around.
SUSPENSION Independent by coil springs and wishbones all around.
MAXIMUM SPEED 155–200 mph (249–322 km/h, depending on gearing)
0-60 MPH (0-96 KM/H) 4.5 sec
0-100 MPH (0-161 KM/H) 8.5 sec
A.F.C. 12–16 mpg

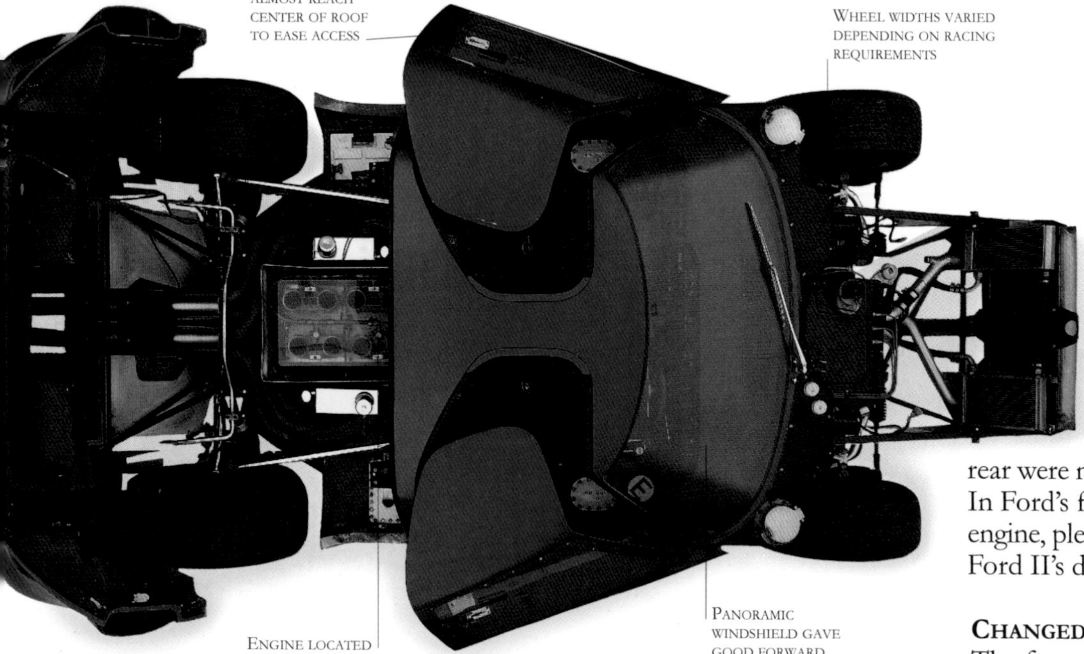
LARGE DOORS ALMOST REACH CENTER OF ROOF TO EASE ACCESS
WHEEL WIDTHS VARIED DEPENDING ON RACING REQUIREMENTS
ENGINE LOCATED ALMOST EXACTLY IN MIDDLE OF CAR
PANORAMIC WINDSHIELD GAVE GOOD FORWARD VISION

DESIGN SECRETS
Design of the GT40 was based on an earlier British Lola. Features such as mid-engined layout with gearbox/transaxle at the rear were now standard race-car practice. In Ford's favor were the powerful V-8 engine, plenty of bucks, and Henry Ford II's determination to win Le Mans.

CHANGED APPEARANCE
The front section is the easiest way to identify various developments of the GT40. First prototypes had sharp snouts; squared-off nose, as shown here, first appeared in 1965; the road-going MkIII was smoother, and the end-of-line MkIV rounder and flatter.

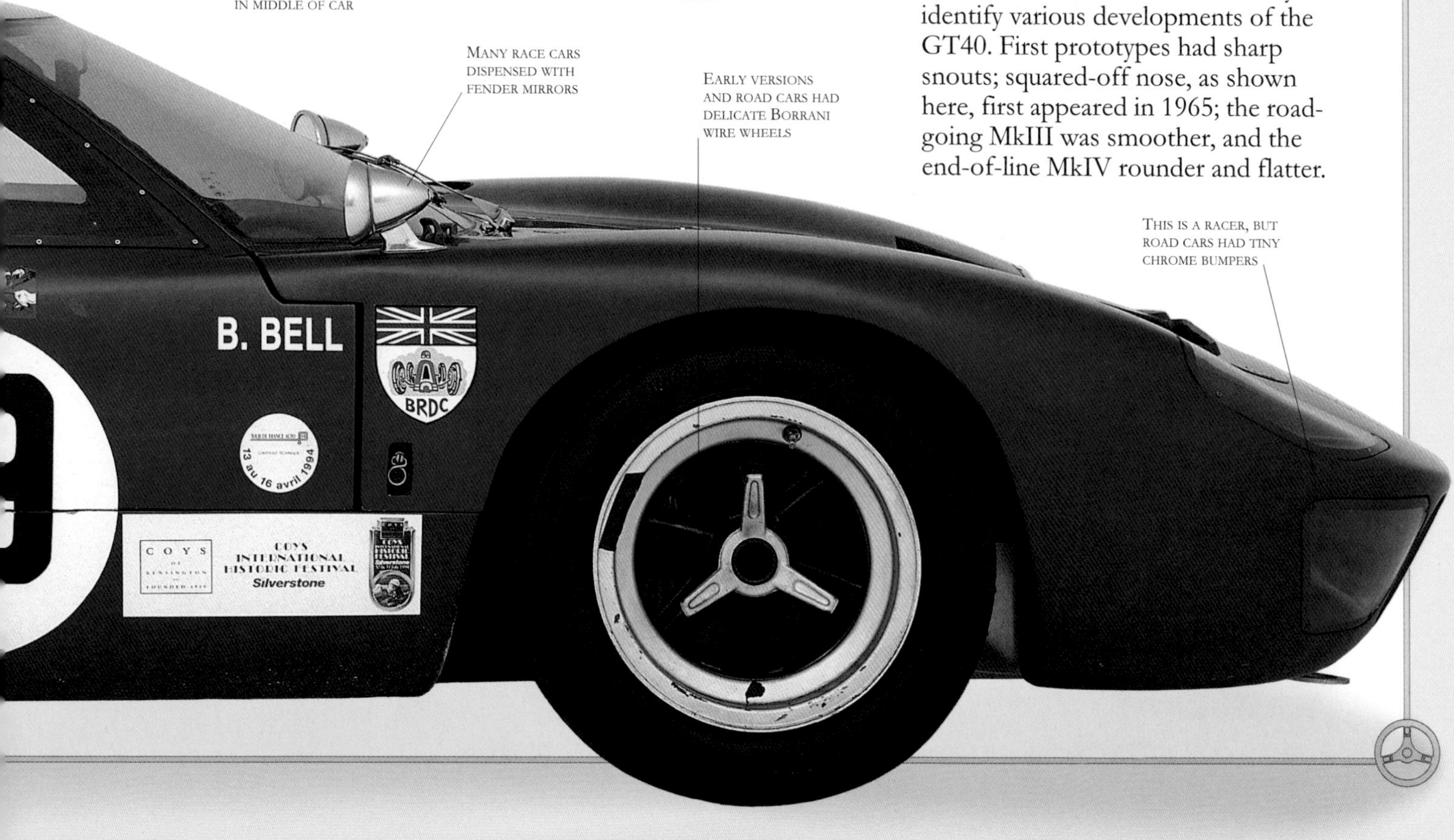
MANY RACE CARS DISPENSED WITH FENDER MIRRORS
EARLY VERSIONS AND ROAD CARS HAD DELICATE BORRANI WIRE WHEELS
THIS IS A RACER, BUT ROAD CARS HAD TINY CHROME BUMPERS
B. BELL
BRDC
13 au 16 avril 1994
COYS
INTERNATIONAL HISTORIC FESTIVAL
Silverstone

THE ROAD TO LE MANS

Le Mans laurels looked a long way off when Ferrari rebuffed Ford's overtures, but with unwavering determination Henry Ford II pursued his goal and created a Le Mans legacy that will live forever.

HENRY FORD'S grandson, Henry Ford II, figured the quickest and easiest way of achieving his ultimate Le Mans goal would be to buy the company that was already doing all the winning in the current endurance classics – Ferrari. The Commendatore, Enzo Ferrari, would not sell to the Americans, so they were forced to look elsewhere. Unsuccessful overtures were also made to Colin Chapman's Lotus in England.

The project finally started to gain momentum when Ford took over a race-car project begun by the small British firm of Lola, which by coincidence used a Ford V-8 racing engine. Other British racing people were hired to join the team based near London and to produce a Ferrari-beater. American input was in the form of the V-8 racing engine, and the distinctive body design. Everything else was created in England, and the

GT40 AT LE MANS, DRIVEN BY MAGLIOLI AND CASSONI

first cars were completed there. But it was American determination which insisted that the cars run at Le Mans in 1964, before they were really ready. They were the fastest cars in the race, but did not have the reliability. On the other hand, the American policy which dictated that the early engines be replaced by a monstrous 7-liter unit for

FORD GT40 MK1V AT LE MANS IN 1967

FORD
GT40

FUZZY SLIT ABOVE ENGINE COVER
GIVES JUST ENOUGH REAR VISION
TO WATCH A FERRARI FADE AWAY

EXHAUST NOTE RISES
FROM GRUFF BELLOW
TO EAR-SPLITTING YOWL

VITAL STATISTICS
GT, of course, stands for Grand Touring; 40 for the car's height in inches. Overall length was 13 ft 9 in (4.2 m), width 5 ft 10 in (1 .78 m), and unladen weight 1,835 lb (832 kg).

FELIC

965, brought the first breakthrough –
ctory in the world championship
ound at Daytona in Florida.
Still the Le Mans jewel was elusive;
e cars again broke down after
etting the early pace. But Henry
ord was single-minded, doggedly
ursuing his ambition, and it was a
atter of third time luck for the
nglo-American enterprise, which
nally enjoyed the fruits of its effort

ULF FORD GT40 LE MANS WINNER, 1968

with a stunning Le Mans 1-2 finish
in 1966. Now that Ford had cracked
the formula, it could not be beaten –
it won in 1967, 1968, and 1969 as well,
when the 24-hour enduro fell to Ford.
The last two victories were achieved
after the Ford company, honor
satisfied, had withdrawn from the fray

1966 FORD GT40 AT SPA, BELGIUM

and left the operation in the hands of
the independent Gulf team. Headed
by John Wyer, who had been the first
manager of the GT40 racing team,
Gulf achieved the incredible
distinction of winning at Le Mans
two years in a row – with the same car.

GT40'S LE MANS VICTORIES
966: CHRIS AMON (NZ)/BRUCE
CLAREN (NZ); 1967: A.J. FOYT (US)/
AN GURNEY (US); 1968: PEDRO
ODRIGUEZ (MEX)/LUCIEN
IANCHI (B); 1969: JACKY
CKX (B)/JACKIE
LIVER (GB).

THE LUCKY FEW WHO HAVE
DRIVEN THE GT40 REPORT
PLEASINGLY LIGHT STEERING

DUCTS HELPED HOT AIR
ESCAPE FROM RADIATOR

ONE OF THE SEVEN
MKIII ROAD CARS
WAS ACTUALLY FITTED
WITH A TV

FEL 1C

GORDON KEEBLE *GT*

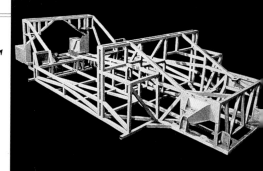

COMPOSITE
SKELETON OF
SQUARE TUBES

IN 1960, THIS WAS THE MOST electrifying car the British magazine *Autocar & Motor* had ever tested. Designed by Giugiaro in Italy and built in an aircraft hanger in Southampton, it boasted good looks, a fiberglass body, and a 5.4-liter, 300 bhp V-8 Chevrolet Corvette engine *(see pages 62–63).*

But, despite plenty of publicity, good looks, epic performance, and a clientele as glamorous as Jackie Kennedy and Diana Dors, the Gordon Keeble was a commercial disaster, with only 104 built.

"The car built to aircraft standards," read the advertising copy. And time has proved the Keeble's integrity; a space-frame chassis, fiberglass body, and that unburstable V-8 has meant that over 90 Gordons have survived, with 60 still in regular use. The Gordon Keeble was born in an era where beauty mattered more than balance sheets. It failed for two reasons. Firstly, the workers could not make enough of them, and secondly, the management forgot to put a profit margin in the price. How the car industry has changed...

SPACE FRAME
The space-frame chassis was finished in February 1960, flown to France, then driven to Turin, where Giugiaro added a handsome GT body.

HIGH-QUALITY BODY
In its day, the Keeble's hand-finished, glass-reinforced plastic body was among the best made.

CARTER FOUR-BARREL CARBURETOR LIVES UNDER
RESPLENDENT CHROMED AIR CLEANER

WINDOWS
Electric windows used the same motors as the Rolls-Royce Silver Shadow.

ENGINE
The small block Sting Ray engine, supplied by General Motors, is an aristocrat among American V-8s, delivering a huge 300 bhp of high compression power. Brutal performance means 70 mph (113 km/h) in first gear and a mighty wall of torque which, even when flooring the throttle in top gear, meant you could annihilate most other cars.

LIGHTS
Twin slanted headlights were distinctly sporting in the 1960s.

BUMPERS
The Keeble's delicate three-piece chrome bumpers were specially hand-made.

FEW 555

FUEL TANKS
Twin fuel tanks say much about an era when fuel cost 30 cents a gallon and 15 mpg was considered reasonable.

SPECIFICATIONS

MODEL Gordon Keeble GT (1964–67)
PRODUCTION 104
BODY STYLE Four-seater fiberglass GT.
CONSTRUCTION Multitubular chassis frame, GT body.
ENGINE 5.3-liter V-8.
POWER OUTPUT 300 bhp at 5000 rpm.
TRANSMISSION Four-speed all synchromesh.
SUSPENSION Independent front, de Dion rear end.
BRAKES Four-wheel disc.
MAXIMUM SPEED 141 mph (227 km/h)
0–60 MPH (0– KM/H) 7.5 sec.
0–100 MPH (0–161 KM/H) 13.3 sec.
A.F.C. 14 mpg

POWER
Despite restrained elegance and concealed twin exhausts, the Keeble could top 140 mph (225 km/h).

GORDON KEEBLE GT
Only 21 when he designed the car, Giugiaro gave the hood a dummy intake scoop and fashionably raked twin headlights. The roof was lengthened and the slant of the C pillar decreased to give wider glass areas and maximum visibility.

FOUR-SPEED CHEVROLET GEARBOX WAS UNBREAKABLE

LAVISHLY EQUIPPED, THE KEEBLE CAME WITH A PUSH-BUTTON RADIO, SEAT BELTS, AND A FIRE EXTINGUISHER

AERO VENTILATION
Built at Eastleigh airport, Southampton, England, many aircraft parts found their way into the Keeble, like this period swivelling ventilation nozzle.

INTERIOR
The inside is like the flight deck of an old luxury jet – quilted aircraft PVC, black-on-white gauges, toggle switches, and that *de rigueur* accessory of all 1960s GT cars, a wood-rimmed steering wheel.

THIS IRONIC BADGE WAS CHOSEN AFTER A TORTOISE WALKED INTO VIEW DURING THE PHOTO SHOOT FOR THE SALES BROCHURE

STYLE
For a '60s design, the Gordon Keeble is crisp, clean, and timeless.

HOLDEN *FX*

AT THE END OF WORLD WAR II, Australia was up against a problem – an acute shortage of cars and a newly discharged army with money to burn. Loaded with government handouts, General Motors-Holden came up with a four-door, six-cylinder six-seater that would eventually become an Australian legend on wheels.

Launched in 1948, the 48-215, more generally known as the FX, was Australia's Morris Minor *(see pages 178–81).* Tubby, conventional, and as big as a Buick, it had a sweet, torquey engine, steel monocoque body, hydraulic brakes, and a three-speed column shift. Light and functional, the FX so impressed Lord Nuffield (of Morris fame) with its uncomplicated efficiency that he had one shipped to England for his engineers to pull apart. The Australians did not care about the FX's humble underpinnings and bought 120,000 with grateful enthusiasm.

SPEEDOMETER CALIBRATED TO 100 MPH (161 KM/H) WAS A TAD OPTIMISTIC

WHITE STEERING WHEEL WAS AN AMERICAN INHERITANCE

DASHBOARD
The dash echoes the Australian culture for utilitarianism, with central speedometer, two occasional gauges, precise three-speed colu[m] changer, and only five switches. The umbre[l] handbrake and chrome horn ring were holdovers from Detroit design influences.

DOOR HANDLE
The extravagant prewar door handle looked strangely out of place on such an austere shape and was one of the FX's few styling excesses.

FRONT SUSPENSION
Front springing was by tough coil and wishbone with lever arm shocks.

ENGINE
Power came from a sturdy 2170cc cast-iron straight six, which developed a modest 60 bhp, with an integral block and crankcase, pushrod overhead valves, and a single-barrel downdraft Stromberg carburetor.

WARNING
Strident horn mounted behind the front grille was to warn roaming wildlife in the Australian outback.

TK·377 NSW

HANDLING
The Holden was too powerful for its suspension and many ended up on their roofs.

LIGHTING
Simple and unadorned, the FX had no turn signals or parking lights, just a six-volt electrical system with a single rear light.

SPACE
Endlessly practical, the FX had a cavernous luggage compartment.

BROCHURES
General Motors-Holden started life as an Adelaide saddlery and leather goods manufacturer, later diversifying into Holden Motor Body Builders – the sole supplier to General Motors Australia.

ECONOMY
Postwar fuel shortages meant that the Holden was economical.

HOLDEN 48-215 FX

The "Humpy Holden" was a warmed-over prewar design for a small Chevrolet sedan that General Motors US had created in 1938. A Detroit-Adelaide collaboration, the FX emerged as a plain shape that would not date, with high ground clearance for bad roads and dustproof body. It became the standard transportation of the Australian middle classes.

BODY FLEX
Taxi drivers complained of body flexing – doors could spring open on corners.

MASCOT
Recumbent lion hood mascot gave the FX an illusion of pedigree. In reality, Holden had no bloodline at all.

REAR STYLING
Rear fender line was cut into the rear doors but was much milder than Detroit's styling men would have liked. Rear fender skirts made the car look lower and sleeker.

CHROME
Lavish Baroque grille looks like a stylistic afterthought.

REAR FENDER STONE-GUARDS WERE MADE NOT FROM CHROME BUT RUBBER

HUDSON *Super Six*

IN 1948, HUDSON'S FUTURE could not have looked brighter. The feisty independent was one of the first with an all-new postwar design. Under the guidance of Frank Spring, the new Hudson Super Six not only looked stunning, it bristled with innovation. The key was its revolutionary "step-down" design, based on a unibody construction with the floor pan suspended from the bottom of the chassis frame. The Hudson was lower than its rivals, handled with ground-hugging confidence, and with its gutsy six-cylinder engine, outpaced virtually all competitors. In 1951, it evolved into the famous Hudson Hornet, dominating US stock car racing from 1951 to 1954. But the unibody design could not adapt to the rampant demand for yearly revision; the 1953 car looked much like the 1948. In 1954 Hudson merged with Nash, disappearing for good in 1957.

POSTWAR PIONEER
Along with Studebaker the 1948 Hudson departed from the design of prewar cars. It created a sensation, but its complex structure made it difficult to update.

BIG SIX
The gutsy new 262cid six arrived the same year as the new-style Hudsons in 1948. It made the Hudson one of the swiftest cars on America's roads and, bored out to 308cid for the 1951 Hornet, it became a racing legend.

WOOD-GRAIN DASH
This is not wood at all, but painted metal. Main instruments are a speedometer, and 30-hour windup clock, both later moved in front of the driver. "Idiot lights," rather than gauges, for oil pressure and amperage were a traditional Hudson feature.

THIS IS A RARE RIGHT-HAND DRIVE CAR, ORIGINALLY EXPORTED TO SOUTH AFRICA, NOW IN THE UK

LOW RIDER
Chassis frame runs outside the rear wheels, serving as "invisible side bumpers" and contributing to low height.

HEIGHT
The Super Six stood only 60.4 in (1.53 m) high when contemporary Buicks and Chryslers were more than 15 in (38 cm) taller. Yet Hudson's interior space was exceptional.

LOGO
Hudson triangle dated back to 1909 when department store owner Joseph L Hudson gave his name and financial backing to the venture. White triangle is illuminated.

INTERIOR
All passengers were cradled between axles for comfort. Reviewers raved that rear passengers were treated to a front-seat ride.

SPECIFICATIONS

MODEL Hudson Super Six (1948–51)
PRODUCTION 180,499
BODY STYLES Four-door sedan, Brougham two-door sedan, Club coupe, hardtop coupe, two-door Brougham convertible.
CONSTRUCTION Unit chassis/body.
ENGINE 262cid L-head straight-six.
POWER OUTPUT 121 hp at 4000 rpm.
TRANSMISSION Three-speed manual, optional overdrive; semiautomatic.
SUSPENSION *Front:* independent, wishbones, coil springs, telescopic shocks, antiroll bar. *Rear:* live-axle, semielliptic leaf springs, telescopic shocks, antiroll bar.
BRAKES Hydraulic drums all around.
MAXIMUM SPEED 90 mph (145 km/h)
0–60 MPH (0–96 KM/H) 14–18 sec (depending on transmission)
A.F.C. 15–20 mpg

HUDSON SUPER SIX

It is the smooth beauty of the profile that really marks the Hudson. The design team was led by Frank Spring, a long-time Hudson fixture, whose unusual blend of talents combined styling and engineering. He had also designed airplanes. The new Hudson shape that evolved from a series of wartime doodles was one of the most aerodynamic of its time. The famed "step-down" chassis kept the center of gravity and overall height low without compromising levels of comfort.

MONOBILT
All Hudsons from 1932 had unit chassis and body, Monobilt in company speak. Many figured the Super Six's step-down design made it the safest automobile of its time.

REAR ASPECT
The rear of the Hudson is least pleasing, a slightly settled soufflé; but it is the view most other motorists and stock car racers saw.

SPLIT SCREEN
Each segment of the split screen was curved for partial wraparound effect and good visibility.

JAGUAR *XK120*

A CAR-STARVED BRITAIN, still trundling around in perpendicular, prewar hangover cars, glimpsed the future in October 1948 at the Earl's Court Motor Show in London. The star of the show was the Jaguar Super Sports. It was sensational to look at from any angle, with a purity of line that did not need chrome embellishment. It was also sensationally fast; in production as the Jaguar XK120, it would soon be proven that 120 really did stand for 120 mph (193 km/h), making it the fastest standard production car in the world.

Once again Jaguar boss William Lyons had pulled off his favorite trick: offering sensational value for money compared with anything else in its class. In fact this time there was nothing else in its class. The only trouble was that you could not actually buy one. Lyons had planned the XK120 as a short-production-run, prestige show-stopper, but overwhelming interest at the 1948 show changed all that. Hand-built aluminum-bodied cars dribbled out of the Jaguar factory in 1949, and you needed a name like Clark Gable to get your hands on one. In 1950, tooling for steel-bodied cars was ready and the XK120 took off as an export earner, with over 85 percent of all XK120s going to foreign countries. Today the XK120 is as stunning as ever, still thrilling owners and enthusiasts.

HANDSOME
SMITH DIALS

WALNUT TRIM WAS
A FEATURE OF
HARDTOP COUPES
AND DROPHEADS ONLY

CAT MOTIF
ON IMPOSING
STEERING WHEEL

THE ENGINE
The famed XK six-cylinder engine was designed by Bill Heynes and Wally Hassan, and went on to power the E-type *(see pages 140–43)* and other Jaguars up until 1986. Even this was "styled"; William Lyons insisted it had twin camshafts to make it resemble Grand Prix cars of the 1930s.

CLASSIC SIMPLICITY
Surrounded by leather and thick-pile carpet, you feel good just sitting in an XK120. With its lush interior, purposeful instruments, and the bark of the exhaust from behind, you will hardly notice that it is a little cozy – if not downright cramped.

REAR VIEW
Hardtop coupes had limited rear vision.

SELLING THE DREAM
The original sales brochure for the XK120 used airbrushed photographs of the very first car built.

JAGUAR XK120 HARDTOP COUPE

Many rate the hardtop coupe as the most gorgeous of all XK120s, with a roofline and teardrop window reminiscent of the beautiful Bugatti Type 57SC Atlantic. The hardtop model did not appear until March 1951 and is much rarer than the roadster. Even though numbers were trimmed further in the late 1980s' scramble to restore roadsters, their flowing curves and perfect proportions are now more widely appreciated.

PARKING LIGHTS
This is clearly a 1953 XK120 because of the body-colored parking lights fared into the fender. Early XKs had chrome parking light pods.

THE CAT'S PAWS
Skinny cross-ply tires gave more thrills than needed on hard cornering.

WHEELS
Standard wheels were the same steel discs as on the Jaguar sedans. Wire wheels were a popular option and helped to counter alarming fade by reducing heat buildup in the brake drums.

XK120 HALLMARKS
Slim split bumpers and thin grille slats distinguish the XK120 from the thicker bumpered XK140, which superseded it.

JAGUAR *XK150*

THE XK150 APPEARED IN THE SPRING of 1957 and was the most refined of the XK trio. One of the last Jaguars to have a separate chassis, it carried four-wheel Dunlop disc brakes, a 210 bhp version of the legendary XK straight six power plant, and an optional Borg Warner automatic gearbox. The 150 marked the beginning of the civilization of the Jaguar sports car. With its wider girth and with more creature comforts, it was to hold the market's interest until the then-secret E-Type project *(see pages 140–43)* was ready to unveil in 1961.

In the late 1950s, the XK150 was a glamorous machine, almost as flashy as an Aston Martin, but $3,000 cheaper. March 1958 saw more power in the form of the "S" performance package, which brought the 3.4 up to 250 bhp. In 1959 the 3.8's output soared to a heady 265 bhp. Available as a roadster, drophead, or hardtop coupe, the 150 sold 9,400 examples in its four-year run, the rarest model being the XK150S hardtop coupe, with a mere 193 cars built. Despite being eclipsed by the sinewy E-Type, the 150 was charismatic enough to be the personal transportation of '50s racing ace Mike Hawthorn and starlet Anita Ekberg. Currently undervalued, a well-restored 150 costs half the price of the equivalent E-Type and is much more individual.

INTERIOR
The interior was much more refined than previous XKs, with a wrap-around windshield and adjustable steering column. On the last 1960 cars, the turn signal switch was on the steering column instead of the dashboard.

LIGHT INDICATOR
A tiny red peak on the parking light reminded the driver that lights were on.

The XK150 Roadster

SLEEK PROMOTION
Introduced in 1958, the two-seater XK150 Roadster was the last model in the series and also the sportiest. Ever since the 120, all XKs had been a hit in America and the 150 was no exception.

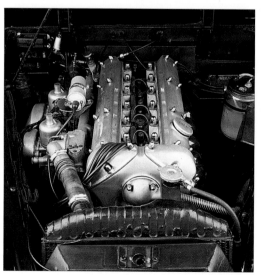

ENGINE
This classic, twin overhead cam design first saw the light of day in 1949, and was phased out in 1986. Some say it is one of the finest production engines of all time. Sturdy, powerful, and handsome, the 3.8 powered the legendary D-Type Jaguars which could top 197 mph (317 km/h).

TIRES
Standard tires were Dunlop crossply RS5s.

REAR VIEW
From the rear, the hardtop has definite sedan lines, with a curved rear window, big wraparound bumper, wide track, and cavernous trunk.

JAGUAR XK150
The gorgeous curved body sits on a conventional chassis. Joints and curves were smoothed off at the factory using lead. The 1950s car industry paid little thought to rustproofing, so all Jaguars of the period are shamefully rust-prone.

WHEELS
Wire wheels were the most common, although steel wheels with hubcaps were available.

BODYWORK
The body is mounted on a massive box-section chassis, which hardly differs from the original XK120 design. All the XK150's body panels were new, with a higher cowl and fender line, wider hood, and broader radiator grille than earlier models.

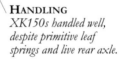

HANDLING
XK150s handled well, despite primitive leaf springs and live rear axle.

VENTILATION
Vent in front fender was to provide air to passenger compartment.

RACING SUCCESS
Jaguar XKs won laurels all over the world.

SO MUCH FOR SO LITTLE
At $3,600, the 150 was a resounding value. This is a very early car wearing a 1958 Coventry-issued registration number, probably a factory demonstrator.

SPECIFICATIONS
MODEL Jaguar XK150 FHC (1957–61)
PRODUCTION 9,400
BODY STYLES Two-seater roadster, drophead, or hardtop coupe.
CONSTRUCTION Separate pressed-steel chassis frame with box section side members.
ENGINE Straight six, twin overhead cam 3442cc or 3781cc.
POWER OUTPUT 190 bhp at 5500 rpm (3.4); 210 bhp at 5500 rpm (3.8); 265 bhp at 5500 rpm (3.8S).
TRANSMISSION Four-speed manual, with optional overdrive, or three-speed Borg Warner Model 8 automatic.
SUSPENSION Independent front, rear leaf springs with live rear axle.
BRAKES Dunlop front and rear discs.
MAXIMUM SPEED 135 mph (217 km/h)
0–60 MPH (0–96 KM/H) 7.6 sec (3.8S)
0–100 MPH (0–161 KM/H) 18 sec
A.F.C. 18 mpg

JAGUAR *C-Type*

THE C-TYPE IS THE CAR that launched the Jaguar racing legend and began a Le Mans love affair for the men from Coventry. In the 1950s, Jaguar boss Bill Lyons was intent on winning Le Mans laurels for Britain, just as Bentley had done a quarter of a century before. After testing mildly modified XK120s in 1950, he came up with a competition version, the XK120C (C-Type) for 1951. A C-Type won that year, failed in 1952, then won again in 1953. By then the C-Type's place in history was assured. It had laid the cornerstone of the Jaguar sporting legend that blossomed through its successor, the D-Type, which bagged three Le Mans 24-hour wins in four years. C-Types were sold to private customers, most of whom used them for racing rather than road use. They were tractable road cars though, often driven to and from races; after their days as competitive racers were over, many were used as high-performance highway tourers.

THE CAT FAMILY
Grille reflects family resemblance to the XK120 production model, which compan[y] head Bill Lyons had insisted on

HOME COMFORTS
Snug-fitting seats supported well during hard cornering.

POWERPLANT
The engine was taken from the XK120 and placed into the competition version. Horsepower of the silky six was boosted each year until some 220 bhp was available.

AERO HERITAGE
Designer Malcolm Sayer's aircraft industry background shows in the smooth aerodynamic styling.

FAST FUELING
Quick-release gas cap was another racing feature, and could save valuable seconds in a race.

ACCESSIBILITY
It was easier to step over the door than open it; passenger did not even get one.

HOOD IS HINGED FORWARD TO EASE MID-RACE ADJUSTMENTS

ENGINE SNUGGLES NEATLY INTO ITS BAY, READY FOR ACTION

WIRE WHEELS HAVE KNOCK-OFF HUBCAPS FOR QUICK TIRE CHANGES

JAGUAR C-TYPE
Jaguar's Bill Lyons dictated that the C-type racer should bear a strong family resemblance to production Jaguars. The Malcolm Sayer body, fitted to a special frame, achieved that aim. The clever blend of beauty and function retained the pouncing-cat Jaguar "look," while creating an aerodynamically efficient tool for the high-speed Le Mans circuit. In racing trim, cars ran with a single windshield; our car has a second full-width windshield.

PUR 120

SPECIFICATIONS

MODEL Jaguar C-Type (1951–53)
PRODUCTION 53
BODY STYLE Two-door, two-seater sports racer.
CONSTRUCTION Tubular chassis, aluminum body.
ENGINE Jaguar XK120 3442cc, six-cylinder, double overhead camshaft with twin SU carburetors.
POWER OUTPUT 200–210 bhp at 5800 rpm.
TRANSMISSION Four-speed XK gearbox with close ratio gears.
SUSPENSION Torsion bars all around; wishbones at front, rigid axle at rear.
BRAKES Lockheed hydraulic drums; later cars used Dunlop discs all round.
MAXIMUM SPEED 144 mph (232 km/h)
0–60 MPH (0–96 KM/H) 8.1 sec
0–100 MPH (0–161 KM/H) 20.1 sec
A.F.C. 16 mpg

ON THE TRACK
The C-Type was always most at home on the track, though more at Le Mans – where it won the 24-hour classic twice in three attempts – than on shorter circuits such as Silverstone, where this picture was taken in July 1953.

INTERIOR
Cockpit was designed for business, not comfort, but was roomy enough for two adults; passengers were provided with a grab-handle in case the driver thought he was at Le Mans.

LUGGAGE SPACE
A car built for racing does not need to carry baggage; rear deck covers the massive fuel tank.

BRAKE LIGHTS
Brake lights were a racing necessity as well as safety feature for road use, particularly with later disc-braked versions.

SPARE WHEEL
Removable panel in the tail hides the spare wheel.

ATTENTION TO DETAIL
Louvers on the hood help hot air escape; engine cover is secured by quick-release handles and leather safety straps.

PUR 120

SUSPENSION
Telescopic shocks smoothed the ride; C-Type introduced disc brakes to road racing as a secret weapon in 1952, though most examples used drums.

JAGUAR *E-Type*

WHEN JAGUAR BOSS WILLIAMS LYONS, by now Sir William, unveiled the E-Type Jaguar at the Geneva Motor Show in March 1961, its ecstatic reception rekindled memories of the 1948 British launch of the XK120 *(see pages 134–35)*. The E-Type, or XKE as it is known in the US, created a sensation. British motoring magazines had published road tests of preproduction models to coincide with the launch – and yes, the hardtop coupe really could do 150 mph (242 km/h). OK, so the road-test cars were probably tuned a little and early owners found 145 mph (233 km/h) a more realistic maximum, but the legend was born. It was not just a stunning, svelte sports car, though; it was a trademark Jaguar sporting package, once again marrying sensational performance with superb value for money. Astons and Ferraris, for example, were more than twice the price.

HARDTOP
A two-seater hardtop coupe was available from the outset. In 1966, a hardtop two-plus-two with a longer wheelbase was added to the line and it was this longer wheelbase that the V-12 adopted at its launch in 1971.

DETACHABLE HARDTOP WAS AVAILABLE AS A FACTORY OPTION

INTERIM MODEL
Our featured 1965 car is still a Series 1, even though it features the 4.2-liter engine, better brakes and an all-synchromesh gearbox

SIMPLICITY OF LINE
Designer Malcolm Sayer insisted he was an aerodynamicist and hated to be called a stylist. He claimed the E-Type was the first production car to be "mathematically" designed.

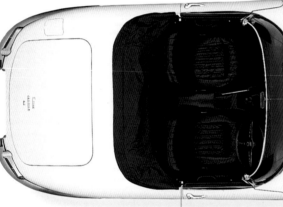

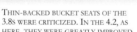
THIN-BACKED BUCKET SEATS OF THE 3.8S WERE CRITICIZED. IN THE 4.2, AS HERE, THEY WERE GREATLY IMPROVED

TELL TAIL
The thin bumpers with lights above are an easy giveaway for E-Type spotters. In 1968, with the introduction of the Series 2, bulkier light clusters appeared below the bumpers.

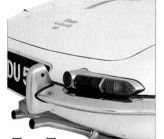

WIRE WHEELS WERE STANDARD ROAD WEAR FOR SIX-CYLINDER E-TYPES; STEEL DISCS WERE FITTED TO V-12S

XK Engines

The twin-overhead cam, six cylinder was a development of the original 3.4-liter XK unit fitted to the XK120 of 1949. First E-Types had a 3.8-liter unit, then 4.2 after 1964. Configuration changed in 1971 to a new V-12.

TRIPLE SU CARBURETORS ON UK SIXES; LESS OOMPH FROM TWIN STROMBERGS ON SOME US CARS

ENGINE ACCESS LOOKS GOOD, BUT WATCH YOUR HEAD

SPECIFICATIONS

MODEL E-Type Jaguar (1961–74)
PRODUCTION 72,520
BODY STYLES Two-seater roadster and hardtop coupe, 2+2 hardtop coupe.
CONSTRUCTION Steel monocoque.
ENGINE 3781cc straight six; 4235cc straight six; 5343cc V-12.
POWER OUTPUT 265 to 272 bhp.
TRANSMISSION Four-speed manual, optional automatic from 1966.
SUSPENSION *Front:* independent, wishbones, and torsion bar; *Rear:* independent, coil and radius arm.
BRAKES Discs all around.
MAXIMUM SPEED 150 mph (241 km/h), 3.8 & 4.2; 143 mph (230 km/h) 5.3.
0–60 MPH (0–96 KM/H) 7–7.2 sec.
0–100 MPH (0–161 KM/H) 16.2 sec (3.8)
A.F.C. 16–20 mpg

Handling

Jaguar designed an all-new independent setup at the rear. Handling in the wet and on the limit is often criticized, but for its day the E-Type was immensely capable.

Racing

Although intended as a roadgoing sports car, light-weight and racing E-Types performed creditably on the track in the hands of amateurs.

Cockpit

The interior of this Series 1 4.2 is the epitome of sporting luxury, with leather seats, wood-rim wheel, and an array of instruments and toggle switches – later replaced by less sporting and less injurious rocker switches.

CENTER PANEL HINGES FOR ACCESS TO ELECTRICS

3.8S HAD ALUMINUM-FINISHED CENTER CONSOLE PANEL AND TRANSMISSION TUNNEL

Hood

On a sunny day, the view over the long hood from the driving seat is one of the great motoring sensations – but not in congested traffic.

WITH NO SUN VISORS, TINTED GLASS IS DESIRABLE

LOUVERS ARE NOT FOR LOOKS; E-TYPES, PARTICULARLY EARLY ONES, TENDED TO OVERHEAT IN HOTTER CLIMATES

STANDARD FOUR-WHEEL DISC BRAKES WERE PART OF THE SPEC FROM FIRST E-TYPES

THE EXHILARATING JAGUAR

Most enthusiasts would settle for any E-Type Jaguar, but through the years the curvaceous Cat transformed, and for the later part of its life Americans had to make do with detoxed XKEs as emissions laws emasculated the wild Cat.

E – IT IS ONLY A LETTER, but when you attach it to the trunk lid of a sporting Jaguar it stands for exhilaration, excitement, ecstasy, and entertainment.

1955 JAGUAR D-TYPE

E also comes after D and that is where all these sporting superlatives have their roots, in the D-Type sports racers of the 1950s that dominated Le Mans with wins in 1955, '56 and '57.

In its early development stages, the E-Type was seen as a successor to the D-Type (and the rare XKSS roadgoing D-Type), but as Jaguar abandoned racing, the road-car project developed along different lines. There

FIXED-HEAD E-TYPE AT GENEVA MOTOR SHOW, 1961

was no doubt though, that racing had improved the breed. For a start, the lovely lines of the E-Type displayed a direct lineage from the D-Type. That is no surprise as the C, D, and E-Types were penned by aerodynamicist Malcolm Sayer. Under the skin, the E-Type chassis evolved from the D-

JAGUAR
E-Type

AS LEGISLATORS GANGED UP ON THE E-TYPE, THESE ELEGANT LIGHTS WERE REPLACED BY BULKIER ITEMS

ULTIMATE E
The 4.2 is often seen as the most complete driving package, but most prized are the first 3.8s, especially the earliest "flat-floor" models.

HDU 555C

THIS BULGE LOOKS PURPOSEFUL, BUT IS NOTHING MORE IMPORTANT THAN THE FUEL TANK DRAIN PLUG

e's monocoque and front-
frame structure. Of course
re were the four-wheel disc
kes and that fabulous XK six
nder overhead cam engine.
he impact the shape made at
aunch on March 15, 1961, at
Geneva Motor Show is now
stuff of Jaguar lore. Those first
ype roadsters and hardtop
pes, produced until June 1962, are
v referred to as "flat-floor" models,
are the most prized of all. In fact,
r flat floor was something of a
v, as recessed foot wells were later
orporated to increase comfort for
er drivers. In 1964, the 4.2-liter
ine supplanted the 3.8. It was
ntly more torquey and now had an

1972 JAGUAR E-TYPE SERIES 3

all-synchromesh box. One of the many
E-Type watersheds was in 1967 with the
so-called Series 1½ models, which lost
those characteristic headlight covers in
the interests of better illumination. From
there, US Federal safety regulations took
control and the Series 2 featured altered
bumpers and lights. By now the Cat was

putting on weight and girth. In 1971,
as US emission regulations were
increasingly strangling the Cat's
performance, the Series 3 emerged with
a 5.3-liter V-12 based on the layout of
the longer 2+2 hardtop. Production
ceased in 1974, ending a distinguished
life and a remarkable export success
story. For every three E-Types built,
two were exported – most of those to
the US. There is one more
telling fact, when deciding
on which E-Type to
choose. The 150 mph
(242 km/h) performance
of the very first 3.8-
liter E-Types was
never matched by
later models.

NVERTIBLE COUNT
rdtop coupes actually
ounted for a little
er half of all E-Type
duction, yet the
dster was the
or export winner,
h most going to
US.

UNUSUAL AND SPORTY-
LOOKING TRIPLE WIPERS
GAVE WAY TO A TWO-
BLADE SYSTEM WITH
THE 1971 V-12

THE STYLISH BUT
INEFFICIENT LENS
COVERS WERE
REMOVED IN 1967

HDU 555C

JENSEN *Interceptor*

THE JENSEN INTERCEPTOR was one of those great cars that comes along every decade or so. Built in a small Birmingham, England, factory, a triumph of tenacity over resources, the Interceptor's lantern-jawed looks and tire-smoking power made the tiny Jensen company a household name. A glamorous cocktail of an Italian-styled body, American V-8 engine, and genteel British craftsmanship, it became the car for successful swingers of the late 1960s and 1970s.

The Interceptor was handsome, fashionable, and formidably fast, but its tragic flaw was a singlefigure appetite for fuel – 10 mpg if you enjoyed yourself. After driving straight into two oil crises, a worldwide recession, and suffering serious losses from the ill-starred Jensen-Healey project, Jensen filed for bankruptcy in 1975 and finally closed its doors in May 1976.

<table>
<tr><td colspan="2" align="center">— SPECIFICATIONS —</td></tr>
<tr><td>MODEL</td><td>Jensen Interceptor (1966–76)</td></tr>
<tr><td>PRODUCTION</td><td>1,500</td></tr>
<tr><td>BODY STYLE</td><td>All-steel occasional four-seater coupe.</td></tr>
<tr><td>CONSTRUCTION</td><td>Separate tubular and platform type pressed steel frame.</td></tr>
<tr><td>ENGINE</td><td>V-8, 6276cc.</td></tr>
<tr><td>POWER OUTPUT</td><td>325 bhp at 4600 rpm.</td></tr>
<tr><td>TRANSMISSION</td><td>Three-speed Chrysler Torqueflite automatic.</td></tr>
<tr><td>SUSPENSION</td><td>Independent front with live rear axle.</td></tr>
<tr><td>BRAKES</td><td>Four-wheel Girling discs.</td></tr>
<tr><td>MAXIMUM SPEED</td><td>135 mph (217 km/h)</td></tr>
<tr><td>0–60 MPH (0–96 KM/H)</td><td>7.3 sec</td></tr>
<tr><td>0–100 MPH (0–161 KM/H)</td><td>19 sec</td></tr>
<tr><td>A.F.C.</td><td>13.6 mpg</td></tr>
</table>

ADWEST POWER STEERING WAS ALSO USED IN THE CONTEMPORARY JAGUAR XJ6

BODYWORK
Bodies were all-steel, with scant attention paid to corrosion proofing.

INTERIOR
Road testers complained that the Interceptor's dash was like the flight deck of a small aircraft, but the interior was beautifully hand-made with the finest leather and plush Wilton carpets.

SUSPENSION
Front suspension was coil spring, wishbone and lever arm shocks borrowed from the Austin Westminster.

TIRES
Original skinny Dunlop RS5 Crossplies had, by 1968, changed to wider Dunlop SP Radials.

ENGINE
The lazy Chrysler V-8 of 6.2 liters gives drag strip acceleration along with endless reliability. With one huge carburetor and only a single camshaft, the Interceptor has a simple soul.

JENSEN INTERCEPTOR
The Interceptor's futuristic shape hardly changed over its 10-year life span and was widely acknowledged to be one of the most innovative designs of its decade. The rear window lifted up to reveal a large luggage compartment.

STYLING
The classic shape was crafted by Italian styling house Vignale. From bare designs to running prototype took just three months.

GEARING
Most Interceptors were automatic apart from 24 ultra rare cars fitted with four-speed manual gearboxes.

LAMBORGHINI *Espada*

FERRUCCIO LAMBORGHINI'S AIM OF out-Ferrari-ing Ferrari took a sidestep with the four-seater Espada. It was a first and a last for the tractor manufacturer turned dream-maker; the first and only true four-seater Lamborghini, and the last of the front-engined cars, along with the Jarama. Perhaps underrated today, it was nevertheless the biggest-selling Lamborghini ever until the Countach *(see pages 148–49)* overtook it.

With the design constraint of seating four adults in a VIP road rocket, the Espada was never going to have conventional 2+2 beauty, but it is still an exhilarating executive express. Propelled by the Miura's muscular four-liter V-12, the fastest boardroom on wheels will eat up the autostrada at 140 mph (225 km/h) all day long. Where other cars are merely labeled GTs, this Bertone beauty needs no acronyms on its rump to excel as the epitome of the term Grand Tourer.

SPECIFICATIONS

MODEL Lamborghini Espada (1968–78). S1 1968–70; S2 1970–72; S3 1972–1978.
PRODUCTION 1,217
BODY STYLE Two-door, four-seater fastback sedan.
CONSTRUCTION Pressed-steel platform frame, integral steel body with aluminum hood.
ENGINE Four-cam V-12 of 3929cc.
POWER OUTPUT 325–365 bhp at 6500 rpm.
TRANSMISSION Five-speed manual or, from 1974, Chrysler TorqueFlite auto.
SUSPENSION All independent by unequal-length wishbones & coil springs.
BRAKES Discs on all four wheels.
MAXIMUM SPEED 150–155 mph (241–249 km/h)
0–60 MPH (0–96 KM/H) 7.8 sec
0–100 MPH (0–161 KM/H) 16 sec
A.F.C. 10–15 mpg

EXECUTIVE LUXURY
Sumptuous fittings included leather upholstery and electric windows. The dash improved on later cars, as seen here.

SMOOTH POWER
The engine was borrowed from existing models – the 400GT and the Miura. Power from the 4-liter V-12 grew from 325 bhp for the first models, through 350 bhp for the S2, to 365 bhp for the last of the S3s.

FAT FEET
Fat tires, supple ride, and a fine chassis add up to exceptional handling.

DEEP BREATHS
Six greedy twin-choke Webers gulp in air through hood air ducts.

POISE
Four headlights, blacked-out grille, and low stance make for a formidable road presence.

LAMBORGHINI ESPADA
The Espada's styling was created by Marcello Gandini from Bertone's "Marzal" show car. Lamborghini's first true passenger car could carry four people comfortably, as long as two of them were not too tall.

LAMBORGHINI *Miura*

THE LAUNCH OF the Lamborghini Miura at the 1966 Geneva Motor Show was the decade's driving sensation. Staggeringly beautiful, technically pre-eminent, and unbelievably quick, it was created by a triumvirate of engineering wizards all in their twenties. For the greater part of its production life the Miura was considered the most desirable car money could buy, combining drop-dead looks, awesome performance, and unerring stability, as well as an emotive top speed of 175 mph (282 km/h).

From its dramatic swooping lines – even Lamborghini thought it was too futuristic to sell – to its outrageously exotic colors, the Miura perfectly mirrored the middle 1960s. But, as the oil crises of the 1970s took hold, the Miura slipped into obscurity, replaced in 1973 by the unlovely, and some say inferior, Countach *(see pages 148–49).*

INTERIOR
The cockpit is basic but finely detailed, with a huge Jaeger speedometer and tachometer. Six minor gauges on the left of the console tell the mechanical story. Only the gearbox is a disappointment, with a trucklike, sticky action that does not do the Miura's gorgeous engine justice.

ALUMINUM GEAR-LEVER
GATE IS A HAND-MADE
WORK OF ART

ENGINE
The V-12 4.0-liter engine was mid-mounted transversely to prevent the car's wheelbase from being too long. The gearbox, final drive, and crankcase were all cast in one piece to save space. Beneath all that pipery slumber 12 pistons, 4 chain-driven camshafts, 24 valves, and 4 carburetors.

BERTONE DESIGN
Long, low, and delicate, the Miura is still considered one of the most handsome automotive sculptures ever.

TAIL-END ACTION
Because the Miura sits so low, it displays virtually zero body roll; therefore there is little warning before the tail breaks away.

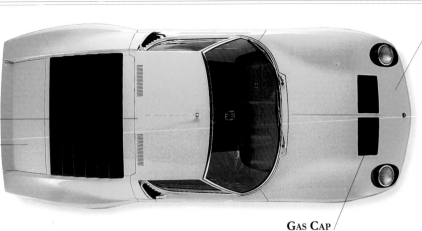

SOUND INSULATION
In an attempt to silence a violently loud engine, Lamborghini put 4 in (10 cm) of polystyrene insulation between engine and cabin.

LIGHT POWERHOUSE
The Miura has a very impressive power-to-weight ratio – output of 385 bhp, yet it weighs only 2,646 lb (1,200 kg).

LAMBORGHINI MIURA SV

In looks and layout the mid-engined Lambo owes much to the Ford GT40 *(see pages 124–27)*, but was engineered by Gianpaolo Dallara. At the core of the Miura is a steel platform chassis frame with outriggers front and rear to support the major mechanicals. The last-of-the-line SV was the most refined, with more power, a stiffer chassis, and redesigned suspension. Other changes included wider wheels and a different rear fender profile.

FRONT-END LIFT
Treacherous aerodynamics meant that approaching speeds of 170 mph (274 km/h) both front wheels could actually lift off the ground.

GAS CAP
The gas cap hides under one of the hood slats.

SPECIFICATIONS

MODEL Lamborghini Miura (1966–72)
PRODUCTION Approx. 800
BODY STYLE Two-seater roadster.
CONSTRUCTION Steel platform chassis, light aluminum and steel bodywork.
ENGINE Transverse V-12 4.0-liter.
POWER OUTPUT P400, 350 bhp at 7000 rpm; P400S, 370 bhp at 7700 rpm; P400SV, 385 bhp at 7850 rpm.
TRANSMISSION Five-speed with transaxle.
SUSPENSION Independent front and rear.
BRAKES Four-wheel ventilated disc.
MAXIMUM SPEED P400SV, 175 mph (282 km/h)
0–60 MPH (0–96 KM/H) 6.7 sec
0–100 MPH (0–161 KM/H) 15.1 sec
A.F.C. 16 mpg

SV MARQUE
The Miura SV is the most desirable of the species, with only 150 built.

AIR DUCTS
Ducts in front of the rear wheels channel air for cooling the rear brakes.

HEADLIGHT POSITION
The car was so low that headlights had to "pop-up" to raise them high enough for adequate vision.

LIGHTS
Standard Miura headlights were shared by the Fiat 850.

LAMBORGHINI *Countach 5000S*

THE COUNTACH IS a prodigious antique. First unveiled at the 1971 Geneva Motor Show as the Miura's replacement, it was engineered by Giampaolo Dallara and breathtakingly styled by Marcello Gandini of Bertone fame. For a complicated, hand-built car, the Countach delivered all the reliable high performance that its swooping looks promised. In 1982, a 4.75-liter 375 bhp V-12 was shoehorned in to give the upcoming Ferrari Testarossa *(see pages 110–11)* something to reckon with. There is no mid-engined car like the Countach. The engine sits longitudinally in a multi-tubular spaceframe, with fuel and water carried by twin side-mounted tanks and radiators. Weight distribution is close to 50/50, which means that the Countach's poise at the limit is legendary. On the down side, it takes forever to get used to the extra wide body, visibility is appalling, steering is heavy, gear selection difficult and, for all its tremendous cost, the cockpit is cramped, with luggage space restricted to an overnight bag. Yet such faults can only be considered as charming idiosyncrasies when set against the Countach's staggering performance – a howling 187 mph (301 km/h) top speed and a 0–60 belt of 5 seconds.

NOT ONE BUT FOUR
Everything on the Countach is built on a grand scale. Four exhausts, four camshafts, 12 cylinders, six 45DCOE Webers, a rev line of 8000 rpm, 26-gallon fuel tank, single figure thirst, and the widest track of any car on the road.

MANEUVERABILITY
Reversing the Countach is like launching the Queen Mary. Preferred technique is to open the door and sit on the sill while looking over your shoulder.

WHEELS
Steamroller-like 12J five-porthole aluminum wheels sit on ultra-low profile Pirelli P7 tires.

CELEBRATIONS

The 25-year anniversary of Lambo production in 1985 was celebrated with the 5000S and the elite Quattrovalvole 5000S.

SPECIFICATIONS

MODEL Lamborghini Countach (1973–90)
PRODUCTION Approx 1,000
BODY STYLE Mid-engined, two-seater sports coupe.
CONSTRUCTION Aluminum body, space-frame chassis.
ENGINE 4754cc four-cam V-12.
POWER OUTPUT 375 bhp at 7000 rpm.
TRANSMISSION Five-speed manual.
SUSPENSION Independent front and rear with double wishbones and coil springs.
BRAKES Four-wheel vented discs.
MAXIMUM SPEED 187 mph (301 km/h)
0–60 MPH (0–96 KM/H) 5.1 sec
0–100 MPH (0–161 KM/H) 13.3 sec
A.F.C. 9 mpg

BODY VULNERABILITY
Scant body protection means that most Countachs acquire a tapestry of scars and scratches that require the cost of a Ford Escort to repair.

INTERIOR
The cabin is crude, with unsubtle interior architecture. Switches and stalks are Fiat- and Lancia-sourced.

HANDLING
The Countach goes exactly where it is pointed with unerring precision thanks to almost perfect weight distribution.

SOUND EFFECTS
Inches away, all occupants are able to hear exactly what this engine has to say.

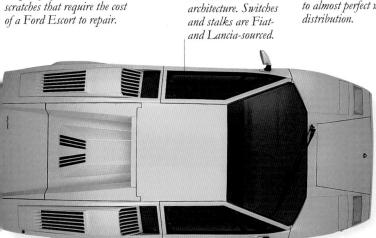

DOORS
Pivoting doors are works of art that worked perfectly from the earliest prototypes.

LAMBORGHINI COUNTACH 5000S

The shape is a riot of creative genius that ignores all established rules of car design. Air scoops behind the body's side windows break up the wedge-shaped line and form a readymade indent for a compact door catch and an ideal hand-hold for the huge gullwing doors. Under the aluminum panels nestles a birdcage spaceframe chassis of great complexity.

LANCIA *Aurelia* B24 *Spider*

BEAUTY IS MORE THAN just skin deep on this lovely little Lancia, for underneath those lean Pininfarina lines, the Aurelia's innards bristle with innovative engineering. For a start there is the compact aluminum V-6. Designed under Vittorio Jano, the man responsible for the great racing Alfas of the 1920s and '30s, this free-revving, torquey little lump was the first mass-produced V-6. The revolution was not just at the front though, for at the back were the clutch and gearbox, housed in the transaxle to endow the Aurelia with near perfect weight distribution. Suspension, although hardly run-of-the mill, was typically Lancia, with the front sliding pillars that Lancia had first employed in the 1920s.

These innovations were first mated with the Pininfarina body in 1951, with the Aurelia B20 GT coupe. And the point of it all becomes clear when you climb behind the wheel, for although the Aurelia was never the most accelerative machine, its handling was so impeccable that 40 years later it still impresses with its cornering poise. The B20 GT is often credited as the first of the new breed of modern postwar GTs. With the B24 Spider you got fresh air too, and today this charismatic roadster is the most prized of this illustrious family.

FLEXIBLE V-6
Aurelias featured an all-aluminum unit that grew from 1754cc to 1991cc and then 2451cc, which was fitted to the B24 Spider. The flexible 60-degree V-6 could pull the Spider from 20 mph (32 km/h) in top gear, yet ran to 5500 rpm.

ELEGANT, ADJUSTABLE NARDI STEERING WHEEL WAS STANDARD EQUIPMENT ON THE SPIDER

SPARTAN INTERIOR
The panel has just three major dials and a clutch of switches on a painted metal dash. It was devoid of the walnut-leather trimmings that British car makers of the time considered essential for a luxury sports car.

LUGGAGE ROOM
The Aurelia Spider scored well in luggage-carrying capabilities compared with other two-seaters of the time.

TWIN TAILPIPE
As you pile on the revs, the throbbing, gruff sound rises to a rich gurgle that is singularly tuneful from the twin exhausts.

ROADHOLDING
Handling, the Spider's best feature, was helped by racing tires being fitted as part of the original spec.

BALANCE
For perfect balance, the weight of the engine was offset by locating clutch and gearbox in a unit with the differential at the rear.

CROSSED FLAGS
These represent the joint input of Lancia, responsible for design and manufacture of the mechanical parts, and Pininfarina, who not only styled the body but also built the cars.

RIGHT-HAND DRIVE
Until the Aurelia, Lancia had eccentrically persisted with right-hand steering, even for the Italian market. The adoption of left-hand drive makes this right-hander a real rarity.

SPECIFICATIONS

MODEL Lancia Aurelia B24 Spider (1954–1956)
PRODUCTION 330
BODY STYLE Two-seater sports convertible.
CONSTRUCTION Monocoque with pressed steel and box-section chassis frame.
ENGINE Twin-overhead-valve aluminum alloy V-6, 2451cc.
POWER OUTPUT 118 bhp at 5,000 rpm.
TRANSMISSION Four-speed manual.
SUSPENSION Sliding pillar with beam axle and coil springs at front, De Dion rear axle on leaf springs.
BRAKES Hydraulic, finned aluminum drums, inboard at rear.
MAXIMUM SPEED 112 mph (180 km/h)
0–60 MPH (0–96 KM/H) 14.3 sec
A.F.C. 22 mpg

LANCIA AURELIA B24 SPIDER
The Spider bears a passing family resemblance to the Aurelia sedan, and even more so to the GT models. Neither of the closed versions had the wraparound windshield though, or the equally distinctive half-bumpers; the Spider's radiator grille was a slightly different shape, too. The curvaceous Pininfarina profile is characterized by the sweeping front fenders and long luggage compartment. High-silled monocoque construction meant small doors; the Spider had a basic hood with plastic side-screens.

SPIDER SPOTTING
The Spider's hood-top air-scoop was a unique feature among Aurelia models.

LANCIA STRATOS

THE LANCIA STRATOS was built as a rally-winner first and a road car second. Fiat-owned Lancia took the bold step of designing an all-new car solely to win the World Rally Championship and, with a V6 Ferrari Dino engine *(see pages 108–09)* on board, the Stratos had success in 1974, '75 and '76. Rallying rules demanded that at least 500 cars be built, but Lancia needed only 40 for its rally program; the rest laid unsold in showrooms across Europe for years. Never a commercial proposition, the Stratos was an amazing mix of elegance, hard-charging performance, and thrill-a-minute handling.

RALLY SUCCESS
Lancia commissioned Bertone to build a rally weapon, and the Stratos debuted at the 1971 Turin Show. Despite scooping three World Championships, sales of Stratos road cars were so slow that they were still available new up until 1980.

INTERIOR
The Stratos is hopeless as a day-to-day machine, with a claustrophobic cockpit and woeful rear vision. The width of 67 in (1.72 m) and the narrow cabin mean that the steering wheel is virtually in the middle of the car.

ENGINE
Factory rally versions had a four-valve V-6 engine.

REAR COWL
Molded fiberglass rear cowl lifts up by undoing two clips, giving access to midships-mounted power plant.

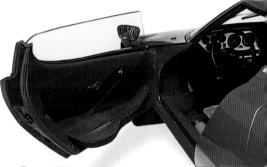

DEEP WINDOWS
Plastic side windows are so deeply recessed within the bodywork that they can be fully opened without causing any wind turbulence.

SHARP END
Flimsy nose section conceals spare wheel, radiator, and twin thermostatically controlled cooling fans.

WHEELS
Campagnallo aluminum wheels with Pirelli P7F tires – F stands for a softer compound to give a gentler loss of adhesion.

LANCIA STRATOS

Shorter than a Mk II Escort, and with the wheelbase of a Fiat 850, the stubby Stratos wedge looks almost as wide as it is long. Front and back are fiberglass with a steel center section.

COMFORT
Truncated cabin is cramped, cheap, nasty, and hot.

WEIGHT
The Stratos is a two-thirds fiberglass featherweight, tipping the scales at a little over 2,000 lb (908 kg).

SPECIFICATIONS

MODEL Lancia Stratos (1973–80)
PRODUCTION 492
BODY STYLE Two-seater, mid-engined sports coupe.
CONSTRUCTION Fiberglass and steel unit construction body chassis tub.
ENGINE 2418cc mid-mounted transverse V-6.
POWER OUTPUT 190 bhp at 7000 rpm.
TRANSMISSION Five-speed manual in unit with engine and transaxle.
SUSPENSION Independent front and rear with coil springs and wishbones.
BRAKES Four wheel discs.
MAXIMUM SPEED 143 mph (230 km/h)
0–60 MPH (0–96 KM/H) 6.0 sec
0–100 MPH (0–161 KM/H) 16.7 sec
A.F.C. 18 mpg

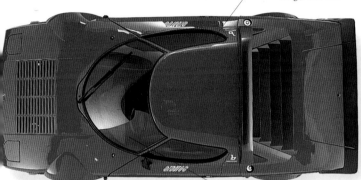

WINDSHIELD
Windshield is cut from thin cylindrical glass to avoid distortion.

ENGINE

Lifted straight out of the Dino 246, the 190 bhp transverse, mid-mounted V-6 has four chain-driven camshafts spinning in aluminum heads, which sit just 6 in (15 cm) from your ear. Clutch and throttle are incredibly stiff, which makes smooth driving an art form.

SLATS
A 1970s fad, matte black plastic rear window slats do little for rearward visibility.

REAR SPOILER
Raised rear spoiler does its best to keep the rear wheels stuck to the road like lipstick on a collar.

SUSPENSION
Rear springing was by Lancia Beta-style struts, with lower wishbones, and had anti-dive and anti-squat geometry.

LOTUS *Elite*

IF EVER A CAR WAS A MARQUE landmark, this is it. The Elite was the first Lotus designed for road use rather than out-and-out racing, paving the way for a string of stunning sports and GT cars that, at the least, were always innovative. But the first Elite was much more than that. Its all-fiberglass construction – chassis as well as body – was a bold departure which, coupled with many other innovations, marked the Elite as truly exceptional, especially considering the small-scale operation that created it. What's more, its built-in Lotus race-breeding gave it phenomenal handling and this, together with an unparalleled power-to-weight ratio, brought an almost unbroken run of racing successes. It also happens to be one of the prettiest cars of its era; in short, a superb GT in miniature.

WINDOW DESIGN
The door shape did not allow for conventional windup windows. Wing windows opened, but on early cars the main side windows were fixed. This later car has a catch to allow outward opening.

CUBBY-HOLES APLENTY WERE PROVIDED TO SUPPLEMENT TRUNK SPACE

SE (SPECIAL EQUIPMENT) MODELS HAD A SILVER ROOF AS A "DELETE OPTION"

QUICK-RELEASE FUEL CAP WAS AN OPTION MANY CHOSE

LOW DRAG
Low frontal area, with air intake below the bumper lip, was a major contribution to Elite speed and economy. Drag coefficient was 0.29, a figure most other manufacturers would not match for 20 years.

LENGTH IS ONLY 12 FT (3.66 M), YET THE TRUNK IS VERY USABLE; SPARE WHEEL IS IN THE CABIN

BOTH FRONT AND REAR BUMPERS HID BODY MOLDING SEAMS

FIBERGLASS FACTS
Fiberglass was used to avoid both the tooling costs of traditional construction and to build in lightness. In reality, the Elite was not cheap to produce but, at around 1,300 lb (590 kg), it was certainly light.

INTERIOR

Even tall owners were universal in their praise for driving comfort. The award-winning interior is crisp and neat, with light, modern materials. Main instruments were a speedometer reading to 140 mph (225 km/h) and an 8000 rpm tachometer.

OUTLINE OF INSTRUMENT PANEL MIMICS PROFILE OF THE ELITE BODY

WOOD-RIM WHEEL IS THE ONE TRADITIONAL TOUCH ON THE INTERIOR

SPECIFICATIONS

MODEL Lotus Elite (1957–63)
PRODUCTION 988
BODY STYLE Two-door, two-seater sports coupe.
CONSTRUCTION Fiberglass monocoque.
ENGINE Four-cylinder single ohc Coventry Climax, 1216cc.
POWER OUTPUT 75–105 bhp at 6100–6800 rpm.
TRANSMISSION Four-speed MG or ZF gearbox.
SUSPENSION Independent all around; wishbones and coil springs at front and MacPherson-type "Chapman strut" at rear.
BRAKES Discs all around (inboard at rear).
MAXIMUM SPEED 118 mph (190 km/h)
0–60 MPH (0–96 KM/H) 11.1 sec
A.F.C. 35 mpg

VENTILATION

Built-in cockpit ventilation system was fed by an intake on the cowl; outlet vents were above the rear window.

CIRCUIT SUCCESS

Elites were seen on the track even before they were available for sale. They were uncatchable in their class, claiming Le Mans class wins six years in a row from 1959 to 1964, and often embarrassing bigger GT Ferraris and Jaguars.

COVENTRY CLIMAX ENGINE BADGE SHOWS LADY GODIVA, WHO PARADED NAKED THROUGH THE CITY'S STREETS

ENGINE

The lightweight 1216cc four-cylinder engine was developed by Coventry Climax from its successful racing units. Power rose from an initial 75 bhp to 83 bhp in the second series, but over 100 bhp was possible with options.

THE COVENTRY CLIMAX ENGINE WAS DEVELOPED FROM A WARTIME FIRE-PUMP ENGINE

CONCEALED STEEL HOOP AROUND WINDSHIELD ADDED STIFFNESS AND GAVE SOME ROLLOVER PROTECTION

CONTEMPORARY ROAD TESTS RECORDED A REMARKABLE 25 MPG AT A STEADY 100 MPH (161 KM/H)

48-SPOKE CENTER-LOCK DUNLOP WIRE WHEELS WERE STANDARD

THE FIRST LOTUS FOR THE ROAD

Against the odds the elegant Elite launched the tiny Lotus company into the world of production car maufacturing with a blend of almost amateur enthusiasm, race-bred engineering expertise, dedication, and sure intuition.

THE ELITE WAS THE brainchild of company founder and great racing innovator, Anthony Colin Bruce Chapman. The elegant coupe was a remarkable departure for the small company – and, to most, a complete surprise when it appeared at the London Motor Show in October 1957. Even more surprising was the nature of the package, for it was not professionally styled, but drawn up initially by a friend of Chapman's, Peter Kirwan-Taylor, an accountant and design hobbyist.

It bristled with innovation too, for its fiberglass monocoque – not just body – was an amazing industry first. The engine was the lightweight Coventry Climax unit that Chapman knew well in competition Lotuses. It really was developed from a wartime fire-pump engine. Suspension was derived from the Lotus Formula 2 car of 1956, with that elegant weight-saving Chapman strut at the rear. The result was a light fantastic, so nimble and precise that it gave road users an insight into racing car dynamics. On the race track it was a giant-killer.

That is the glory of the Elite, but in reality, customers had to wait to find out. The Elite was already a race winner, but the first customer cars – only two of them – did not go out

COLIN CHAPMAN AT TRACKSIDE

LOTUS
Elite

AT ITS LAUNCH, THE ELITE COST MORE THAN A JAGUAR XK150

MANY ELITES FROM 1961 ONWARD WERE SOLD AS NEAR-COMPLETE KITS, WHICH, THE ADVERTISING SAID, COULD BE ASSEMBLED IN 25 MAN-HOURS

STRESSED ROOF
The roof was part of the Elite's stressed structure, which meant that popular calls for a convertible – especially from America – could not be answered.

TINY DOOR HANDLE IS LIT MORE THAN A HO

LJC 322

until December 1958, more than a year after the launch. And the Elite's exceptional qualities came at an exotic price, initially a little more than a Jaguar XK150, and twice the price of an MGA. In the end, it was a triumph that 988 were built at all, against a backdrop of early production problems and Lotus' characteristically convoluted finances and organization – even the production total is far from certain.

But the ultimate testimony to the Elite is the number of survivors – at least 660, possibly 750. It had made its mark and when the end came, the American magazine *Road & Track* published a full-page obituary that serves as a fine epitaph: "A beautiful design was the Elite ... one that seems certain to be looked back upon as a landmark of some sort in automobile design. Without question it was the best, if not the very best looking Grand Touring car ever built." But it was also a beginning. Built along with the Elite was the cult-status Lotus 7, and the Elite laid the foundations for future Lotuses – the Elan, then Europa, Elite again, Eclat, Esprit, and back to a new Elan.

LOTUS 7

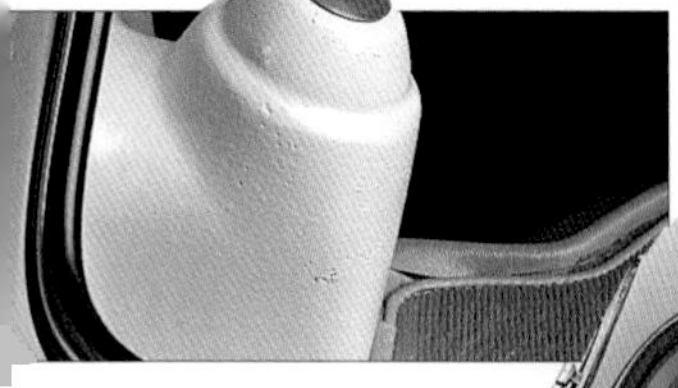

SUSPENSION STRUT
Curious conical bulges cover the coil springs and telescopic shocks.

AIR CHEATER
The Elite's aerodynamic makeup is remarkable considering that there were no full-scale wind tunnel tests, only low-speed airflow experiments. Height of just 46 in (1.17 m) helped, as did the fully enclosed undertray below.

A 2-LITER ENGINE WAS TOYED WITH FOR A WHILE, BUT IT UPSET THE ELITE'S FINE BALANCE

LJC322

LOTUS *Elan Sprint*

THE LOTUS ELAN RANKS as one of the best handling cars of its era. But not only was it among the most poised cars money could buy, it was also drop-dead gorgeous. Conceived by engineering genius Colin Chapman to replace the race-bred Lotus 7, the Elan sat on a steel backbone chassis, was clothed in a slippery fiberglass body, and was powered by a 1600cc Ford twin-cam engine. Despite a high price tag, critics and public raved and the Elan became one of the most charismatic sports cars of its decade, selling over 12,000 examples.

Over an 11-year production life, with five different model series, it evolved into a very desirable and accelerative machine, culminating in the Elan Sprint, a 120 mph (193 km/h) banshee with a sub-seven second 0–60 time. As one motoring magazine of the time remarked, "The Elan Sprint is one of the finest sports cars in the world." Praise indeed.

ENGINE
The "Big Valve" engine in the Sprint pushed out 126 bhp and blessed it with truly staggering performance. Twin 40 DCOE Weber carburetors were hard to keep in tune. The ribbed cam covers were designed to prevent oil leaks. Power assisted disk brakes provided tremendous stopping power.

CLASSY INTERIOR
The Sprint's interior accommodation was refined and upmarket, with all-black trim, wood veneer dashboard, and even electric windows. Safer recessed rocker switches were a legal requirement in most markets.

WHEEL RESPECT
Colin Chapman's signature on the aluminum steering wheel.

TRUNK SPACE
The Elan was popular as a touring car because, despite housing the battery, its trunk was larger than average.

HEADLIGHTS
The pop-up headllights worked via a vacuum system, but often failed.

SPORTY PIPE
The rakishly angled exhaust left no doubt about the car's performance.

LOTUS ELAN SPRINT

The two-tone paint with dividing strip was a popular factory option for the Sprint. The red and gold combination had racing associations – the same color scheme as the Gold Leaf racing team cars. Everyone agreed that the diminutive Elan had an elfin charm.

WRAP-AROUND BUMPERS
Front bumper was foam-filled fiberglass. The Elan was one of the first cars to be fitted with bumpers that followed the car's contours.

STYLING
Perfectly proportioned from any angle, the Elan really looked like it meant business.

WORLD CHAMPION BADGE

Never slow to sing its own praises, Lotus fitted many Elans with this badge as a reminder of the company's string of Grand Prix victories.

WORLD CHAMPION CAR CONSTRUCTORS 1970 1968 1965 1963

SPECIFICATIONS

MODEL Lotus Elan Sprint (1970–73)
PRODUCTION 1,353
BODY STYLE Two-seater drophead.
CONSTRUCTION Steel box section backbone chassis.
ENGINE Four-cylinder twin overhead cam, 1558cc.
POWER OUTPUT 126 bhp at 6500 rpm.
TRANSMISSION Four-speed manual.
SUSPENSION Independent front and rear.
BRAKES Discs all around.
MAXIMUM SPEED 121 mph (195 km/h)
0–60 MPH (0–96 KM/H) 6.7 sec
0–100 MPH (0–161 KM/H) 15 sec
A.F.C. 24 mpg

MASERATI *Ghibli*

MANY RECKON THE GHIBLI is the greatest of all road-going Maseratis. It was the sensation of the 1966 Turin Show, and 30 years later is widely regarded as Maserati's ultimate front-engined road car, a supercar blend of luxury, performance, and stunning good looks that never again quite came together so sublimely on anything with the three-pointed trident. Pitched squarely against the Ferrari Daytona *(see page 104)* and Lamborghini Miura *(see page 146)*, it outsold both. Its engineering may have been dated, but it had the perfect pedigree, with loads of grunt from its throaty V-8 engine and a flawless Ghia design. It is an uncompromised supercar, yet it is also a consummate continent-eating grand tourer with 24-karat panache. Muscular and perhaps even menacing, but not overbearingly macho, it is well mannered enough for the tastes of the mature super-rich with hectic social timetables. There will only be one dilemma; do you take the windy back roads or blast along the autoroutes? Why not a bit of both.

GHIBLI NAME
Like the earlier Mistral, the Ghibli takes its name from a regional wind.

QUAD-CAM
The potent race-bred quad-cam V-8 is even-tempered and undemanding, delivering loads of low-down torque and accelerating meaningfully from as little as 500 rpm in fifth gear. The "dry sump" arrangement allowed for a low hood-line.

FOUR GREEDY TWIN-CHOKE WEBER CARBS SIT ASTRIDE THE V-8

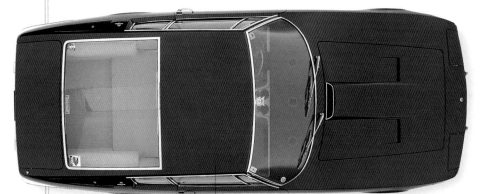

OPEN MASER
Most prized of all Ghiblis are the 125 convertible Spiders.

WIDE VIEW
The front windshield is huge but the big hood can make the Ghibli difficult to maneuver.

STEERING
Power steering was a later, desirable option.

HIDE-AWAY HEADLIGHTS
Pop-up headlights improve looks when not needed, but take their time to pop up.

LIFT OFF
Wide front has a tendency to lift above 120 mph (193 km/h) as the steering can become disconcertingly light.

TRIDENT
Masers are instantly recognizable by the three-pointed trident.

FLIGHT DECK
A cliché certainly, here you really do feel you are on an aircraft flightdeck. The high center console houses air-conditioning, which was standard Ghibli equipment.

MASERATI GHIBLI SS
The Ghibli's dramatic styling is uncompromised, a sublime and extravagant 15 ft (4.57 m) of attitude that can only accommodate two people. From its blade-like front to its short bobbed tail, it looks fast even standing still. It has also aged all the better for its lack of finicky detail; the Ghibli's detail is simple and clean, worn modestly like fine, expensive jewelry.

SPECIFICATIONS

MODEL Maserati Ghibli (1967–73)
PRODUCTION 1,274
BODY STYLE Two-door sports coupe or open Spider.
CONSTRUCTION Steel body and separate tubular chassis.
ENGINE Four-cam 90-degree V-8, 4719cc, 4930cc (SS).
POWER OUTPUT 330 bhp at 5000 rpm (4719cc), 335 bhp at 5500 rpm (4931).
TRANSMISSION ZF five-speed manual or three-speed Borg-Warner auto.
SUSPENSION Wishbones and coil-springs at front; rigid axle with radius arms/semi-elliptic leaf springs at rear.
BRAKES Girling discs on all four wheels.
MAXIMUM SPEED 154 mph (248 km/h), 168 mph, SS (270 km/h)
0–60 MPH (0–96 KM/H) 6.6 sec, 6.2 sec (SS)
0–100 MPH (0–161 KM/H) 15.7 sec
A.F.C. 10 mpg

THIRSTY
The Ghibli was a gasoline guzzler, but when was there an economical supercar?

EARLY GIUGIARO
Coachwork by Ghia was one of the finest early designs of its brilliant young Italian employee, Giorgetto Giugiaro.

MASERATI *Kyalami*

MASERATI 300S
Maserati's racing bloodline goes back to 1930, when it won five Grand Prix events in a row. After the war, Juan Fangio trounced the opposition in the legendary 250F, and the 300S sports racing car went on to secure success at Le Mans.

THE 1970S PRODUCED some automotive lemons. It was a decade when bare-faced label engineering and gluttonous V-8 engines were all the rage, and nobody cared that these big bruisers cost three arms and a leg to run. The Kyalami is one such monument to excess, a copy of the De Tomaso Longchamp with Maserati's all-aluminum V-8 on board instead of Ford's 5.8 liter cast-iron lump.

The Kyalami was meant to take on the Jaguar XJS but failed hopelessly. Plagued with electrical gremlins, this was a noisy, bulky, and unrefined machine that was neither beautiful nor poised. Yet for all that, it still sports that emotive trident on its nose and emits a deep and strident V-8 bark. The Kyalami might not be a great car but most of us, at least while looking at it, find it hard to tell the difference.

REAR LIGHTS
Dainty rear light clusters were borrowed from the contemporary Fiat 130 Coupe.

MASERATI KYALAMI
Maserati designer Pietro Frua retouched the De Tomaso Longchamp design, turning it into the Kyalami. He gave it a new lower nose with twin lights, full width hood, new rubber-cap bumpers with integral turn signals, and deleted the extractor vents from the C-pillars. By the time he had finished, the only shared body panels were the door panels.

THIRSTY
The Kyalami guzzled liquid gold at the rate of 14 miles per gallon.

PRECISION INTERIOR
In the Fifties, the bechromed dash was pure sci-fi. The large two-spoked white wheel gives a good view of the dials. On some cars, mostly for the US, the wheel tilted to ease access and became known as 'the fat man's wheel.'

PASSENGER AND DRIVER GET EQUAL SHARE OF THE CLOCK.

AERODYNAMIC STYLING
Mercedes insisted that the "eyebrows" over the wheel arches were aerodynamic aids; it is more likely they were US-aimed styling touches.

IF YOU FLIP IN A GULLWING THERE IS NO GETTING OUT UNTIL SOMEONE COMES ALONG

SPECIFICATIONS
MODEL Mercedes-Benz 300SL (1954–57)
PRODUCTION 1,400
BODY STYLE Two-door, two-seat coupe.
CONSTRUCTION Multitubular space-frame with steel and aluminum body.
ENGINE Inline six-cylinder overhead camshaft, 2996cc.
POWER OUTPUT 240 bhp at 6100 rpm.
TRANSMISSION Four-speed all synchromesh gearbox.
SUSPENSION Coil springs all around, with double wishbones at front, swinging half-axles at rear.
BRAKES Finned aluminum drums.
MAXIMUM SPEED 135–165 mph (217–265 km/h), depending on gearing.
0–60 MPH (0–96 KM/H) 8.8 sec
0–100 MPH (0–161 KM/H) 21.0 sec
A.F.C. 18 mpg

ROAD CARS DEVELOPED 240 BHP, MORE EVEN THAN THE RACING VERSIONS OF JUST TWO YEARS EARLIER

PIPEWORK ON THE SIDE IS FOR FUEL INJECTION

STAR IDENTITY
The massive three-pointed star dominated the frontal aspect and was repeated in enamel on the hood edge.

ENGINE BAY COULD GET VERY HOT, SO GILL-LIKE SIDE VENTS WERE MORE THAN A MERE STYLING MOTIF

PRODUCTION ENGINE
The engine was derived originally from the 300-Series 3-liter sedans, then developed for the 1952 300SL racer. Two years later it was let loose in the road-going Gullwing, with fuel injection in place of carburetors.

SILVER WAS THE OFFICIAL GERMAN RACING COLOR

HD·WD 34

THE FLIGHT OF THE GULLWING

The might of Mercedes had been brought low by the ravages of war, but the launch of the staggering 300SL Gullwing prototype at the 1954 New York Auto Show also announced to the world that Mercedes was back – with a bang.

STIRLING MOSS AT THE 1955 MILLE MIGLIA

MERCEDES' RECOVERY had been based on its trademark solid and well-engineered sedans, but with the Gullwing, its proud sporting tradition was once more in full flight. The

STIRLING MOSS AT START OF 1955 MILLE MIGLIA

awesome Silver Arrows were no longer just a misty memory of yesterday's podium glory; here in the 300SL was tomorrow's supercar, today.

The Gullwing is certainly magical and bathed in its own folklore, which centers on the involvement of a New York sports car importer with a coast-to-coast smile – Max Hoffman.

In 1952, Mercedes stormed back into autosports with a space-frame chassised car that

did not allow for conventional doors. Its engine was a development of the 3-liter engine of the 300-Series sedans. This aluminum-bodied car was called the 300SL – SL stood for Super Leicht – and it was right straight out of the box. In its first race, the 1952 Mille Miglia, it finished second, snatched outright victory at the Berne Grand Prix, took a 1–2 at Le Mans, won at the Nürburgring, and finished the year with 1–2 in the Carrera Panamericana Mexican road race. Mercedes had proved its point, and in 1954 concentrated on Grand Prix goals.

MERCEDES
300SL Gullwing

SMOOTH REAR
The Gullwing's smooth styling extended to the uncluttered rear; the trunk lid suggests ample luggage space, but this was not the case.

REAR VIEW GIVES A GOOD IDEA OF THE WIDTH OF THE SILL

COZY COCKPIT BECAME PRETTY HOT; AIR VENTS AT REAR HELPED REMOVE STALE AIR

LIMITED SPACE
With the spare tire mounted atop the fuel tank, there was very little room for luggage.

HD-WD·34

ERCEDES AT THE 1955 MILLE MIGLIA

ON THE TRACK AT THE 1955 MILLE MIGLIA

Meanwhile, something that looked like a Gullwing was making waves again in autosports. It was the 300SLR of 1955, which with its straight-eight actually owed more to the Mercedes W196 Grand Prix car. It won the Targa Florio, and, in the hands of Stirling Moss, the 1955 Mille Miglia.

The 300SL reestablished Mercedes' position at the pinnacle of sporting excellence. Yet it had a wider appeal, for wherever the jet setters gathered there also seemed to be a 300SL nearby, often drawing more camera flashes than the stars themselves. A youthful King Hussein of Jordan owned one, along with Stirling Moss, British comedian Tony Hancock, and numerous film stars.

But the story did not end there, for in 1969 gullwings appeared again on a Mercedes; but the rotary-engined C111 was a research project that was never seriously contemplated for production.

ut the 300SL Gullwing was about to nter a new life. Max Hoffman was so onvinced of the 300SL's appeal that e was willing to back up his word ith a large order, if Mercedes would uild them. The road-going 300SL as clearly based on the racer, with the ddition of luxury refinements. Hoffman's hunch was right, for over alf of the 1400 Gullwings built from 954 to 1957 went straight to American customers. As Gullwing production wound down in 1957, a roadster version was introduced, which lasted until 1963.

00SL ROADSTER

s Gullwing production wound own, Mercedes introduced he 300SL Roadster, which rom 1957 to 1963 sold ,858, compared to the Gullwing's 1,400. From 955 to 1963 the 190SL Roadster served as he "poor man's" 00SL.

ALL GULLWINGS WERE ONLY AVAILABLE IN LEFT-HAND DRIVE

ONE HOOD BULGE WAS FOR AIR INTAKES, THE OTHER FOR AESTHETIC BALANCE

MOST OF THE BODY WAS MADE OF STEEL, BUT HOOD, TRUNK LID, AND DOORS WERE ALUMINUM

HD · WD 34

MERCEDES *280SL*

THE MERCEDES 280SL has mellowed magnificently. In 1963, the new SLs took over the sporting mantle of the aging 190SL. Named W113 in Mercedes parlance, they evolved from the original 230SL, through the 250SL, and on to the 280SL. The most remarkable thing is how modern they look. With their uncluttered, clean good looks, it is hard to believe that the last one was made in 1971. Underneath the timelessly elegant sheet metal, they were based closely on the earlier "fintail sedans," sharing even the decidedly unsporting recirculating ball steering.

Yet it is the looks that mark this Mercedes as something special. The enduring design, with its distinctive so-called "pagoda roof," is credited to Frenchman Paul Bracq. Some macho types may dismiss it as a "woman's car" and it is certainly not the most hairy-chested sporting Mercedes. But this well-manicured car is a beautifully built boulevardier that will induce a sense of supreme self-satisfaction on any journey.

JBW 620

SL MOTIF
In Mercedes parlance, the S stood for Sport or Super, L for Leicht (light) and sometimes Luxus (luxury), although at well over 3,000 lb (1,362 kg) it was not particularly light.

US-MARKET CARS HAD A MILDER CAMSHAFT

BRAKES ARE POWER ASSISTED

ENGINE
The six-cylinder overhead camshaft engine saw a process of steady development starting in July 1963, with the 2281cc, 150 bhp, 230SL. In December 1966 came the 2496cc 250SL, with the same power but slightly more torque. From January 1968 to March 1971 the final 2778cc, 170 hp 280SL shown here was produced. All had Bosch electronic fuel injection.

CITY SLICKER
With standard power steering and a turning circle of less than 33 ft (10 m), the SL handled city streets with aplomb.

JBW 62

MODEL Mercedes-Benz 280SL (1968–71)
PRODUCTION 23,885
BODY STYLE Two door, two seat convertible with detachable hardtop.
CONSTRUCTION Pressed-steel monocoque.
ENGINE 2778cc inline six; two valves per cylinder; single overhead camshaft
POWER OUTPUT 170 bhp at 5750 rpm.
TRANSMISSION Four- or five-speed manual, or optional four-speed auto.
SUSPENSION *Front:* Independent, wishbones, coil springs, telescopic shocks. *Rear:* Swing axle coil springs, telescopic shocks.
BRAKES Front discs & rear drums.
MAXIMUM SPEED 121 mph, auto (195 km/h)
0–60 MPH (0–96 KM/H) 9.3 sec
0–100 MPH (0–161 KM/H) 30.6 sec
A.F.C. 19 mpg

...FE SPENSION
...ng axle rear ...pension was ...ed to provide ...ural ...dersteer.

OPTIONAL THIRD
The SL was essentially a two-seater, although a third, sideways-facing rear seat was available as a (rare) optional extra.

CLAP HANDS
Windshield wipers are of the characteristic "clap hands" pattern beloved by Mercedes.

MERCEDES 280SL

The most distinctive design feature of the 280SL is the so-called "pagoda-roof" removable hardtop. It is said to have evolved from the need to provide relatively deep windows for a more balanced side view of the car, without at the same time making it look topheavy from the front or rear. The layout also provided a remarkably efficient way of keeping rain away.

LEATHER LOOK
Seats were trimmed in leather-look vinyl or, at extra cost, real leather.

TRADEMARK LIGHTS
"Stacked" headlights are unmistakable Mercedes trademarks. Each outer lens concealed one headlight, turn signal and parking lights.

CHROME BUMPER
The full width front bumper featured a central recess just big enough for a standard license plate; the quality of the chrome, as elsewhere on the car, was first class.

THE D-SHAPED HORN RING ALLOWS AN UNOBSTRUCTED VIEW OF THE INSTRUMENTS

ILLUMINATED HEATER CONTROLS ARE COMMON TODAY, BUT IN THE 1960S WERE A STEP FORWARD

ONLY THE 280 AUTOMATIC AND SOME OF THE LAST 250S HAD THE ILLUMINATED GEARSHIFT SHOWN HERE

INTERIOR
With the huge steering wheel (albeit attached to an energy-absorbing column), the painted dash, and the abundance of chrome, the interior is one area where the 280SL shows its age. It is still elegant, though. Relatively few cars were ordered with manual gearboxes, underlining the public perception of the SL as more a grand tourer than a genuine sports car.

MG *TC*

EVEN WHEN IT WAS NEW, the MG TC was not new. The TC, introduced in September 1945, displayed a direct lineage back to its prewar ancestors. If you were a little short on soul, you might even have called it old fashioned. Yet it was a trailblazer, not in terms of performance, but in opening up new export markets. Popular myth has it that American GIs stationed in England fell in love with these quaint sporting devices, when they left for home they were eager to take a little piece of England with them.

Whatever the reality, it was the first in a long line of MG export successes. The average American family car of the time could drag a TC off the line, but there was simply nothing remotely like this TC toy car coming out of Detroit. It had a cramped cockpit, harsh ride, and minimal creature comforts, but when the road got twisty the TC could show you its tail and leave soft-sprung sofa-cars lumbering in its wake. Yet it was challenging to drive, and all the more rewarding when you got it right. Mastering an MG was a thrill in its own right, for in a TC you did not need to joust with other jalopies; the TC and its cracking exhaust note were enough to give you hours of solo driving enjoyment.

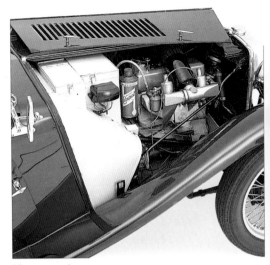

ENGINE ACCESS
Ease of accessibility and maintenance was another of the TC's attractions. The XPAG engine, first used on some TB Midgets in 1939, then became standard on MGs until it was replaced by a 1500cc version in 1955.

POWER BOOST
Though not a factory option, Shorrock superchargers were often fitted.

ALTHOUGH OVER 2,000 WERE SOLD IN AMERICA, ALL TCS WERE RIGHT-HAND DRIVE

RACERS' FAVORITE
The TC was a popular race car, especially in the US, where it launched many careers and one world champion, Phil Hill.

COCKPIT
Roomier than earlier Midgets, the TC cockpit was still more cramped than less sporting contemporaries.

SPORTING DIALS
Big Jaeger dials were in true British sporting tradition; the driver got the tachometer, while the speedometer was in front of the passenger. Closeup *(right)* shows the warning light that came on if you exceeded Britain's 30 mph (48 km/h) town speed limit.

RAIN OR SHINE
Hood up or hood down, the TC looked sportier than its performance figures proved it to be.

SPECIFICATIONS

MODEL MG TC (1947–49)
PRODUCTION 10,000
BODY STYLE Two-door, two-seater sports.
CONSTRUCTION Channel-section ladder-type chassis; ash-framed steel body.
ENGINE Four-cylinder overhead valve 1250cc, with twin SU carburetors.
POWER OUTPUT 54 bhp at 5200 rpm.
TRANSMISSION Four-speed gearbox with syncromesh on top three gears.
SUSPENSION Rigid front and rear axles on semielliptic springs, lever-type shock absorbers.
BRAKES Lockheed hydraulic drums.
MAXIMUM SPEED 73 mph (117 km/h)
0–60 MPH (0–96 KM/H) 22.7 sec
A.F.C. 28 mpg

MG TC

With its squarerigged layout, the TC is traditional with a capital T, and certainly a "classic" before the term was applied to cars. With its square front and distinctive headlights, sweeping front fenders, and cutaway doors, it is short on sophistication. Yet these are the essential elements that marked it as a true enthusiast's sporting car in the car-starved late 1940s.

OVERSEAS WINNER
The British bought one TC for every two exported.

REPLACEMENT
The TC was replaced by the TD which, with its smaller disc wheels, and chrome hubcaps and bumpers, was considered less pure by some aficionados. The export trend begun by the TC took off with the TD, which sold three times the number.

FBT 112

MGA

LAUNCHED IN SEPTEMBER 1955, the MGA was the first of the modern sporting MGs. The chassis, engine, and gearbox were all new, as was the smooth, Le Mans-inspired bodywork. Compared to its predecessor – the TF, which still sported old-fashioned running boards – the MGA was positively futuristic. Buyers thought so too, and being cheaper than its nearest rivals, the Triumph TR3 and Austin-Healey 100, helped MG sell 13,000 cars in the first year of production. The company's small factory at Abingdon, near Oxford, managed to export a staggering 81,000 MGAs to America. The car also earned an enviable reputation in competition, with the Twin Cam being the most powerful of the MGA engines.

SPECIFICATIONS

MODEL MGA (1955–62)
PRODUCTION 101,081
BODY STYLES Two-door sports coupe.
CONSTRUCTION Steel.
ENGINE Four-cylinder/1489cc; 1588cc; 1622cc (Twin Cam).
POWER OUTPUT 72 bhp; 80 bhp; 85 bhp.
TRANSMISSION Four-speed manual.
SUSPENSION *Front:* Independent . *Rear:* Leaf-spring.
BRAKES Rear drums, front discs. All discs on De Luxe and Twin Cam.
MAXIMUM SPEED 100 mph (161 km/h); 113 mph (181 km/h) Twin Cam.
0–60 MPH (0–96 KM/H) 15 sec (13.3 sec Twin Cam)
0–100 MPH (0–161 KM/H) 47 sec (41 sec Twin Cam)
A.F.C. 20–25 mpg

HORN BUTTON IS LOCATED IN THE CENTER OF THE DASHBOARD AND CAN BE WORKED BY EITHER DRIVER OR PASSENGER

LIMITED SPACE
The trunk is deceptively shallow and filled by the spare wheel.

NO HANDLES
The uncluttered design means no door handles – doors are opened by pulling a cable reached from inside the car.

WHEELS
Perforated steel wheels are standard.

DASHBOARD
The simple dashboard has no glove compartment, but the MG badge and center grille are for a radio and speaker. Passengers have a map light, but little else.

HAND-FINISHED
Although the MGA's steel panels were hand-pressed, bodies were finished by hand and no two are quite the same.

VENTILATION
The chromed, shroud-panel vents at the front are for engine bay ventilation.

ENGINE
The tough B-Series, pushrod engine goes well and lasts forever. A heater unit in front of the bulkhead was an optional extra.

MGA
The slippery, wind-cheating shape of the MGA was created for racing at Le Mans – an early prototype achieved 116 mph (223 km/h). Production MGAs were very similar and the smooth hood and sloping fenders aid both top speed and fuel consumption.

STARTING HANDLE
Hole is for a starting handle.

BSK 215

MG*B*

WIDELY ADMIRED FOR its uncomplicated nature, timeless good looks, and brisk performance, the MGB caused a sensation back in 1962. The now famous advertising slogan "Your mother wouldn't like it" was quite wrong. She would have wholeheartedly approved of the MGB's reliability, practicality, and good sense.

In 1965 came the even more practical hardtop MGB GT. These were the halcyon days of the MGB – chrome bumpers, leather seats, and wire wheels. In 1974, in pursuit of modernity and US safety regulations (the US was the MGB's main market), the factory gave the B ungainly rubber bumpers, a higher ride height, and garish striped nylon seats, making the car slow, ugly, and unpredictable at the limit. Yet the B became the best-selling single model sports car ever, finding 512,000 grateful owners throughout the world.

SPECIFICATIONS

MODEL MGB Tourer (1962–80)
PRODUCTION 512,243
BODY STYLE Steel front-engined two seater with aluminum hood.
CONSTRUCTION One-piece monocoque bodyshell.
ENGINE Four-cylinder/1798cc.
POWER OUTPUT 92 bhp at 5400 rpm.
TRANSMISSION Four-speed with overdrive.
SUSPENSION *Front:* Independent coil; *Rear:* Semielliptic leaf springs.
BRAKES Lockheed discs front, drums rear.
MAXIMUM SPEED 106 mph (171 km/h)
0–60 MPH (0–96 KM/H) 12.2 sec
0–100 MPH (0–161 KM/H) 37 sec
A.F.C. 25 mpg

AGELESS DESIGN
The MGB's shape was a miracle of compact packaging. One-piece steel monocoque bodyshell was strong and roomy.

MIRROR SUPPORT
The line down the center of the windshield is a mirror support rod.

DASHBOARD
This is vintage traditionalism at its best. Leather seats, crackle black metal dash, nautical-sized steering wheel, and minor controls are strewn about the dash like boulders with scant thought for ergonomics. The radio speaker is almost Art Deco.

EBW 45B

ADDITIONAL HOOD
To supplement the hood a fiberglass detachable hardtop was an option in 1962.

SOFT TOP
Early cars had a "packaway" hood made from ICI Everflex.

HOOD
Hood is made out of lightweight aluminum.

SUSPENSION
Front suspension was coil spring with wishbones, and dated back to the MG TF of the 1950s.

MGB TOURER
All MGBs had the simple 1798cc B-series four-cylinder engine with origins going back to 1947. This Tourer's period charm is enhanced by the rare Iris Blue paintwork and seldom seen pressed-steel wheels – most examples were fitted with optional spoked wire wheels.

MORGAN *Plus Four*

IT IS REMARKABLE THAT THEY still make them, but there are many men with cloth caps and corduroys who are grateful that they do. Derived from the first four-wheeled Morgans of 1936, this is the car that buoyed Morgan after the war while many of the old mainstays of the British motor industry wilted around it. Tweedier than a Scottish moor on the first day of the grouse shooting season, it is as quintessentially British as a car can be. It was a hit in America and other foreign countries. It has also remained the backbone of the idiosyncratic Malvern-based company that refuses to move with the times. Outdated and outmoded it may be, but there is still a very long waiting list to purchase a Morgan. First introduced in 1951, the Plus Four, with a series of Standard Vanguard and Triumph TR engines, laid the foundations for the modern miracle of the very old-fashioned Morgan Motor Company.

LIKE ALL FOUR-WHEELED MORGANS, THE PLUS FOUR HAD A TWO-PIECE HOOD WITH A PIANO HINGE IN THE MIDDLE

— OTHER MODELS —

Today, the company builds just two cars: the four-cylinder Ford Zetec-engined Plus Four, with a top speed of 111 mph (179 km/h), and the Plus Eight.

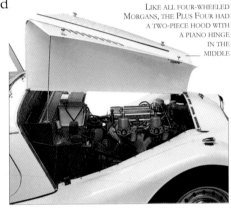

MORGAN PLUS EIGHT
The 3.5-liter Rover V-8-engined Plus Eight is slower today, at 121 mph (195 km/h), than it was 20 years ago, but accelerates to 60 mph (96 km/h) in just 6.1 seconds.

ENGINE
The later Triumph TR3A 2138cc engine, as here, gave increased torque. The 2138cc engine was available in the TR3A from summer 1957. The earlier Triumph 1991cc engine was still available for those wishing to compete in classes below two liters.

INTERIOR
From 1958 onward, all Plus Fours had wider cockpits with a new dash, identifiable by the cubbyhole on the passenger's side. Speedometer, switches, warning lights, and minor gauges were grouped in a central panel on the dash.

"SUICIDE" DOORS
The earlier two-seat drophead coupe retained rear-hinged "suicide" doors with framed, sliding windows, but the sleeker two- and four-seat sports models had front-hinged doors with removable sidescreens.

ON THE RACK
Morgans have limited luggage capacity, so many owners fitted external racks.

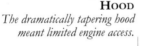

LIGHT WORK
Headlights are big, bold affairs set in pods on the front fenders, but sidelights are about as visible as a pair of lightning bugs.

REAR ILLUMINATION
Rear lights have never been a Morgan strong point. Amber signals are a good 6 in (15 cm) inboard of the stop/tail lights, and are partially obscured by the luggage rack.

SPECIFICATIONS

MODEL Morgan Plus Four (1951–69)
PRODUCTION 3,737
BODY STYLES Two- and four-seater sports convertible.
CONSTRUCTION Steel chassis, ash frame, steel and aluminum outer panels.
ENGINE 2088cc overhead valve inline four (Vanguard); 1991cc or 2138cc overhead valve inline four (TR).
POWER OUTPUT 105 bhp at 4700 rpm (2138cc TR engine).
TRANSMISSION Four-speed manual.
SUSPENSION *Front:* Sliding stub axles, coil springs, and telescopic shocks. *Rear:* Live axle, semielliptic leaf springs, and lever-arm shocks.
BRAKES Drums front and rear; front discs standard from 1960.
MAXIMUM SPEED 100 mph (161 km/h)
0–60 MPH (0–96 KM/H) 12 sec
A.F.C. 20–22 mpg

MORGAN PLUS FOUR

The second generation Plus Four was the first of what are generally considered the "modern looking" Morgans – if that is the right expression for a basic design which, still in production today, dates back to 1936. Distinguishing features are the cowled radiator grille and, from 1959 onward, a wider body (as here) to provide more elbow room for driver and passenger.

HOOD
The dramatically tapering hood meant limited engine access.

WHERE'S THE CATCH?
Traditional latches – two for each hood half – are among the most tactile features of the Plus Four.

MIRROR POSITION
Doors were the only sensible places for exterior rear view mirrors; the tops of the front fenders were miles away.

TRADITIONAL ASH FRAME
The current four-cylinder Morgan is built in exactly the same manner as most of its predecessors. The chassis is made from "Z"-section steel members, and on it sits a 94- or 114-piece wooden framework (two- and four-seat cars, respectively) clothed in a mixture of steel and aluminum panels.

SUSPENSION
The Plus Four retained a simple sliding-pillar front suspension.

FULL-UP POSITION

COUP DE VILLE POSITION

BEST OF BOTH WORLDS
Unlike most convertible cars, the Plus Four has a hood that can be partially folded back. It provides fresh air without being too drafty.

MORRIS MINOR MM *Convertible*

THE MORRIS MINOR is a motoring milestone. As Britain's first million seller it became a "people's car," staple transportation for everyone from midwives to builder's suppliers. Designed by Alec Issigonis, the genius who later went on to pen the Austin Mini *(see pages 40–41)*, the new Series MM Morris Minor of 1948 featured the then-novel unit chassis-body construction. The 918cc side-valve engine of the MM was rather more antique, a hang-over from the pre-war Morris 8.

Its handling and ride comfort more than made up for the lack of power. With independent front suspension and crisp rack-and-pinion steering it embarrassed its rivals and even tempted the young Stirling Moss into high-speed cornering antics that lost him his license for a month. Of all the 1.5 million Minors the most prized are the now rare Series MM convertibles. Rag-tops remained part of the Minor model line-up until 1969, two years from the end of all Minor production. So desirable are these open tourers that in recent years there has been a trade in rogue rag-tops, chopped sedans masquerading as original factory convertibles.

TURN SIGNALS
With no door pillars above waist height, semaphore turn signals were mounted lower down on the tourers; flashers eventually replaced semaphores in 1961.

RAG-TOP RARITY
Convertibles represent only a small proportion of Minor production. Between 1963 and 1969 only 3,500 soft-tops were produced, compared with 119,000 two-door sedans.

CHOICE OF MODELS
At its launch the Minor was available as a two-door sedan and as a convertible (Tourer). Four-door, wagon, van, and pick-up complete the range.

ORIGINAL MM TOURER HAD SIDE CURTAINS, REPLACED BY GLASS REAR WINDOW IN 1952

MORRIS BEAM COUNTERS DICTATED OLD-FASHIONED LIVE AXLE AND LEAF SPRINGS AT REAR

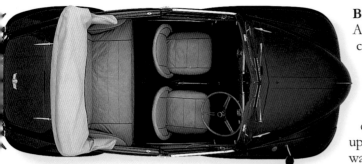

BODY WIDTH
At 61 in (155 cm) the production car was 4 in (10 cm) wider than the prototype.

DASHBOARD
This simple early dashboard was never really updated, but the speedometer was later moved to the central console.

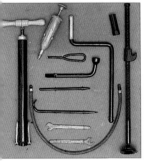

TOOLED UP
A complete original tool kit is a rarity, a prize companion piece for any owner.

THE SPRUNG-SPOKE STEERING WHEEL IS TRADITIONAL, BUT RACK-AND-PINION STEERING GIVES A CRISP, LIGHT FEEL

MINOR MOTORS
The original 918cc side-valve engine was replaced progressively in 1952 and 1953 by the Austin A-series 803cc overhead valve engine, then by the A-series 948cc, and finally the 1098cc.

SPECIFICATIONS

MODEL Morris Minor (1948–71)
PRODUCTION 1,620,000
BODY STYLES Two- and four-door sedan, two-door convertible (Tourer), wagon (Traveller), van, and pick-up.
CONSTRUCTION Unit body/chassis; steel.
ENGINE Straight-four, 918cc, 803cc, 948cc, and 1098cc.
POWER OUTPUT 28 bhp (918cc); 48 bhp (1098cc).
TRANSMISSION Four-speed manual.
SUSPENSION Torsion bar independent front suspension; live-axle leaf-spring rear.
BRAKES Drums all around.
MAXIMUM SPEED 62–75 mph (100–121 km/h)
0–60 MPH (0–96 KM/H) 50+ sec for 918cc, 24 sec for 1098cc.
A.F.C. 36–43 mpg

UNDER-HOOD SPACE AND EASY ENGINE ACCESS MAKE THE MINOR A DIY FAVORITE

EVEN ON CROSS-PLY TIRES THE ORIGINAL MINOR WON PRAISE FOR ITS HANDLING AND COMPETED WITH DISTINCTION IN THE MONTE CARLO RALLY

BRITAIN'S FIRST MILLION SELLER

The Morris Minor owes much of its success to the singular vision of one shy man, Alex Issigonis, the Greek-born son of an itinerant marine engineer.

UNDER THE PATRONAGE of Morris vice-chairman, Sir Miles Thomas, the young and talented Alex Issigonis, already a respected suspension engineer, was entrusted with the task of developing a small new Morris.

Prototypes of the car that was to become the Morris Minor had already been built in 1943. Back then it was to be called the Mosquito, but the name was abandoned in the ramp up to its launch as several other companies claimed rights to the name. Issigonis had wanted a flat-four water-cooled engine and his rear suspension was also compromised, but the car that made its debut at Britain's first post-war motor show, in London in 1948, was still very much his in concept, design, and execution – he had even designed the door handles. The Jaguar XK120 *(see pages 134–35)* was the show-stopper, the car that everyone wanted, but the Morris Minor was the car ordinary people needed. Unusually for a small utility car, its merits were appreciated quite early on, even though

WORLDWIDE MINOR EXPORTS, FROM 1950s SALES BROCHURE

MORRIS
*Minor MM
Convertible*

MINOR WATERSHED
The split windshield was replaced by a curved glass in 1956.

BOTH FRONT AND REAR FENDERS ARE EASILY REPLACED, BOLT-ON ITEMS

LGO 786

THE FILLET IN THE BUMPER IS ANOTHER EXAMPLE OF THE WIDENING OF THE BODY

THE MILLIONTH MINOR ROLLS OFF THE PRODUCTION LINE

Morris boss Lord Nuffield dismissed it as a "poached egg." But there was no stopping the Minor. After its official launch as a two-door sedan and convertible Tourer, a four-door sedan, van, pick-up, and Traveller wagon followed, so that in one guise or another the Minor met the needs of every ordinary motorist.

On December 22, 1960, the millionth Minor was made, spawning a limited edition of 349 Minor Millions, painted a sudden lilac and badged "Minor 1000000" on the rear.

As the Minor's fortunes dimmed through the Sixties until its eventual demise in 1971, another Issigonis design, the Mini *(see pages 40–41)*, was on the rise. The Mini eventually outstripped the Minor's 1,620,000 sales total to become Britain's best-seller ever, but the Minor will always be remembered as Britain's first million seller and its first "people's car."

EXTRACT FROM A 1950s FRENCH SALES BROCHURE – "THE BEST LITTLE CAR IN THE WORLD"

LA PETITE VOITURE LA PLUS AVANTAGEUSE DU MONDE

"LOW LIGHTS"
In 1950, the headlights on all Minors were moved to the top of the fenders. Earlier models such as our featured car are now dubbed "low lights."

LGO 786

STARTER HANDLE
Most Minor engines are willing starters, but all models to the end of production came with a starter handle in the tool kit.

SYMBOLS OF AN OX AND A FORD REPRESENT MORRIS'S HOME TOWN OF OXFORD

LGO 786

ISSIGONIS WAS ORIGINALLY A SUSPENSION ENGINEER AND INDEPENDENT FRONT SUSPENSION IS A CREDIT TO HIS GENIUS

ORIGINAL SLIMLINE BUMPERS LATER ACQUIRED OVER-RIDERS AS THE MODEL WAS UPDATED

NSU *Ro80*

ALONG WITH THE Citroën DS *(see pages 72–75),* the NSU Ro80 was ten years ahead of its time. Beneath that striking, wind-cheating shape was an audacious two rotor engine, front-wheel drive, disc brakes, and a semiautomatic clutchless gearbox. In 1967, the Ro80 won the acclaimed "Car of the Year" award and went on to be hailed by many as "Car of the Decade." Technical preeminence aside, it also handled like a racer. But NSU's brave new Wankel power unit was flawed and, due to acute rotor tip wear, would expire after only 15–20,000 miles (24–32,000 km). NSU honored its warranty claims until it went broke. Eventually Audi/VW took over, axing the Ro80 in 1977.

INTERIOR
Power steering was by ZF. Dashboard was a paragon of Teutonic efficiency which would later be mirrored by Mercedes and BMW. With no transmission tunnel or driveshaft, plenty of headroom, and a long wheelbase, rear passengers found the Ro80 thoroughly accommodating.

TO AVOID OVER-REVVING THE ENGINE, A WARNING BUZZER WOULD SOUND AT 7000 RPM

ENGINE HAD TWO SPARK PLUGS PER ROTOR AND BREATHED THROUGH SOLEX TWO-STAGE CARBURETORS

ENGINE POSITION
Engine was mounted on four progressive-acting rubber mounts with telescopic shocks on each side of the gearbox casing.

ENGINE
Designed by Felix Wankel, the brilliant twin rotor engine was equivalent to a two-liter reciprocating piston unit. Drive was through a torque converter with a Fichel & Sachs electro-pneumatic motor to a three speed NSU gearbox.

CORNERING
The Ro80's stability, roadholding, ride, steering, and dynamic balance were exceptional, and far superior to most sports and GT cars.

NSU Ro80
In 1967, the Ro80 looked like a vision of the future with its low center of gravity, huge glass area, and sleek aerodynamics. The high rear end, widely imitated a decade later, held a huge, deep trunk.

LIGHTS
Hella headlights give fine nighttime light.

BRAKES
ATE Dunlop with twin circuits and inboard discs at the front.

WHEELS
Five-spoke aluminum wheels were optional.

HYU 975K

SPECIFICATIONS
MODEL NSU Ro80 (1967–77)
PRODUCTION 37,204
BODY STYLE Front engine five-seater sedan.
CONSTRUCTION Integral chassis with pressed steel monocoque body.
ENGINE Two rotor Wankel, 1990cc.
POWER OUTPUT 113.5 bhp at 5500 rpm.
TRANSMISSION Three speed semiautomatic.
SUSPENSION Independent all around.
BRAKES Four wheel discs.
MAXIMUM SPEED 112 mph (180 km/h)
0–60 MPH (0–96 KM/H) 11.9 sec
0–100 MPH (0–161 KM/H) 25 sec
A.F.C. 20 mpg

PANHARD *PL17 Tigre*

PANHARD WAS ONE of the world's oldest names in car manufacturing, dating back to 1872. But by 1955 it had lost its upmarket image and had to be rescued by Citroën, which eventually bought it out completely in 1965. The Dyna, produced after the war in response to a need for a small, practical, and economical machine, had an aluminum alloy frame, bulkhead, and horizontally opposed, air-cooled, two cylinder engine.

In 1954, the Dyna became front-wheel drive, with a bulbous but streamlined new body. The 848cc flat twin engine was a gem and in post-1961 Tigre form pushed out 60 bhp; this gave 90 mph (145 km/h), enough to win a Monte Carlo Rally. Advertised as "the car that makes sense," the PL17 was light, quick, miserly on fuel, and years ahead of its time.

EFFICIENT DESIGN
Simple design meant fewer moving parts, more power, and more miles to the gallon.

DESIGN
Front-wheel drive guaranteed stability and safety, with class-leading space for an 848cc car.

STEERING
The steering was rack and pinion, with only two turns lock-to-lock and large Bendix hydraulic brakes.

PANHARD PL17 TIGRE
With its aerodynamically shaped body, Panhard claimed the lowest drag coefficient of any production car in 1956. Emphasis was on weight saving and, despite its quirky looks, the PL17 was a triumph of efficiency.

ENGINE
The engine design dates back to 1940. Cylinders were cast integral with their heads in light aluminum, cooling fins and cast iron liners. Heads had hemispherical combustion chambers and valve gearing incorporating torsion bars. Carburetor was Zenith 38 NDIX twin choke.

INTERIOR
The unusual interior had bizarre oval-shaped pedals, column shifter, and an unsuccessful collection of American styling themes.

SPECIFICATIONS

MODEL Panhard PL17 Tigre (1961–64)
PRODUCTION 130,000 (all models).
BODY STYLE Four door, four seater sports sedan.
CONSTRUCTION Separate chassis with steel and aluminum body.
ENGINE 848cc twin horizontally opposed air cooled.
POWER OUTPUT 60 bhp at 5800 rpm.
TRANSMISSION Front-wheel drive four-speed manual.
SUSPENSION Independent front with twin transverse leaf, torsion bar rear.
BRAKES Four-wheel drums.
MAXIMUM SPEED 90 mph (145 km/h)
0–60 MPH (0–96 KM/H) 23.1 sec
A.F.C. 38 mpg

PEUGEOT 203

COMPARED TO THE SCORES of upright postwar sedans that looked like church pews, Peugeot's 203 was a breath of fresh air. As well as being one of the French car maker's most successful products, the 203's monocoque body and revolutionary engine set it apart. In its day, the 1290cc overhead valve powerplant was state-of-the-art, with an aluminum cylinder head and hemispherical combustion chambers, said to be the inspiration for the famous Chrysler "Hemi" unit. With a range that included two- and four-door cabriolets, a family wagon, and a two-door coupe, the French really took to the 203, loving its tough mechanicals, willing progress, and supple ride. By its demise in 1960, the 203 had broken records for Peugeot, with nearly 700,000 sold.

PEUGEOT 203 AT THE MONTE CARLO RALLY
In the '50s there were plenty of firms who could give the 203 more urge. Many were tuned and campaigned by amateurs in rallies like the Monte Carlo.

TURN SIGNAL
The 203's turn signals were operated by a vacuum from the inlet manifold.

INTERIOR
With postwar steel in short supply, aluminum was used to good effect in the under-dash handbrake and column-mounted gear changer. The handsome fastback body gave plenty of cabin room.

ROOMY
Clever use of space meant 203 was spacious.

PEUGEOT'S LION LABEL DATES BACK TO 1906, WHEN ROBERT PEUGEOT STARTED UP HIS OWN COMPANY CALLED LION-PEUGEOT

PAINTWORK
A high gloss finish was achieved with several coats of synthetic lacquer.

ENGINE
The 49 bhp ohv pushrod engine was the 203's most advanced feature. With wet piston liners, low compression ratio, and aluminum head, it was smooth, free-revving and long-lasting. The four-speed gearbox is really a three with overdrive. The basic design was still used in the 1980s for Peugeot's 1971cc 505 model.

OAA 95

PEUGEOT 203 CABRIOLET

The 203 Cabriolet turned out as a 2+2 but was originally planned to have a rumble seat. Colors were cheerful pastels instead of dull grays and blacks.

WINDSHIELD WIPERS

"Clap hand" windshield wipers may look dated, but the motor was so robust that it was still in use 43 years later on the tailgate wiper of the 504 model.

BUDGET INTERIOR

Interior was built to a budget with rubber mats, metal dash, and cloth seat facings.

SPECIFICATIONS

MODEL Peugeot 203 (1948–60)
PRODUCTION 685,828
BODY STYLES Two-door coupe, two- or four-door convertible, family wagon.
CONSTRUCTION All-steel monocoque rigid one-piece body shell.
ENGINE Four-cylinder ohv 1290cc.
POWER OUTPUT 42–49 bhp at 3500 rpm.
TRANSMISSION Four-speed column change with overdrive.
SUSPENSION Transverse leaf independent front, coil spring rear with Panhard rod.
BRAKES Drums all around.
MAXIMUM SPEED 73 mph (117 km/h)
0–60 MPH (0–96 KM/H) 20 sec
A.F.C. 20–35 mpg

STYLING

These stylish sweeping curves were influenced by the 1946 Chevrolet.

GAS TANK

This was concealed under a flush-fitting flap – unheard of in 1948.

SMART DESIGN

The hood swings up on counterbalanced springs and the front grille comes away by undoing a wing nut.

PEUGEOT 203

Widely acclaimed at the 1948 Paris Motor Show, the 203's slippery shape was wind tunnel tested in model form and claimed to have a rather optimistic drag coefficient of just 0.36 – lower than a modern Porsche 911 *(see pages 194–95)*. Quality touches abound, such as the exterior brightwork in stainless steel and integral mounting points for a roof rack.

TRUNK

A vast trunk with a low-loading sill made the 203 the ideal family car.

OAA 950

PLYMOUTH *Barracuda*

BACK IN 1964, IT WAS Ford's Mustang *(see pages 120–23)* that gave its name to a new breed of sporty compact. But Chrysler was quick with its own "pony car," the Plymouth Barracuda, launched for the 1965 model year. Admittedly, Chrysler had hastily revised its Valiant tooling to reach the starting gate in the pony car stakes, but there is no doubt the Barracuda was a worthy contender. Over the years it grew in stature, and in 1970 really came of age with a complete redesign that was altogether more purposeful-looking. The Barracuda never matched the Mustangs and Camaros *(see pages 66–67)* in sales terms, but it attracted a loyal band of followers with its clean, lean looks. It was a brief flowering though, for the Barracuda's fate was sealed when insurance companies took exception to muscle cars and government emission laws started to strangle the performance. The fuel crisis of 1973–74 finished it off once and for all.

INTERIOR
Many ordinary buyers were attracted by Plymouth successes on the NASCAR stock-car circuit and having tried out the cockpit, valued the "race-bred" features. These included a three-spoke wood rim steering wheel, 150 mph (241 km/h) speedometer, and high-backed bucket seats with headrests.

STREAMLINING
Attention to aerodynamics included retractable antenna, streamlined door mirrors, and hidden windshield wipers.

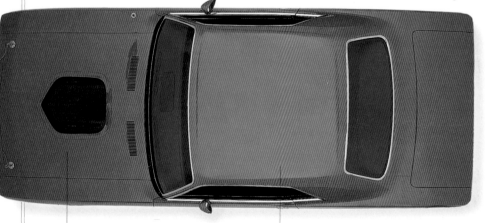

WIDE DOORS
The huge doors give access to low front seating and make rear entry manageable.

GO-FASTER PINS
External hood pins are a racing-style accessory.

HEMI OPTION
One engine option was the famous Chrysler Hemi, so named for its hemispheral combustion chambers.

OVERHEAD VIEW
From the top the Barracuda could be a different car; compared to its slim and lean side aspect the top view is almost completely rectangular.

SLOPING TAIL
The first Barracudas had a glass-filled roof sloping gently back to the tail. The hardtop option, introduced as part of the 1970 redesign, became more popular.

SHARED SHELL
The Barracuda shared the same bodyshell as another Chrysler pony car, the Dodge Challenger.

SPECIFICATIONS

MODEL Plymouth Barracuda (1970–74)
PRODUCTION 102,786
BODY STYLES Two-door fastback coupe, convertible, or hardtop.
CONSTRUCTION Unibody shell.
ENGINE Inline six, 224cid, or 90-degree V-8, 318cid, 339cid, 383cid, 426cid, or 440cid.
POWER OUTPUT 110–145 hp at 4000 rpm (six), 150–390 hp (V-8).
TRANSMISSION Torqueflite automatic or four-speed manual.
SUSPENSION *Front*: independent, unequal length wishbones, with torsion bar and antiroll bar. Live rear axle, semielliptic leaf springs.
BRAKES *Front*: disc; *Rear*: drums.
MAXIMUM SPEED 137 mph (220 km/h)
0–60 MPH (0–96 KM/H) 5.9 sec (7212cc)
A.F.C. 10–23 mpg

PLYMOUTH BARRACUDA

The Plymouth Barracuda range was developed from the Valiant to become Chrysler's prime pony car contender. With its rivals, the 'Cuda shared the then-popular two-door coupe styling on a short-wheelbase chassis. The post-redesign, second-generation cars, built to 1974, are favored by many devotees. This is a top-of-the-line Cuda 440, with the biggest (7.2-liter) engine and special bodywork package. Power and handling options made Barracudas great performers.

NAME ORIGINS
The name came from Plymouth Rock, where the first white settlers landed.

"SHAKER HOOD"
Engine options ranged from "small" six to V-8 of seven liters plus. The air cleaner for the triple carburetors protruded through the hood, and could be seen vibrating; hence the term "shaker hood" for this feature.

PONTIAC *Trans Am*

THE BIG-HEARTED Pontiac Trans Am was born in those heady days when America's "big three" (Ford, General Motors, and Chrysler) built bold-as-brass, brawny machines. GM's Pontiac Division, under the dynamic John Z. DeLorean, adopted a sporting image across its whole range in this era. The first Pontiac "muscle car" was the 1964 GTO *(see pages 190–91)*, followed in 1967 by the Firebird "pony car." Pontiac raced this in the Trans Am championship and before long a higher-performance version was put on sale, with go-faster stripes, trunk spoiler, and sports cockpit.

But the classic Pontiac Trans Am was much more, with a stiffened chassis and better brakes to cope with the 350 hp engine. By the mid-1970s, the fuel crisis and US emission laws turned it from a roaring lion into a tame pussycat.

HOLLYWOOD STAR
The Trans Am was a Hollywood favorite, a four-wheeled film star in its own right. One of i biggest roles was in *Smokey and the Bandit*, in whic it upstaged Burt Reynolds. The Firebird, on whi the Trans Am was based, was made famous in t television detective series, *The Rockford Files*.

SPORTS CONTROLS
Leather-rimmed steering wheel, floor shift, groov dashboard, and bucket seats make the Trans Am cockpit about as sporting as that of any Americ car – even if the seats are vinyl trimmed.

PONTIAC CALLED THIS INSTRUMENT PACKAGE ITS "RALLY CLUSTER"; IT WAS OPTIONAL ON SOME OTHER PONTIACS

BIG V-8s (400 OR 455 CID) PROVIDED TRANS AM POWER

AROUND 350 HP WAS AVAILABLE FROM THE VARIOUS ENGINE OPTIONS, BUT 1973 EMISSION LAWS TAMED THE BEAST

FRONTAL FEATURE
All post-1964 Pontiacs were quickly identifiable from the front by the divided air intake. The 1969–73 "bull-nose" Trans Am was more attractive head on than some of its successors, which almost became cartoon versions of the original. Early Trans Ams all came with white paintwork and blue flashes.

PARKING LIGHTS
Front parking lights were a distinguishing feature of the very first Trans Ams, as the early base Firebird models had none.

DLR 30
MASSACH

PONTIAC TRANS AM

Clean Trans Am styling was welcomed by at least some sectors of the American market as a departure from the finned and chromed monsters which still made up the bulk of Detroit production at the time. Family resemblance to other GM "pony cars" of the time, such as the Chevrolet Camaro (see pages 66–67) and Pontiac's own Firebird, is clear, sharing their chic Coke-bottle shape.

DEBUT
The first Trans Ams appeared in 1969, two years after the Firebird.

FIREBIRD
The logo was based on Indian firebird legend; it is often affectionately referred to as a "chicken" or even "dead eagle."

FISHER BODYWORK
Fisher was the coachbuilding division of GM; the logo appeared on top-line models.

BULL-NOSE
Post-1973 models were given a more sloping front end.

RACING MIRRORS
Streamlined mirrors were another tell-tale Trans Am feature.

SPECIFICATIONS

MODEL Pontiac Firebird Trans Am (1969–73)

PRODUCTION 12,097

BODY STYLE Two-door, four-seat sports coupe.

CONSTRUCTION Steel-bodied monocoque with engine subframe.

ENGINE 90-degree V-8, 400cid; 455cid option from 1971.

POWER OUTPUT 345 hp at 5400 rpm (400cid); 335 hp at 4800 rpm (455cid).

TRANSMISSION Three- or four-speed manual or Hydramatic automatic.

SUSPENSION Independent front by wishbones and coil springs, beam axle on semielliptic leaf springs at rear.

BRAKES *Front:* Power-assisted front discs; *Rear:* drums.

MAXIMUM SPEED 112–132 mph (180–212 km/h) depending on spec.

0–60 MPH (0–96 KM/H) 5.4–6.0 sec.

A.F.C. 10–15 mpg

HIDDEN WIPERS
The Trans Am's concealed windshield wipers aided aerodynamic efficiency and enhanced the uncluttered appearance of the whole package.

HARD TOP
Although convertible Firebirds were freely available at the time, only eight rag-top Trans Am versions were built, all in the first year of production.

LUGGAGE SPACE
Small by US standards, but bigger than most European cars.

REAR VIEW
Another advantage over many European sporting cars was adequate rear visibility.

PONTIAC *GTO*

GTO 6·5 LITRE

THE CAR THAT STARTED the whole muscle car movement was really just a piece of corporate defiance. When General Motors clamped down on performance cars, Pontiac chief engineer John Z. DeLorean skirted the edict by simple "hot-rod" methods, placing the biggest engine available into its medium-sized Tempest Le Mans range. The GTO immediately hit home, especially in the youth market, and it was the first to offer near-race performance and roadholding in a full-sized car. Americans lined up to buy: 207,000 chose the GTO option in the first three years. From the original option package, the GTO was elevated to a separate Tempest model in 1966, and became a model in its own right in 1968. It faded back into the Le Mans line in 1972, but in the course of its joyride, the GTO had created a uniquely American expression of performance driving.

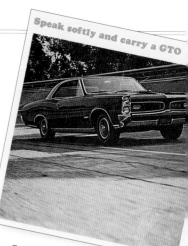

Speak softly and carry a GTO

IMAGES OF ADVERTISING
In this 1966 advertisement, the GTO was described as "A Pontiac in a saber-toothed tiger skin." Whatever it meant, the GTO upheld Pontiac's recent strong following in the youth market.

INTERIOR
The interior looks more like a speedboat than a car. The Tempest was a six seater with front bench; Tempest Le Mans, on which the GTO was based, was a five seater with separate front seats.

WALNUT GRAIN DASH

WIPER MOVE
For the 1968 facelift, disappearing wipers cleaned up the cowl area.

POWER TOP
Apart from the first few, all GTO convertibles came with power-operated top.

GTO NICKNAME
The GTO very quickly earned the nickname of "Goat," as it was agile for its size.

TIRE CHOICE
For many production years, GTO buyers could choose between red-line or whitewall-stripe tires.

HARD FACTS
Pillarless hardtop coupes often outsold convertibles by nearly 10 to 1.

SPACIOUS
Bowling-alley rear deck enclosed spacious trunk.

HEADLIGHTS
Twin lights were horizontal in 1964, then vertical for 1966 and 1967, before reverting to side-by-side format in line with GM design trends.

PONTIAC GTO

While the GTO was by no means a giant in American terms, at a little over 17 ft (5.18 m) long, it was a step up in size from the "pony cars" of the period. With routine annual updates, GTO spotters can identify model years with ease. The car featured here is from 1966; the grille, different from the preceding and following year models, is one giveaway. The slab sides of 1965 have a "Coke bottle" treatment. After various facelifts, an all-new design appeared for 1970. From 1969 to 1971, the ultimate GTO was the "The Judge," with all top GTO options as standard. They are rare too – only 11,000 were built.

POWER BULGE
Hood scoop in various forms easily distinguished the GTO from the Tempest Le Mans.

SPECIFICATIONS

MODEL Pontiac GTO (1964–71)
PRODUCTION 497,122
BODY STYLES Two door, five seat coupe, hardtop, or convertible.
CONSTRUCTION Semi-unit chassis/body.
ENGINE V-8; 326cid, 389cid, 400cid, or 456cid.
POWER OUTPUT 250–280 hp at 4600–4800 rpm; 325 hp at 4800 rpm; 335–350 hp at 5000 rpm; 360 hp at 5000 rpm.
TRANSMISSION Three- or four-speed manual; two-speed automatic.
SUSPENSION *Front:* independent, coil springs. *Rear:* live axle, coil springs, upper and lower trailing arm links.
BRAKES Drums all around, front discs from 1968.
MAXIMUM SPEED 135 mph (217 km/h)
0–60 MPH (0–96 KM/H) 6.6 sec
A.F.C. 8–12 mpg

GRAN TURISMO
The GTO name ("Gran Turismo Omologato") was hijacked by GM from Ferrari.

ENGINE
GTO engines were always the most powerful in the Pontiac range. This 1966 car has that year's standard GTO 389cid V-8 (6.5-liter), pumping out 335 hp.

PORSCHE *356B*

VOLKSWAGEN BEETLE designer Ferdinand Porsche may have given the world the "people's car," but it was his son Ferry who, with longtime associate Karl Rabe, created the 356. These days a Porsche stands for precision, performance, purity, and perfection, and the 356 is the first chapter in that story. Well not quite. The 356 was so named because it was actually the 356th project from the Porsche design office since it was set up in 1930. It was also the first car to bear the Porsche name. Postwar expediency forced a make-do reliance on Beetle underpinnings, but the 356 is much more than a Bug in butterfly's clothes. Its rear-engined layout and design descends directly from the father car, but in the athletic son the genes are mutated into a true sporting machine. A pert, nimble, tail-happy treat, the pretty 356 is the foundation stone of a proud sporting tradition.

TRACK RECORD
Here Porsches are seen retro racing at Palm Springs, California in 1990. The first Porsche 356s distinguished themselves immediately with a 1951 Le Mans class win and a 20th overall finish. Since then, Porsche has always been associated with performance, boasting an enviable track and rally victory tally.

SPLIT-SCREEN DECEIT
On convertibles, the rear view mirror is attached to a slim chrome bar that gives a deceptive split-screen appearance from the front.

1949 PORSCHE 356
This original incarnation of the 356 has slimmer wheels, split screen, lower bumpers, and is a more bulbous shape.

REDESIGN
On the 356B, headlights and bumpers moved higher up the fender.

INTERIOR
The interior is delightfully functional, unfussy, unfaddish, and, because of that, enduringly fashionable. Below the padded dash are the classic green-on-black instruments. Seats are wide and flat, and the large, almost vertical, steering wheel has a light feel. Passenger gets a grab handle.

TRANSMISSION LOCK WAS A USEFUL SECURITY FITTING AVAILABLE ON LATER CARS

SLICK CHANGES
The lever is long, but the patented Porsche split-ring synchromesh gives smooth changes with quick and positive engagement.

DYU 400

EXTRA LUGGAGE
With limited luggage accommodation in the front, the rear rack provides useful extra luggage space.

ACCESS COVER
Not a covered jacking point but an access cover to allow you to retrieve the torsion bar.

BRAKES
Drum brakes gave way to four-wheel discs with the 356C in 1963.

PORSCHE 356B SUPER 90

The first Porsche 356 was a triumph of creative expediency and inspired engineering, taking basic VW Beetle elements to create a new breed of sports car. Aficionados adore the earliest cars, often affectionately dubbed "jelly molds," and, like a jelly settling on a plate, the shape settled and spread out over the years to become flatter and sleeker.

EXHAUSTS
On the 356B, twin exhausts exit on each side through bumper overriders.

ENGINE

The rear-engined layout was determined by reliance on VW Beetle mechanicals and running gear. The flat-four engine, with its so-called "boxer" layout of horizontally opposed cylinders, is not pure Beetle, but a progressive development. Engines grew from 1086cc producing 40 bhp, to 1996cc in the final versions. This is the 1582cc engine of the 1962 356B.

SPECIFICATIONS

MODEL Porsche 356B (1959–63)
PRODUCTION 30,963
BODY STYLES Two-plus-two hardtop coupe, convertible, and Speedster.
CONSTRUCTION Unit steel body with integral pressed steel platform chassis.
ENGINE Aircooled, horizontally opposed flat four 1582cc.
POWER OUTPUT 90 bhp at 5500 rpm (Super 90).
TRANSMISSION Four-speed manual, all synchromesh, rear wheel drive.
SUSPENSION *Front:* Independent, trailing arms with transverse torsion bars and anti-roll bar. *Rear:* Independent, swing half axles, radius arms, and transverse torsion bars. Telescopic shocks.
BRAKES Hydraulic drums all around.
MAXIMUM SPEED 110 mph (177 km/h)
0–60 MPH (0–96 KM/H) 10 sec
A.F.C. 30–35 mpg

PORSCHE *Carrera 911 RS*

AN INSTANT LEGEND, the Carrera RS became the classic 911, and is hailed as one of the ultimate road cars of all time. With lighter body panels and bare bones interior trim, the RS is simply a featherweight racer. The classic flat-six engine was bored out to 2.7 liters and equipped with uprated fuel injection and forged flat-top pistons – modifications that helped to develop a sparkling 210 bhp.

Porsche had no problem selling all the RSs it could make. A total of 1,580 were built and sold in just 12 months. Standard 911s were often criticized for tail-happy handling, but the Carrera RS is a supremely balanced machine. Its race-bred responses offer the last word in sensory gratification. With one of the best engines ever made, an outstanding chassis, and 150 mph (243 km/h) top speed, the RS can rub bumpers with the world's finest. Collectors and Porsche fans consider this the pre-eminent 911, with prices reflecting its cult-like status, The RS is the original air-cooled screamer.

INTERIOR
Touring or road versions of the RS had creature comforts like sunroof, electric windows, and radio cassette. Large central tachometer and "dog-leg" gear shift are RS trademarks. Leather seats and steering wheel are non-standard later additions.

RACING 911
The RS outclassed everything else on the track, winning the Daytona 24-hours in 1973 and beating heavyweights like the Ferrari 365 GTB/4.

ENGINE
The bored-out, air-cooled 2.7-liter opposed six produces huge reserves of power. Externally, it is identifiable only by extra cylinder cooling fins. Internally, things are very different from the stock 911 unit.

WINDSHIELD
Steeply raked glass helps the 911's wind-cheating shape.

GoldStar

LIGHTS
Classic slanted headlights betray 911's VW Beetle origins.

VENTILATION
Cockpit ventilation is through tiny louvers above the rear window.

WHEEL ARCHES
Rear wheel arches are flared to accommodate 7-in (18-cm) rims.

PORSCHE CARRERA 911 RS 2.7

The plastic bumpers, thin steel bodywork, and lightweight "Glaverbell" glass help the RS to weigh in at just over 1,984 lb (900 kg). Standard Porsches tip the scales at 2,194 lb (995 kg). In addition, the weight distribution and rear engine layout demand some very gentle treatment of the throttle. Handle the 911 roughly and it will understeer, eventually breaking away with savage violence. 911s need great respect in the rain.

SPECIFICATIONS

MODEL Porsche Carrera 911 RS (1972–73)
PRODUCTION 1,580
BODY STYLES Two door, two seater coupe.
CONSTRUCTION Thin-gauge steel panels.
ENGINE Flat-six, 2687cc.
POWER OUTPUT 210 bhp at 5100 rpm.
TRANSMISSION Close-ratio, five-speed manual.
SUSPENSION Front and rear torsion bar.
BRAKES Ventilated discs front and rear, with aluminum calipers.
MAXIMUM SPEED 150 mph (243 km/h)
0–60 MPH (0–96 KM/H) 5.6 sec
0–100 MPH (0–161 KM/H) 12.8 sec
A.F.C. 23 mpg

TARGA STAMP
The 911 Targa had a lift-out roof panel and built-in roll bar. But enthusiasts preferred the Beetle-backed lines of the closed 911.

INTERIOR
Racing RSs do not even have headlining, sun visors, or sound-proofing.

REAR SPOILER
The RS has a fiberglass Burzel rear spoiler, fitted to reduce rear-end lift at speed. This boosted the RS's maximum speed by 2 mph (3 km/h).

RENAULT *Alpine A110*

THE RENAULT ALPINE A110 may be diminutive in its proportions but it has a massive and deserved reputation, particularly in its native France. Although wearing the Renault label, this pocket rocket is a testimony to the single-minded dedication of one man – Jean Redélé, a passionate sports car enthusiast and son of a Dieppe Renault agent. As he took over his father's garage he began to modify Renault products for competition, then develop his own machines based on Renault engines and mechanicals. The A110, with its fiberglass body and backbone chassis, was the culmination of his effort, and from its launch in 1963 went on to rack up a massive list of victories in the world's toughest rallies. On the public roads, it had all the appeal of a thinly disguised racer, as nimble as a mountain goat, with sparkling performance and just about the most fun you could have this side of a Lancia Stratos *(see pages 152–53)*.

SAFETY CUT OUT
External cut out switches are a competition requirement, allowing outsiders to switch off the engine to prevent fire in an accident.

INTERIOR
Instrument layout is typical of sports cars of the period, and the stubby gear lever is handily placed for ease of operation. Getting in and out was not easy though, because of the low roof and high sills. Examples built for road rather than race use lacked the racing seats but were better trimmed and were still fun cars to drive.

ALPINE ACTION
The Alpine was most at home in rally conditions and won everything on the world stage, including a staggering 1–2–3 at the 1971 Monte Carlo Rally. The picture shows this featured car on the way to winning the Millers Oils RAC Rally Britannia in England in November 1994.

COMPACT SIZE
It is a compact little package, just 44.5 in (1.16 m) high, 60 in (1.5 m) wide, and 151.5 in (3.85 m) in length.

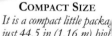

Richard Tyzack
Mick Briggs

MILLERS OILS
RAC International Historic Rally
of Great Britain

104

LEFT HOOKERS
Sadly for British enthusiasts, the Alpine A110 was only available in left-hand drive.

RENAULT ENGINES
Myriad engine options mirrored Renault's offerings but, in Alpine tune – by Gordini or Mignotet – it really flew. First models used Dauphine engines, progressing through R8 and R16 to R12 power. This 1967 car sports the 1442cc unit. Engines were slung behind the rear axle, with drive taken to the gearbox in front of the axle.

RENAULT ALPINE A110

Squat, nimble and slightly splay-footed on its wide tires, the Alpine looks purposeful from any angle. Climb into that tight cockpit and you soon feel part of the car; start it up and there is a delicious barrage of noise. On the move, the sting in the Alpine's tail is exhilarating as it buzzes behind you like an angry insect. The steering is light too, and the grip tenacious, but when it does let go that tail wags the dog in a big way. Its singular appearance remained intact through its production life, with only detail changes to the trim, which these days is hard to find.

NAME
Cars were known at first as Alpine Renaults, then became Renault Alpines as Renault influence grew.

TRUNK AJAR
Competition versions had engine covers fixed slightly open to aid cooling.

SPECIFICATIONS

MODEL Renault Alpine A110 Berlinette (1963–77)
PRODUCTION 8,203
BODY STYLE Two-seater sports coupe.
CONSTRUCTION Fiberglass body integral with tubular steel backbone chassis.
ENGINE Four cylinder, 13 options ranging from 956cc to 1796cc.
POWER OUTPUT 51–170 bhp (depending on engine size).
TRANSMISSION Four- and five-speed manual, rear-wheel drive.
SUSPENSION *Front:* Coil springs all around, with upper/lower control arms. *Rear:* Trailing radius arms and swing-axles.
BRAKES Four-wheel discs.
MAXIMUM SPEED 132 mph (212 km/h) 1595cc.
0–60 MPH (0–96 KM/H) 8.7 sec (1255cc)
A.F.C. 27 mpg

ROLLS-ROYCE *Silver Cloud*

IN 1965, $8,000 BOUGHT a large house, 11 Austin Minis, eight Triumph Heralds, or a Rolls-Royce Silver Cloud. The Rolls that everybody remembers was the ultimate conveyance of landed gentry and captains of industry. But, by the early '60s, Britain's social fabric was shifting. Princess Margaret announced she was to marry a divorcé, and aristocrats were so short of old money that they had to sell their crumbling country houses to celebrities and entrepreneurs. Against such social revolution the Cloud was a resplendent anachronism.

Each Cloud took three months to build, weighed over two tons, and had 12 coats of paint. The body sat on a mighty chassis and drum brakes were preferred because discs made a vulgar squealing noise. Beneath the hood slumbered straight six or V-8 engines, whose power output was never declared, but merely described as "sufficient." The Silver Cloud stands as a splendid monument to an old order of breeding and privilege.

OTHER MODELS
The Silver Cloud was replaced in 1966 by the more modern-looking, and monocoque-constructed, Silver Shadow – Rolls-Royce's most successful and profitable product.

R-R SILVER WRAITH II
Silver Wraith was meant to be a limo version of the Shadow with longer wheelbase and smaller rear window.

R-R SILVER SHADOW
The Shadow was more socially acceptable and technically superior, with disc brakes and hydraulic suspension.

GEAR SELECTOR
All Clouds were automatic, using a four-speed GM Hydramatic box which R-R used under license, but made itself.

DASHBOARD
A haven of peace in a troubled world, the Silver Cloud's magnificent interior was a veritable throne room, with only the finest walnut, leather, and Wilton carpeting.

WIDE REAR THREE-QUARTER PANEL WAS DESIGNED SO REAR OCCUPANTS COULD BE OBSCURED FROM PRYING EYES

ROLLS CLAIMED ITS CHROME PLATING WAS THICKER THAN ON ANY OTHER CAR IN THE WORLD

LEATHER COMFORT
The rear compartment might have looked accommodating, but Austin's little 1100 actually had more legroom.

QUALITY TOOLS
Every Cloud had a complete tool kit. So obsessed was Rolls-Royce with integrity that it tested every tool to destruction.

STANDARD WALNUT PICNIC TABLES WERE IDEAL FOR CHAMPAGNE AND CAVIAR PICNICS

EVERYTHING ABOUT THE CLOUD'S STYLING WAS ANTIQUE, LOOKING MORE LIKE A PIECE OF ARCHITECTURE THAN AN AUTOMOBILE

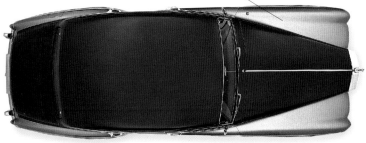

ENGINE
Cloud IIs and IIIs – aimed at the American market – had a 6230cc five-bearing V-8 power unit squeezed into a cramped engine bay. Cloud Is had a straight-six, 4.9-liter engine that could trace its origins back to before the Second World War.

BODYWORK
Standard steel bodies were made by the Pressed Steel Co. of Oxford, England, with the doors, hood, and trunk lid hand-finished in aluminum to save weight.

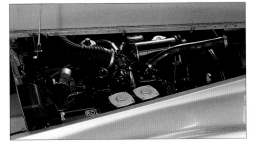

SPECIFICATIONS
MODEL Rolls-Royce Silver Cloud III (1962–65)
PRODUCTION 2,044 Standard Steel
BODY STYLE Five-seater, four-door sedan.
CONSTRUCTION Girder chassis with pressed-steel body.
ENGINE 6230cc five bearing V-8.
POWER OUTPUT 220 bhp (estimate)
TRANSMISSION Four-speed automatic.
SUSPENSION Independent front with coils and wishbones, rear leaf springs and hydraulic shock absorbers.
BRAKES Front and rear drums with mechanical power assist.
MAXIMUM SPEED 116 mph (187 km/h)
0–60 MPH (0–96 KM/H) 10.8 sec
0–100 MPH (0–161 KM/H) 34.2 sec
A.F.C. 12.3 mpg

MASCOT
Perhaps the most famous car mascot in the world, the Spirit of Ecstasy graced a German silver patrician radiator shell that took several men five hours to polish.

THE FRONT FENDERS LOOKED AS IF THEY WERE SEPARATE FROM THE REST OF THE BODY

DEEPLY RESISTANT TO CHANGE, ROLLS-ROYCE MADE THE CLOUD'S HOOD OPEN SIDEWAYS IN THE BEST PREWAR TRADITION

MASCOT WAS ATTACHED BY A SPRING AND WIRE TO DETER SOUVENIR-HUNTERS

THE NOUVEAU ROLLER

*Launched in 1955, styled like Big Ben, and with Stone Age mechanicals,
the Silver Cloud was old before its time.*

THE CLOUD I had a venerable straight-six 4.9-liter engine (conceived as early as 1938), heavy separate chassis, drum brakes, and no power steering. Its postwar engineering survived until the end of the decade, when Rolls was forced to pay lip service to modernity and exchange its ancient six for a V-8 and make power steering standard. Cloud IIs ran until 1962, when the car enjoyed its first major facelift – a lowered hood line and radiator shell, with the addition of twin headlights as a concession to the all-important American market. But, for those who thought the Cloud's architecture was a bit flamboyant, there was the more discreet Bentley S-Series. At $250 less than the Cloud, it was identical, apart from the round-shouldered radiator, hubcaps, and labeling. But even the Bentley's self-conscious restraint could not protect it from a changing world.

ADVERTISEMENT FOR 1965 ROLLS-ROYCE SILVER CLOUD

ROLLS-ROYCE *Silver Cloud*

MAX HEADROOM
The roofline was high in the best limousine tradition. Rear passengers had enough room to wear top hats

DOORS WERE SECURED BY THE HIGHEST QUALITY YALE LOCKS

ROMAN NUMERALS WERE CHOSEN FOR THE CLOUD III SCRIPT TO LEND AN AIR OF DIGNITY

EEL 800C

GB

Silver Cloud III

Previously, Royces had been driven by chauffeurs, but the Cloud was one of the first Rollers to be driven by owners. In the early '60s, a British film called *Man at the Top* was released, featuring a new breed of thrusting executive at the wheel of a Regal Red Cloud III. The film showed him driving the car himself, filling it up with gas, even breaking down and picking up hitchhikers. At roughly the same time, John Lennon decided to give his Phantom a psychedelic paint job. Both these events triggered a huge change in public perception of the Silver Cloud. It instantly slipped a social rung, and it was new rather than

inherited money that now prized Rolls-Royces from showrooms.

By the late '60s the Cloud, looking like a prodigious antique, fell rapidly from grace and could be bought from downmarket car dealers for a few thousand dollars. In the '70s, many met with a low-rent end, stripped of

JOHN LENNON AND HIS PSYCHEDELIC R-R PHANTOM

their haughty Edwardian dignity, whitewashed, ribboned, and harnessed into service as wedding workhorses.

NEW IMPROVED

When the Cloud II was unveiled in 1962, one magazine saw the changes as "more power, more passenger space, better lighting and easier steering."

TURN SIGNALS WERE MOVED FROM THE FOGLIGHT TO THE FRONT FENDER ON THE CLOUD III

ON THE VERY LAST CLOUDS, THE REAR-VIEW MIRRORMOUNTING WAS MOVED FROM THE DASHBOARD TO THE ROOF LINING

150-WATT 5.25-IN (14-CM) LUCAS DOUBLE HEADLIGHTS WERE NECESSITATED BY NORTH AMERICAN SAFETY REQUIREMENTS

EEL 800C

SAAB *99 Turbo*

EVERY DECADE OR SO, one car comes along that overhauls accepted wisdom. In 1978, the British motoring magazine *Autocar* wrote, "this car was so unpredictably thrilling that the adrenaline started to course again, even in our hardened arteries." They had just road-tested a Saab 99 Turbo. Saab took all other car manufacturers by surprise when it announced the world's first turbocharged family car, which promptly went on to be the first "blown" car to win a World Championship rally.

Developed from the fuel-injected EMS model, the Turbo had Bosh-K-Jetronic fuel injection, a strengthened gearbox, and a Garrett turbocharger. A hundred prototypes were built and between them they covered 2.9 million miles (4.8 million km) before Saab was happy with their prodigy. Priced at $9,998 it was expensive, but there was nothing to equal its urge. Rare, esoteric, and historically significant, the mold-breaking 99 Turbo is an undisputed card-carrying classic.

ENGINE
The five-bearing, chain-driven single overhead cam engine was an 1985cc eight-valve, water-cooled four cylinder unit, with low compression pistons and altered cam timing. The result was 145 bhp and 122 mph (196 km/h).

RALLY BREAKTHROUGH
Stig Blomqvist won the 1977 Swedish Rally and the next year gave the 99 Turbo some serious exposure. He made a thunderous run down Esgair Dafydd in Wales on the first televised rally sprint – with a punctured front tire.

RARE TWO-DOOR
Hatchback three-door versions are the most common 99 Turbo incarnation. The faster and lighter two-door cars are much rarer, with only 1,000 made.

BODYSHELL
Shell is stiff and light and a full four-seater. It is remarkably durable, too, with factory underseal and cavity wax injection.

When the turbo boost gauge needle swept up its arc, all hell would break loose

INTERIOR
1970s interior looks tacky now, with red velour seats and imitation wood. Buyers did get a leather steering wheel and heated driver's seat.

STYLING
Never as visually threatening as the Audi Quattro (see pages 32–35), the 99 is pleasantly rounded but unremarkable.

SAAB 99 TURBO

The car appeared at the 1978 Frankfurt Show as a three-door EMS. The body has a certain business-like presence, helped by specially made Inca alloys designed to mimic the shape of turbocharger blades, standard front and rear spoilers, and a sliding steel sunroof. Colors were chosen to be deliberately assertive – only red and black. The chassis was a peach, with taut high-speed steering, four-wheel discs, minimal understeer, and incredible levels of grip. Between 40 mph (65 km/h) and 100 mph (161 km/h) it accelerated faster than any other four-seater of its day.

TURBOCHARGER
The turbo is reliable, but its Achilles heel is a couple of seconds lag on hard acceleration.

HANDLING
The 99 Turbos were poised. Crisp handling came from front-wheel drive, with prodigious adhesion courtesy of 195/60 Pirelli P6s.

COMMON PARTS
Turbo shared most parts with the Saab 99 EMS Sedan. But camshaft valves and pistons were uprated for performance and durability.

SUSPENSION
Independent front suspension was the usual wishbone and coil spring setup, with a dead beam axle at the rear.

SIMCA *Aronde Plein Ciel*

BY APING AMERICAN 1950s styling trends and regular face-lifts, Simca metamorphosed from a company building Fiats under license into France's top privately owned car maker. And the Aronde was the car that turned the tide. Brainchild of Henri-Théodore Pigozzi, the comely Aronde was the first popular French car to have postwar transatlantic style. Over a 12-year lifespan, 1.3 million Arondes were sold. By 1955 it had put Simca ahead of both Peugeot and Citroën.

With bodywork by Facel of Facel Vega fame *(see pages 94–97)*, the Aronde was an affordable *haute couture* confection based on run-of-the-mill components. 1958 saw a complete US-influenced redesign, with engine names such as "Flash Special." Even so, the Aronde is a quaint hybrid that stands as a testament to the penetrating influence of 1950s Detroit design.

(see pages 94–97)

OTHER MODELS

Plein Ciel Coupe and Ocean Convertible were rebodied Arondes, available up until 1963, when the range disappeared in favor of the 1300 and 1500 models.

SIMCA OCEAN
The 1957 Ocean bears a deliberate resemblance to the Ford Thunderbird (see pages 116–17).

(see pages 116–17).

DASHBOARD

The interior is pure Pontiac pastiche, with no less than six different types of plastic – the Aronde's cabin is a riot of two-tone synthetic.

THE ARONDE NAME

A delicate birdlike thing, Aronde is French for swallow.

ENGINE

"Flash Special" had a four-cylinder, 57 bhp pushrod engine bored out to 1288cc, with a Solex carburetor. Four-speed manual gearbox had obligatory American-style column shifter.

WHEEL EMBELLISHMENT

Full-width polished chrome hub-caps and wheel trims were an American fad, embraced by European imitators.

WHAT'S IN A NAME?

Plein Ciel ("open air") motif accords with the airy cockpit and generous glass area.

SIMCA ARONDE PLEIN CIEL

The Facel Vega connection is unmistakable, especially in the steep wraparound windshield and bubblelike cockpit. The finned rear, flowing script on the front fenders, liberal use of chrome, and raked rear lights would not look out of place on a 1957 Chevrolet. The moustachelike, eggcrate grille and recessed parking lights lend the Aronde an air of class and quality.

HANDLING
The Aronde handled as well as it looked but, because it did not have a smooth ride, the French motoring press disapproved. Despite conventional underpinnings, it felt sporting with positive, if unpowered, brakes, and a firmly tied-down chassis.

SPECIFICATIONS

MODEL Simca Aronde Plein Ciel (1957–62)
PRODUCTION 170,070 (Facel-bodied Arondes)
BODY STYLES Cabriolet or hardtop sports coupe.
CONSTRUCTION Steel body over separate steel chassis frame.
ENGINE 1288cc four-cylinder pushrod.
POWER OUTPUT 57 bhp at 4800 rpm ("Flash Special").
TRANSMISSION Four-speed manual.
SUSPENSION *Front*: Independent by coil springs and wishbones. *Rear*: Semielliptic leaf springs.
BRAKES Four-wheel drums.
MAXIMUM SPEED 87 mph (140 km/h)
0–60 MPH (0–96 KM/H) 15.6 sec
A.F.C. 28 mpg

COLOR
The Aronde was available in 22 different two-tone color schemes.

SEATING
Despite a sloping rear roof line, the Aronde was just about a four seater.

REFINEMENTS
"Flash Special" engine had punchier low-range torque, stronger crankshaft and big-end journals, plus an improved lubrication system.

LUGGAGE CAPACITY
The elongated rear meant that the trunk was surprisingly ample, even though the sill meant loading baggage required some serious lifting.

MODERNISM
Flush-fitting, lockable gas cap-flap was surprisingly avant garde for 1958.

SUNBEAM *Tiger*

THERE WAS NOTHING NEW about placing an American V-8 into a pert English chassis. After all, that is exactly what Carroll Shelby did with the AC Ace to create the awesome Cobra *(see pages 22–23)*. When Rootes in Britain decided to do the same with its Sunbeam Alpine, it also commissioned Shelby to produce a prototype and although Rootes already had close links with Chrysler, the American once again opted for a Ford V-8. To cope with the 4.2-liter engine, the Alpine's chassis and suspension were beefed up to create the fearsome Tiger late in 1964. In 1967, the Tiger II arrived with an even bigger 4.7-liter Ford V-8, but this was a brief swan song as Chrysler took control of Rootes and was not going to sanction a car powered by a Ford engine. Often dubbed "the poor man's Cobra," the Tiger is still a lot of fun to grab by the tail.

— SPECIFICATIONS —

MODEL Sunbeam Tiger (1964–67)
PRODUCTION MkI, 1964–67, 6,496; MkII, 6,083
BODY STYLE Two-plus-two roadster.
CONSTRUCTION Steel monocoque.
ENGINE Ford V-8 4261cc or 4727cc.
POWER OUTPUT 164 bhp at 4400 rpm (4261cc), 200 bhp at 4400 rpm (4727cc).
TRANSMISSION Four-speed manual.
SUSPENSION Coil springs and wishbones at front, rigid axle on semielliptic leaf springs at rear.
BRAKES Power-assisted front discs, rear drums.
MAXIMUM SPEED 117 mph (188 km/h) (4261cc), 125 mph (201 km/h) (4727cc)
0–60 MPH (0–96 KM/H) 9 sec (4261CC), 7.5 sec (4727CC).
A.F.C. 20 mpg

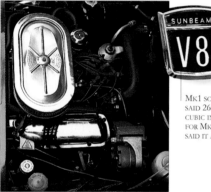

MK1 SCRIPT SAID 260 FOR CUBIC INCHES; FOR MK2, V-8 SAID IT ALL

POWERED BY FORD
The first Tigers used 4.2-liter Ford V-8 engines, replaced later – as shown here – by a 4727cc version, the famous 289. It was not, however, in the same state of tune as those fitted to the Shelby Cobras.

SUNBEAM TIGER
MkII Tiger had an eggcrate grille to distinguish it from the Alpine. Earlier cars were less easy to tell apart: a chrome strip along the Tiger's side was the giveaway, plus discreet labeling.

ADAPTED ALPINE
Alpine chassis and suspension had to be beefed up to cope with the weight and power of the V-8. Modifications included heavy-duty rear axle, sturdier suspension, and chassis stiffening.

STEERING
The Tiger's steering system was rack-and-pinion, as the normal Alpine recirculating-ball gear would not fit with the V-8 engine. Wood-rim steering wheel was standard.

HOTHOUSE
Tigers often suffered overheating, which was not surprising as the Alpine engine bay originally accommodated a 1494cc four-cylinder engine.

RACE HOOD
Race and rally Tigers had improved air-flow with slightly raised hood.

OPC 53E

TOYOTA *2000 GT*

TOYOTA'S 2000GT is more than a "might have been" – it is a "should have been." A pretty coupe with equipment and performance to match its good looks, it predated the rival Datsun 240Z *(see pages 84–87),* which was a worldwide sales success. The Toyota failed to reach much more than 300 sales, partly because of low capacity at its Yamaha factory, but even more because the car was launched before Japan was geared to export. That left only a domestic market, largely uneducated in the finer qualities of sporting cars, to make what they could of the offering. As a design exercise, the 2000GT proved that the Japanese motor industry had reached the stage where its products rivaled the best in the world. It is just a pity that more people were not able to appreciate this fine car at first hand.

FASHIONABLE THREE-SPOKE WOOD-RIM WHEEL WAS LINKED TO PRECISE RACK-AND-PINION STEERING

SPEEDOMETER SHOWED AN OPTIMISTIC 160 MPH (257 KM/H)

SHORT-THROW WOODEN-TOP GEAR LEVER OPERATED A FIVE-SPEED, ALL-SYNCHROMESH BOX

ROLE MODEL
The 2000GT's snug cockpit featured a walnut veneer instrument panel, sporty wheel, stubby gear lever, form-fitting seats, and deep footwells. The eight-track stereo is a nice period touch.

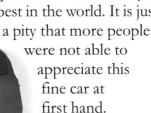

YAMAHA ENGINE
The engine was a triple-carburetor six-cylinder Yamaha, which provided 150 bhp. A competition version boosted output to 200 bhp.

TOYOTA 2000GT
The design of the Toyota 2000 GT is based on an earlier prototype penned by Albrecht Goertz, creator of the BMW 507 and Datsun 240Z. When Nissan rejected the design, it was offered to Toyota and evolved into the 2000 GT.

LIGHTING
Unusual combination of hightech pop-up and fixed headlights gives the front a fussy look.

TOPLESS STAR
A modified convertible starred with Sean Connery in the James Bond film, You Only Live Twice.

SIDE BOXES
Panel on the right conceals the battery; on the left is the air cleaner. This arrangement enabled the hood to be kept low.

SPECIFICATIONS

MODEL Toyota 2000GT (1965–68)
PRODUCTION 337
BODY STYLE Two-door sports coupe.
CONSTRUCTION Steel body on backbone frame.
ENGINE Yamaha inline DOHC six, 1988cc.
POWER OUTPUT 150 bhp at 6600 rpm.
TRANSMISSION Five-speed manual.
SUSPENSION Fully independent by coil springs and wishbones all around.
BRAKES Hydraulically operated discs all around.
MAXIMUM SPEED 128 mph (206 km/h)
0–60 MPH (0–96 KM/H) 10.5 sec
A.F.C. 31 mpg

TRIUMPH *TR2*

IF EVER THERE WAS A SPORTS CAR that epitomized the British bulldog spirit it must be the Triumph TR2. It is as true Brit as a car can be, born in the golden age of British sports cars, but aimed at the lucrative American market, where the Jaguar XK120 *(see pages 134–35)* had already scored a hit. At the 1952 Earl's Court Motor Show in London, the Healey 100 had been transformed overnight into the Austin-Healey, but the "Triumph Sports" prototype's debut at the same show was less auspicious. It was a brave attempt to create an inexpensive sports car from a company with no recent track record in this market segment.

With its dumpy *derriere*, the prototype was no oil painting; as for handling, incoming chief tester Ken Richardson described it as a "bloody deathtrap." An all-new chassis, revised rear, and other modifications saw Standard-Triumph's new TR2 emerge into a winner at the Geneva Motor Show in March 1953. No conventional beauty certainly, but a bluff-fronted car that was a worthy best-of-breed contender in the budget sports car arena, and the cornerstone of a stout sporting tradition.

OTHER MODELS

The TR2 began a fine tradition of sporting TRs that was only eventually let down by the controversially styled, wedge-shaped TR7 of the 1970s.

TRIUMPH TR3
The TR3 was the first development, with more power and front disc-brakes on later cars. External door handles and lift-off hardtop were options.

TRIUMPH TR3A
The most obvious difference from the TR3 was the full-width grille. The TR3A was produced from 1957–61.

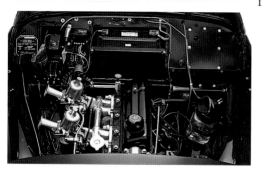

ENGINE
Legend says that the TR2 engine came from a Ferguson tractor – in fact it and the tractor were developed from a Standard Vanguard engine. The twin-carburetor TR2 was reduced to just under two liters.

SPORTING PROWESS
The car on these pages was a "factory built" competition car, pictured here with its driver, Ken Richardson.

FOR RACING
The TR2 came with small holes drilled in the cowl to fit racing windshields.

THE TR2 CHASSIS WAS PRAISED FOR ITS TAUTNESS AND FINE ROAD MANNERS

LIKE THE AUSTIN-HEALEY' THE TR CHASSIS RUNS UNDE THE AXLE AT THE REAR

STOCK DESIGN
There is nothing revolutionary in the design of the pressed-steel chassis; a simple ladder with X-shaped bracing. It was a transformation, though, from the prototype's original chassis

TRIUMPH TR2
The design, by Walter Belgrove, was far cry from the razor-edged Triump Renown and Mayflower sedans that he had previously styled. If not beautiful, the TR2 has chunk good looks with a bluff, honest demeanor. Unusual recessed grille presents a slightly grumpy disposition but the low front helped the car to top 100 mph (161 km/h). Equipment was spartan – you did not even ge external door handles.

INTERIOR
Stubby gear lever and full instrumentation gave TR a sports car feel. The steering wheel was large, but the low door accommodates vintage "elbows out" driving style.

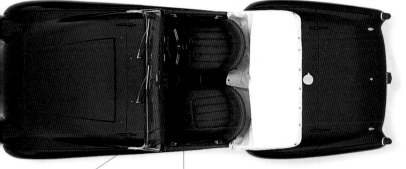

WINDSHIELD
It looks flat, but the windshield actually has a slight curve; this prevents it from bowing at speed, which is what the prototype's flat screen did.

LOW-CUT DOORS
You could reach out over the doors and touch the road. External door handles only arrived with the TR3A of 1957.

LUGGAGE SPACE
The prototype had a stubby tail with exposed spare wheel; the production model had a real opening trunk and locker below for spare wheel.

OVC 276

SPECIFICATIONS

MODEL Triumph TR2 (1953–55)
PRODUCTION 8,628
BODY STYLE Two-door, two-seater sports car.
CONSTRUCTION Pressed-steel chassis with separate steel body.
ENGINE Four-cylinder, overhead valve, 1991cc, twin SU carburetors.
POWER OUTPUT 90 bhp at 4800 rpm.
TRANSMISSION Four-speed manual with Laycock overdrive option, initially on top gear only, then on top three (1955).
SUSPENSION Coil spring and wishbone at front, live rear axle with semielliptic leaf springs.
BRAKES Lockheed hydraulic, drums.
MAXIMUM SPEED 105 mph (169 km/h)
0–60 MPH (0–96 KM/H) 12 sec
A.F.C. 30+mpg

SPORTY TRIUMPH
The Triumph sporting tradition was firmly established when TR2s came first and second in the 1954 RAC Rally.

WHEEL CHOICE
The first TR2s came with pressed-steel disc wheels, complete with chrome hubcaps, but most customers preferred the option of wire wheels, which were considered much sportier.

OVC 276

TRIUMPH *TR6*

TO MOST TR TRADITIONALISTS this is where the TR tale ended, the final flourishing of the theme before the TR7 betrayed an outstanding tradition. In the mid-1960s, the TR range was on a roll and the TR6 continued the upward momentum, outselling all earlier offerings. Crisply styled, with chiseled-chin good looks and carrying over the 2.5-liter six-cylinder engine of the TR5, the TR6 in early fuel-injected form heaved you along with 150 galloping horses. This was as hairy chested as the TR got. It was a handful, with some critics carping that, like the big Healeys, its power outstripped its poise. But that just made it more fun to drive.

OTHER MODELS

The TR6 was a natural progression from the original TR2; the body evolved from the TR4/5, the 2.5-liter six-cylinder engine from the TR5.

TRIUMPH **TR4**
The TR4 of 1961 was the first TR to carry all-new Michelotti-styled bodywork, updated by Karmann into the Triumph TR6.

TRIUMPH **TR5**
In 1967 the TR5 became the first of the six-cylinder TRs, its 2.5-liter engine going on to power the TR6.

ENGINE
The first engines, as on this 1972 car, produced 150 bhp, but public pressure for something more well-mannered resulted in a 125 bhp version in 1973.

AMERICAN VERSIONS HAD CARBURETORS RATHER THAN FUEL INJECTION AS HERE

INTERIOR
The interior is still traditional but more refined than earlier TRs. Yet with its big dials, wooden dash, and short-throw gear knob, its character is still truly sporting.

EASY ACCESS
Big, wide-opening doors gave easy access to the TR6, a long cry from the tiny doors of the TR2 and TR3.

FAT WHEELS
Wider wheels were a TR6 feature, as was the antiroll bar at the front.

POWER DROP
Revised injection metering and reprofiled camshaft reduced power from 1973; US carburetor versions were more sluggish (and thirstier) still, but sold many more.

SALES FIGURES
British sales stopped in February 1975, but continued in the US until July 1976. Ten times as many TR6s were exported as remained in Britain.

SPECIFICATIONS

MODEL Triumph TR6 (1969–76)
PRODUCTION 94,619
BODY STYLE Two-seat convertible.
CONSTRUCTION Ladder-type chassis with integral steel body.
ENGINE In-line six-cylinder, 2498cc, fuel-injection (carburetors in US).
POWER OUTPUT 152 bhp at 5500 rpm (1969–1973), 125 bhp at 5250 rpm (1973–1975), 104 bhp at 4500 rpm (US).
TRANSMISSION Manual four-speed with optional overdrive on third and top.
SUSPENSION Independent by coil springs all around; wishbones at front, swing-axles & semitrailing arms at rear.
BRAKES *Front:* discs; *Rear:* drums.
MAXIMUM SPEED 119 mph (191 km/h, 150 bhp) , 107 mph (172 km/h, US)
0–60 MPH (0–96 KM/H) 8.2 sec (150 bhp); 9.0 sec (125 bhp); 10.6 sec (104 bhp).
0–100 MPH (0–161 KM/H) 29 sec
A.F.C. 25 mpg

TRIUMPH TR6

There is an obvious difference between the TR4/5 and the later TR6, restyled by Karmann; sharper, cleaner lines not only looked more modern, but also gave more luggage space. The chopped-off tail was an aerodynamic aid. One-piece hardtop was available as an option, and was more practical than the two-piece seen on earlier models. The TR6's good looks, and a long production run, made this model the biggest selling of all TR models.

ENGINE NOISE
Deep-throated burble is still a TR6 come-on.

ROOMY INTERIOR
The cockpit was more spacious than earlier TRs, providing excellent driving position from comfortable seats.

MERGER
The TR6 was launched just after the 1968 merger of Leyland and BMC.

VOLKSWAGEN *Beetle Karmann*

BEETLE PURISTS MAY WAX LYRICAL about the first-of-breed purity of the original split rear-screen Bugs and the oval window versions of 1953 to 1957, but there is one Beetle that everybody wants – the Karmann-built Cabriolet. Its development followed that of the sedans through a bewildering series of modifications, but it always stood apart. With its hood retracted into a bulging bustle, this Beetle was not only cheerful, but chic too, a classless cruiser equally at home on Beverly Hills boulevards, Cannes, and the Kings Road. The final incarnation of the Karmann convertible represents the ultimate development of the Beetle theme, with the peppiest engine and improved suspension and handling. This model is from the final year of manufacture, the most refined Bug of all, but still true to its original concept. It's strange to think that once, long ago, the disarming unburstable Bug was a vehicle of fascist propaganda, branded with the slogan of the Hitler Youth, "Strength through Joy." Today, its strength has given joy to millions of motorists as the undisputed people's car.

OTHER MODELS

The Beetle was subjected to a bewildering 78,000-plus modifications through its production life, but somehow managed to retain its essential character.

VW BEETLE SEDAN
This 1131cc Beetle from 1947 shows how the myriad modifications amount to minor detailing only.

DASHBOARD

The Beetle is still bare, its dash dominated by the one minimal instrument; on this model the speedometer incorporates a fuel gauge. It also has a padded dash, replacing the original metal version.

FOUR-SPOKE STEERING WHEEL IS NOT AS CLASSIC AS EARLIER THIN-RIMMED TWO- AND THREE-SPOKED WHEELS

CURVED "PANORAMIC" WINDSHIELD REPLACED FLAT GLASS IN 1972

PRODUCTION PLANS

Before Karmann chopped the lid off the Bug, there had been plans for a Beetle-based roadster which in some ways foreshadowed later custom Bugs. The prototypes inspired coachbuilders Joseph Hebmüller & Sons to build a short-lived roadster, but just 696 were built before a factory fire ended the project. That opened the door for the four-seater Karmann convertible.

ORIGINAL 16-IN (40-CM) WHEELS WERE REDUCED TO 15 IN (38 CM) IN 1952. FRONT DISC BRAKES WERE INTRODUCED IN 1966

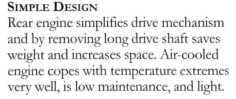

SIMPLE DESIGN
Rear engine simplifies drive mechanism and by removing long drive shaft saves weight and increases space. Air-cooled engine copes with temperature extremes very well, is low maintenance, and light.

THE WORLD RECORD FOR A BEETLE ENGINE SWAP IS JUST OVER THREE MINUTES

ENGINE
You can always tell that a Beetle is on its way before it comes into sight thanks to the distinctive buzzing of the air-cooled, horizontally opposed four-cylinder engine. Its capacity grew from 1131cc to 1584cc and the engines have a deserved reputation as robust, high-revving units.

FIRST CARS HAD FLAG TURN SIGNALS, THEN LIGHTS WERE FENDER-MOUNTED, AND IN SOME CASES PLACED WITHIN FRONT BUMPERS

SPECIFICATIONS
MODEL VW Beetle Karmann Cabriolet (1972–80)
PRODUCTION 331,847 (all Karmann Cabriolets from 1949 to 1980).
BODY STYLE Four-seater cabriolet.
CONSTRUCTION Steel-bodied, separate chassis/body.
ENGINE Rear-mounted, air-cooled flat four, 1584cc.
POWER OUTPUT 50 bhp at 4000 rpm.
TRANSMISSION Four-speed manual.
SUSPENSION *Front:* independent MacPherson strut; *Rear:* independent trailing arm and twin torsion bars.
BRAKES *Front:* disc; *Rear:* drums.
MAXIMUM SPEED 82.4 mph (133 km/h)
0–60 MPH (0–96 KM/H) 18 sec
A.F.C. 24–30 mpg

ONE-MODEL POLICY
The one-model policy that VW adopted in its early years was successful while Beetle sales soared, but by 1967 Fiat had overtaken VW as Europe's biggest car manufacturer. VW's new models had failed to displace the Beetle and it was not until 1974 that the Golf and Polo revived the company's fortunes.

ON ALL CABRIOLETS THE ENGINE BREATHES THROUGH SLOTS ON THE ENGINE COVER

THE WORLD BEATER

The VW Beetle is one bug they can't find a cure for. Hitler's vision of a "people's car" has become just that and more — the world car to beat all other contenders.

PRODUCED CONTINUOUSLY since 1945, every Beetle that rolls off the remaining Mexican and Brazilian production lines sets a new production record that is unlikely ever to be beaten. With production running as high as 1,000 a day, the Beetle is a 21-million-plus world beater.

But the Beetle had a long and painful birth. In the early 1930s, Hitler's vision for mass motoring began to take shape when he entrusted Dr. Ferdinand Porsche with the project.

1935 TATRA 77

Both Hitler and Porsche were influenced by the fabulous streamlined Czechoslovakian Tatras. Hitler, a keen automobile enthusiast, had ridden in Tatras on political tours of Czechoslovakia. He had often dined with Tatra designer Hans Ledwinka. After one of these dinner-table conversations Hitler is reported to have remark to Porsche, "This is t car for my roads." Of Ledwinka, Porsche was reported as saying "Well, sometimes I looked over his shoulder and

VOLKSWAGEN
Beetle Karmann

FRESH AIR
With the hood raised, the Karmann cabriolet is a bit claustrophobic, but it comes into its own as a timeless top down cruiser that is still a full four-seater.

CABRIOLETS LIKE THIS CALIFORNIA-REGISTERED CAR ARE A MAINSTAY OF SURFING CULTURE ALL OVER THE WORLD

KARMANN

COACHBUILDER
As well as the Beetle convertible, Karmann also buil the Type 1 VW Karmann-Ghia, a two-seater based on Beetle running gear.

MANY LATER DESIG CHANGES LIKE THE "ELEPHANT FOOTPRINT" REAR LIGHT CLUSTERS WERE DRIVEN BY US REGULATIO

CALIFORNIA
1RWL494

sometimes he looked over mine." There is also no doubt that the Beetle bore a marked resemblance to earlier Tatras, both in shape and concept. In fact, after the war a large out-of-court settlement was made to Tatra. Although the Tatra influenced the Beetle, it served as a departure point for a unique car, developed by Porsche and his team into a machine-age artifact. Some 630 or so Beetles had been made before hostilities disrupted production. Back then, Beetles were propaganda wagons, too, named KdF-Wagen, after the slogan of the Hitler Youth, "*Kraft durch Freude*," which

HITLER AND
FERDINAND PORSCHE

means strength through joy. When production resumed in 1945 the Beetle, now a more friendly Volkswagen, gathered an irresistible momentum, notching up 10,000 sales

in 1946, 100,000 by 1950 and a million by 1955. In 1972, it overtook the Model T Ford's production record of 15 million. Today, the amazing story of the world's most popular car is not yet over.

BEETLE PRODUCTION LINE

STATE OF PLAY

Although the Beetle is still in production, Karmann stopped making the elegant cabriolet in 1980. In 1994, combined daily Mexican-Brazilian Beetle production exceeded 1,000 on a good day.

REAR VISION WITH THE HOOD RAISED IS NOT MUCH BETTER THAN ON EARLY SPLIT-SCREEN AND OVAL-WINDOWED MODELS

FROM 1967, THICKER SO-CALLED EUROPA BUMPERS WERE FITTED

VOLKSWAGEN GOLF GTi

EVERY DECADE or so a really great car comes along. In the Seventies it was the Golf. Like the Beetle *(see pages 212–15)*, the Golf was a car designed to make deep inroads into world markets. Yet while the Beetle evolved into the perfect consumer product, the Golf was designed and planned to be one. The idea of a "hot" Golf was not part of the grand design. It came about almost accidentally, the brainchild of a group of enthusiastic VW engineers who worked weekends and evenings, impressing the management so much that it became an official project in May 1975.

Despite its extreme youth, the Golf GTi is as much a classic as any Ferrari. Its claim to fame is that it spawned a traffic jam of imitators and brought an affordable mix of performance, handling, and reliability to the mass-market buyer. Few other cars have penetrated the suburban psyche as deeply as the original VW Golf GTi.

INTERIOR
With its dark headlining and trim, the cockpit may be austere, but features like the golfball-shaped gear lever add a touch of humor.

ALUMINUM
Much admired cross-spoke BBS aluminum wheels were both factory and aftermarket options.

SIMPLE FRONT DESIGN
Factory spec Golfs were understated, with just a GTi label and a thin red stripe around the grille. Owners who wanted to show off would bolt on aftermarket front spoilers and twin headlight kits.

REAR VIEW
The Giugiaro-designed Mk I Golf was neat, roomy, and compact, admirably predicting the then burgeoning 1970s craze for hatchbacks.

Volkswagen Golf GTi

GTi suspension was lower and firmer than the standard Golf, with wider tires and wheels. Front disc brakes were ventilated along with a larger motor, but keeping standard drum brakes at the rear was a big mistake – early Golfs were very disinclined to stop.

SPECIFICATIONS

MODEL Volkswagen Golf GTi MkI (1976–83)
PRODUCTION 400,000
BODY STYLE All steel sedan
CONSTRUCTION All steel/ monocoque body.
ENGINE Four-cylinder 1588cc/1781cc.
POWER OUTPUT 110–112 bhp at 6100 rpm.
TRANSMISSION Four- or five-speed manual.
SUSPENSION *Front:* Independent; *Rear:* Semi-independent trailing arm.
BRAKES *Front:* disc; *Rear:* drum.
MAXIMUM SPEED 111 mph (179 km/h)
0–60 MPH (0–96 KM/H) 8.7 sec
0–100 MPH (0–161 KM/H) 18.2 sec
A.F.C. 29 mpg

WIPERS
Driver's windshield wiper had a small aerodynamic wing. The faster you went, the more wind pressure pushed the wiper down onto the glass.

ENGINE SUCCESS
Initially, only 5,000 GTis were to be built for racing homologation, but the silky smooth engine and poised handling meant that sales went crazy.

ENGINE
Easily capable of 150,000 miles (240,000 km) in its stride, the 1588cc four-cylinder power unit breathed through Bosch K-Jetronic fuel injection, pushing out 110 bhp. Later cars had five-speed gearbox and more willing 1781cc engines.

SPOILER
Standard Golfs had a tiny front spoiler. This larger after-market BBS add-on makes the car look lower and meaner.

VOLVO *P1800*

THERE HAS NEVER BEEN a Volvo like the P1800, for this was a one-time flight of fancy by the sober Swedes, who already had a reputation for building sensible sedans. As a sports car the P1800 certainly looked stunning. Every sensuous curve and lean line suggests athletic prowess. But under that sharp exterior were most of the mechanicals of the Volvo Amazon, a worthy workhorse sedan. Consequently, the P1800 was no road-burner; it just about had the edge on the MGB *(see page 175)*, but only in a straight line. Another competitor, the E-Type Jag *(see pages 140–43)*, was launched in 1961, the same year as the P1800 and at almost the same price, but there the comparison ends. The P1800 did have style, though, and its other virtues were pure Volvo – strength, durability, and reliability. These combined to create something quite singular in the sporting idiom – a practical sports car.

LUGGAGE
As you would expect, the sensible sports car has a decent-sized trunk, although the spare wheel lies flat on the trunk floor and takes up space

INTERIOR
The instrumentation has a real flight-deck feel; revs, oil pressure, and oil temperature are all displayed on a well laid-out dash. Although you are sitting low to the floor, the leather seats are comfortable.

JENSEN'S SIGNATURE
Early cars like this were built in Britain by Jensen, identified by Volvo label on rear pillar.

SUPPORTING ROLE
The P1800 is eternally typecast as the "Saint Volvo" after appearing alongside Roger Moore in the long running television series, *The Saint*. The producers actually wanted to use the "sexiest car of 1961", the E-Type Jag; Jaguar declined and Volvo leapt at the chance. Roger Moore drove a P1800 off screen for many years.

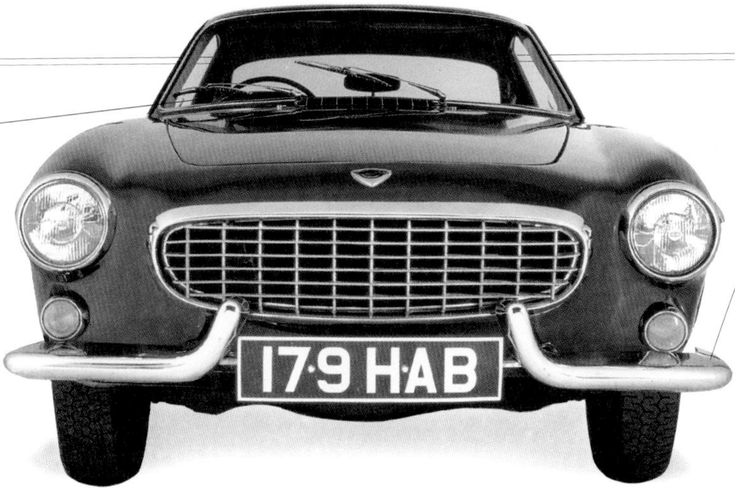

STEERING
Big, upright vertical wheel looks sporty, with twin spokes seemingly drilled for lightness.

COW HORNS
Attractive cow-horn bumpers became simpler, straight affairs in 1964.

TWO-PLUS-TWO COUPE
Space for two children only in the back, or one adult sitting sideways; rear seat folds down flat to increase load capacity.

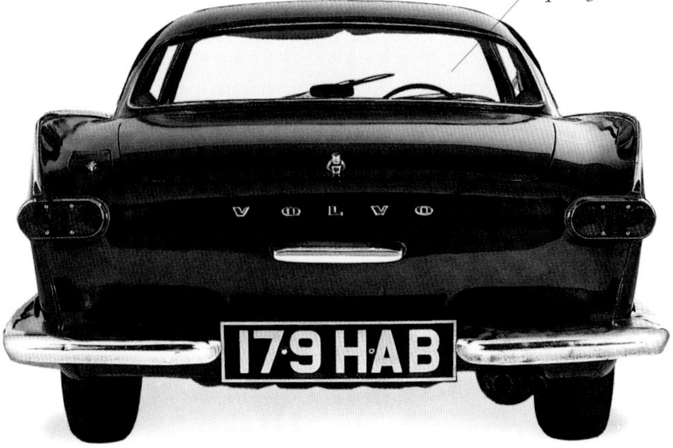

SPECIFICATIONS

- MODEL Volvo P1800 (1961–73)
- PRODUCTION 47,707 (all models)
- BODY STYLES Two-plus-two fixed-head coupe; sports wagon (P1800ES).
- CONSTRUCTION Unit steel body/chassis.
- ENGINE 1778cc straight four, overhead valves; 1985cc from 1968–73.
- POWER OUTPUT 100 bhp at 5,500 rpm (P1800); 124 bhp at 6,000 rpm (P1800E, P1800 ES).
- TRANSMISSION Four-speed manual with overdrive/optional automatic.
- SUSPENSION *Front:* independent coil-sprung with wishbones. *Rear:* rigid axle, coil-sprung, Panhard rod.
- BRAKES Front discs, rear drums.
- MAXIMUM SPEED 105 mph (169 km/h, P1800); 115 mph (P1800 E/ES).
- 0–60 MPH (0–96 KM/H) 9.7–13.2 sec
- 0–100 MPH (0–161 KM/H) 31.4–53 sec
- A.F.C. 20–25 mpg

VOLVO P1800

Official Volvo history credits the award-winning design of the P1800 to Frua of Italy, but it is not as simple as that. In 1957 Volvo approached Ghia to style a two-plus-two coupe and the assignment fell to chief designer Pietro Frua. However, he walked out halfway through, set up his own studio in Turin, and tendered his own proposals. The chosen design was actually created by young Swede Pelle Petterson, then a trainee at Ghia. The Italian influences are obvious in the final form.

ROBUST ENGINE
Early cars had 1778cc four-cylinder units with twin SU carburetors, as shown here; the 1985cc unit came later, followed by electronic fuel injection.

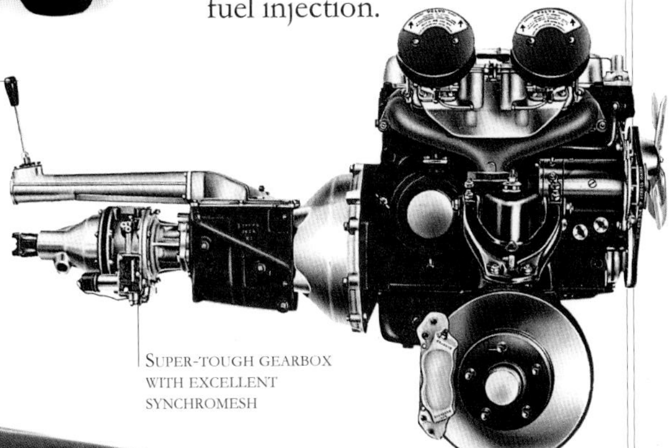

SHORT, STUBBY LEVER GAVE POSITIVE, SHARP CHANGES THAT FELT TRULY SPORTING

SUPER-TOUGH GEARBOX WITH EXCELLENT SYNCHROMESH

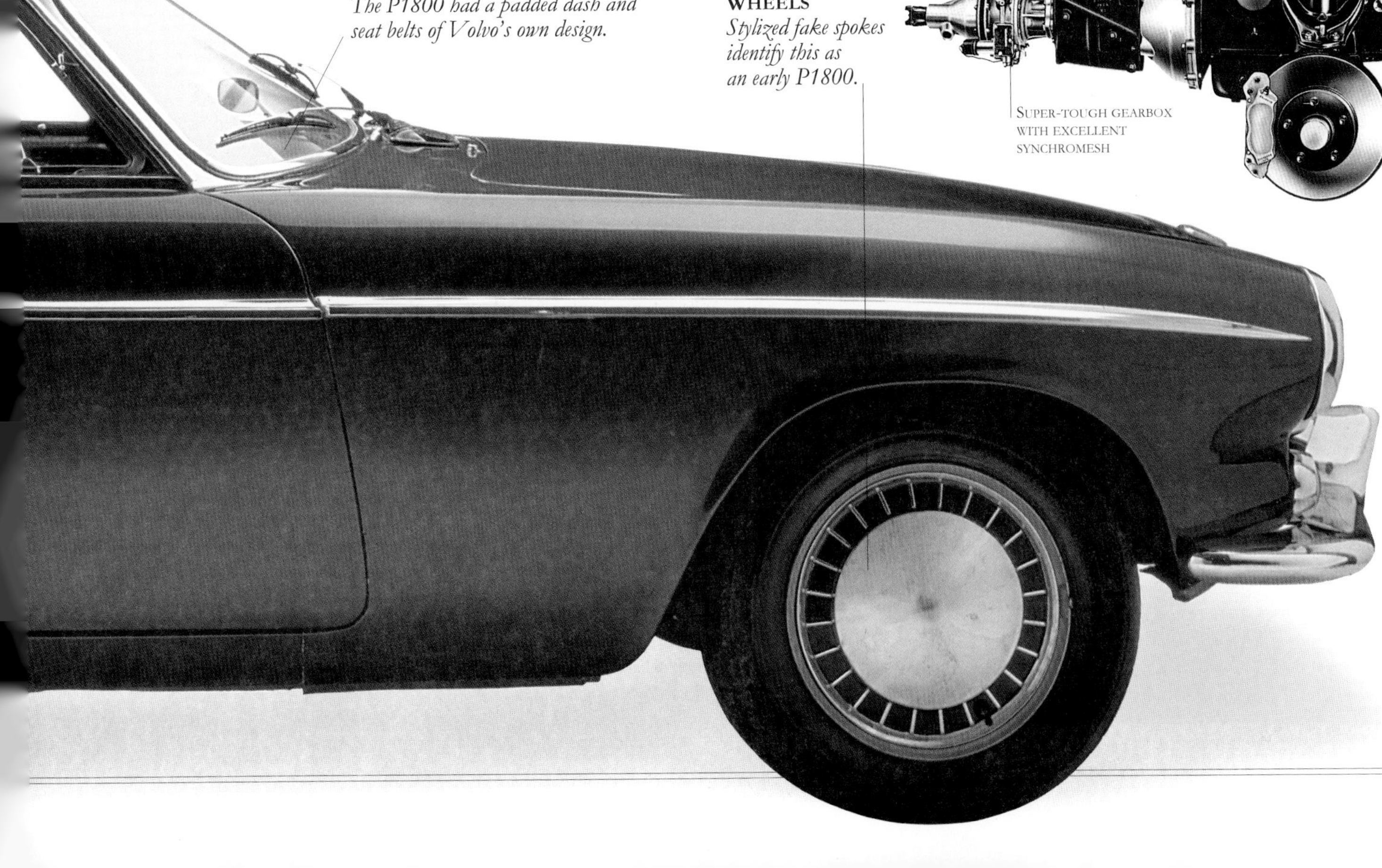

SAFETY MEASURES
The P1800 had a padded dash and seat belts of Volvo's own design.

WHEELS
Stylized fake spokes identify this as an early P1800.

THE INNOVATORS

From ground-breaking design to heroic failure, the following figures have all played their part in the development of some of the classic cars included in this book.

COLIN CHAPMAN *(1928–1982)*
Son of an innkeeper, engineering graduate Colin Chapman founded the Norfolk Lotus company which produced fiberglass pocket rockets like the trend-setting 1960s Elite and Elan. Lotus won the World Championship and Constructors Championship twice running.

ANDRÉ CITROËN *(1878–1935)*
Known as the French Mr. Ford, André Citroën started producing silent-meshing chevron-toothed gear wheels and went on to build the legendary 2CV, Traction Avant, and DS. An innovator rather than an accountant, his company was taken over by Michelin in 1934 and he died a year later.

JOHN DELOREAN *(1925–)*
John Zachary DeLorean headed a business empire funded by $500 million of other people's money. His Belfast-built gullwing stainless steel sports car failed along with his company, leaving a paper trail of skulduggery. He was indicted in a $24 million cocaine sting and, after a 63 day hearing, was acquitted.

HARLEY EARL *(1893–1969)*
Harley Earl designed the Cadillac Eldorado, Chevrolet Corvette and Buick Skylark and gave the American car its chrome pomp and ceremony. As General Motors' Chief of Design, he was responsible for the shape of 50 million cars. Few men have had such an influence on man-made objects.

HARRY FERGUSON *(1884–1960)*
Eccentric, irascible and rude, Ferguson built plows and tractors and sued Ford for $9.25 million for infringement of patents. His greatest achievement was the incorporation of his four-wheel drive system into the Jensen FF, the world's first successful production four-wheel drive car.

ENZO FERRARI *(1898–1988)*
Known as *Il Commendatore*, Enzo Ferrari gave his name to one of the most emotive cars in the world. As well as making extraordinary cars, he could pick skillful racing drivers, like Ascari,

HARLEY EARL ALONGSIDE A PROTOTYPE.

Fangio and Lauda. A silver-haired recluse in dark glasses, Ferrari was as passionate and charismatic as the cars he made.

DANTE GIACOSA *(1905–)*
One of Italy's most outstanding designers, Giacosa helped establish Fiat as an Italian national institution. Obsessed with the economies of scale, he came up with the Topolino of 1936, the 600 of 1955, and the 500 of 1957, the first very small cars to really be refined and the first to be free of the savage compromises of size and usability.

DONALD HEALEY *(1898–1988)*
Donald Healey, a sharply dressed bon vivant, designed the rally-winning Austin Healey in his attic. The Healey-Austin alliance spawned one of the most successful and charismatic British sports cars of the 1950s and 1960s. After designing the Jensen-Healey, he went into retirement and died in the late 1980s.

LEE IACOCCA *(1924–)*
Originator of the Ford Thunderbird, Iacocca was a marketing genius. He saw a huge vacuum in the American youth market of the 1960s and promptly plugged it with one of the most perfectly conceived consumer products ever, the Pony Mustang.

SIR ALEC ISSIGONIS *(1906–1988)*
Alexander Issigonis, a charming, eloquent and artistic man, conceived the million-selling Morris Minor and that miracle of automotive packaging, the Mini. His basic design philosophy was always

stiff structure, independent suspension, low weight and high torque. He was knighted in 1969.

SIR WILLIAM LYONS *(1901–1985)*
An elder statesman of the British auto industry, Sir William Lyons was an inspirational engineer who single-handedly masterminded the Jaguar phenomenon. From SS100 through XK120, E-Type and XJ6, Lyons was the creator of one of the most admired marques in the world which won Le Mans five years in a row.

HEINZ NORDHOFF *(1899–1968)*
An ex-Opel executive, Nordhoff took over the war-ravaged Wolfsburg Volkswagen factory in 1948. Under his direction the Volkswagen Beetle became the largest-selling single car in the world with an estimated quarter of a million people earning their living directly from VW.

FERDINAND PORSCHE *(1875–1952)*
Son of a tinsmith, Porsche was the most versatile car engineer in history, working for Mercedes, Volkswagen, Auto Union and Cisitalia as well as designing the World War II Tiger tank. Despite creating the Beetle, one of the most famous cars in the world, his association with Hitler caused him to be imprisoned for two years by the Allies after the war.

CARROLL SHELBY *(1925–)*
A smooth-talking Texan chicken farmer and race driver, Shelby was responsible for the wild AC Cobra and Shelby Mustang. Firmly believing that there was no substitute for cubic inches, he was a seminal figure in the Sixties' American muscle car movement.

INDEX

ACKNOWLEDGMENTS

DORLING KINDERSLEY WOULD LIKE TO THANK THE FOLLOWING:

Helen Stallion for picture research; Mick Hurrell for setting the editorial ball in motion; Maryann Rogers of production for overseeing the book in its early stages; Colette Ho for additional design assistance; Ken McMahon of Pelican Graphics for a superb electronic retouching job; Gerard Maclaughlan, Cangy Venables, Tracie Lee, Sharon Lucas and Annabel Morgan for additional editorial assistance; Daniel McCarthy for additional DTP assistance; Clive Webster and Miriam Sharland for additional picture research; Kilian and Alistair Konig of Konig Car Transport for vehicle transportation and invaluable help in locating cars; Steve at Trident Recovery; Jenny Glanville at Plough Studios; Ashley Straw for assisting Matthew Ward; Garry Ombler, Andy Brown and Sarah Ashun for assisting Andy Crawford; George Solomonides for help with locating images; Antony Pozner at Hendon Way Motors for helpful advice and supply of nine cars; Phillip Bush at Readers Digest, Australia for supervising the supply of the Holden; Derek Fisher; Bill Medcalf; Terry Newbury; John Orsler; Paul Osborn; Ben Pardon; Derek Pearson; Peter Rutt; Ian Smith; John Stark; Richard Stephenson; Kevin O' Rourke of Moto-technique; Rob Wells; Colin Murphy; Bill McGarth; Ian Shipp; Jeff Moyes of AFN Ltd; Rosie Good of the TR Owners Club; Bob and Ricky from D.J. Motors; Acorn Studios PLC; Straight Eight Ltd; Action Vehicles of Shepperton Film Studios and John Weeks of Europlate for number plate assistance; and Peter Maloney for compiling the index. Ron Stobbart for jacket design.

DORLING KINDERSLEY WOULD LIKE TO THANK THE FOLLOWING FOR ALLOWING THEIR CARS TO BE PHOTOGRAPHED:

Page 20 courtesy of Anthony Morpeth; p. 22 A J Pozner (Hendon Way Motors); p. 24 Louis Davidson; p. 26 Richard Norris; p. 28 Brian Smail; p. 30 Desmond J Smail; p. 32 David and Jon Maughan; p. 36 restored and owned by Julian Aubanel; p. 38 courtesy of Austin-Healey Associates Ltd, Beech Cottage, North Looe, Reigate Road, Ewell, Surrey, KT17 3DH; p. 40 Tom Turkington (Hendon Way Motors); p. 42 courtesy of Mr Willem van Aalst; p. 46 A J Pozner (Hendon Way Motors); p. 50 Terence P J Halliday; p. 52 L & C BMW Tunbridge Wells; p. 54 "57th Heaven" Steve West's 1957 Buick Roadmaster; p. 56 Stewart Homan, Dream Cars; p. 58 Garry Darby, American 50's Car Hire; p. 62 Benjamin Pollard of the Classic Corvette Club UK (vehicle preparation courtesy of Corvette specialists D.A.R.T Services, Kent, UK); p. 66 car owned and restored by Bill Leonard; p. 68 on loan from Le Tout Petit Musée/Nick Thompson, director Sussex 2CV Ltd; p. 70, 72 courtesy Classic Restorations; p. 76 Derek E J Fisher; p. 78 Daimler SP 250 owned by Claude Kearley; p. 82 Steve Gamage; p. 84 Kevin Kay; p. 88 D Howarth; p. 90 Lewis Strong; p. 92 Neil Crozier; p. 94 owned and supplied by Straight Eight Ltd (London); p. 104, 106, 108 A J Pozner (Hendon Way Motors); p. 105 Dr Ismond Rosen; p. 110 by kind permission of J A M Meyer; p. 112 Janet & Roger Westcott; p. 114 Stu Segal; p. 116 Teddy Turner Collection; p. 118 Stewart Homan, Dream Cars; p. 120 Max & Beverly Floyd; p. 124 Bell & Colvill PLC, Epsom Road, West Horsley, Surrey KT24 6DG, UK; p. 128 Gordon Keeble by kind permission of Charles Giles; p. 132 David Selby; p. 134 Jeff Hine; p. 136 c/o Hendon Way Motors; p. 140 owner Phil Hester; p. 144 John F Edwins; p. 146 privately owned; p. 148 A R J Dyas; p. 150 courtesy of Ian Fraser, restoration Omicron Engineering, Norwich; p. 152 courtesy of Martin Cliff; p. 154 Geoff Tompkins; p. 158 owner Phillip Collier, rebuild by Daytune; p. 160 Alexander Fyshe; p. 162 Edwin J Faulkner; p. 164 Irene Turner; p. 170 Mrs Joan Williams; p. 172 courtesy of Chris Alderson; p. 174 John Venables; p. 175 John Watson, Abingdon-on-Thames; p. 176 Martin Garvey; p. 178 E.J. Warrilow saved this car from the scrapyard in 1974; restored by the owner in 1990, maintaining all original panels and mechanics; winner of many concourse trophies; p. 182 NSU Ro80 1972 David Hall; p. 183 Panhard PL17 owned by Anthony T C Bond, Oxfordshire, editor of "Panoramique" (Panhard Club newsletter); p. 184 Nick O'Hara; p. 186 Alan Tansley; p. 188 owner Roger Wait, Backwell, Bristol; p. 190 courtesy of Peter Rutt; p. 192 owner Mr P G K Lloyd; p. 194 c/o Hendon Way Motors; p. 196 Richard Tyzack's historic rally Alpine; p. 198 owned by Ian Shanks of Northamptonshire; p. 202 David C Baughan; p. 204 Julie A Lambert (formerly Julie A Goldbert); p. 206 Peter Matthews; p. 207 Lord Raynham of Norfolk; p. 208 E A W Holden; p. 210 Brian Burgess; p. 212 Nick Hughes & Tim Smith; p. 216 Roy E Craig; p. 218 Kevin Price, Volvo Enthusiasts' Club.

PHOTOGRAPHIC CREDITS

t= top b= bottom c= center l= left r= right a= above

All photography by Andy Crawford and Matthew Ward except:
Linton Gardiner: pp. 64–65, 114–115
National Motor Museum: pp. 11t, 13b, 167c, b
Nick Goodall: pp. 15br, 22cr, 38c, 79tl, tr, 118r, 128t, 132t, 135tc, 166tl, tr, 167t, cr, 168cr, 180t, 181tr, 185c, 190tr, 195cr, 206cr, 208cr, 222–23, 224
Clive Kane: 130–31

PICTURE CREDITS

AC Cars: 8t. Adams Picture Library: 56tr. Advertising Archives: 8b; 54cl; 118tr; 135tr; 200tr, b; 223t. Aerospace Publishing: 3; 48tl, tr, cl, cr; 48–49; 49t, cl, cr; 76tr, cr; 76–77; 77tl, tr, cl, crb; 90tl, tr, cl, cr; 90–91; 91t, cr, crb, 94cl, cr; 94–95; 95t, cl, cr, crb; 96c, b; 97b; 102t, cl, crb; 103tl, tr, c, b; 138t, 138tl, ca, cb; 138–139; 139tr, cl, cr; 145t, cra, clb, crb, b; 148c; 148tr; 148–149; 149tl, tr, cl, cr; 166cl; 167cla, crb; 168b; 169b; 207cl, cr, b. Allsport: 2; 123tr; Allsport/Mike Pavell: 192tr. Art Directors: 137cb. Autosport Photographic 35tr; Doug Baird: 40cl, b. Bell & Colvill 125tl; BMW : 50tr; 52tr. British Film Institute: *Back to the Future*/Copyright © by Universal City Studios, Inc. Courtesy of MCA Publishing Rights, a Division of MCA Inc. All Rights Reserved 88tr. Neill Bruce: 9t; 20bl; 26cr; 30tr; 44t; 66tr; 70tl; 79t; 106tr; 107crb; 110tr; 142tl; 176tr; 208t; 224b. Neill Bruce/Peter Roberts Collection 14t; 37br; 38cr; 45t; 60c; 61tl, c; 70tl; 80t; 86t; 87tl; 168tl; 169tl, tr; 215tr. *Classic and Sportscar*: 141clb; 155c. Ford Motor Company: 114cb; 127cr. General Motors/Pontiac Division: 190tr. Gordon Keeble Cars: 128t. Ronald Grant Archive: *The Living Daylights*/Danjaq 31cr; *Pink Cadillac*/Malpaso 59cl; *Bullit*/Warner Brothers Pictures 92tr; *Smokey and the Bandit*/Raspar 188tr. Haymarket Publishing: 12c; 28tr; 94tr. David Hendley: 177cr. Eddy Holden: 208clb. Hulton Deutsch Collection: 81t; 97t; 215tl; 220tr. Jaguar Cars: 143cr. LAT Photographic: 126tr. Ludvigsen Library: 42c; 85tr; 123tc; 140ct; 202c; 214t. Mathewson Bull: 213tr. Mercedes Benz: 166tl, tr; 167t, cr; 168cr; 222b. Don Morley: 35tl; 87tr; 162tr. National Motor Museum/Motoring Picture Library: 9b; 22tr; 26tr; 47c; 50cr; 58tr; 62bl; 64bl; 70tr; 73tl, crb; 79cl; 80c; 81c; 96t, 98tr, cr; 99cra; 101tl; 104cra; 113cr; 114bl; 121ct; 122tr; 123tl; 126c; 136cl; 139tl; 152tr; 156t; 166–167; 167cl; 181tl; 182cra; 184tr; 192cr; 194ca; 204tr; 210tr, cra. Peugeot: 185ca; 221b; Phillip Porter: 142tr. Popperfoto :124cl. Quadrant Picture Library: 10t; 11b; 12t; 17b; 18b; 26cl; 34t; 62tr; 74t; 75t; 76cl; 91cl; 112tr; 127c; 140tr; 143tl; 157tl, tr; 182 cla; 198tr, cr; 208cra; 212tl, tr. Readers Digest: 130tl, tr, ct, cl, cr; 131tl, tc, ca, cb, b. Rex Features: 100t; 101tr; 168tr; 201tr. Triumph: 15br; 208crb. Richard Tyzack: 196c. Volvo UK Ltd: 218cr; 219cb. Matthew Ward: 10b; 12b.

NOTE
Every effort has been made to trace the copyright holders. Dorling Kindersley apologizes for any unintentional omissions and would be pleased, in such cases, to add an acknowledgment in future editions.

Classic
AMERICAN
Cars

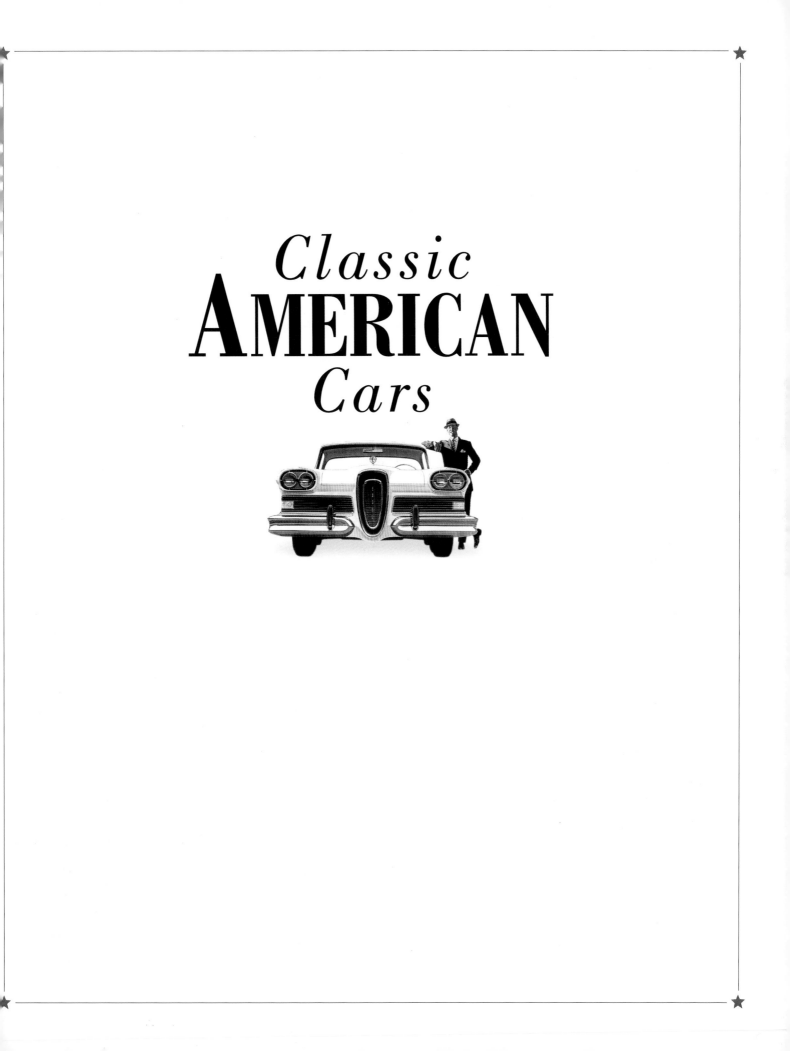

QUENTIN WILLSON

Classic AMERICAN *Cars*

Photography by
Matthew Ward

[DK]

DK PUBLISHING, INC.

A DK PUBLISHING BOOK

PROJECT EDITOR
PHIL HUNT
ART EDITOR
KEVIN RYAN
EDITOR
JILL FORNARY
DESIGNER
CLARE DRISCOLL
MANAGING EDITOR
FRANCIS RITTER
MANAGING ART EDITOR
DEREK COOMBES
DTP DESIGNER
SONIA CHARBONNIER
PICTURE RESEARCHER
SAM RUSTON
PRODUCTION CONTROLLERS
RUTH CHARLTON, ROSALIND PRIESTLEY
US EDITOR
MARY SUTHERLAND

First American Edition, 1997
2 4 6 8 10 9 7 5 3 1

Published in the United States by DK Publishing Inc.,
95 Madison Avenue, New York, New York 10016

Visit us on the World Wide Web at
http://www.dk.com

Copyright © 1997 Dorling Kindersley Limited, London

Text copyright © 1997 Quentin Willson

Library of Congress Cataloging-in-Publication Data

Willson, Quentin.
Classic American Cars / by Quentin Willson. -- 1st American ed.
p. cm.
Includes index.

1. Automobiles--United States.   I. Title.
TL23.W583 1997   97-16172
629.222 ' 0973--dc21   CIP

Color reproduction by Colourscan, Singapore
Printed and bound in Hong Kong

NOTE ON SPECIFICATION BOXES
Every effort has been made to ensure that the information
supplied in the specification boxes is accurate. Unless otherwise indicated,
all figures pertain to the actual model in the specification box.
A.F.C. is an abbreviation for average fuel consumption.

CONTENTS

FOREWORD
J.D. Power

AMERICAN CARS HAVE TAKEN A BAD RAP over the past half century. Yet, for all the criticisms, it's fair to say that the American motor industry brought us the things we love most about the automobile.

American cars gave us electrically adjustable seats, windows, and mirrors, automatic transmission, air-conditioning, two-tone paint, and Wonder Bar radios. More recently, they've provided us with remote buttons to lock and unlock the doors, airbags, and catalytic converters. They might not be highly regarded for engine efficiency, pin-sharp handling, or stunning looks, but, when it comes to delivering what customers want in an easy and reliable package, American cars have always led the world.

Aficionados may balk at accepting the cardinal role that US iron has played in the development of today's reliable, safe, comfortable, and convenient machines, but they should read this book with an open mind. Many of the innovative automotive features we take for granted originated in American cars. A technological history that started back in 1911 with the development of the electric starter fast-forwards through this book's pages to today's symbol of convenience – the cup holder.

Now is the perfect time, as we near the millennium, to look back at the evolution of America and her cars and reflect on her contribution to the advancement and refinement of the automobile. Quentin Willson's nostalgic look at the American classic car is for most of us a delicious and delightful trip back to a world that will never be the same again. Enjoy the ride.

J.D. POWER III
CHAIRMAN OF J.D. POWER ASSOCIATES

AUTHOR'S PREFACE

T WAS THE LONG, HOT SUMMER of '69 that did it. I was a wide-eyed English 11-year-old at grade school in a small town 50 miles outside of Chicago. Dad was doing a sabbatical year lecturing at the local University, and I was having the time of my life driving in American cars.

I'd fallen in with a kid called Nicky, whose father owned the biggest GM dealership in Illinois. Their vast clapboard house sat in 10 acres with a huge yard strewn with Pop's trade-ins. There'd be lines of cast-off 'Cudas, Firebirds, Caddys, and Continentals, and each with the keys temptingly hidden under the sun visor. Nicky was the sort of kid my parents had spent months warning me against, which is why I liked him on sight. He could tell a 260 V8 from a 289 with his back turned, and he'd spend hours explaining about hemi-heads and Positraction. I was a mightily impressed 11-year-old.

And that year was what really got me into cars. Every day after school I'd cycle up to Nicky's place and we'd borrow a Fairlane, a Mustang, or an Eldorado and practice power slides and handbrake turns. Nobody wanted old muscle cars, and every week Nicky's Dad would bring home yet another load of heavy metal. Boss Mustangs, Coronet Hemis, Chevelle SSs, Pontiac GTOs: we drove them all. I owe Nicky a big debt of gratitude. He showed a shy English kid in short pants two of the wildest things in life: America and American cars.

This book is a tribute to those formative years, an homage to all those wicked wheels. It's not meant to be the definitive list of best or worst, rather a nostalgic trawl through some of the most captivating and compelling cars ever.

Quentin Willson

THE MOST INFLUENTIAL CARS IN THE WORLD

1951 CHRYSLER IMPERIAL

FOR THE BEST PART OF THREE decades the world has snickered up its sleeve at American cars. To listen to the torrent of ridicule, you'd think Detroit's offerings of the Forties, Fifties, and Sixties were designed by madmen on their way to the asylum. The British sneered at their unseemly girth, weight, and size; the Germans mocked Motown's build quality; and the Italians would rather have walked than commit stylistic suicide behind the wheel of a Cadillac Eldorado. Even some Americans joined the chorus of dissenters. John Keats in *The Insolent Chariots* remarked with rancor that "American automobiles are not reliable machines for reasonable men, but illusory symbols of sex, speed, wealth, and power for daydreaming nitwits." Only the French, bless them, actually reckoned a Pontiac Parisienne was glamorous enough for posing on the Périphérique. But were American motor cars as dire as the pundits said? Were they really that ridiculous?

Perhaps jealousy is the word we're looking for. America's prosperity

IKE ARRIVES IN STYLE
In November 1952, an impressed world watched Dwight Eisenhower celebrate his election to the presidency of the most powerful nation on earth in a shining Lincoln Capri Convertible the size of a small house.

in the postwar years was all spangled exuberance and cheerful opulence. While Europe trundled about in dumpy little gray-and-black boxes with all the charisma of church pews, Americans squealed around in glittering, pastel-colored rocketships. Europe was winding her windows down by hand, while Americans were operating not just their windows but their seats, trunk releases, and transmissions at the touch of a chromium-plated button. The nearest Europeans got to American cars was on the flickering screen. We envied all those lantern-jawed heroes who could one-hand huge Chevrolets around corners while smoking a cigarette and still manage to feign an expression of complete and utter boredom.

1949 CADILLAC SERIES 62
While Europe was filling in the bullet holes and struggling to rebuild her devastated cities with money borrowed from America, Americans were tooling around in dreamboats like the '49 Cadillac.

ower-sliding never looked so easy or so much fun.
he cars we watched in the movies seemed to be
uilt on the same grand scale as the stars who drove
em and, if we'd been honest, we would have cut
ff bits of our anatomy just to sit in the passenger
eat. Americans were living the good life through
eir cars, and Europe's resentment was nothing
ore than old-fashioned envy.

Keeping the Customer Satisfied

retrospect, the cars that Detroit rolled out in the
ree decades after World War II were shining stars
f the world's automotive firmament. This was the
ost imaginative and fertile period of car design
ver, when every stylistic sleight of hand, and then
ome, was used in the deepest and most inventive
xamination of the consumer psyche by any
dustry in the history of the world. Simply put,
merican automobiles defined the vernacular of
he modern motor car. They not only gave us
anoramic windscreens, two-tone paint, and
hitewalls but also those little touches that mean
o much, like cruise controls, air-conditioning,
M/FM radios, power windows and
eats, not to mention automatic
ansmission and power steering.

In 1959, the buyer of a
hevrolet Impala was faced
vith an embarrassment of
iches of factory and dealer-
nstalled optional equipment.

HARLEY J. EARL
1893–1969

HARLEY EARL, GM's chief stylist, was the man who shaped millions of American cars. "You design a car so that every time you get in it's a relief – you have a little vacation for a while." The first motor mandarin to really understand that consumers don't buy cars with their heads but their trousers, Harley Earl invented automotive attitude.

In 1956, Earl headed GM's state-of-the-art $125 million Tech Center and led a styling team of 1,200 people. Every year they took automotive design over the edge and back again.

In the chain of command, Earl was somewhere between God and

HARLEY J. EARL

President, without the latter's limitations. GM's corporate culture elevated stylists over engineers, who were relegated to the role of rude mechanics employed to turn Earl's whims of steel into production realities. In his tenure at GM, Harley Earl took the solemnity out of the American car and replaced it with a chromium smile.

EARL'S PROTOTYPE LE SABRE SHOW CAR BOASTED A CONVERTIBLE TOP THAT CLOSED AUTOMATICALLY WHEN IT SENSED RAIN

1954 CHEVROLET CORVETTE
The '54 drastic plastic Corvette is a perfect example of Earl's stylistic audacity. He knew there was a whole raft of buyers out there bursting for some automotive bravado, so he layered on the charisma with a trowel.

The order form listed 78 different accessory choices ranging from a Super Turbo-Thrust V8, Positraction rear axle, and Turboglide automatic transmission, through power steering, brakes, windows, and seats, to electric rear-tailgate glass on station wagons. The roster of comfort and vanity options offered was even longer. Consumers could enrich their lives with de luxe steering wheels, shaded rear windows, air-foam seat cushions, tri-volume horns, simulated wire-wheel covers, tissue dispensers, Magic-Aire heaters, tinted Soft Ray glass, and Strato-Rest headrests. The culture of convenience was running riot.

By the time the Mustang appeared in mid-'64, Ford had turned the option list into an arcane art form. Not only could you choose from a whole hill of engines, transmissions, and axles but there were now specially named generic option groups to

THE RISE OF THE MOTORING PRESS
By the mid-Fifties, the public was obsessed with automobile styling, and the shape of cars to come was a national gambit. The newsstands groaned with auto magazines, and GM was spending $162 million a year on advertising to persuade consumers to debauch themselves with tail fins.

consider. The GT Equipment Group, the Handling Package, the Rally Pack, the Visibility Group, and the Interior Decor Group were all part of the pony car building-block philosophy: give buyers a sexy-looking car as a platform and allow them to customize it to their own individual specifications. Not for nothing did the Ford ads trumpet "Mustang – Designed To Be Designed By You." With so many options available, the San Jose factory could literally churn out an entire year's Mustang production without any two cars ever being exactly the same.

Power to the People

Transatlantic metal gave the world much more than just chrome and creature comforts. American cars also gave us fun in the form of the ever-higher numbers at the tips of their speedometer needles. Detroit's horsepower gallop began in '51 when Chrysler let loose its 180 bhp Fire-Dome V8.

RAYMOND LOEWY
1893–1987

RAYMOND LOEWY DESIGNS REPRESENT the articulation of plenty that hallmarks postwar America. He shaped everything from pencil sharpeners, Studebakers, the interior of Skylab, and Coca-Cola dispensing-machines to the inside of JFK's official jet, Air Force One.

Many of Loewy's creations have become foundation stones of modern design; the Studebaker Avanti of '63, the Coldspot refrigerator, the Greyhound Scenicruiser bus, and the Hallicrafter radio all illustrate his key contribution to American design. His motoring credits include the Studebaker Commander, Starliner, Golden Hawk, and Champion. A maverick to the last, he reckoned design was "far too important to be left in the careless hands of company men in suits." He will be remembered as one of the prime architects of the American Dream.

LOEWY DESIGNED COCA-COLA DISPENSER

LOEWY AND HIS FAMILY POSE BY THE SENSATIONAL AVANTI

THE '57 STUDEBAKER GOLDEN HAWK

MOTORAMA
GM's Motoramas were the wildest car shows ever conceived. Regularly pulling up to two million visitors, there were dancers, actors, musical stage shows, and amazing displays of postwar technical prowess. From 1949 to 1961, they showcased new products and were GM's most powerful weapon in the marketing war.

FUTURISTIC CHASSIS
The gadget-laden '57 Mercury Turnpike Cruiser was hailed as "space age design for earth travel." Apart from a chassis like the Brooklyn Bridge, it had Air Cushion suspension and push-button automatic transmission.

This was followed by Chevy's small-block V8 of '55. Five years later, the Chrysler 300F was stampeding out 400 bhp, and by '63 a Hi-Po T-Bird was displacing 427 cubes and red-lining the dynamometer at a jaw-dropping 425 bhp. Then in '66 Chrysler went ballistic with their 426 Hemi, firing the first serious salvo of the performance war that was to send horsepower ratings spiraling through the stratosphere. The heat had been turned up to the max, and by the late sixties a super-warm Chevy Chevelle SS was pumping out a thundering 450 bhp.

Those were the days when anyone with enough bucks could saunter into their local showroom, check all the right boxes on the options list, and find themselves master of absolutely apocalyptic horsepower. They were mass-produced cars that, in a straight line, could run bumper-to-bumper with handcrafted Ferraris, Jaguars, and Aston Martins. Today those performance figures are impressive enough, but back then they were heart-stoppingly quick. Even the monikers were enough to hurry the hormones. Eliminator, Marauder, Cougar, Cyclone, Thunderbolt, and Charger were machines that could accelerate to 60 in the time it took to say their

names. The world's greatest democracy really did offer power to the people, and it came in the wrapping of the muscle car. Never had so much heave been available to so many for so little.

Behind a Painted Smile

Automotive historians may claim that Europe was more technically audacious with its unitary bodies, radial-ply tires, and four-wheel drive. Certainly the British pioneered disc brakes and fuel injection, the Germans perfected millimetrically precise build quality, and the Italians made V12 engines almost reliable. But Detroit could come up with plenty of wizardry too. Look at some of the show cars, particularly from GM's Motoramas, and you'll see that innovation was not only being actively pursued, it was in rude health. These cars were plugged up like the Pentagon, with transistorized electrical systems, magnesium bodies, automatic transaxles, special tiny engines to drive accessories, TVs instead of rearview mirrors, and even gas turbine engines. Harley Earl's 1951 Le Sabre, named after the F-86 jet fighter, stood no higher than a mailbox, had built-in automatic jacks for changing wheels, and a power-operated convertible top that automatically raised when it sensed rain on the console.

1957 CADILLAC COUPE DE VILLE
The '57 Coupe de Ville came with air-conditioning as standard. In Britain, the amount of buildings with air-con could be counted on the fingers of one hand.

POWER BRAKES
Stopping a Detroit dinosaur took some effort, and by the mid-Fifties most cars had power drum brakes as an option. As the picture shows, power-assisted brakes were meant to help "the lady."

POWER WINDOWS
Electric windows appeared in the late Forties and, by 1955, were de rigueur. This was an age when almost every minor control was designed to be activated by a dainty finger.

MITCHELL'S CLASSIC BUICK RIVIERA

BILL MITCHELL
b.1912

BILL MITCHELL TOOK OVER as Vice-President of GM's styling division after Harley Earl retired in 1959. He claimed that to be a real car designer you had to have "gasoline in your veins." Under Earl he designed the 1938 Cadillac 60 Special, but went on to oversee the Chevrolet Corvair of 1960, the Buick Riviera of '63, the split-window Corvette Sting Ray of '63, the Oldsmobile Toronado of '66, and the Chevrolet Camaro of '67. He admired clean, sculptured lines and rejected the bosomy, rounded shapes favored by Earl.

In the 1970s he bemoaned the blandness of Detroit's offerings. "They all look alike. I have to read the goddam badges to know what they are." After his retirement, Mitchell still rode a Yamaha 1000 motorbike and enjoyed a much modified Pontiac Trans Am powered by a Ferrari Daytona engine.

MITCHELL WITH HIS MAKO SHARK SHOW CAR, WHICH WAS SAID TO BE HIS ALL-TIME FAVORITE DESIGN

Mercedes, 47 years later, has just gotten around to using rain sensors to actuate the windshield wipers on their E-Class range.

In 1959, GM touted its Firebird III at the New York and Boston Motorama shows. Billed as "Imagination In Motion," it had an ultrasonic key that you aimed at the door, a cockpit pre-heater, a formed plastic interior, and the steering wheel, transmission lever, brake, and throttle were all worked from a single joystick control. The Whirlfire GT 305 regenerative gas turbine unit developed 220 bhp through a differential-mounted gearbox and De Dion transaxle. Braking was courtesy of an aluminum drum antilock system with a grade retarder on the differential. This was wildly futuristic gadgetry that in 1959 must have seemed as if it came straight out of the pages of *Buck Rogers and the Forgotten Planet*. Behind the revolving stage shows and the pageantry, Motoramas showed America and the rest of the world that the white-coated eggheads in GM's technical labs were slipstreaming a vapor-trail into the future. Against Detroit's backdrop of prodigious innovation, the European motor industry's efforts looked almost tame.

DRIVE-IN MOVIES
In 1955, Detroit rolled out eight million new cars, and teenagers with after-school jobs were a perfect target market. The automobile allowed youth to escape the middle-aged morality of Main Street America and savor the romance and passion of the drive-in.

Sultans of Style

But the Big Three auto manufacturers – GM, Chrysler, and Ford – knew that technical features alone wouldn't move metal. What buyers wanted was street-strutting style, and nobody supplied dash and flash like Uncle Sam. The postwar American Dream was founded on the concept of "populuxe," or luxury for all. By the late '50s, the average Chevrolet or Buick was groaning under the weight of 44 lb (20 kg) of twinkling chrome and luxury add-ons. In 1949, Harley Earl's finny Cadillac was considered the last word. By '55, its styling motifs had percolated to even the humblest Chevy. Fins, sweepspears, and the two front-end protuberances known as Dagmars gave customers an extra receipt for their money, and sales of new cars in '55 totalled $65 billion, or 25 percent of the Gross National Product. Americans were willing, even grateful, to spend vast amounts of money on two-and-a-half tons of candy-pink space rocket simply because it transported them into another world.

GLIMPSE OF THE FUTURE
The Firebird II, III, and XP-21 were all GM show cars displayed at the Motorama exhibitions of the Fifties. Incredibly futuristic, they boasted technical wizardry like automatic steering sensors and gas turbine engines.

SPACE CULTURE
Space-age styling metaphors were plastered over the Fifties American car. Speed, rocket ships, and outer space became the national narcotic.

Despite what the sceptics would have us believe and behind all that gratuitous glitz were some of the world's most significant cars. You simply can't deny the huge influence of creations like the Mustang, Corvette, Jeep, GTO, and Thunderbird. They were pioneering designs that changed the shape and styling of cars forever. And every last one of them was conceived and built in America. Europeans may have been envious, but they were quick enough to mimic what they saw. By the Sixties, the British had two-tone Vauxhall Crestas, finned Zephyrs and Zodiacs, sweepspears on Sunbeam Rapiers, and quad headlights on Rolls-Royces. The French pasted Detroit's styling cues onto the Simca Aronde, Vedette, and Facel Vega, and even the Germans couldn't claim they weren't occasionally inspired. In 1961, Mercedes launched their four-door 190 sedan. Teutonic perfection incarnate maybe, but what were those two weird little flourishes on the rear? Dainty little tail fins. The world's oldest car maker had publicly admitted that when it came to style, Detroit

had taught all there was to know. The influence of America's auto stylists was incredibly far-reaching, and there wasn't a car company in the world that didn't cull something from Motown's awesome aesthetic arsenal.

Britain might have been first with the sports car and Italy the coupe, but America came up with machines that could literally be all things to all men. Reacting exactly to what the market wanted, Detroit fielded the personality car. Thunderbirds, Rivieras, Cougars, Barracudas, Camaros, and Firebirds were brilliant niche products that offered consumers cars that were distinctive and separate. One ad for the Dodge Challenger promised "a car you buy when you don't want to be like everyone else." And by offering a raft of options longer than the Gettysburg Address, Dodge was telling the truth.

1957 DODGE CUSTOM ROYAL
Dodge's '57 model range had a lowered silhouette, "Swept Wing" styling, and taillights that looked like jet-engine afterburners. The F-86 Sabre jet fighter in the background was meant to reinforce the tenuous relationship between car and plane.

sculptors in steel and visionaries driven from within. One contemporary said of Earl: "He was like a Roman Emperor in Constantinople. Nobody in the history of industry ever had such an incredible effect over man-made objects like Earl." Raymond Loewy, creator of the Studebaker Avanti, also designed streamlined trains and the Lucky Strike cigarette pack. Loewy once said, "Pride, social consciousness, and the desire to serve mankind better are the only inspirations a designer needs." History will rank luminaries like these as the grand masters of design who between them changed the face of 20th-century consumer culture irreversibly. They gave the American car its dazzle and swagger; they lowered, lengthened, and widened it, gave it half a hundred stylistic metaphors more glass than a greenhouse, and pushed the envelope of design to its absolute limit. They gave the automobile optimism and hope. They made it a machine that promised unlimited possibilities.

Bucket seats, mag wheels, center consoles, and various instrument packs all gave buyers more choice than there were atoms in the universe. The Ford Mustang was the world's fastest-selling car, not because it was dynamically special but because its appeal was wider than that of any other car before or since. And Motown's trick of piling on the personality undeniably influenced everything from the Ford Cortina to the BMW 3-Series. The modern cult of auto individuality began in the US.

Gurus of Glitz

One reason why American cars of the period were so remarkably influential was the quality of their designers. Men like Harley Earl, Raymond Loewy, Lee Iacocca, Bill Mitchell, and Virgil Exner were

THE ROLE OF VOLKSWAGEN
Detroit ignored the VW Beetle, seeing it as a car for cranks. Ford was even offered the Volkswagen factory free of charge but declined because Henry Ford II called the car "a little shit box." By '57, 79,000 Beetles were imported into the US, accelerating the rise of economy compacts.

NEW TRENDS
By 1964, Detroit was selling distinction and individuality. Chrome and tail fins were out while bucket seats, center consoles, and floor-shifters were in. The lantern-jawed '64 Pontiac Bonneville was sold on elegance and sophistication.

GLAMOUR AT THE TOP
The baby boomers of the Sixties bought US iron in vast numbers. John and Jackie Kennedy personified the new-age Camelot dynasty and swept around in glamorous Lincoln Continental Convertibles. With a matinee idol as President, life took on the excitement of a Hollywood movie.

LEE A. IACOCCA
b.1925

IACOCCA'S ORIGINAL PONY LOGO

LEE IACOCCA IS WIDELY regarded as the father of the greatest automotive success in postwar history, the Ford Mustang. As Ford's precocious General Manager in 1961, the 36-year-old Iacocca came up with the idea of a sporty compact to woo the burgeoning youth market. He reasoned that if the performance of a car like the Corvette could be stuffed into an affordable car for the masses, it would sell like hotcakes. And it did.

The Mustang remains the world's fastest-selling car; by its first birthday, it had racked up nearly half a million sales. It was the first of the pony cars, a breed of two-door personal coupes that went on to wow America for the best part of 20 years. Without Iacocca's vision, determination, and tenacity, one of the world's most memorable cars might well have remained just a doodle on the back of an envelope.

IACOCCA IS SEEN AS THE "FATHER" OF THE MUSTANG

And America's preoccupation with how things looked wasn't just self-obsessed narcissism, it helped keep the machinery of mass consumption turning. Good design was the American Way and a million miles from Europe's puritanical austerity of line. This was the great liberal phase of American styling, and it flourished because it was essential to the nation's economic health. Yearly model changes, or what Harley Earl chose to call "dynamic obsolescence," guaranteed not only an annual orgy of buying but also the less affluent could purchase last year's cast-offs at used-car prices. The designer anticipated the public's desires and kept his creations just an arm's length away, so the buyer always had next year's model to look forward to, yet another dream to pursue.

Dreaming Out Loud

For three decades, Detroit fueled a massive metallic fantasy that Americans believed in and the rest of the world desired. And it was a fantasy engineered by a deliberate corporate policy of encouraging dreams. Detroit invented the "dream car" at a moment in American history when the future looked bright, exciting, and almost close enough to touch. American cars looked the way they did because that was the way America looked. Scholars who trawl through the social history of the United States could do worse than study her cars, because American automobiles tell us more about America's past than a whole library of history books ever could.

ORIGINAL MUSCLE
John DeLorean, Pontiac's Chief Engineer, shoe-horned the division's biggest V8 into the timid little Tempest, creating one of the first muscle cars, the Pontiac GTO. It was an instant hit with speed-thirsty youngsters.

After World War II, America didn't have a single bomb crater anywhere, and the '49 Roadmaster mirrored a population looking forward to a brave new world of plenty. The happy and handsome '55 Chevrolet Bel Air epitomized the confident consumption of the Fifties boom years, while the baroque '59 Cadillac revealed a nation so near to satiety that it had forgotten the itch of desire. By 1960, America was losing her arrogance, and the austere and anxious 1962 Chevy Corvair reflected a society in the grip of paranoia. While Vietnam and race riots raged, the belligerent Dodge Charger R/T of 1968 betrayed a country at war with itself. After the fat and glittery Fifties and Sixties dreamboats came the lean and hungry Chevrolet Vegas and Ford Pintos. And by the time the abstemious and severe Cadillac Seville debuted in 1975, the dream had evaporated completely. And that's maybe the most fascinating and compelling thing about watching American cars. They've always precisely mirrored the highs and lows of the American Way.

Uniquely American

The cynics should remember that while it's easy to snicker at machines that turned dreams into dollars, it's even easier to lose sight of the purity of vision, the genius, and the humanity that made Detroit's tremendous achievements possible. American cars may have been continually satirized for the vice of flamboyance, but it was exactly that florid styling that gave them their greatest virtue. It blessed them with a genuinely

GLAMOROUS AND FUN
This Chrysler 300X research car is bring tried out by the 1966 Miss World. Even though the extreme experimentation of the Fifties had gone, research projects still offered publicity for manufacturers in the Sixties.

hopeful, twinkling innocence. And it doesn't matter that all those strident Oldsmobiles, DeSotos, and Plymouths didn't obey European strictures of order and elegance. They had an infectious optimism and cheer that actually made Americans feel better about themselves and the nation they lived in; Detroit was selling a welcome distraction from heartbreak. As Virgil Exner once said, "A well-styled car will make a man feel better at the end of his journey than when he started." For 30 years the American automobile hasn't only entertained millions of Americans, it's given the rest of the world a unique glimpse behind the curtain of the American Dream. Motown's glory years may have gone, but they'll never be forgotten.

1966 FORD MUSTANG
This milestone car was born halfway through 1964 and continues to this day. If any car sums up the spirit of American auto manufacturing, it must be the Mustang. In automotive history no other car has flown from the showrooms faster than Ford's pony prodigy.

CLASSIC CAR GALLERY

The following sixty cars are a vivid memorial to America's most colorful decades. Quirky, ingenious, excessive, and built on the grand scale, nothing sums up America like her cars.

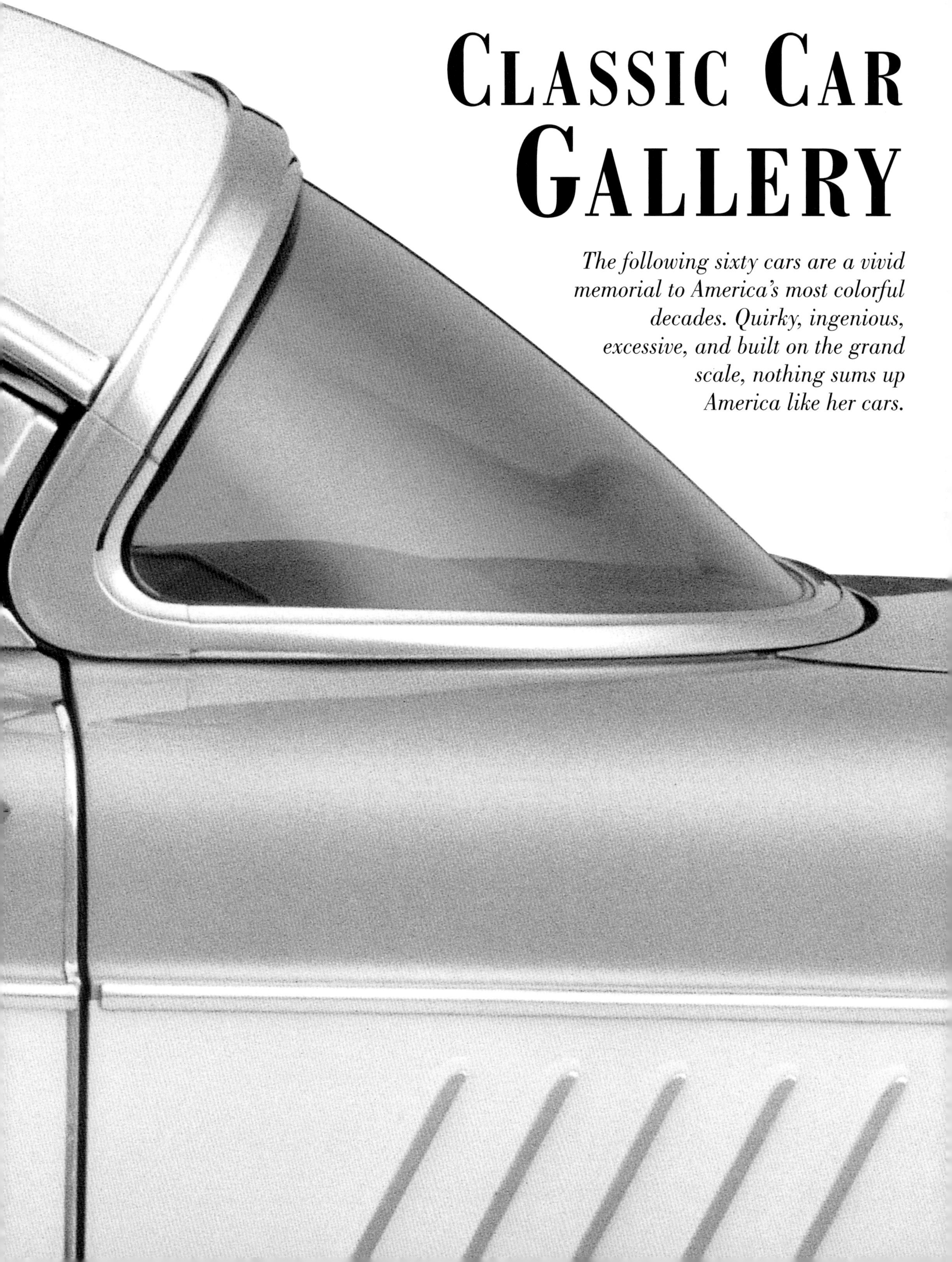

The Forties

America's intervention in World War II filled the nation with a self-confidence that would fertilize phenomenal postwar industrial growth. The automobile industry never had it so good.

CHRYSLER'S 25TH ANNIVERSARY MODEL WAS THE FIRST ALL-NEW POSTWAR STYLING CHANGE

MODERN AMERICA began in 1945. Postwar austerity didn't last long, and by the late Forties American workers produced 57 percent of the world's steel, 60 percent of the oil, and 80 percent of all the cars on the planet. In the five short years after the end of the war, Americans were able to buy electric clothes dryers, long-playing records, Polaroid cameras, frozen foods, and automatic garbage-disposal units. It was a brave new world of miracle materials like plastics, nylon, Styrofoam, vinyl, and chrome. What had once seemed science fiction was suddenly everyday life.

The GI Bill of Rights in 1945 invigorated the economy and stimulated education, industry, and business, kick-starting the biggest consumer boom the world has ever seen. Houses for heroes became a national priority and, between 1945 and 1950,

15 million shot up all over America. The Levitts of Levittown fame could build one in just 16 minutes, charging $7,990 for a four-and-a-half room, two-story with central heating, refrigerator, washing machine, and an eight-inch Bendix television set. Marriage rates soared and American newlyweds

1941 LINCOLN ZEPHYR V12
Lincoln's '41 Zephyr V12 carried over many prewar styling elements. Tall, long, and boxy, it wasn't until 1942 that it got a mild facelift. The last prewar Lincoln rolled out of the factory on February 10 the same year.

	1940–1945	1946	1947	1948	1949
AUTOMOTIVE	• Streamlining percolates down even to lowly **Chevrolet**s • Harley Earl and design team view P-38 Lightning pursuit plane • Supercharged **Graham** is fastest car powered by side-valve six • **DeSoto** builds fuselage sections for the Martin B-26 • **Chrysler** resumes car production in 1945	• 50th Anniversary of US car industry • **Ford** is biggest manufacturer, producing 468,022 cars • Steel strike and shortage of materials affect car industry • **Lincoln** Continental is pace car at Indianapolis 500 • **Mercury** launches Sportsman Convertible with wood body panels • **Pontiac** dusts off prewar Silver Streak styling	• **Chevrolet** now America's No. 1 car maker with 671,546 cars • **Frazer** and **Kaiser** are first US cars to exhibit new postwar styling with unbroken lines • Virgil Exner designs new enclosed-body **Studebaker** Champion • **Pontiac** builds a rear-mounted straight-eight engine • Woodie look is all the rage • Whitewall tires now available • Henry Ford dies	• **Cadillac** brings out dramatic new 62 Series with dorsal fins • **Hudson** launches famous "Step-Down" body • **Pontiac** introduces Hydra-Matic automatic transmission • Rare and radical **Tucker** Torpedo unveiled • Charles Nash dies • **Willys** launches the Jeepster, America's last true touring car	• **Ford** returns to the top spot, making an extraordinary 1,118,308 cars • **Buick** debuts new Roadmaster • **Chevrolet** makes first major restyle since the war 1949 HUDSON SUPER SIX
HISTORICAL	• Japanese bomb Pearl Harbor (1941) • First US troops land in Europe (1942) • US miners strike (1943) • Eisenhower masterminds D-Day (June 6, 1943) • Glenn Miller disappears over English Channel (1944) • A-bomb on Hiroshima (1945) GENERAL DWIGHT D. EISENHOWER	• United Nations holds first session • IBM introduces electronic calculator • First subsurface atomic explosion at Bikini Atoll • Ten Nazi war criminals executed at Nuremburg • *Road to Utopia* opens with Bob Hope and Bing Crosby	• Marshall Plan offers massive aid for postwar Europe • US crusade against Communism begins • Soviets test A-bomb • Plutonium is discovered • John Cobb sets land speed record of 394 mph (634 km/h) • Bell XI plane breaks the sound barrier at over 600 mph (965 km/h) • Rita Hayworth divorces Orson Welles	• Soviets blockade Berlin, and their envoy to the UN walks out • Truman wins Presidency • Transistor is invented • Kinsey Report on American sexual mores is published • Kansas ends prohibition • Tennessee Williams wins Pulitzer Prize for *A Streetcar Named Desire* • George Orwell publishes *1984* • Norman Mailer publishes *The Naked and the Dead*	• Berlin blockade ends • Truman says he won't hesitate to use the A-bomb again but publicly tries to calm "red hysteria" • Einstein publishes Theory of Gravitation • Actor Robert Mitchum jailed for smoking marijuana • RCA launches new system for broadcasting color TV pictures • 7" vinyl records first available

1948 LINCOLN CONTINENTAL COUPE
Although largely unchanged from 1946 models, the $4,662 '48 Continental was considered one of the most glamorous cars you could buy at the time. The Metropolitan Museum of Modern Art selected it as one of the eight automotive "works of art." Time magazine also ranked it in their top 10 of 100 best-designed products.

RITA HAYWORTH'S CONTINENTAL
Movie star Rita Hayworth had the necessary $2,812 to buy one of only 850 '41 Lincoln Continentals, as did architect Frank Lloyd Wright who described it as "the last classic car built in the United States." This was one of the final cars produced before the US entered the war.

locked to the suburbs. Precisely nine months after VJ-Day, the cry of the baby rang out across the land; by the end of '46, 3.4 million had been born. Radio shows like *The Adventures of Ozzie and Harriet* portrayed a cozy domestic idyll of plenty and normalcy. In 1948, some 172,000 American households each paid $200 to buy a television set. By 1950, 7½ million families were glued to the tube. And, looking through that new window on the world, American expectations grew grander and grander.

The Rebirth of the Industry

Clearly, the nation now needed a different kind of mobilization. In steel-starved 1945, new car sales totaled just 69,500. By 1949, this had risen to a staggering 5.1 million. Buyers were so desperate to own new Chevys and Fords that they not only paid full list price but slipped the dealer a fan of dollars to jump the line. An ad for the 1945 model Buick featured a shimmering car emerging from a gloomy scene of war. The copy read, "Buicks are for the lively, exciting, forward-looking world so many have fought for." In a *Saturday Evening Post* article titled "Your Car After the War," a man called Harley Earl prophetically predicted low, futuristic machines with curved windshields and slipstream bodies.

Although the metal in showrooms after 1945 was mainly a prewar lunch warmed over, aerodynamic styling and technical advancement gradually seeped into the brochures. Two significant engineering developments dominated the decade: the V8 engine and the automatic gearbox. It was General Motors that pioneered a generation of V8s, along with the seminal Hydra-Matic and Dynaflow self-shifters. Innovation was everywhere, not least in Preston Tucker's spectacular helicopter-engined Tucker Torpedo of 1948.

But it was Harley Earl who came up with probably the greatest automotive innovation of the late Forties, the infant fin. His '48 Cadillac wore two strange little bumps on its rear, and from that point the vernacular of the postwar American automobile was defined. Cars would never be mere transportation again.

1947 CHRYSLER TOWN AND COUNTRY
Chrysler's Town and Country series of 1947 was a new departure from prewar designs. Wood had previously been used only on station wagons, but the T & C Sedan had unique wood-bodied sides.

1943 WILLYS
Jeep MB

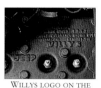

WILLYS LOGO ON THE
ENGINE BLOCK

AS ONE WAR CORRESPONDENT said, "It's as faithful as a dog, as strong as a mule, and as agile as a mountain goat." The flat-fendered Willys Jeep is one of the most instantly recognizable vehicles ever made. Any American TV or movie action hero who wasn't on a horse was in a Jeep. Even General Eisenhower was impressed, saying "the three tools that won us the war in Europe were the Dakota and the landing craft and the Jeep."

In 1940, the American Defense Department sent out a tough spec for a military workhorse. Many companies took one look at the seemingly impossible specification and 49-day deadline and turned it down flat. The design that won the contract and made it into production and the history books was a mixture of the ideas and abilities of Ford, Bantam, and Willys-Overland. A stunning triumph of function over form, the Jeep not only won the war but went on to become a cult off-roader that's still with us today. The Willys Jeep is surely the most original 4x4 by far.

THE JEEP AT WAR

OVER 635,000 MB JEEPS were built, and they immediately became the workhorse of the Allied armies during World War II. Jeeps completed some extraordinary operations in North Africa, where the British would load them with extra fuel, water, and munitions, and ferry the Special Air Service Regiment deep into the desert for weeks on end to harry the Germans. In the Pacific, Jeeps ran supply convoys from the coral sand beaches to the muddy jungles. Jeeps hauled trains, delivered the mail, carried generals, and were parachuted to battlefields by air. They fought their way through sand, snow, mud, and water, and became a symbol of hope for the war-battered Allies. The Jeep has also completed tours of duty in Korea and Vietnam.

PRESIDENT-ELECT EISENHOWER VISITING
TROOPS IN KOREA IN 1952

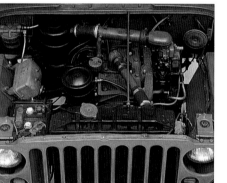

ENGINE
Power came from a Ford straight four, which took the Jeep to around 60 mph (96 km/h), actually exceeding US Army driving regulations. The hardy L-head motor developed 60 bhp, and the Warner three-speed manual box was supplemented by controls allowing the driver to select two- or four-wheel drive in high or low ratios.

DUAL-PURPOSE HEADLIGHT
The headlight could be rotated back to illuminate the engine bay.

QUICK-RELEASE CLUTCH DISENGAGES ENGINE FAN FOR FORDING STREAMS AND RIVERS

FRONT VIEW
Earlier Jeeps had a slatted radiator grille instead of the pressed steel bars shown here. The silhouette was low but ground clearance high to allow driving in streams as deep as 21 in (53 cm). Weather protection was vestigial.

LEFT-HAND SUSPENSION SPRINGS HAD A STIFFER
RATING TO COPE WITH THE WEIGHT OF THE ENGINE

DORCAS

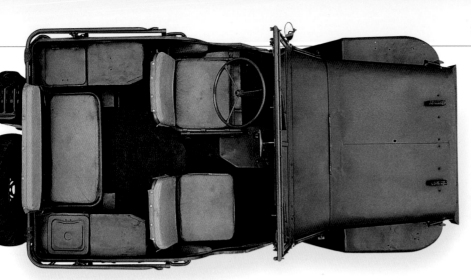

...DY FOR
...YTHING,
...PS CAME
...TH GAS
...N,
...OVEL,
...NG-
...NDLED
..., AND
...AB BARS

EXTENDED LIFESPAN

The Jeep was a brilliantly simple engineering solution to the problem of rugged mobility at war, but the life expectancy of an average vehicle was expected to be less than a week! In practice, many have survived to this day.

SPECIFICATIONS

MODEL 1943 Willys Jeep MB
PRODUCTION 586,000 (during World War II)
BODY STYLE Open utility vehicle.
CONSTRUCTION Steel body and chassis.
ENGINE 134cid straight four.
POWER OUTPUT 60 bhp.
TRANSMISSION Three-speed manual, four-wheel drive.
SUSPENSION Leaf springs front and rear.
BRAKES Front and rear drums.
MAXIMUM SPEED 65 mph (105 km/h)
0–60 MPH (0–96 KM/H) 22 sec
A.F.C. 16 mpg (5.7 km/l)

EXPOSED COLUMN

Driver safety wasn't a Jeep strong point. Many GIs ended up impaled on the steering column even after relatively low-speed impacts. Only the generals fought the war in comfort, and Jeeps were strictly no frills. Very early Jeeps had no glove compartment.

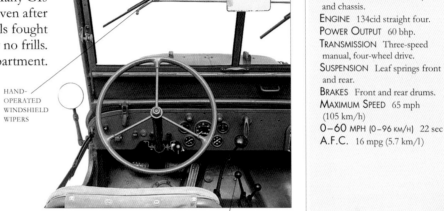

HAND-OPERATED WINDSHIELD WIPERS

FIRST PRODUCTION JEEP MODEL, THE MA, HAD A COLUMN CHANGE

WHAT'S IN A NAME?

Jeeps were first called General Purpose cars, then MA, and finally standardized as MB, but to this day nobody's sure from where the unofficial Jeep name originated. Some say it is a phonetic corruption of GP, or General Purpose, others that it was named after a curious little creature called Eugene the Jeep who appeared in a 1936 Popeye cartoon.

DOORS WOULD HAVE ADDED WEIGHT, SO SIDE STRAPS WERE A TOKEN GESTURE TOWARD DRIVER SAFETY

BOX-SECTION CHASSIS WAS TOUGH, YET FLEXIBLE ENOUGH TO ALLOW THE FRAME TO TWIST FOR MAXIMUM WHEEL ARTICULATION

HIGH CLUTCH, NARROW FOOTWELL, AND UNMOVABLE SEAT FORCED A DRIVING POSITION WITH KNEES SPLAYED

1943 WILLYS JEEP MB

EVOLUTION OF THE JEEP

THAT THE LEGENDARY quarter-ton Jeep was in fact a mishmash of available components virtually thrown together at record speed is amazing enough. But no one could have predicted that it would eventually create a whole new market for lifestyle leisure vehicles. Willys was to survive into the Fifties and Sixties, but investment was lacking until Chrysler acquired Jeep in the Eighties. Now the brand is in the ascendancy and giving rival Land Rover some stiff opposition.

1942

WILLYS AND FORD JEEPS saw service in every theater of war, and the two versions were almost identical. By August 1945, when wartime production of the Jeep ended, the two companies together had manufactured over 600,000 Jeeps. The US Army continued using Jeeps well into the Sixties, and some European armies still use them now.

KEY FEATURES
• Wartime Jeeps used the L-head straight four from production cars of the early '40s
• Willys bid lowest for the Jeep contract, but the Defense Department included Ford
• Tiny Bantam company produced 3,000 Jeeps

1950

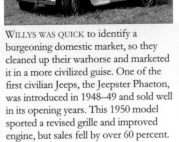

WILLYS WAS QUICK to identify a burgeoning domestic market, so they cleaned up their warhorse and marketed it in a more civilized guise. One of the first civilian Jeeps, the Jeepster Phaeton, was introduced in 1948–49 and sold well in its opening years. This 1950 model sported a revised grille and improved engine, but sales fell by over 60 percent.

KEY DEVELOPMENTS
• High-compression 7.0:1 cylinder head option available
• Split windshield rigid with chrome edging
• Mechanically operated soft-top
• Rear wheels gain fenders

WILLYS TRIED TO broaden the Jeep's appeal by bringing out a small Jeep-based station wagon. It was a longer car, built on the same wheelbase, and sold from 1946 to 1951. All were painted maroon with wood trim and had dual wipers, front bumper guards, and rails. Six-cylinders had wheel trim rings, cigarette lighter, and whitewalls.

KEY DEVELOPMENTS
• Restyled grille is divided by five horizontal bars
• New center gauge dashboard design and wrap-around rear bumper
• The first Jeep with a single-piece windshield

1943 WILLYS *Jeep MB*

WAR HERO
World War II made the Jeep's reputation – it was used in every theater of war in which GIs served, and appears in this poster recruiting soldiers to fight in China.

THE JEEP MAY HAVE HAD COMPETENCE AND CHARISMA, BUT IT ALSO HAD A PRODIGIOUS THIRST FOR FUEL

JOINT EFFORT
Of the 135 manufacturers contacted by the Defense Department, only Willys and Bantam rose to the challenge. Ford presented their version some time later

DAMPING IS BY LEAF SPRINGS AND HYDRAULIC SHOCKS WHICH GIVE A SURPRISINGLY GOOD RIDE

1962

P PREDATED the Range Rover by a
...de with its oversized, go-anywhere
...-wheel drive station wagon. With
...le room for at least five and a
...sive luggage deck, it became
...vorite of intrepid outdoor types.
...n levels could be specified, marking
...Jeep's most significant departure
...n its utilitarian military image.

Y DEVELOPMENTS
...led the Wagoneer, this new Jeep was
...-new in a market all on its own
...adiator pickup available
...llys name was dropped in 1963 and
...anged to Kaiser-Jeep Corporation

1971

BY THE MID-SIXTIES, manufacturers
were seeing a new all-terrain leisure
market emerge. International Harvester
launched the Scout, and Ford joined
in with the Bronco. Lacking real
investment, Jeep based a new car, the
Jeepster Commando, on the Wagoneer's
wheelbase. A roadster, station wagon,
and convertible were offered.

KEY DEVELOPMENTS
- Five engines offered, from a 134cid four
  to a 304cid V8
- Press acclaims new Jeeps, saying "passenger
  comfort is way above average"
- Jeepster had a 101 in (257 cm) wheelbase

1976

BASED ON JEEP's hefty Cherokee station
wagon, the Honcho was the company's
big pickup for the Seventies. The most
popular engine was the V8. Jeep got the
luxury sport utility vehicle ball rolling
with the full-size Cherokee, but
it wasn't until the compact four-door
models were introduced that sales
really took off.

KEY DEVELOPMENTS
- AMC acquires Kaiser-Jeep Corporation and
  becomes largest 4x4 manufacturer in US
- Range Rover's success in the UK expands
  the off-road market

1994

AFTER YEARS OF SUCCESS with the
smaller Cherokee, Jeep came up with
the larger and more luxurious Grand
Cherokee in the mid-Eighties. With
every possible luxury, it was strong
competition for the big Japanese 4x4s
and now-legendary Range Rover.
Priced competitively, it was adopted
as a very practical suburban trinket.

KEY DEVELOPMENTS
- Jeep now a division of the Chrysler Corp.
- Grand Cherokee with V8 now has
  125 mph (201 km/h) performance
- Antilock braking system (ABS), low-emission
  engine, and air-conditioning are added

...Y ACCESS
...e Jeep's hood was
...d down using
...ck-release sprung
...ches. The upper
...ch held the fold-
...wn windshield.

...ENDSETTER
...ose stark fenders and
...e all-terrain tires
...y look humble and
...ctional, but the
...p's claim to fame
...hat it spawned
...ity vehicles from
...ssans and Isuzu
...Discoverys and
...nge Rovers.

JEEP FIREPOWER
The Jeep remains very
popular with fans of
military memorabilia,
especially in its various
specialty guises. This
archive shot – taken in
Germany – shows
a Jeep equipped
with a potent
antitank cannon.

LONG-STROKE SIDE-
VALVE FLAT-TOP FOUR
DEVELOPED PLENTY
OF STUMP-PULLING
TORQUE

AXLES ARE FULLY
FLOATING WITH
BENDIX-WEISS,
RZEPPA, OR
SPICER CONSTANT
VELOCITY JOINTS

1948 TUCKER
Torpedo

EXTRAVAGANT ORNAMENTATION

THERE'S NO OTHER POSTWAR CAR that's as dramatic or advanced as Preston Tucker's futuristic '48 Torpedo. With four-wheel independent suspension, rear-mounted Bell helicopter engine, pop-out safety windshield, and uncrushable passenger compartment, it was 20 years ahead of its time.

"You'll step into a new automotive age when you drive your Tucker '48," bragged the ads. It was a promise that convinced an astonishing 300,000 people to place orders, but their dreams were never to be realized. Problems with the engine and Tuckermatic transmission, plus a serious cash-flow crisis, meant that only 51 Torpedos left the Chicago plant. Worse still, Tucker and five of his associates were indicted for fraud by the Securities Exchange Commission. Their acquittal came too late to save America's most eccentric car from an undignified end.

HOLLYWOOD PORTRAYAL
The 1988 film *Tucker: The Man and His Dream* starred Jeff Bridges and told a none-too-accurate story of an impassioned genius thwarted by Detroit's Big Three. In reality, Tucker failed because the project was underfunded.

FAMILY CREST
The horn on the steering wheel lay flush for safety, and was adorned with the Tucker family crest in injection-molded acrylic, suggesting a Cadillac-type bloodline.

INTERIOR
Some say Detroit conspired to destroy Tucker, but steering wheels on Torpedos were from the Lincoln Zephyr, given freely by Ford as a gesture of help. Although the interior was groaning with safety features, the Tucker sales team felt that it was too austere.

REAR LIGHT, LIKE MUCH OF THE TUCKER, WAS BOUGHT IN AND WAS A PREWAR DODGE DESIGN

REAR ENGINE WAS PLACED CROSSWISE ON THE OVERHANG BETWEEN THE TWO INDEPENDENTLY SPRUNG REAR WHEELS

SPECIFICATIONS

MODEL 1948 Tucker Torpedo
PRODUCTION 51
BODY STYLE Four-door sedan.
CONSTRUCTION Steel body
and chassis.
ENGINE 335cid flat six.
POWER OUTPUT 166 bhp.
TRANSMISSION Three-speed
Tuckermatic automatic, four-speed
manual.
SUSPENSION Four-wheel
independent.
BRAKES Front and rear drums.
MAXIMUM SPEED 120 mph
(193 km/h)
0–60 MPH (0–96 KM/H) 10.1 sec
A.F.C. 30 mpg (10.6 km/l)

LOW PROFILE

One of the fastest cars on American roads, the Tucker had a low floor that gave it a huge aerodynamic advantage. The roof tapered in two directions to reduce lift forces, and the drag coefficient was as low as 0.30. The Torpedo's top speed was 120 mph (193 km/h), and an astonishing 30 mpg (10.6 km/l) was possible.

AN INSTANT HIT

The public loved the Tucker not only for its comfort, power, and safety but also because the styling was completely free from the usual prewar clichés. The prototype was ready in 60 days, and more than 5,000 people attended the launch.

WHEN THE TUCKER WAS PREVIEWED TO THE PRESS, THE FRONT BUMPER WAS MADE OF WOOD

DARING CYCLOPS HEADLIGHT SWIVELED WITH THE FRONT WHEELS

STEERHORN BUMPER GAVE THE CAR A DRAMATIC FRONT VIEW

WITH NO ENGINE UP FRONT, LUGGAGE SPACE WAS COMMODIOUS

ENGINE

The first Tucker engine was a monster 589cid aluminum flat six that proved difficult to start and ran too hot. It was replaced by a 6ALV 335cid flat six, developed by Air-Cooled Motors of Syracuse. Perversely, Tucker later converted this unit to a water-cooled system.

SLIPPERY FRONT WAS DESIGNED TO CLEAVE THE AIR

THE CAR OF THE FUTURE HELD BACK IN THE PAST

ARTWORK OF A
PROTOTYPE
1947 TUCKER
TORPEDO

PRESTON TUCKER WAS AN EXTRAORDINARY automotive maverick. An unlettered engineer whose favorite phrase was "our boss is bigger than all of us, and it's the automobile," he was a well-connected wheeler-dealer who'd made a fortune from the design of a gun-turret mounting for World War II bombers. Obsessed by a dream of building the most advanced passenger car in the world, he secured a lease on a vast plant in Chicago, previously used to build engines for Boeing Superfortresses. A born deal-maker, he'd shrewdly raised $8 million franchising 1,800 Tucker dealerships before his automotive vision of the future was even in running prototype form.

The Torpedo was so different from anything else on four wheels that it was a complete sensation.

PRESTON TUCKER

The work of former Auburn-Cord-Duesenberg stylist Alex Tremulis, it was so low it only came up to a man's shoulder, had the widest track of any car, could crack over 120 mph (193 km/h), and had all-around independent suspension sprung by rubber-in-torsion units similar to those of Issigonis's Mini.

But the much-vaunted 589cid helicopter power plant was a nightmare, as was the troublesome Tuckermatic transmission, which was later replaced by a modified Cord gearbox. Tucker's tribulations soon leaked out to the press, who'd heard that prototypes sent to dealerships were plagued with glitches.

1948 TUCKER
Torpedo

INTERIOR WAS DESIGNED BY
AUDREY MOORE, WHO HAD
WORKED WITH RAYMOND
LOEWY ON STUDEBAKERS

NOVEL ENGINE WAS
POSITIONED LOWER
THAN THE REAR
PASSENGER SEAT TO
DIMINISH NOISE,
HEAT, AND FUMES

REAR DEFROSTER WAS
ONE OF ONLY FOUR
OPTIONS AVAILABLE

PRESTON TUCKER
DEMANDED A
"SASSY" REAR
END FROM HIS
DESIGN TEAM

HELICOPTER HELL
The early 589cid modified helicopter engines were a bit of a disaster. One test driver, Gene Haustein, described them as "slow as the moon coming up, making a noise like a barrel full of monkeys with the lid propped open."

MANUFACTURER
1 5
ILLINOIS 48

The situation got worse. Tucker had raised capital by a conventional stock market issue, but he ran afoul of the Securities Exchange Commission because the production cars didn't include all the audacious technical features he'd listed in his prospectus: direct fluid drive, disc brakes, sealed cooling system, electronic ignition, and fuel injection. The suits from Wall Street claimed that the cars being offered to the public did not fulfill Tucker's grandiose promises. The Tucker Corporation was therefore guilty of fraud.

PRESTON IN HIS DREAM CAR

After an essential $30 million loan was refused, Tucker was forced into voluntary liquidation. The tragedy was that Tucker could have sold every car he made, and he even had a float of several million dollars in the bank. The Chicago plant closed in the summer of 1948, by which time 37 Torpedos had been produced. In the end, volunteer workers assembled another 14 cars from remaining parts.

TUCKERS WAIT OUTSIDE COURT DURING THE TRIAL

Fifty-odd years later, the Torpedo remains one of America's most charismatic classics, and mint specimens can sell for up to $300,000. Many are proudly exhibited in museums, and some have even racked up a quarter of a million miles without incident. The Torpedo was meant to herald the brave new world of postwar America but failed because it was too complicated, too daring, and too under-resourced. A perfect example of American automotive genius, Tucker's precocious prodigy was guilty of just one sin – it bloomed too soon. Five years later the story might have been very different.

UNIQUE AND EXCITING

The front was like no other American car, with a fixed circular headlight lens that pivoted with the steering and a front panel that blended artfully into the bumper and grille.

FRONT AND REAR SEAT CUSHIONS COULD BE INTERCHANGED TO SPREAD WEAR AND TEAR

SEAT BELTS WERE NEVER INSTALLED BECAUSE THEY WERE THOUGHT TO SUGGEST THAT THE CAR WAS UNSAFE

RADIO WAS AN OPTIONAL EXTRA

THE TORPEDO WAS ONE OF THE FIRST WIDE-TRACK CARS AND HAD EXCEPTIONAL CORNERING ABILITY

THE TORPEDO COULD BRAKE TO A STOP IN HALF THE DISTANCE OF AN AVERAGE CAR

1949 BUICK
Roadmaster

THE '49 ROADMASTER TOOK the market's breath away. With a low silhouette, straight hood, and fastback styling, it was a poem in steel. The first Buick with a truly new post-war look, the '49 was designed by Ned Nickles using GM's new C-body. It also boasted two bold new styling motifs: Ventiports and an aggressive 25-tooth "Dollar Grin" grille. Harley Earl's aesthetic of aeronautical entertainment worked beautifully, and Buick notched up nearly 400,000 sales that year. Never mind that the windshield was still two-piece, that there was no power steering, and the engine was a straight eight – it looked gorgeous and came with the new Dynaflow automatic transmission. The Roadmaster, like the '49 Cadillac, was a seminal car and the first flowering of the most flamboyant decade of car design ever seen.

GUN-SIGHT HOOD DECORATION

DASHBOARD
The instrument panel was new for '49 and described as "pilot centered" because the speedo was positioned straight ahead of the driver through the steering wheel. The design was taken straight from Harley Earl's Buick Y-Job.

REAR LIGHT CLUSTER
The Art Deco taillights looked upscale and blended smoothly into the rear fenders. Nobody could have guessed that they were emergent fins that, in 10 years, would mushroom to almost comical proportions.

VENTIPORTS
Open Ventiports were sealed mid-year because a high-school principal complained that male students used those on his Roadmaster to relieve themselves.

SPOTLIGHT WITH MIRROR WAS A $25 OPTION

VENTIPORTS GAVE THE IMPRESSION OF A FIRE-BREATHING JET ENGINE

Roadmaster

BUICK

Less expensive Buicks had only three ventiports, but the lavish Roadmaster sported four

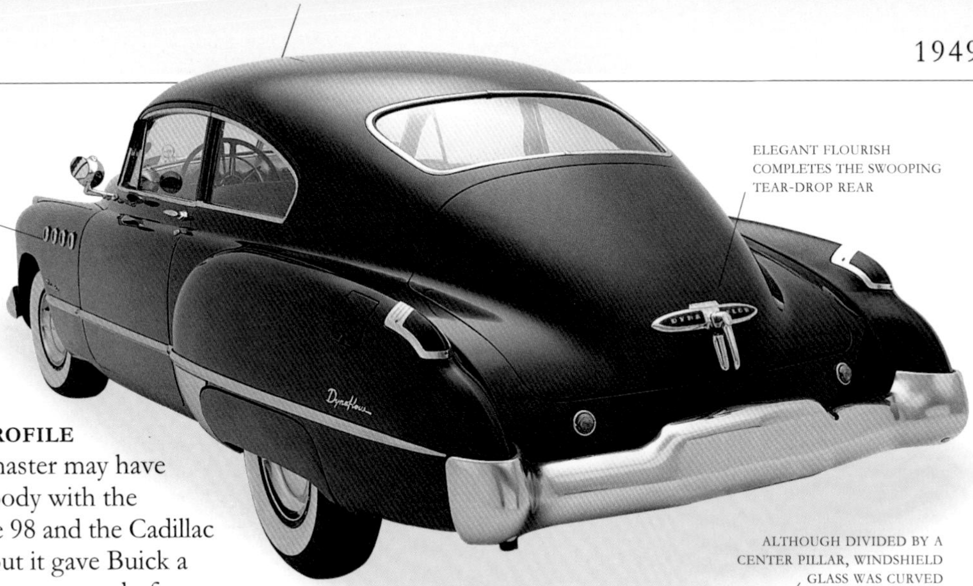

Elegant flourish completes the swooping tear-drop rear

Specifications

Model 1949 Buick Roadmaster Series 70
Production 18,415
Body Style Two-door fastback coupe.
Construction Steel body and chassis.
Engine 320cid straight eight.
Power Output 150 bhp.
Transmission Three-speed Dynaflow automatic.
Suspension Front and rear coil springs.
Brakes Front and rear drums.
Maximum Speed 100 mph (161 km/h)
0–60 mph (0–96 km/h) 17 sec
A.F.C. 20 mpg (7 km/l)

Raised Profile
The Roadmaster may have shared its body with the Oldsmobile 98 and the Cadillac Series 62, but it gave Buick a distinction never seen before.

New Automatic
Dynaflow automatic transmission was introduced in 1948 as an option on the Roadmaster. By '49 it had become standard equipment on the Series 70 Roadie and an immensely popular option on Series 50 and, later, Series 40 models.

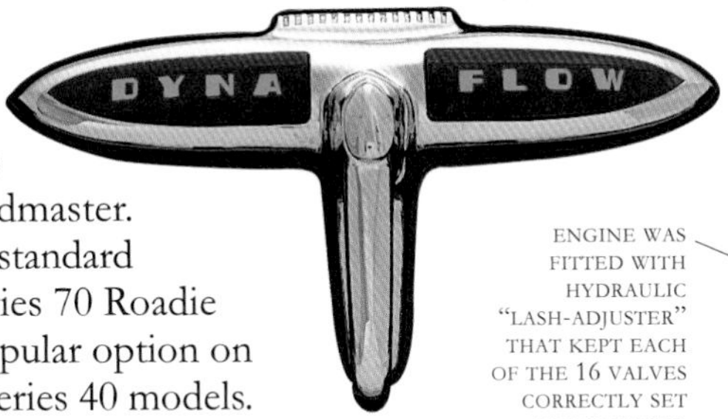

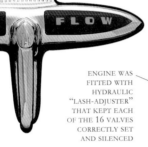

Although divided by a center pillar, windshield glass was curved

Engine was fitted with hydraulic "lash-adjuster" that kept each of the 16 valves correctly set and silenced

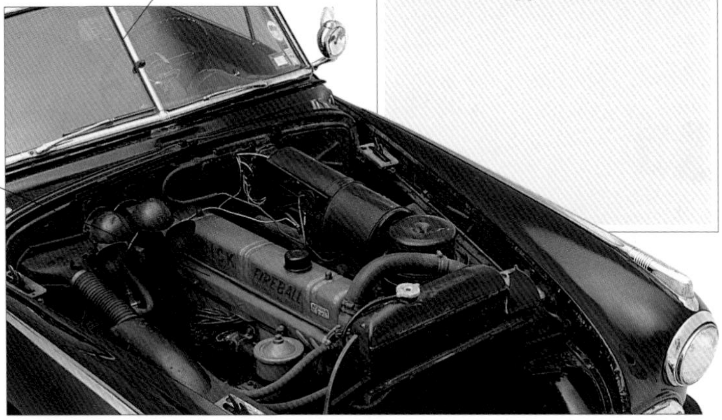

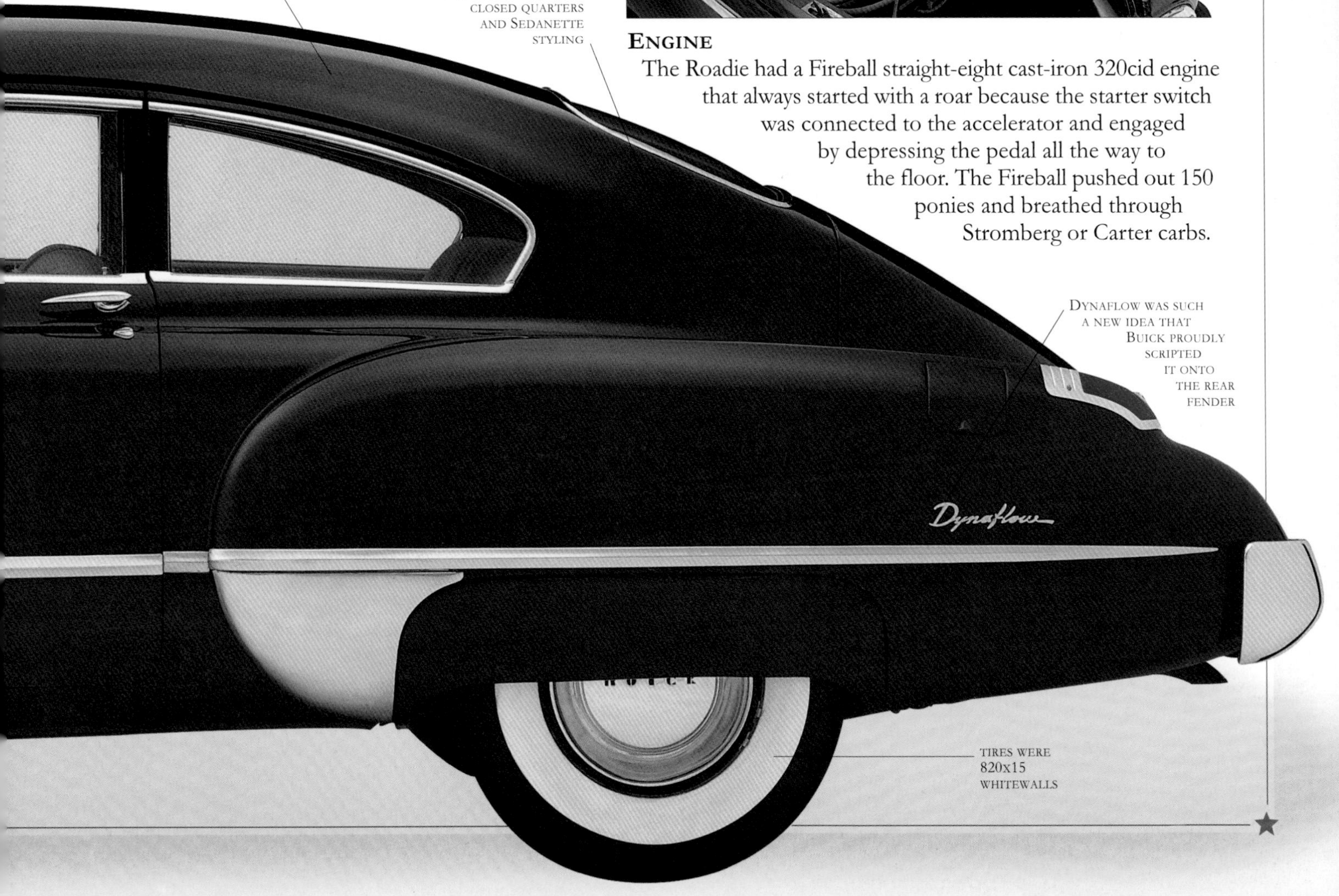

Engine
The Roadie had a Fireball straight-eight cast-iron 320cid engine that always started with a roar because the starter switch was connected to the accelerator and engaged by depressing the pedal all the way to the floor. The Fireball pushed out 150 ponies and breathed through Stromberg or Carter carbs.

The Roadmaster began the trend for lower, sleeker styling

The GM C-body had closed quarters and Sedanette styling

Dynaflow was such a new idea that Buick proudly scripted it onto the rear fender

Tires were 820x15 whitewalls

EVOLUTION OF THE BUICK ROADMASTER

FOR YEARS GM'S COPYWRITERS crowed that "when better cars are built, Buick will build them," and in a sense that hyperbole was true. In its day, the gloriously voluptuous Roadmaster was a serious set of wheels, only one step down from a Cadillac, and to own one meant you had really arrived. Big, bold, and brash, the '49 was perfect for its time. Optimistic, opulent, and glitzy, it carried flamboyant styling cues that told people a block away that this was no ordinary car – this was a Buick; even better, the very best Buick money could buy.

AD FOR THE 1956 ROADMASTER STRESSED THAT IT WAS THE "BUICK OF BUICKS"

1945–46

THE FIRST POSTWAR Buicks were practically unchanged from 1942, with engines that dated back to 1936 and chassis frames that originated in 1933. But they did have all-coil suspension and Harley Earl styling, and the Roadmaster Convertible was Buick's fastest and most glamorous car. Buick did well in '46, producing more than 156,000 cars.

KEY FEATURES
- Permi-Firm steering on all models
- Two-tone instrument panel with wood grains
- Only three-speed manual transmission available
- Standard vacuum-operated windshield wipers

1953

IN '53 THE ROADMASTER gained the firs Buick V8, nicknamed the "Nail-Head" because of the small diameter of its valve heads. The nose was shortened to accommodate the smaller lump, an power steering, power brakes, and Dynaflow drive became standard. This was Buick's 50th anniversary, celebrate by the seven millionth Buick built.

KEY DEVELOPMENTS
- New V8 engine goes into 50 percent of all Buicks
- Calendar year production total tops 485,000
- Dynaflow gets twin turbines, which increases torque by 10 percent
- 80 percent of Buicks have Dynaflow

1949 BUICK Roadmaster

A CAR TO ASPIRE TO Roadmaster was a brilliant name for the top-of-the-line Buick and soon became the preferred choice of professionals who couldn't quite make it to Cadillac territory.

PRISMATIC REARVIEW MIRROR WAS AN OPTIONAL EXTRA

THE '49 ROADIE WAS THE PUREST AND MOST BEAUTIFUL BUICK EVER MADE

18 363 52 WYOMING

1955

[M]AJOR FACE-LIFT for '55 didn't do [mu]ch for the Roadmaster. The vertical [gri]lle bars were replaced by a tight mesh, [and] the body styling was distinctly [slab]-sided. The Ventiports and hood [orn]aments stayed, but the result was a [mu]ch blander machine. The public cared [no]t, buying nearly 800,000 Roadies to [put] Buick in industry third place.

[KE]Y DEVELOPMENTS
- [G]old-colored Roadmaster desk script [an]d hood ornament
- [C]onvertible gets standard leather
- [1]0 choices of interior trim
- Eight-millionth Buick rolls off the line

1957

LOWER AND SMOOTHER, with a more dramatic sweepspear that kicked up violently over the rear wheel arch, the restyle of '57 made the Roadmaster look a lot like every other American car. Gone was that chaste individuality, and Buick began to lose its reputation as a maker of high-quality cars. Production was down 24 percent.

KEY DEVELOPMENTS
- Revised front suspension with ball-joint mounting
- Grille reverts to vertical bars
- New two-piece torque tube
- New engine mountings
- Nine-millionth Buick hits the showroom

1991

BUICK RESURRECTED the Roadmaster name for 1991 after a foolish and inexplicable 33-year hiatus. Riding on a body-on-chassis design dating back to '77, the '91 Roadmaster was a shadow of its former self. Long, heavy, and ungainly, it bore too obvious a resemblance to other GM products and had completely lost all character.

KEY DEVELOPMENTS
- Roadmaster name first appears on aero-look eight-passenger station wagon
- Fuel-injected 5.0 V8
- Driver's-side airbag and ABS standard
- Improved suspension gives better stability
- Same chassis and mechanicals as Chevrolet Caprice

1994

THERE WERE ONLY minor changes to the Roadmaster in '94, the main one being the optional Corvette-based 260 bhp V8. The rear-drive sedan and station wagon continued, and stock power was from the 5.7 V8. This year's models returned only 16 mpg (5.7 km/l) in urban driving. Alas, the once great name had been sacrificed on the altar of badge engineering.

KEY DEVELOPMENTS
- Station wagons get rear-facing two-place third seat and vista roof
- Solar-Ray tinted windshield
- Improved sound deadening
- Lockout switch for power windows
- Sedan roof pillars hinder visibility

[L]OUD AND PROUD
[T]he center of the steering [w]heel was one of five [p]laces where Dynaflow [w]as written on the car. [T]he steering itself was [u]nassisted and required [a] hefty five turns [l]ock-to-lock.

INTERIOR FABRICS WERE PLUSH, WITH A CUSTOM TRIM OPTION

FULL-WIDTH BENCH SEATS WERE STANDARD ON THE '49 ROADIE

BUICK STYLING
Gun-sight hood ornament, bucktooth grille, and Ventiports were flashy styling metaphors that would become famous Buick trademarks.

BUICK EIGHT

ROAD MASTER

18 363
52 WYOMING

1949 CADILLAC
Series 62

THE CADILLAC SCRIPT IS FAMOUS THE WORLD OVER

WE OWE A LOT TO the '49 Cadillac. It brought us tail fins and a high-compression V8. Harley Earl came up with those trendsetting rear rudders and John F. Gordon the performance motor. Between them they created the basic vernacular of the postwar American car.

In 1949 the one millionth Caddy rolled off the production line, and the stunning Series 62 Fastback or Sedanette was born. Handsome and quick, with Hydra-Matic transmission, curved windshield, and hydraulically operated front seats and windows, it was a complete revelation. Everybody, including the haughty British and Italians, nodded sagely in admiration and, at a whisker under $3,000, it knocked the competition dead in their tracks. As Cadillac ads boasted: "The new Cadillac is not only the world's most beautiful and distinguished motor car, but its performance is a challenge to the imagination." The American Dream and the finest era in American cars began with the '49 Cadillac.

BENTLEY CONNECTION

THE CLASSIC 1952 BENTLEY R-TYPE Continental certainly bears a startling similarity to the '49 Cadillac. Motoring academics have frequently hinted at plagiarism, suggesting that the Bentley's comely teardrop shape was inspired by Harley Earl's design. Naturally, the boys at Bentley declined to comment, but nonetheless the two cars do display an uncanny kinship of line. However, far from waving writs about, Earl, Cadillac, and GM took a philosophical approach and simply smiled quietly to themselves. For after all, we all know that imitation is the most sincere form of flattery.

1952 BENTLEY R-TYPE CONTINENTAL

GLORIOUS TAPERING ROOF LINE MADE DUMPY EUROPEAN CARS LOOK LIKE CHURCH PEWS

CADILLAC CREST
The V emblem below the crest denoted V8 power, and the basic badge design remained unaltered until 1952.

BODY STYLE
Hugely influential body design was penned by Harley Earl and Julio Andrade at GM's styling studios. Many of the '49 features soon found themselves on other GM products such as Oldsmobile and Buick.

TIRES RAN AT ONLY 24 PSI, MAKING UNASSISTED STEERING HEAVY

MASCOT

The famous streamlined Art Deco goddess hood ornament first appeared after World War II and continued unchanged until 1956. America's most prestigious car wore its mascot with pride.

INTERIOR

The cabin was heavily chromed and oozed quality. Colors were gray-blue or brown with wool carpets to match and leather or cloth seats. Steering was Saginaw, with standard four-speed auto transmission.

ACCOLADES

British motoring journalist S.C.H. Davis rated the '49 one of the six outstanding cars of the two postwar decades. *Motor Trend* magazine named it "Car of the Year."

WHILE STYLING WAS SIMILAR TO THAT OF THE '48 MODEL, THE NEW OHV V8 IN THE '49 WAS AN INNOVATION

CHROME SLASHES WERE INSPIRED BY AIRCRAFT AIR INTAKES

FUEL FILLER-CAP WAS HIDDEN UNDER TAILLIGHT, A CADILLAC TRAIT SINCE 1941

FIN STYLING

The rear fins, inspired by the Lockheed P-38 aircraft, became a Caddy trademark and would reach a titanic height on '59 models.

SPECIFICATIONS

MODEL 1949 Cadillac Series 62
PRODUCTION 92,554
BODY STYLE Two-door, five-seater fastback.
CONSTRUCTION Steel body and chassis.
ENGINE 331cid V8.
POWER OUTPUT 162 bhp.
TRANSMISSION Four-speed Hydra-Matic automatic.
SUSPENSION *Front:* coil springs; *Rear:* leaf springs.
BRAKES Front and rear drums.
MAXIMUM SPEED 100 mph (161 km/h)
0–60 MPH (0–96 KM/H) 13.4 sec
A.F.C. 17 mpg (6 km/l)

EVOLUTION OF THE CADILLAC SERIES 62

Maybe <u>This</u> Will Be The Year!

1955 ADVERTISING BROCHURE

'48 WAS THE YEAR of the fin and the year of the crème de la Cads. Cadillac designers Bill Mitchell, Harley Earl, Frank Hershey, and Art Ross had been smitten by a secret P-38 Lockheed Lightning fighter plane. Mitchell admitted that the P-38's fins "handed us a trademark nobody else had." Cadillac also had Ed Cole's OHV V8, some 10 years in the making. With a brief to reduce weight and increase compression, the end result was an engine with more torque and better mileage than any other at the time.

1941

THE '41 CADILLACS had a powerful, sweeping glamour that was the envy of custom coachbuilders the world over. Hopes of returning to the wheel of a romantic '41 Series 62 Convertible kept many a GI sane. With egg-crate grille, swooping fenders, concealed gas filler, and Hydra-Matic shifting, it was the last word in modernity.

KEY FEATURES
• Horsepower up from 135 to 150 bhp
• New coffin-nose hood
• Optional Hydra-Matic transmission
• Record 59,572 models sold
• Genuine top speed of 100 mph

1947

AFTER A FOUR-YEAR consumer droug[ht] Cadillac found itself with about 200,000 orders and only 104,000 cars Although a warmed-over prewar design, the '46 and '47 Caddies had sleek, wind-cheating smoothness fu[ll] of rapid purpose. They were classica[lly] correct and aesthetically stunning – n[ot] bad for a car with two tons of bulk.

KEY DEVELOPMENTS
• First true "jellybean" body shape
• Smoothest car engine of its day
• Sombrero deep-dish wheel covers
• Modified Cadillac V crest
• Grille bars reduced from six to five

1949 CADILLAC
Series 62

BELIEVE THE HYPE
Cadillac advertisements trumpeted that the 1949 was "the world's most beautiful car," and the simple yet elegant styling caught the public's imagination.

AMONG MINOR DE[SIGN]
CHANGES FROM 19[48]
WAS THE MORE
SQUARED-OFF REA[R]

LG·136
NY EMPIRE STATE 57

1949 CADILLAC SERIES 62

1948

THE '48 CADILLAC was first to define the vernacular of the typical post-war American family sedan. A magnificent design package, it was clean, curvaceous, and beautiful, and that '49 engine was a honey. With the best styling and the finest engine in the business, Cadillac became the zenith of good taste.

KEY DEVELOPMENTS
• First of the fins
• First-generation modern GM OHV V8
• Class-leading economy and performance
• Distinctive fastback styling
• First luxury hardtop
• Front fender line within bodywork

1955

'55 WAS A BANNER year for the motor industry as well as Cadillac's most successful to date, with 141,000 units built. Horsepower was up to 250 (270 in the Eldorado), and the Florentine roof was extended to sedans. Even the Dagmars were bigger, causing many complaints from other drivers savaged in parking lots.

KEY DEVELOPMENTS
• Eldorado has all accessories as standard except air-conditioning
• Compression ratio improved
• Redesigned egg-crate grille
• New rectangular sidelights under headlights
• Extended side molding

1959

STRIDENT AND BAROQUE, the '59 Cadillac had ridiculously extravagant tail fins. The ultimate iron dinosaur, it was soon pilloried as proof that late Fifties America was out to lunch. But because of its flamboyance, the '59 is now a fiercely prized collector's car, with Biarritz Convertibles fetching as much as Ferraris.

KEY DEVELOPMENTS
• New 390cid engine
• Improved power steering
• Revised suspension
• World's highest tail fins
• 14 models in four series available

1961

ALL '61 MODELS CAME with the 390cid, 325 bhp V8, and the new, crisp styling was inspired by GM's Bill Mitchell, who had begun to clean up the Caddy look in 1960. Family resemblance was strong, with the Series 62 hardtop coupe looking very much like the upscale de Ville, and the Eldorado Biarritz almost identical to the Series 62 Convertible.

KEY DEVELOPMENTS
• Rubberized front and rear coil springs replace problematic air suspension system
• Wheelbases shorter on most models
• Self-adjusting brakes from 1960 on, plus an automatic vacuum parking-brake release
• All Caddies offer lifetime chassis lubrication
• Dual exhausts no longer available

NEW POWER UNIT

The trendsetting new OHV 331cid V8 developed 160 bhp and weighed 188 lb (85 kg) less than the reliable but bulky L-head design. It made the '49 one of the fastest cars on the road.

CURVED WINDSHIELD WAS A NOVELTY FOR A 1949 CAR

PROTOTYPE ENGINE WAS RUN FOR 541 HOURS AND FOUND TO BE IN PERFECT CONDITION

GRILLE WAS HEAVIER ON THE '49 THAN ON THE '48, AFTER FRANK HERSHEY TOLD HARLEY EARL THAT HE DID NOT LIKE THE ORIGINAL DESIGN

LG·136
NY EMPIRE STATE 57

1949 PONTIAC
Chieftain

STYLISH CHIEFTAIN LOGO

UP TO '49, PONTIACS looked and felt like prewar leftovers. Sure, they were reliable and solid, but they had a reputation as middle-of-the-road cars for middle-aged, middle-class buyers. Pontiac was out of kilter with the glamour boom of postwar America. 1949 was a watershed for Pontiac – the first postwar restyles were unveiled, with the new Harley Earl-designed envelope bodies trumpeted as "the smartest of all new cars." In reality, their Silver Streak styling was old hat, tracing its origins back to the Thirties. But although mechanically tame – with aged flathead sixes and eights – the '49 Chieftain Convertibles mark the transition from upright prewar designs to postwar glitz. These were the days when the modern convertible really came into its own.

INTERIOR
A three-speed manual gearbox was standard, but Hydra-Matic automatic was available as a $159 option. There was no power steering or power brakes.

CHIEFTAIN ORNAMENT
The Indian chief mascot never smiled, but the head was illuminated at night by a 2-watt bulb that gave a warm, yellow glow.

WINDSHIELD
This was called the Safe-T-View and was one of a series of gimmick Pontiac names that also included Carry-More trunk, Tru-Arc Saf Steering, and Easy-Access doors.

REAR AXLE
Optional rear axle ratios were Standard, Economy, and Mountain.

DECORATION
The five parallel chrome bars were a Silver Streak hallmark and were aped by the British Austin Atlantic.

ENGINE
Six-cylinder engines were cast iron with four main bearings, solid valve lifters, and a puny Carter one-barrel carb. Choosing the straight eight gave you a measly extra 13 bhp but cost only $23 more. Pontiac did not offer a V8 unit in any of their models until 1955.

SPOTLIGHTS
Dual side-mounted spotlights were trigger-operated.

1949 PONTIAC CHIEFTAIN CONVERTIBLE DE LUXE
Ads promised that "Dollar for Dollar, You Can't Beat a Pontiac," and the Chieftain was proof that Pontiac wasn't bluffing. Convertibles cost just $2,183 for the six and $2,206 for the eight and were a great bargain for the price. The engine was set well forward in a very rigid cantilever box girder frame, and the rear seat was positioned ahead of the rear axle and fender to give what Pontiac dubbed a "cradle ride."

CHROME PANEL
Extravagant mudguards only appeared on the De Luxe and added a classy flourish.

REAR BUMPER
Intricate bumper was designed to prevent girls in full skirts from getting them caught in the bumper when opening the trunk.

SPECIFICATIONS
MODEL 1949 Pontiac Chieftain Convertible
PRODUCTION Not available
BODY STYLE Two-door convertible.
CONSTRUCTION Steel chassis and body.
ENGINE 239cid straight six, 249cid straight eight.
POWER OUTPUT 90–103 bhp.
TRANSMISSION Three-speed manual, optional four-speed Hydra-Matic automatic.
SUSPENSION *Front:* coil springs; *Rear:* leaf springs.
BRAKES Front and rear drums.
MAXIMUM SPEED 80–95 mph (129–153 km/h)
0–60 MPH (0–96 KM/H) 13–15 sec
A.F.C. 15 mpg (5.3 km/l)

The Fifties

The postwar feel-good factor made the Fifties a decade of unprecedented leisure and prosperity. In this heady new world of television, rock 'n' roll, nuclear power, and the space race, Americans reached for the moon.

FAIRLANE, "THE TOUCH OF TOMORROW" IN '57

NEVER AN ERA remembered for highbrow culture, life in Fifties America did imitate art – but it was art viewed through a flickering screen. Shows like Walt Disney's weekly *Disneyland*, the *I Love Lucy* sitcom, and the *Ed Sullivan Show* changed the country's mindset. Television became a national narcotic and the tube of plenty. With seven million sets sold every year, the old order had no choice but to quietly evaporate. Television changed America's consciousness forever.

Although McCarthyism, the shadow of nuclear terror, and the Korean War dominated headlines, most Americans were busy having a good time with their bobby socks, Tupperware parties, barbecued steaks, and Billy Graham's way to God without sacrifice. These were the years of rampant consumerism, when the country binged on a decade-long spending spree. In 1952, Americans spent $255 million on chewing gum, $235 million on greeting cards, and a staggering $23 million on mouthwash. The most stable and prosperous time in Uncle Sam's history, the Fifties promised a brave new world.

Between 1950 and 1958, the economy was riding high. Pent-up postwar demand, $100 billion worth of personal savings, the baby boom, Ike's

ATOMIC ERA
The nuclear specter haunted the Fifties. America regularly tested her arsenal of A- and H-bombs, in readiness for the widely anticipated confrontation with the Soviet Union.

AUTOMOTIVE	1950	1951	1952	1953	1954
	• **Chevrolet** is America's No.1 car maker with 1,498,590 cars • First Motorama show opens at New York Waldorf • Only 333 **Volkswagen** Beetles sold in entire US • First modern compact introduced, the **Nash** Rambler • **Ford** wins coveted Fashion Academy award for styling • **Chevrolet** offers new fully automatic Powerglide transmission	• Ford-O-Matic is **Ford**'s first fully automatic transmission • **Chrysler** announces all-new 331cid hemi-head V8 for the New Yorker, plus power steering for first time • *Hop Up* magazine launched, for hot-rodders and customizers • Office of Price Stabilization allows some car manufacturers to raise prices • One in three cars is automatic	• National steel strike and Korean War slow auto production • **Buick** is third largest maker of convertibles and largest hardtop builder • **Ford**'s first totally new body since 1949 features one-piece curved windshield • 95 percent of all **Fords** have V8s • Office of Price Stabilization drops pegging of new car prices • War cuts make whitewalls scarce	• **GM** loses $10 million • **Dodge** launches famed Hemi V8 and new option, air-conditioning • More chrome as war eases • **Chrysler** introduces PowerFlite automatic 1953 CADILLAC ELDORADO	• **Ford** overtakes **Chevrolet** as top maker, with 1,165,942 cars • Spinner hubcap becomes most popular accessory in America • Harley Earl previews first Firebird experimental car at Motorama
HISTORICAL	• President Truman sanctions building of US's first H-bomb • Mao Zedong and Stalin sign Mutual Defense Treaty • Joseph McCarthy launches crusade against Communism • First major US battle in Korea • First kidney transplant • Drive-in movie theaters being built at rate of 2,200 a year • Nuclear test in Nevada desert • *The Third Man* wins Oscar for black-and-white photography	• Average salary is $1,456 p.a. • *A Streetcar Named Desire* voted best film of 1951 • US Atomic Energy Commission says it can produce electric power from nuclear reactors • *Betty Crocker's Picture Cookbook*, first out in '50, sells its millionth copy	DWIGHT EISENHOWER CELEBRATES ELECTION VICTORY IN 1952 • Eisenhower elected President with largest-yet popular vote • Contraceptive pill introduced • Gene Kelly stars in *Singin' in the Rain* • TWA launches tourist class air travel • Nationally televised detonation of atomic bomb in Nevada desert	• Marilyn Monroe is America's favorite pinup and appears on the cover of *Playboy* • Khrushchev new Communist Party leader after Stalin's death • Levis are America's No.1 jeans • A young Elvis Presley walks into Sun Studios, Memphis • *From Here to Eternity* premieres • Soviets admit they have H-bomb • Cinemascope launched • New "stiletto" heels panned as dangerous	• First McDonald's is born • Eisenhower proposes new Interstate highway system • IBM launches first computer • Boeing unveil prototype 707 • Second H-bomb exploded at Bikini Atoll • Elvis sings "That's All Right" • Racial segregation outlawed in US schools • Premiere of *Seven Brides for Seven Brothers* • First nuclear sub launched

DOMESTIC UTOPIA
Set pieces such as this illustrated the Fifties suburban dream, with well-appointed house, Mom with her "New Look" clothes, and Dad and Junior admiring the family's shiny new 1951 Ford Custom.

were buffed to a high sheen or swathed in chrome so a narcissistic nation could admire its reflection.

The middle-class suburbanite looked out of his window and coveted his neighbor's possessions. Success was measured in material terms – a gas barbecue, a swimming pool, a white Corvette. This credo of instant gratification changed everything, including the nation's eating habits. In 1954, Ray Kroc of San Bernadino, a high-school dropout, came up with a newfangled stand for selling French fries, soda, and 15¢ hamburgers. Today it's a fast-food empire known as McDonald's.

nterstates, and new technology meant that by he end of the decade more than 80 percent of Americans had not only electric lighting but also efrigerators, telephones, and televisions. Suburbia became a paradise of comfort and convenience, with ranch-style homes, double garages, expansive front lawns, and kitchens with a new state-of-the-rt Colorama Frigidaire.

Bright New World

Consumer durables were curvy, bosomy, and brightly colored. Buyers had had enough of the austere penury of khaki and navy blue and wanted up-to-the-minute modish pastels to show that their purchases were brand-new. Pink became the color, as worn by Elvis, Mamie Eisenhower, Cadillacs, steam irons, and even Dad's button-downs. Surfaces

LUSHLY-UPHOLSTERED LOOKS
The mildly rounded 1950 Nash Rambler shows the first flowerings of curvilinear, volumetric design. By the end of the decade, an obsession with full contours would change the American car into a four-wheeled bordello.

1955	1956	1957	1958	1959
Highest **Ford** output since 1923, but **Chevrolet** is back on top, producing 1,704,667 cars Big Three auto manufacturers dominate 97 percent of market US production at postwar high Auto makers agree to ban advertisements promoting performance and horsepower **Cadillac** sales peak at 141,000 Chic new **Ford** Fairlane launched 60,000 foreign cars imported into US, including 25,000 **VW** Beetles	• **GM** spends $125 million on new technical center in Michigan • Federal Highway Act passed • Raymond Loewy blasts "jukeboxes on wheels" LIMITED EDITION 1956 DESOTO ADVENTURER	• **Ford**, with all-new styling, outsells **Chevrolet** 1.67 million to 1.5 • New **Ford** Skyliner is world's first hardtop convertible • **Chevrolet** offers fuel injection and first 1 hp/cu in engine • Thunderbird sales up by half • Edsel launched • New magazine *Custom Cars*	• **Chevrolet** regains lead in car manufacture, with 1,142,460 built • Industry-wide recession; sales worst since World War II • **Chevrolet** introduces highly unpopular seat belts • Thunderbirds get four seats • **Ford** offers Level-Air ride for one year only • 50th birthday for **Chevrolet** • **GM** employs four women in their design department • **Studebaker** offers compact Lark	• Virgil Exner admits that with fins he'd "given birth to a Frankenstein" • Highest fins ever on 1959 Cadillac, although **Ford**, **Lincoln**, and **Mercury** fins almost disappear • **Chevrolet** shows its controversial "batwing" fins • **Chrysler** offers Golden Lion V8 • Compact **Ford** Falcon introduced • Flat-six **Chevrolet** Corvair launched • **Chrysler** 300D gets fuel injection • Britain launches the Mini • **Plymouth** Sport Fury introduced
Disneyland opens in California James Dean dies in car crash New phrase "Rock 'n' Roll" coined by DJ Alan Freed 3-D movies launched *Billboard* introduces Top 100 record chart; Bill Haley's "Rock Around the Clock" is No.1 for 25 weeks Marlon Brando wins Best Actor for *On the Waterfront* Soviets test H-bomb	• Martin Luther King Jr. fights for black rights using peace • JFK goes for Vice-President nomination • Elvis buys his first pink Cadillac • First video tape shown • *My Fair Lady* opens • 60 percent of Americans are homeowners JAMES DEAN	• USSR first in space with Sputnik • Eisenhower and Nixon sworn in for second term • Jack Kerouac's novel *On the Road* published • Breathalyzer tested to measure alcohol on drivers' breath • "Cat," "dig," "cool," "square," and "hip" enter the language • Elvis in first film, *Jailhouse Rock* • Bogart dies of throat cancer • Jerry Lee Lewis sings "Great Balls of Fire"	• First US satellite launched • Pan American World Airways begins first transatlantic flights • NASA created • Elvis drafted • First stereo record on sale • Hope Diamond donated to Smithsonian Institution • *West Side Story* opens • Danny and the Juniors have smash hit with "At the Hop" • Last Communist newspaper, *The Daily Worker*, folds	• Fidel Castro becomes Cuban premier • Nixon and Khrushchev hold "kitchen debate" • First Russian rocket to reach moon • Hawaii proclaimed 50th US state • Buddy Holly dies • Bobby Darin wows with "Mack the Knife" HULA HOOP

PATRIOTIC PURCHASING
The auto industry was the biggest player in the nation's economy, and consumers obsessed with keeping up to date were persuaded that buying a new car every year would help to build a stronger America.

NEW ROCK 'N' ROLL AGE
The name of Bill Haley's group, the Comets, echoed America's fascination with rockets and the space age. Between 1955 and 1957 their hit "Rock Around the Clock" was on the US charts for 37 weeks.

With less time spent on cooking and eating, Americans had more time for shopping. Parents raised in the Depression had no problem swallowing the mantra that more was most definitely better. Teenagers and adults alike gorged on everything from Bill Haley records and hula hoops to cashmere sweaters, trips to Hawaii, and hot-rods. Madison Avenue spent $10 billion a year to persuade consumers that improving their lives with material possessions wasn't just okay, it was the American Way. This illusion of fulfillment was made possible by a small rectangle of plastic dubbed the credit card. Diners' Club appeared in 1950, followed by the American Express card, and by the end of the decade Sears Roebuck alone had over 10 million credit accounts.

Prosperity brought leisure, and American consumers spent $30 billion a year killing time. Sales of power tools, model kits, stamp albums, and painting sets soared. In two years Craftmaster sold Paint By Numbers sets to the value of

MAGIC KINGDOM
Disneyland, opened in 1955, was like a living TV, where visitors could change channels from medieval castles to rocket ships, with souvenir shops serving as "commercials."

$10 million and even Eisenhower was a regular dauber. For Americans wanting somewhere to go to spend time and money, the $17 million Disneyland was opened by Walt Disney on July 13, 1955, watched by 24 live ABC cameras and hosted by none other than Ronald Reagan. Two years later Disney's dream world had welcomed 10 million visitors, most of whom arrived by car.

Freedom on Wheels

The massive American automobiles of the Fifties, although they looked like rocket-launchers with 38D cups, were built as family cars, perfect for weekend outings and vacations. As one Ford ad of the period put it, the car promised "freedom to come and go as we please in this big country of ours." A freedom from the sameness of the suburbs and the ennui of prosperity, the car became a symbol of blissful escapism.

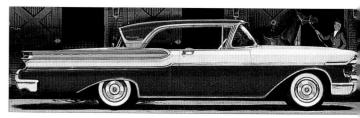

LOW-SLUNG PROFILE
By mid-decade, American cars had become so long and low that many reached only to shoulder height. The car manufacturers followed a dramatic "squashing" policy all through the Fifties, and this 1957 Mercury Turnpike Cruiser is as squat as they come. The Turnpike Cruiser boasted gadgets such as a retractable Breezaway rear window and a 49-position driver's seat.

HARD-SELL WITH CLASS
Cars were sold hard on television, and Lincoln used the Ed Sullivan Show to highlight their 1955 line-up. Their elegant spokeswoman, Julia Meade, wearing an evening dress and running her gloved hands over the upholstery, was the first TV personality to be wholly identified with a single product.

BIZARRE CREATIONS
By the end of the Fifties, automotive styling had become so extravagant that panning the American car became a pastime that threatened to replace baseball as a national sport. Within a few short years of its launch, this outlandish 1959 Cadillac Series 62 would be lampooned as a figure of fun.

By 1956 America owned three-quarters of all the cars in the world. Freeways, multilevel parking lots, shopping centers, drive-ins, and movie theaters sprouted like mushrooms after rain. Americans got high on an orgy of vinyl and power steering.

Buying into the American Dream

Suddenly stylists replaced designers, and the car shed its machinelike properties to become an instrument of fantasy. Not everyone was enthralled; Woodrow Wilson called the American car "a picture of the arrogance of wealth," and John Keats in his *Insolent Chariots* said "there is little wrong with the American car that is not wrong with the American public."

But Americans were willing, indeed eager, to spend vast amounts each year on a machine that symbolized their desires, reflected themselves, and expressed their fantasies. Detroit made them believe that ever-increasing consumption would genuinely help to build a brighter and richer America.

PUTTING ON THE RITZ
The 1953 Packard Caribbean Convertible was one of the most spectacular and lavish cars of the decade. A design that evolved from Packard's recent Pan American show cars, it outsold its arch-rival, the glamorous Cadillac Eldorado.

And buy they did. In 1955 Detroit shipped eight million new cars to showrooms, accounting for $65 billion or 20 percent of the Gross National Product. GM became the first corporation to earn $1 billion in a single year, and their touring Motorama exhibitions drew two million visitors at every stop. The affluent society rolled effortlessly on, cushioned by fat Goodyear whitewalls. The American car of the Fifties may have been all jets and Jane Russell, but it fanned the flames of the new industrial prosperity, created those rows of neat clapboard houses and those miles of arrow-straight freeways, and gave America an upward mobility that was the envy of the world.

1950 CHRYSLER
Imperial

THE IMPERIAL FOUR-DOOR SEDAN COST $3,055 BEFORE OPTIONAL EXTRAS WERE ADDED

IN 1950 CHRYSLER WAS celebrating its silver jubilee, an anniversary year with a sting in its tail. The Office of Price Stabilization had frozen car prices, there was a four-month strike, and serious coal and steel shortages were affecting the industry.

The '50 Imperial was a Chrysler New Yorker with a special roof and interior trim from the Derham Body Company. The jewels in Chrysler's crown, the Imperials were meant to lock horns with the best of Cadillac, Packard, and Lincoln. With Ausco-Lambert disc brakes, Prestomatic transmission, and a MoPar compass, they used the finest technology Chrysler could muster. The trouble was, only 10,650 Imperials drove out of the door in 1950, the hemi-head V8 wouldn't arrive until the next year, buyers were calling it a Chrysler rather than an Imperial, and that frumpy styling looked exactly like what it was – yesterday's lunch warmed up again.

ENGINE
The inline L-head eight developed 135 bhp and had a cast-iron block with five main bearings. The carburetor was a Carter single-barrel, and Prestomatic automatic transmission with fluid drive came as standard.

CHRYSLER LOGO
The celebrated designer Virgil Exner joined Chrysler in 1949 but arrived too late to improve the looks of the moribund Imperial.

INTERIOR
Chryslers interiors were as restrained and conservative as the people who drove them. Turnkey ignition replaced push-button in 1950, which was also the first year of electric windows.

WINDSHIELD
The windshield was still old-fashioned two-piece flat glass, which made the Imperial look rather antiquated.

BRAKES
The industry's first disc brakes came as standard on Chrysler Crown Imperials.

1950 CHRYSLER IMPERIAL

Bulky, rounded Chryslers were some of the biggest cars on the road in 1950. The Imperials had Cadillac-style grilles, and the Crown Imperial was a long limousine built to rival the Cadillac 75. In keeping with its establishment image, an Imperial station wagon was never offered. One claim to fame was that MGM Studios used an Imperial-based mobile camera car in many of their film productions.

REAR WINDOW
New "Clearbac" rear window used three pieces of glass that were divided by chrome strips.

SPECIFICATIONS

MODEL 1950 Chrysler Imperial
PRODUCTION 10,650
BODY STYLE Four-door sedan.
CONSTRUCTION Steel body and chassis.
ENGINE 323cid straight eight.
POWER OUTPUT 135 bhp.
TRANSMISSION Prestomatic semiautomatic.
SUSPENSION *Front:* coil springs; *Rear:* live axle.
BRAKES Front and rear drums, optional front discs.
MAXIMUM SPEED 100 mph (161 km/h)
0–60 MPH (0–96 KM/H) 13 sec
A.F.C. 16 mpg (5.7 km/l)

SEMIAUTOMATIC TRANSMISSION
The semiautomatic gearbox allowed the driver to use a clutch to pull away, with the automatic taking over as the car accelerated. Imperials had Safety-Level ride, Safety-Rim wheels, Cycle-Bonded brake linings, and a waterproof ignition system.

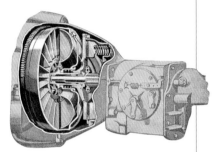

BRIGHTWORK
The brightwork on the door sill runs right through between the mudguards. The theme is reflected on the trailing edges of the front grille.

1950 DeSoto
Custom

HERNANDO ADORNS
THE DESOTO LOGO

THE DESOTO OF 1950 had a glittery glamour that cheered up post-war America. Hailed as "cars built for owner satisfaction," they were practical, boxy, and tough. DeSoto was a longtime taxi builder that, in the steel-starved years of 1946–48, managed to turn out 11,600 cabs, most of which plied the streets of New York.

Despite more chrome up front than any other Chrysler product, DeSotos still labored on with an L-head six-cylinder 250cid mill. The legendary Firedome V8 wouldn't arrive until 1952. But body shapes for 1950 were the prettiest ever, and the American public reacted with delight, buying up 133,854 units in the calendar year, ranking DeSoto 14th in the industry. Top-line Custom Convertibles had a very reasonable sticker price of $2,578 and came with Tip-Toe hydraulic shift with Gyrol fluid drive as standard. The austere postwar years were a sales Disneyland for the makers of these sparkling cars, but DeSoto's roll couldn't last. By 1961 it had disappeared forever.

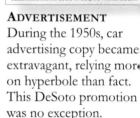

ADVERTISEMENT
During the 1950s, car advertising copy became extravagant, relying more on hyperbole than fact. This DeSoto promotion was no exception.

DESOTO MASCOT
Optional hood ornament was one Hernando DeSoto, a 17th-century Spanish conquistador. The mascot glowed in the dark.

REAR WING
The DeSoto body shape still carried hints of the separate fenders of prewar cars.

GRILLE
The mammoth-tooth grille would be scaled down for 1951. '50 models are easily spotted by their body-color vertical grille divider, unique to this year.

INTERIOR
'50 DeSotos came in two levels of trim. De Luxe, the poverty package, was outsold three to one by the plusher Custom, at $200 more. Direction signals and back-up lights were offered as standard on the Custom, while options included heater, electric clock, and two-tone paint. Convertibles came with whitewalls and wheel covers.

TRUNK
The car's rump was large, round, and unadorned. Trunk space was cavernous.

ENGINE
All '50 DeSotos shared the same lackluster straight-six engine.

1950 DeSoto Custom Convertible

DeSoto's role at Chrysler was much like Mercury's at Ford and Oldsmobile's at GM, to plug the gap between budget models and uptown swankmobiles. The top-of-the-line Custom range fielded a Club Coupe, two huge wagons, a six-passenger sedan, a two-door Sportsman, and a convertible. DeSoto's volume sellers were its sedans and coupes, which listed at under $2,000 in De Luxe form.

ENGINE
The side-valve straight six was stodgy, putting out a modest 112 bhp through the fluid drive gearbox, an innovative semiautomatic pre-selector with conventional manual operation or semiauto kick-down.

SPECIFICATIONS

MODEL 1950 DeSoto Custom Convertible

PRODUCTION 2,900

BODY STYLE Two-door convertible.

CONSTRUCTION Steel body and box-section chassis.

ENGINE 236.7cid straight six.

POWER OUTPUT 112 bhp.

TRANSMISSION Fluid drive semiautomatic.

SUSPENSION *Front:* independent coil springs; *Rear:* leaf springs with live axle.

BRAKES Front and rear drums.

MAXIMUM SPEED 90 mph (145 km/h)

0–60 MPH (0–96 KM/H) 22.1 sec

A.F.C. 18 mpg (6.4 km/l)

1951 WYOMING 18 263

1952 KAISER HENRY J.
Corsair

KAISER LOGO ON THE
STEERING WHEEL

IN THE EARLY 1950s, the major motor manufacturers reckoned that small cars meant small profits, so low-priced transportation was left to independent companies like Nash, Willys, and Kaiser-Frazer. In 1951, a streamlined, Frazerless Kaiser launched "America's Most Important New Car," the Henry J.

An 80 bhp six-cylinder "Supersonic" engine gave the Corsair frugal fuel consumption, with Kaiser claiming that every third mile in a Henry J. was free. The market, however, was unconvinced. At $1,561, the Corsair cost more than the cheapest big Chevy, wasn't built as well, and depreciated rapidly. Small wonder then that only 107,000 were made. Had America's first serious economy car been launched seven years later during the '58 recession, the Henry J. may well have been a best-seller.

PRODUCTION
The Henry J. was buil at the Willow Run factory in Michigan. Despite the caption under the main image that read "Final inspection. Everything must be perfect," quality was poor, and the car quickly earned itself a second-rate reputation

RACING HENRY J.
In 1952, a Henry J. entered th Monte Carlo Rally and, to everybody's surprise, finished in a creditable 20th position.

CHASSIS
The double-channel box chassis was orthodox and sturdy. The 100 in (2.54 m) wheelbase was short but the interior space generous. America's new family car was "long, low, and handsome. The Henry J. is a joy to drive and comfortable to ride in – the Smart Car for Smart People."

INTERIOR
The interior was seriously austere and gimmick-free. Apart from overdrive and automatic transmission, very few factory options were available. The few controls included starter, ignition, light, and choke switches.

REPLACEMENT FENDER
Bolt-on front and rear fenders were part of the Henry J.'s money-saving philosophy.

COLOR SCHEME
*Blue Satin was one of nine
color options available.*

ROOF LINE
*High roof line owed its existence
to the fact that Kaiser's
chairman always wore a hat.*

SPECIFICATIONS

MODEL 1952 Kaiser Henry J.
Corsair Deluxe
PRODUCTION 12,900
BODY STYLE Two-door, five-seater
sedan.
CONSTRUCTION Steel body
and chassis.
ENGINE 134cid four, 161cid six.
POWER OUTPUT 68–80 bhp.
TRANSMISSION Three-speed
manual with optional overdrive,
optional three-speed Hydra-Matic
automatic.
SUSPENSION *Front:* coil springs;
Rear: leaf springs with live axle.
BRAKES Front and rear drums.
MAXIMUM SPEED 87 mph
(140 km/h)
0–60 MPH (0–96 KM/H) 17 sec
A.F.C. 34 mpg (12 km/l)

1952 KAISER HENRY J. CORSAIR DELUXE

The stubborn head of Kaiser industries
insisted that the Henry J., originally designed
as a full-size car by designer Howard "Dutch"
Darrin, be scaled down. American Metal
Products of Detroit created the prototype,
which Darrin then tweaked, not altogether
successfully. Luggage space was among the
largest of any passenger sedan; with the rear
seat folded there were 50 cu ft of trunk area.

FIN FASHION
*Modest dorsal fin was quite
fashionable for 1952.*

BOSS BADGING
The Henry J. nameplate
came from Henry J. Kaiser,
chairman of the Kaiser-
Frazer Corporation.

TIRES
*Corsairs were shod with
skinny 5.9x15 tube tires.*

1954 CHEVROLET
Corvette

CORVETTE FLAGS FOUND
ON THE CAR'S HOOD

A CARICATURE OF A EUROPEAN roadster, the first Corvette of 1953 was more show than go. With typical flamboyance, Harley Earl was more interested in the way it looked than the way it went. But he did identify that car consumers were growing restless and saw a huge market for a new type of auto opium. With everybody's dreams looking exactly the same, the plastic Vette brought a badly needed shot of designed-in diversity. Early models may have been cramped and slow, but they looked like they'd been lifted straight off a Motorama turntable, which they had. Building them was a nightmare though, and for a while GM lost money on each one. Still, nobody minded because Chevrolet now had a new image – as the company that came up with the first American sports car.

INTERNAL HANDLES
Like the British sports cars it aped, the '54 Vette's door handles appeared on the inside. Windows were apologetic side curtains that leaked and flapped; it would take two years for glass windows to come into the equation.

INTERIOR
An aeronautical fantasy, the Corvette's dashboard had a futuristic, space-age feel. Not until 1958 was the row of dials repositioned to a more practical front-of-the-driver location.

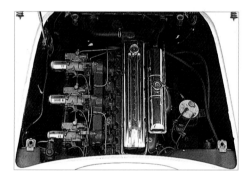

ENGINE
Souped-up Blue Flame Six may have had triple carbs, higher compression, and a high-lift cam, but it was still old and wheezy. Vettes had to wait until 1955 for the V8 they deserved.

ENGINE WAS MOUNTED
WELL BACK IN FRAME TO
IMPROVE HANDLING

SPECIFICATIONS

MODEL 1954 Chevrolet Corvette
PRODUCTION 3,640
BODY STYLE Two-door,
 two-seater sports.
CONSTRUCTION Fiberglass body,
 steel chassis.
ENGINE 235.5cid straight six.
POWER OUTPUT 150 bhp.
TRANSMISSION Two-speed
 Powerglide automatic.
SUSPENSION *Front:* coil springs;
 Rear: leaf springs with live axle.
BRAKES Front and rear drums.
MAXIMUM SPEED 107 mph
 (172 km/h)
0–60 MPH (0–96 KM/H) 8–12 sec
A.F.C. 20 mpg (7 km/l)

SLEEK LINES

The cute little body with minimal glitz was one of Earl's best efforts. But, being smitten with jet styling, he couldn't resist adding the "jet pod" taillights, which spoil the car's symmetry.

ODDLY ENOUGH, 80 PERCENT OF ALL '54 CORVETTES WERE PAINTED WHITE

BUS TIRES LACKED ADHESION, SUSPENSION WAS UNYIELDING, AND TWO-SPEED AUTOMATIC JERKED ALL OVER THE PLACE

OVERVIEW

The cleverly packed fiberglass body was rather tricky to make, with no less than 46 different sections. The convertible top folded out of sight below a neat lift-up panel.

ENTHUSIASTS WERE NOT WILD ABOUT THE SMALL TRUNK, PLASTIC BODY, AND LETHARGIC PERFORMANCE, BUT BETTER THINGS WERE AROUND THE CORNER

PERFORMANCE WAS NOT IN THE JAGUAR XK120 LEAGUE, WITH A MODEST 107 MPH (172 KM/H) TOP SPEED

EXHIBITION SUCCESS

The Vette's shape was based on the 1952 EX-122 show car, and this was one of the few Motorama dream cars to go into production virtually unchanged. The original plan to produce the Vette in steel was shelved after widespread acclaim for the fiberglass body from visitors to Motorama.

OUTBOARD-MOUNTED REAR LEAF SPRINGS HELPED CORNERING STABILITY

1954 CHEVROLET CORVETTE

EVOLUTION OF THE CHEVROLET CORVETTE

HOWLING ALONG the freeways of America, the Vette has always been special. In fact, a whole mystique has grown up around Chevy's wild child. Perhaps it's because of its personification of rebellion, no-compromise attitude, or the people that drive them, but the Vette has endured as America's alter ego – proof positive that not everybody wants to pilot slushy barges half-a-block long. When the motoring day of reckoning comes, the Corvette will be up there with the best of them.

1953

THAT THE VETTE EXISTS at all is due to the genius of one man – Harley Earl. It started life as no more than a half-formed thought, spinning gently on a Motorama turntable. Within months, the Corvette was a reality and proved the perfect product for a generation of suburban good-timers whose beloved Levis were now feeling the strain.

KEY FEATURES
• Polo White EX-122 show car wows the crowds at 1952 Motorama
• Production cars have no exterior door handles or side windows
• Base engine is 150 bhp 235.5cid straight six
• Calendar year sales of 300 cars

1956

THE V8 LUMP & FUEL injection helped, but that swooping, sculpted body of '56 did more than anything to guarantee the Corvette's future. Macho, sexy, and much more refined, the second-generation Vette ('56–'62) could now lock horns with Uncle Henry's T-Bird – and it had windup windows. Today, it is one of the icons of Fifties car design.

KEY DEVELOPMENTS
• New 210 bhp 265cid V8 base engine
• New curved body and taillights
• Outside door handles and windup windows instead of clumsy side curtains
• Exhausts exit through rear bumper guards
• Transistorized radio seek option

1963

THE STING RAY wowed the world like the Jaguar E-Type. For the first time in the Corvette's history it was a sellout. Demand was up by 50 percent and the factory couldn't cope. Waiting lists stretched to infinity, and nobody got a discount. These were the most desirab Corvettes of all, and that magical '63 split-window Coupe was a car to die fo

KEY DEVELOPMENTS
• New body and Sting Ray name
• 327cid V8 option
• Improved interior with dual cockpits
• Unique split rear window
• New chassis frame
• Independent rear suspension
• Bigger drum brakes

1954 CHEVROLET
Corvette

REAR PLATE PROBLEMS
Early cars had license plates in a plastic niche that misted up. Chevrolet inserted two bags of desiccant material to absorb the moisture.

TWIN-COWL DASH WAS PURE BUCK ROGERS

QUALITY STYLING
Rear-fender detailing is glorious, and shows Earl's genius at its very best.

IMPAC
PROTECTIO
MAY HAVE BEE
VESTIGIAL, BU
FIBERGLAS
BODY TOO
MINO
IMPAC
WEL

MN·1744
NY EMPIRE STATE 57

1968

...RVY, CHARISMATIC, but compromised, ...e late '60s Vette was hardly a quantum ...p forward. Emasculated by Federal ...erference and economic, social, and ...ergy neuroses, Chevy was forced to ...ne its bad boy. Suddenly the Vette ...anged from a tire-shredding banshee ...a blow-dried boulevardier. Ironically, ...popularity actually increased.

KEY DEVELOPMENTS
- New "Mako Shark" styling
- Redesigned interior
- New T-Top Sport Coupe model with removable roof panels
- Massive 427cid V8 available
- Wipers now behind vacuum-operated panel

1978

THE CORVETTE celebrated its silver anniversary in '78, marking the moment with a new fastback roof line and wide rear window that tucked around the car's sides. The interior felt more spacious, and rear vision was vastly improved. A Vette was the official Indy pace car in '78 and Chevy produced a run of 6,200 limited edition look-alikes.

KEY DEVELOPMENTS
- Base engine is 350cid V8
- Larger luggage area
- Crossed flags insignia returns to nose and sides
- 500,000th Vette made in 1977
- Optional $995 five-speed gearbox

1984

THE ARRIVAL OF the likes of RX-7s, Datsun Zs, and Porsche 928s meant that America's sports car had to grow up fast. The sixth-generation Vette of '83 was the fastest, best-handling, and most radical ever. Engineered from the ground up and truly sophisticated, it was built to take on the world's elite, while still retaining the Corvette's uniquely American personality.

KEY DEVELOPMENTS
- Hugely improved roadholding
- Steel backbone chassis with unitized body structure
- New Girlock ventilated disc brakes
- New 4+3 gearbox
- Now one of the half-dozen fastest production cars in the world

1992

IN THE WORLD OF THE motor car, 44 years is an eternity for a model name. Yet the Vette has not just survived, it has prospered and become a truly great car. The one-millionth Corvette rolled off the production line in 1992 and, as this book is being written, there's a new Vette poised to steal America's heart all over again.

KEY DEVELOPMENTS
- New 300 bhp V8
- ZR-1 option has twin-cam 32-valve with 405 bhp
- LT1 option has six-speed manual or four-speed automatic gearbox
- ABS and driver's-side airbag standard
- GM's first "passive keyless" entry system

EARLY PRODUCTION
The first cars were literally hand built at the Flint, Michigan, factory. Plans to turn out 1,000 cars a month in 1954 were hit by poor early sales.

GUIDING WORDS
Earl's advice to stylists working on the Corvette was to "go all the way and then back off." They didn't back off much!

EARL ADMITTED THAT SHARK-TOOTH GRILLE WAS ROBBED FROM CONTEMPORARY FERRARIS

...NE-GUARDS ON LIGHTS ...RE CULLED FROM ...ROPEAN RACING CARS, ...CRITICIZED FOR ...NG TOO ...MININE

MN·1744
NY EMPIRE STATE 57

1954 HUDSON
Hornet

BADGE SHOWS TWO
TOWERS AND TWO
GALLEONS

HUDSON DID ITS BEST IN '54 to clean up its aged 1948 body. Smoother flanks and a lower, wider front view helped, along with a new dash and brighter fabrics and vinyls. And at long last the windshield was one piece. Mechanically it wasn't bad either. In fact, some say the last Step-Down was the best ever. With the straight six came a Twin-H power option, a hot camshaft, and an alloy head that could crank out 170 bhp; it was promptly dubbed "The Fabulous Hornet."

The problem was that everybody had V8s, and by mid-1954 Hudson had hemorrhaged over $6 million. In April that year, Hudson, which had been around since 1909, was swallowed up by the Nash-Kelvinator Corporation. Yet the Hornet has been rightly recognized as a milestone car and one of the quickest sixes of the era. If Hudson is to be remembered for anything, it should be for the innovative engineers, who could wring the best from ancient designs and tiny budgets.

INTERIOR
The dash was quite modern and glossy but still used Hudson's distinctive single-digit speedo. The Hornet's interior was liberally laced with chrome, and trim was nylon worsted Bedford cloth and Plastihide in brown, blue, or green. Power steering was offered on Hudsons for the first time in '54.

COLOR CHOICE
Hornets came in Roman Bronze, Pasture Green, Algerian Blue, St. Clair Gray, Lipstick Red, or Coronation Cream as here.

TRIM
Extra chrome trim was new for '54.

ENGINE
Amazingly, Hudson never offered V8 power, which was to hasten its downfall.

LFO 227

Hornet

FRONT VIEW
The grille and front wings were new for 1954 and common to all Hornet shells.

BODY SHAPE
Despite its low, ground-hugging stance, the Hornet had plenty of room inside.

TRUNK MOTIF
The Hornet's rocket motif was a stylish vanity that echoed Hudson's new jetlike look.

ENGINE
The L-section 308cid straight six developed 160 bhp and breathed through a Carter two-barrel. Compression was boosted for '54, with an $86 performance option available.

1954 HUDSON HORNET 7D

These Hudsons were known as "Step-Downs" because you literally stepped down into the car. Among the fastest cars of the Fifties, they boasted above-average power and crisp handling. NASCAR devotees watched many a Hudson trounce the competition, winning 22 out of 37 major races in '53 alone.

SLOPING ROOF
The sloping back on the four-door was very different from the conventional trunk on the two-door. Only the new-for-'54 minifins holding the tail-lights interrupted the flow.

SPECIFICATIONS

MODEL 1954 Hudson Hornet 7D
PRODUCTION 24,833 (1954 Hornets)
BODY STYLE Two-door coupe or convertible, four-door sedan.
CONSTRUCTION Steel body and chassis.
ENGINE 308cid straight six.
POWER OUTPUT 160–170 bhp.
TRANSMISSION Three-speed manual, optional Hydra-Matic automatic.
SUSPENSION *Front:* coil springs; *Rear:* leaf springs.
BRAKES Front and rear drums.
MAXIMUM SPEED 110 mph (177 km/h)
0–60 MPH (0–96 KM/H) 12 sec
A.F.C. 17 mpg (6 km/l)

1954 KAISER
Darrin

"THE SPORTS CAR the world has been awaiting" was a monster flop. Designed by Howard "Dutch" Darrin, Kaiser's odd hybrid came about in 1953 as an accident. Henry J. Kaiser, the ill-mannered chairman of the Kaiser Corporation, had so riled Darrin that he disappeared to his California studio, spent his own money, and created a purse-lipped two-seater that looked like it wanted to give you a kiss.

Its futuristic fiberglass body rode on a Henry J. chassis and was powered by a Willys six-cylinder engine. Alas, the body rippled and cracked, the sliding doors wouldn't slide, and the weedy 90 bhp flathead was no match for Chevy's chic Corvette. At a costly $3,668, the Darrin was in Cadillac territory, and only 435 found buyers. Late in '54, Kaiser-Willys went under, taking the Darrin with it. Few mourned either's demise.

ADS CALLED IT "THE OUTSTANDING PLEASURE CAR OF OUR DAY"

INTERIOR
Standard equipment included electric wipers, tachometer, and a European-style dashboard, with leather trim an optional extra. Whitewall tires, a one-piece windshield, and a three-position convertible hood were also standard.

1953 DARRIN SPORTSTER
In keeping with Kaiser's reputation for wacky, off-the-wall designs, the Darrin Sportster featured sliding doors that disappeared into the front wings. The trouble was that they rattled, jammed, and didn't open all the way.

AN UNHAPPY ALLIANCE
Henry J. Kaiser was livid that Howard Darrin had worked on the car without his permission. In the end, the Darrin was actually saved by Henry J.'s wife, who thought it was "the most beautiful thing" she'd ever seen.

DARRIN BODIES WERE MADE BY BOAT-BUILDERS, GLASSPAR

HOWARD DARRIN FIRST CONCEIVED HIS CONTENTIOUS SLIDING DOORS BACK IN 1922

REAR FENDER AND TAILLIGHT TREATMENT IS RESTRAINED FOR THE YEAR AND REDOLENT OF AN XK JAGUAR

REAR FENDER TAPERS UPWARD TO CREATE A FINE TORPEDO-LIKE SHAPE

THE DARRIN'S FRONT
FENDER SLOPES DOWN
THROUGH THE DOOR
AND MEETS A
DRAMATIC KICK-UP
OVER THE REAR
WHEEL ARCH

BELT UP
The Darrin
was remarkable for
being only the third US
production car to feature seat
belts as standard. The other two
cars were a Muntz and a Nash.

ENGINE
Kaiser opted for an F-head Willys version of the
Henry J. six-cylinder motor, but with just one carb
it boasted only 10 more horses than standard. After
the company folded, Darrin dropped 300 bhp
supercharged Caddy V8s into the remaining cars,
which went like hell.

SPECIFICATIONS

MODEL 1954 Kaiser Darrin 161
PRODUCTION 435 (total)
BODY STYLE Two-seater sports.
CONSTRUCTION Fiberglass body,
  steel frame.
ENGINE 161 cid six.
POWER OUTPUT 90 bhp.
TRANSMISSION Three-speed
  manual with optional overdrive.
SUSPENSION *Front:* coil springs;
  Rear: leaf springs.
BRAKES Front and rear drums.
MAXIMUM SPEED 100 mph
  (161 km/h)
0–60 MPH (0–96 KM/H) 15.1 sec
A.F.C. 27 mpg (9.6 km/l)

STUNNING STYLING
The Darrin was beautifully styled and, unlike
most visions of the future, has hardly dated
at all. The Landau top could be removed
and a hardtop fitted on, and, with its
three-speed floor shift and overdrive,
it could return up to a remarkable
30 mpg (10.6 km/l).

STAR APPROVAL
The French singer Suzanne
Bernard shows off the
Darrin's dubious doors at
the third annual International
Motor Sports Show in
1954. Modern restorations
have since cured the door
problem, but contemporary
owners found them to
be gimmicky, unreliable,
and just plain annoying.

KAISER-FRAZER – A TALE OF MINNOWS AND SHARKS

KAISER MAY HAVE BEEN an imperial name for a motor car, but it wasn't enough to crack the giant American car-maker cartel. Kaiser began auto production in 1946 at Ford's vast Willow Run factory, which had produced Liberator bombers in the war. After the cessation of hostilities, the Government leased the Michigan plant to Henry J. Kaiser and Joe Frazer. Frazer was the president of the Graham Car Company, and Kaiser had earned millions mass-producing ships and houses; he was a "Midas touch" entrepreneur who was seen as serious competition for the market muscle of Ford, GM, and Chrysler.

HENRY J. KAISER

Initially fielding a two-model plan, the Kaiser was the economy car and the Frazer the luxury job. By 1949, the company had scooped 5 percent of the market plus a generous

$44 million loan from the Government Reconstruction Finance Corporation. K-F's products were full of such technical wizardry as independent torsion-bar suspension, front-wheel drive, and two-piece tailgates on station wagons. But by 1950 the dream had peaked, and sales began to evaporate.

The Willow Run monolith turned out to be more efficient as an aircraft plant than a car factory, and costs hit the roof; Ford had wisely turned it down for that very reason. In 1950, sales were 144,000 cars, but K-F posted a $13 million loss.

THE '48 KAISER SPECIAL WAS MEDIOCRE IN DESIGN AND ENGINEERING

1954 KAISER
Darrin

THE 90 BHP DARRIN COST $145 MORE THAN THE 150 BHP CHEVY CORVETTE

REAR VIEW IS SURPRISINGLY BRITISH-LOOKING FOR A CALIFORNIAN DESIGN

LATE DELIVERIES
The Darrin took its time coming. It was first announced on September 26, 1952, with 60 initial prototypes at last displayed to the public on February 11, 1953. Final production cars reached owners as late as January 6, 1954

FLORIDA
9- 8677
19 SUNSHINE STATE 54

THE MANHATTAN OF '53 WAS SERIOUSLY HANDICAPPED BY THE ABSENCE OF A V8

1953, and the Henry J. was finally dropped in favor of the Willys Aero. The merger gave finances a momentary fillip, and Kaisers became sleeker and more luxurious, culminating in the audacious Darrin, which turned out to be another money-loser. Willow Run was bought by GM, and in '55 Kaiser moved to Buenos Aires, where it produced the Carabela model well into the Sixties. Despite burning up $100 million, K-F couldn't break the Big Three's market domination. Apart from being unable to establish a dealer network, the deeply conservative US car buyers resisted its avant-garde models. Had the parsimonious Henry J. appeared in recession-wracked 1958, when the motor market was howling for economy compacts, fortune might have smiled on Kaiser-Frazer.

A hasty restyle in '51 didn't help, and the Henry J., first of the economy compacts, was ugly, overpriced, and slow. The Frazer nameplate was dropped, and the Kaiser empire crumbled fast. Some 3,000 workers were laid off in May 1952 and, despite the addition of a "Penny-Minder" carburetor to the Henry J., it continued to bomb. Kaiser merged with Willys-Overland in

HOWARD DARRIN, WHO HAD A STORMY RELATIONSHIP WITH HENRY J. KAISER

OFFENDING LEGISLATION

The prototype headlight height was too low for state lighting laws, so Kaiser stylists hiked up the front-fender line for the real thing. This offended Darrin, who said it gave the car "an uphill look."

HARDTOP MADE THE CABIN MUCH LESS CLAUSTROPHOBIC AND CRAMPED THAN THAT OF THE SOFT-TOP

SWIVELING ACRYLIC SIDESCREENS REDUCED COCKPIT BUFFETING

FRONT VIEW LOOKS VERY MUCH LIKE AN EARLY VW KARMANN GHIA

1954 MERCURY
Monterey

MERCURY TRADE-IN
VALUES WERE THE HIGHEST
IN THEIR CLASS

FORD'S UPSCALE MERCURY nameplate was on a roll in 1954. Out went their ancient flathead V8, and in came a new 161 bhp Y-block mill. *Motor Trend* magazine said: "That power will slam you back into the seat when you stomp the throttle." Buyers loved the idea of so much heft and drove away Montereys in the thousands, sending Mercury to an impressive seventh slot in the sales league.

Chic, suave, and still glowing from the James Dean association, Montereys were perfect cruisers for these confident, fat years. Unemployment was low, wages were high, and the economy was thumping. Everyone wanted a Merc – "The car that makes any driving easy" – and output for 1954 was a monster 259,300 units. The following year would be the automobile industry's best ever as buyers thronged to showrooms, packing them tighter than Jane Russell's famous brassiere.

HOLLYWOOD GLAMOUR
Film star Gary Cooper poses with his 19
Monterey. Mere mortals vied to win thei
dream car in 1956 when TV host Ed
Sullivan gave away 80 Mercury Phaetons.

CONVERTIBLE AND CLEAR-TOP OPTIONS
This 1954 ad shows the comely Convertible, priced at $2,554. For another $28, you could own America's first transparent-roofed car, the $2,582 Monterey Sun Valley, painted in either pale yellow or mint green. The front half of the roof contained a tinted Plexiglass section that unfortunately raised the interior temperature by about 10 degrees.

INTERIOR
Montereys had optional $140 Bendix power steering, which the industry had only just refined. Road testers of the day thought it to be the best setup around. Bendix also supplied the Monterey's power brakes. Interiors came in a wide variety of solid and two-tone cloth, vinyl, and leather trim combinations.

MERCURY DASHBOARDS
RETAINED THE
INTERCEPTOR-TYPE
AIRPLANE PANEL WITH
JOYSTICK CONTROLS.

CUSTOM CHROME
Montereys were the fanciest Mercs and said as much on their front fenders, which sported a medallion along with the distinctive chrome side trim. All body types in this series, except the station wagons, were called Monterey Customs and had special wide chrome on the windshield and side windows.

HIGH PERFORMANCE

The new V8 was road tested over four million miles, and proved highly competitive on the stock-car circuit, where Mercurys were ranked fifth in the sport.

1954 MERCURY MONTEREY

The Monterey enjoyed enviable success; the four-door sedan was the second most popular model of 1954, with 64,995 made. Customers could choose from 35 different color options – 14 solid shades and 21 two-tones. The car's upscale image was reflected in color names such as Park Lane Green, Yosemite Yellow, and Country Club Tan.

OPTIONAL AUTOMATIC

Options included Merc-O-Matic auto transmission along with power steering, brakes, and four-way seat. The new V161 engine had twin Tornado combustion chambers, alloy pistons, and a four-barrel Holley.

SPECIFICATIONS

MODEL 1954 Mercury Monterey
PRODUCTION 174,238
BODY STYLE Two- or four-door hardtop, station wagon, and convertible.
CONSTRUCTION Steel body and chassis.
ENGINE 256cid V8.
POWER OUTPUT 161 bhp.
TRANSMISSION Three-speed manual with optional overdrive, optional Merc-O-Matic Drive automatic.
SUSPENSION *Front:* independent coil springs; *Rear:* leaf springs.
BRAKES Front and rear drums.
MAXIMUM SPEED 100 mph (161 km/h)
0–60 MPH (0–96 KM/H) 14 sec
A.F.C. 20 mpg (7 km/l)

PILLARLESS COUPE

Two-door models without the central strut had a classic pillarless look with the windows down.

MOODY AND MAGNIFICENT

The heavy grille, chunky hood motif, and slight scowl make the Monterey's front end look more than a bit mean.

HOT-ROD NOSTALGIA

This rear view evokes earlier Mercurys, as loved by roof-chopping hot-rodders and famously driven over the edge by James Dean in Rebel Without a Cause.

1955 FORD
Thunderbird

THE POPULAR
THUNDERBIRD GAINED
ENOUGH EXPOSURE TO BE
INCLUDED ON THIS STAMP

CHEVY'S 1954 CORVETTE may have been a peach, but anything GM could do, Ford could do better. The '55 T-Bird had none of the Vette's fiberglass nonsense, but a steel body and grunty V8 motor. Plus it was drop-dead gorgeous and offered scores of options, with the luxury of wind-up windows. Nobody was surprised when it outsold the creaky Corvette 24-to-one. But Ford wanted volume and two-seaters weren't everybody's cup of tea, which is why by 1958 the Little Bird became the Big Bird, swollen by four fat armchairs. Nevertheless, as the first of America's top-selling two-seaters, the Thunderbird fired the public's imagination. For the next decade American buyers looking for lively power in a stylish package would greedily devour every Thunderbird going.

ENGINE
The T-Bird's motor was the new cast-iron OHV 292cid V8 with dual exhausts and four-barrel Holley carb. Compared to the Vette's ancient six, the T-Bird's mill offered serious shove and played a major role in the car's success.

BADGE
The Thunderbird name was chosen after a southwestern Native American god who brought rain and prosperity.

POWER BULGE
The hood needed a bulge to clear the large air cleaners. It was stylish too.

INTERIOR
Luxury options made the Thunderbird an easygoing companion. On the list were power steering, windows, and brakes, automatic transmission, and even electric seats and a power-assisted top. At $100, the push-button radio was more expensive than power steering.

ENGINE
Power output ranged from 212 to 300 horses. Buyers could beautify their motors with a $25 chrome dress-up kit.

WINDSHIELD
The aeronautical windshield profile is beautifully simple.

COCKPIT
When the top was up, heat from the transmission made for a hot cockpit; as a result, ventilation flaps were introduced on '56 and '57 models.

CAR AND THE STAR
The movie actress Debbie Reynolds loved her Ford Thunderbird. Today, the T-Bird is a fiercely prized symbol of American Fifties utopia. The 1955–57 Thunderbirds are the most coveted – the model turned into a four-seater in 1958.

1955 FORD THUNDERBIRD CONVERTIBLE
The styling was very Ford, penned by Bill Boyer and supervised by Frank Hershey. The simple, smooth, and youthful outer wrapping was a huge hit. A rakish long hood and short rear deck recalled the 1940s Lincoln Continental. Apart from the somewhat prominent exhausts, the rear end is remarkably uncluttered, and the top shot shows that the T-Bird had a bright and spirited personality.

SMOOTH LINES
For 1955, this was an uncharacteristically clean design and attracted 16,155 buyers in its first year of production.

SPECIFICATIONS

MODEL 1955 Ford Thunderbird
PRODUCTION 16,155
BODY STYLE Two-door, two-seater convertible.
CONSTRUCTION Steel body and chassis.
ENGINE 292cid V8.
POWER OUTPUT 193 bhp.
TRANSMISSION Three-speed manual with optional overdrive, optional three-speed Ford-O-Matic automatic.
SUSPENSION *Front:* independent coil springs; *Rear:* leaf springs with live axle.
BRAKES Front and rear drums.
MAXIMUM SPEED 105–125 mph (169–201 km/h)
0–60 MPH (0–96 KM/H) 7–11 sec
A.F.C. 17 mpg (6 km/l)

1956 CONTINENTAL
Mark II

STYLISH
MARK II LOGO

THAT THE 1950s MOTOR industry couldn't make a beautiful car is robustly disproved by the '56 Continental. As pretty as anything from Italy, the Mark II was intended to be a work of art and a symbol of affluence. William Ford was fanatical about his personal project, fighting for a chrome rather than plastic hood ornament costing $150, or the price of an entire Ford grille.

But it was that tenacious attention to detail that killed the car. Even with the Mark II's huge $10,000 price tag, the Continental Division still hemorrhaged money. Poor sales, internal company struggles, and the fact that it was only a two-door meant that by 1958 the Continental was no more. Ironically, one of the most beautiful cars Ford ever made was sacrificed to save one of the ugliest in the upcoming E-Car project – the Edsel.

A CLASSY ACT
The most expensive automobile in America, the pricey $9,695 Continental really was the car for the stars. Elvis tried one as a change from his usual Cadillacs, and Jayne Mansfield owned a pearl-colored '57 with mink trim. The Continental epitomized the concept of "personal luxury."

ENGINE
Engines were Lincoln 368cid V8s, specially picked from the assembly line, stripped down, and hand-balanced for extra smoothness and refinement. With the exception of Packard's 374cid unit, this was the largest engine available in a 1956 production car.

INTERIOR
The classically simple cockpit could have come straight out of a British car. The interior boasted richly grained leathers and lavish fabrics. Autosearch radio, four-way power seat, dual heater, and map lights were among an impressive array of standard features.

TEMPERATURE
Air-conditioning was the only extra-cost option.

TINTED GLASS

This was one of the no-cost extras offered. Other options included two-tone paint, an engraved nameplate, and all-leather trim. The high-quality leather was specially imported from Bridge of Weir in Scotland.

BODY HEIGHT

"Cow belly" frame was specifically designed to allow high seating with a low roof line.

1956 CONTINENTAL MARK II

With a sleek, clean front and simple die-cast grille, the only concession to contemporary Detroit ornamentation was how the turn signals blended into the front bumper. At the rear of the car, trim fins, elegant bumpers, and neat inset taillights meant that the Continental was admired on both sides of the Atlantic. Unlike later models, the stamped-in spare tire cover did actually house the spare.

SPECIFICATIONS

MODEL 1956 Continental Mark II
PRODUCTION 2,250
BODY STYLE Two-door, four-seater sedan.
CONSTRUCTION Steel body and chassis.
ENGINE 368cid V8.
POWER OUTPUT 285 bhp.
TRANSMISSION Turbo-Drive three-speed automatic.
SUSPENSION *Front:* independent coil springs; *Rear:* leaf springs.
BRAKES Front and rear drums.
MAXIMUM SPEED 115 mph (185 km/h)
0–60 MPH (0–96 KM/H) 12.1 sec
A.F.C. 16 mpg (5.7 km/l)

STYLISH REAR

Handsome three-quarter profile echoes some Ferrari 250 models. Note how the gas tank cap hides behind the taillight.

SCRIPT

Continental tag revived the famous 1930s Lincolns of Edsel Ford.

1957 CHEVROLET
Bel Air

CHEVROLET'S FLEUR-DE-LIS, A
REMINDER OF ITS FRENCH ROOTS

CHEVROLET CALLED its '57 line "sweet, smooth, and sassy," and the Bel Air was exactly what America wanted – a junior Cadillac. Finny, trim, and handsome, and with Ed Cole's Super Turbo-Fire V8, it boasted one of the first production engines to pump out one horsepower per cubic inch; it was the first mass-market "fuelie" sedan with Ramjet injection.

Chevy copywriters screamed "the Hot One's even hotter," and Bel Airs became kings of the street. Production that year broke the 1.5 million barrier and gave Ford the fright of its life. The trouble was that the "Hot One" was forced to cool it when the Automobile Manufacturers' Association urged car makers to put an end to their performance hysteria. Today, the Bel Air is one of the most widely coveted US collector's cars and the perfect embodiment of young mid-Fifties America. In the immortal words of Billie Jo Spears, "Wish we still had her today; the good love we're living, we owe it to that '57 Chevrolet."

— ROCK 'N' ROLL CARS —

IN EARLY FIFTIES SITCOMS, teenagers were always seen trying to boost the keys to the Plymouth Fury from dad's pocket. Advertisers ignored them because it was thought that they neither bought new cars nor determined the family's buying decision. But Chevrolet knew better. Its V8 of '55 was the first domestic model aimed as a hot car for boys with hot dates, and college boys with after-school jobs proved to be a huge growth market. In *Rebel Without a Cause*, James Dean drove a customized '49 Merc, while Elvis Presley drove Continentals and Caddys. To Fifties youth, the American car was a duotone fashion bauble with whitewalls – a harbinger of love, sex, money, and success. And the Big Three finally understood.

CARS AND IMAGE WENT VERY MUCH HAND-IN-HAND DURING THE 1950s

ENGINE OPTIONS
The small-block Turbo-Fire V8 packed 185 horsepower punch in base two-barrel trim. With the optional Rochester four-barrel it could muster 270 bhp. Ramjet injection added a hefty $500 to the sticker price; no surprise then that only 1,503 fuel-injected Bel Airs were sold.

IF BUICK COULD ADD VENTIPORTS TO ITS FENDERS, SO COULD CHEVROLET, THOUGH THE BEL AIR'S WOULD LAST ONLY A COUPLE OF YEARS

THE '57 BEL AIR WAS 2.5 (6.3 CM) LONGER THAN TH '56 MOD

SPECIFICATIONS

MODEL 1957 Chevrolet Bel Air Convertible
PRODUCTION 47,562
BODY STYLE Two-door convertible.
CONSTRUCTION Steel box-section chassis, steel body.
ENGINE 265cid, 283cid V8s.
POWER OUTPUT 162–283 bhp (283cid V8 fuel injected).
TRANSMISSION Three-speed manual with optional overdrive, optional two-speed Powerglide automatic, and Turboglide.
SUSPENSION *Front*: independent coil springs; *Rear*: leaf springs with live axle.
BRAKES Front and rear drums.
MAXIMUM SPEED 90–120 mph (145–193 km/h)
0–60 MPH (0–96 KM/H) 8–12 sec
A.F.C. 14 mpg (5 km/l)

STYLISH MOTORING

At $2,511, the Bel Air Convertible was the epitome of budget-priced good taste, finding 47,562 eager buyers. Low, sleek, and flashy, it could almost out-glam the contemporary Caddy ragtop. But the Bel Air was substance as well as style; seat belts and shoulder harnesses were available on the lengthy options list.

BEL AIR HARDTOP

The two-door hardtop model was another of the six body styles available.

INTERIOR

The distinctive two-tone interiors were a delight. Buyers could opt for a custom color interior, power convertible top, tinted glass, vanity mirror, ventilated seat pads, power windows, and even a tissue dispenser.

HIDDEN FUEL CAP

In common with Lincoln and Cadillac, Chevrolet incorporated the fuel filler-cap into the chrome molding at the rear edge of the left tail fin.

ANODIZED RIBBED PANEL SERVED TO COMPLEMENT REAR FENDER TREATMENT AND GAVE THE BEL AIR A TOUCH OF CLASS

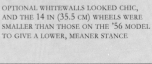

OPTIONAL WHITEWALLS LOOKED CHIC, AND THE 14 IN (35.5 CM) WHEELS WERE SMALLER THAN THOSE ON THE '56 MODEL TO GIVE A LOWER, MEANER STANCE

EVOLUTION OF THE CHEVROLET BEL AIR

THE '57 BEL AIR SUMS UP AMERICA's most prosperous decade better than any other car. Along with hula-hoops, drive-in movies, and rock 'n' roll, it has become a Fifties icon. It was loved then because it was stylish, solid, sporty, and affordable, and it's loved now for more or less the same reasons. Plus, it simply drips with nostalgia. As soon as it was introduced, it was rightly hailed as a design classic. Elegant, sophisticated, and perfectly proportioned, the '57 Bel Air is one of the finest postwar American autos of all. But like so many other drop-dead gorgeous designs, Motown wouldn't and couldn't leave a good thing alone.

CHEVROLET, LIKE EVERYBODY ELSE, WAS EAGER TO CASH IN ON THE JET AGE, BUT IN REALITY THIS '55 BEL AIR LOOKS POSITIVELY DUMPY NEXT TO THE FIGHTER PLANE

Motoramic Chevrolet, stealing the thunder from the high-priced cars!

1953

IN '53, BEL AIRS came in a four-car lineup, and the name now identified the level of trim rather than the body style. At over half a million units, sales were massive, hardly surprising when you could even have the sumptuous two-door ragtop for a smidge over two thousand dollars.

KEY FEATURES
- Available as a two- or four-door sedan, two-door sport coupe, or convertible
- All-new bodies with wrap-around back light on sedans
- Power from 235cid six
- Chevy model year total is 1,356,413

1954

THE '54 LOOKED wider and more modern, the interior was even plusher with wall-to-wall carpets, it had new wheel discs, and the convertible had two-tone, all-vinyl trim. The Bel Air soldiered on with its ancient cast-iron six, but the V8 was just around the corner. Total calendar year sales were slightly up at 1,414,352.

KEY DEVELOPMENTS
- Sport Coupe had special fashion Fiesta upholstery
- An eight-passenger Townsman station wagon joined the lineup
- Four-door Bel Air is Chevrolet's most popular car for 1954

1957 CHEVROLET
Bel Air

STYLISH RESTYLE
'57 Chevys really originated in '55 with a "road-to-roof" redesign of the old line; it's a credit to Chevrolet that the car didn't lose any of its original elegance.

CONTINENTAL SPARE WHEEL CARRIER WAS A DE LUXE OPTION AND MADE THE CONVERTIBLE LOOK LIKE A DREAM COME TRUE

SUBTLE REAR FINS ARE ALMOST DEMURE COMPARED WITH OTHER CONTEMPORARY EFFORTS

THE '57 LOOKS MUCH LEANER THAN THE STOCKIER BEL AIR OF '56

Chevrolet

CALIFORNIA
GUG 562

1957 CHEVROLET BEL AIR

1955	1956	1958	1962

DRAMATIC AND VERY fetching restyle
...ade the '55 Bel Air Chevy's top series
...ain. Things got plushier and plushier,
...th richer upholstery and more
...rome. New for '55 was Chevy's
...illiant 265cid V8, which amazed
...th public and industry alike.
...l Air production this year topped
...staggering 770,955.

EY DEVELOPMENTS
- First year of Chevy's new V8
- Beautiful Nomad wagon joins
  he lineup
- V8 has optional power pack with
  our-barrel carb and twin exhausts
- Bel Air four-door alone sells a
  whopping 354,372

IN '56 THE BEL AIR became a real
honey of a car, taking the nameplate
way upscale. Superbly appointed inside
and out, it was fast, glamorous, and
ultradesirable. And with prices
remaining under $3,000, it was still a
very affordable car. Chevy's model year
production total hit 1,621,004, keeping
it America's number one car maker.

KEY DEVELOPMENTS
- Left-hand taillight now functions as
  a fuel-filler door
- Rear wheel arches are now gently
  scalloped
- Fuel injection available
- V8 Bel Airs now have V-shaped badges
- Nomad wagon sales decline

THIS WAS THE YEAR when the Bel Air
lost its lithe simplicity and looked like
just another big US barge. The all-new
safety girder chassis and body that
looked lower, wider, and longer were
hailed as the new "Dream Car" look.
The Bel Air had shed its youthful
exuberance, passing quietly into
corpulent middle age.

KEY DEVELOPMENTS
- First year of quad headlights
- New gullwing rear fender and
  deck sculpturing
- Impala (right)
  joins the Bel
  Air line

IN COMMON WITH the rest of the
industry, Chevrolet squared off the Bel
Air's lines and chopped off its fins.
Now a midpriced product, the Bel Air
was again one of Chevy's most popular
confections. It was still opulent, with
high-grade cloth interiors and plenty of
stainless steel, chrome, and aluminum,
but it had lost its uniqueness.

KEY DEVELOPMENTS
- Range is now five models, including
  two station wagons
- Chevrolet calendar year output
  peaks at 2,161,398 units

...NAMENTATION

...e rather clumsy bomb-sight hood
...ament could be fairly described as the
... Bel Air's only minor stylistic
...mish. The public liked
...hough.

THE BEL AIR CONVERTIBLE COULD BE FITTED
WITH AN OPTIONAL POWER-OPERATED TOP

WHEN FITTED WITH THE
SOLID-LIFTER FUEL-
INJECTED V8, THE BEL
AIR WAS A DEVASTATINGLY
QUICK CAR

Chevrolet

CALIFORNIA
GUG 562

1957 CHEVROLET
Bel Air Nomad

THE NOMAD'S SLANTING
TAILGATE AND STRIPES
WERE A HALLMARK

IF YOU THOUGHT BMW and Mercedes were first with the sporty upscale station wagon, think again. Chevrolet kicked off the genre as far back as 1955. The Bel Air Nomad was a development of Harley Earl's dream-car wagon based on the Chevrolet Corvette, which he fielded at the four-city Motorama of 1954.

Although it looked like other '55 Bel Airs, the V8 Nomad was the most expensive Chevy ever at $2,571, a whole $265 more than the to-die-for Bel Air ragtop. But despite the fact that *Motor Trend* described the two-door '57 Nomad as "one of the year's most beautiful cars," its appeal was limited, its large glass area made the interior too hot, and the twinkly tailgate let in water. No surprise then that it was one of Chevy's least popular models. Sales never broke the magic 10,000 barrier and, by 1958, the world's first sportswagon, and now a milestone car, had been dropped.

1957 CHEVROLET BEL AIR NOMAD
Although claimed as a Harley Earl design, the Nomad was created by Chevy studio head Claire MacKichen and stylist Carl Renner. Unveiled in January 1954, the Motorama Nomad was such a hit that a production version made it into the '55 brochures. It was essentially a revival of the original Town and Country theme, and a reaction against the utilitarian functionalism of the boxy wooden wagons that had become ubiquitous in suburban America.

STATION WAGONS
FIFTIES CAR ADVERTISERS visualized the dream and wrote the script. The young American family marveled at images of sleek station wagons outside Ivy League country clubs, or the kids and family dog piled into a vast nine-passenger woody. The wagon wasn't a compromise but an entrée into the world of private schools, old money, and wholesome domesticity. And Mom made that buying decision. She'd seen beautifully groomed suburban matrons ferrying nine Little League players to the ballpark in a Country Squire or a Ranchwagon. She cherished her wagon like her hairdresser and rumbled around the parking lots with pride.

1958
DeSoto Firesweep
4-door Explorer

1960 Ford Country Squire

ENGINE

The base engine was a 235cid six, but many Nomads were fitted with the Bel Air's grunty 265cid V8, which had a choice of Carter or Rochester two-barrel carb. For an extra $484 you could even specify fuel injection.

ROOF INNOVATION

The Nomad was the first car to use nonstructural corrugations on a roof.

CARGO FLOOR WAS COVERED WITH LINOLEUM

SPECIFICATIONS

MODEL 1957 Chevrolet Bel Air Nomad

PRODUCTION 6,103

BODY STYLE Two-door station wagon.

CONSTRUCTION Steel body and chassis.

ENGINE 235cid six, 265cid V8.

POWER OUTPUT 123–283 bhp.

TRANSMISSION Three-speed manual with overdrive, two-speed Powerglide automatic, and optional Turboglide.

SUSPENSION *Front:* coil springs; *Rear:* leaf springs.

BRAKES Front and rear drums.

MAXIMUM SPEED 90–120 mph (145–193 km/h)

0–60 MPH (0–96 KM/H) 8–11 sec

A.F.C. 15–19 mpg (5.3–6.7 km/l)

REAR STYLING

The embellished tailgate was lifted straight from the Motorama Vette and was widely praised. Even the roof line had seven transverse fluted pressings, as Harley Earl couldn't bear to see a piece of flat metal unadorned.

VETTE LINES

Motorama Vette roof line was adapted for production Nomads in just two days.

FRONT VIEW

Chevy tried to lower the Nomad's high price by using exterior trim that was identical to the other Bel Air models.

INTERIOR

Inside, the Nomad was very similar to the Bel Air, with distinctive two-tone trim and optional power seat, tinted glass, tissue dispenser, and, for the first time this season, seat belts and shoulder harnesses.

1957 CHEVROLET
3100 Stepside

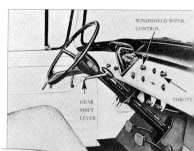

SIMPLE 3100 DESIGNATION DENOTES MODEL NUMBER

CHEVY WAS ON A HIGH in the mid-Fifties. With the Vette, the Bel Air, and the new V8, it was America's undisputed top car manufacturer. A boundless optimism percolated through all divisions, even touching such prosaic offerings as trucks. And the definitive Chevy carry-all has to be the '57 pickup.

It had not only that four-stroke overhead-valve V8 mill but also various options and a smart new restyle. Small wonder it was nicknamed "a Cadillac in drag." Among the most enduring of all American design statements, the '57 had clean, well-proportioned lines, a minimum of chrome, and integrated wings. Chevrolet turned the pickup from a beast of burden into a personalized workhorse complete with all the appurtenances of gracious living usually seen in a boulevard cruiser.

INTERIOR
The car was as stylized inside as out, with a glove compartment, heavy chrome switches, swing-out ashtrays, plus a V-shaped speedometer. De Luxe models had two-tone seats, door trims, and steering wheel.

CHEVY PREDECESSORS
This brochure shows dumpy '54 models, which by '55 would benefit from a dramatic new reskin that changed the Chevy pickup's personality forever.

LIGHTS
*These cowled single
headlights would be
replaced by quad
lights in '58.*

FLOORING
*Wood-bed
floors helped to
protect the load
area and added
a quality feel.*

ENGINE
*The small-block V8 produced 150 bhp
and could cruise at 70 mph (113 km/h).*

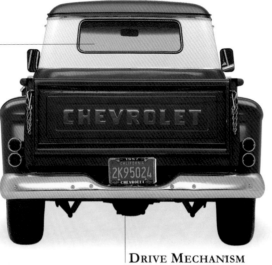

REAR WINDOW
*De Luxe models had a larger,
wrap-around windshield.*

1957 CHEVROLET 3100 STEPSIDE

Chevy's '57 pickups can be identified by the
new trapezoid grille and a flatter hood than
'56 models. Buyers had a choice of short
or long pickup, De Luxe or standard
trim, and 11 exterior colors. Engines
were the 235cid Thriftmaster six or
the 265cid Trademaster V8.

STEP
*This neat rear step allows access to
the load area and gives the pickup
its Stepside name.*

DRIVE MECHANISM
*From '55 on, all Chevys used
open-drive instead of an
enclosed torque-tube driveline.*

SPECIFICATIONS

MODEL 1957 Chevrolet
3100 Stepside
PRODUCTION Not available
BODY STYLE Two-seater,
short-bed pickup.
CONSTRUCTION Steel body
and chassis.
ENGINE 235cid six, 265cid V8.
POWER OUTPUT 130–145 bhp.
TRANSMISSION Three-speed
manual with overdrive,
optional three-speed automatic.
SUSPENSION *Front:* coil springs;
Rear: leaf springs.
BRAKES Front and rear drums.
MAXIMUM SPEED 80 mph
(129 km/h)
0–60 MPH (0–96 KM/H) 17.3 sec
A.F.C. 17 mpg (6 km/l)

1957 CHRYSLER
New Yorker

WHY CAN'T THEY MAKE CARS that look this good anymore? The '57 New Yorker was the first and finest example of Chrysler's "Forward Look" policy. With the average American production worker earning $82.32 a week, the $4,259 four-door hardtop was both sensationally good-looking and sensationally expensive.

THE 1957 NEW YORKER
CONVERTIBLE COUPE

The car's glorious lines seriously alarmed Chrysler's competitors, especially since the styling was awarded two gold medals, the suspension was by newfangled torsion bar, and muscle was courtesy of one of the most respected engines in the world – the hemi-head Fire Power, which in the New Yorker cranked out 325 horses. Despite this, "the most glamorous cars of a generation" cost Chrysler a whopping $300 million and sales were disappointing. One of the problems was a propensity for rust, along with shabby fit and finish; another was low productivity – only a measly 10,948 four-door hardtop models rolled out of the Highland Park factory. Even so, the New Yorker was certainly one of the most beautiful cars Chrysler ever made.

INTERIOR
New Yorkers had it all. Equipment included power windows, a six-way power seat, Hi-Way Hi-Fi phonograph, Electro-Touch radio, rear seat speaker, Instant Air heater, handbrake warning system, Air-Temp air-conditioning, and tinted glass – an altogether impressive array of features for a 1957 automobile.

SUBTLE STYLING
The New Yorker has few styling excesses. Even the seven gratuitous slashes on the rear fender do not look over the top.

ESTATE VERSION
This Town and Country Wagon was another model in Chrysler's 1957 New Yorker lineup and was driven by the same impressive Fire Power V8 found in the sedan and hardtops.

ENGINE
The top-of-the-range model had a top-of-the-range motor. The hemi-head engine was the largest production plant available in 1957. Bore and stroke were increased and displacement raised by nearly 10 percent. It was efficient, ran on low-octane gas, and could be tickled to produce staggering outputs.

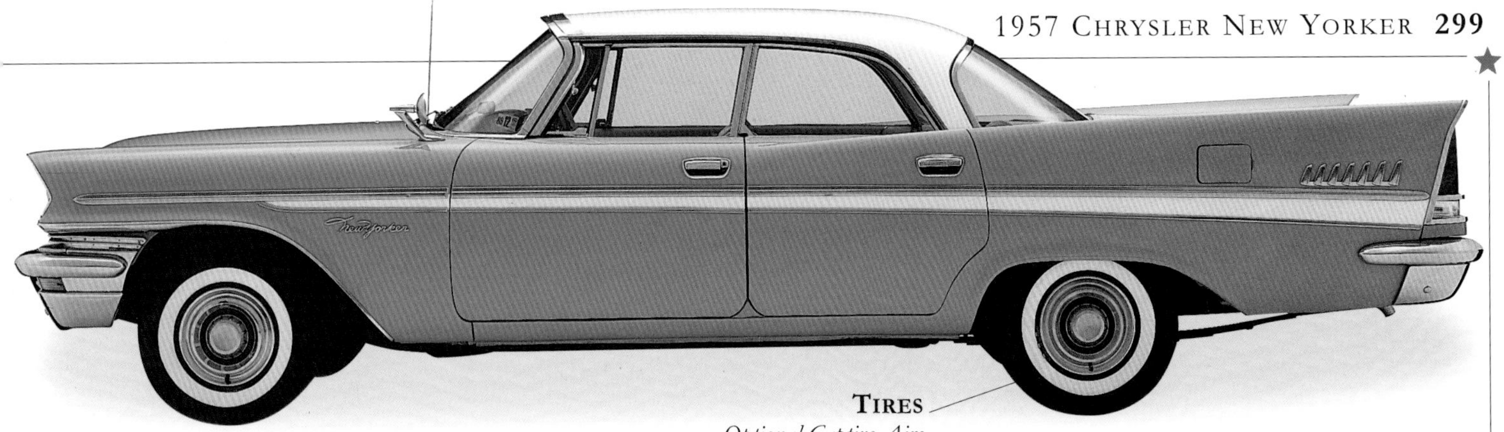

1957 CHRYSLER NEW YORKER

Chrysler stunned the world with its dartlike shapes of 1957. The unified design was created by the mind of one man – Virgil Exner – rather than by a committee, and it shows. Those prodigious rear fenders sweep up gracefully, harmonizing well with the gently tapering roof line. The low belt line, huge expanse of glass, and slinky profile are commendably subtle.

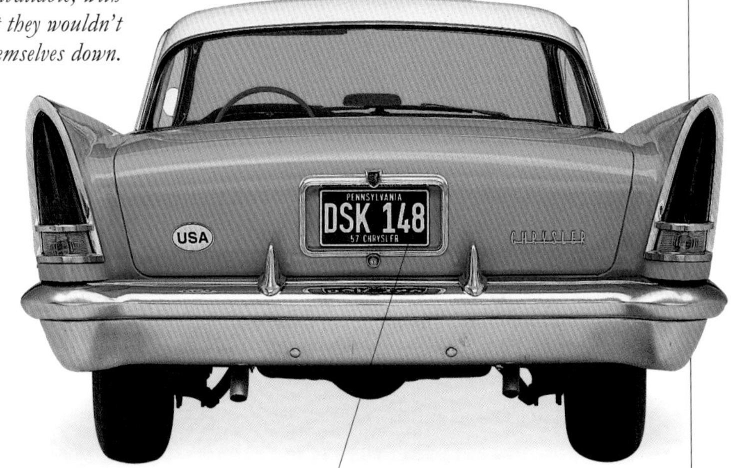

TIRES

Optional Captive-Aire tires were available, with promises that they wouldn't let themselves down.

REAR VIEW

Rather than looking overstyled, the rear end and deck are actually quite restrained. The license plate sits neatly in its niche, the tail pipes are completely concealed, the bumper is understated, and even the rear lights are not too heavy-handed.

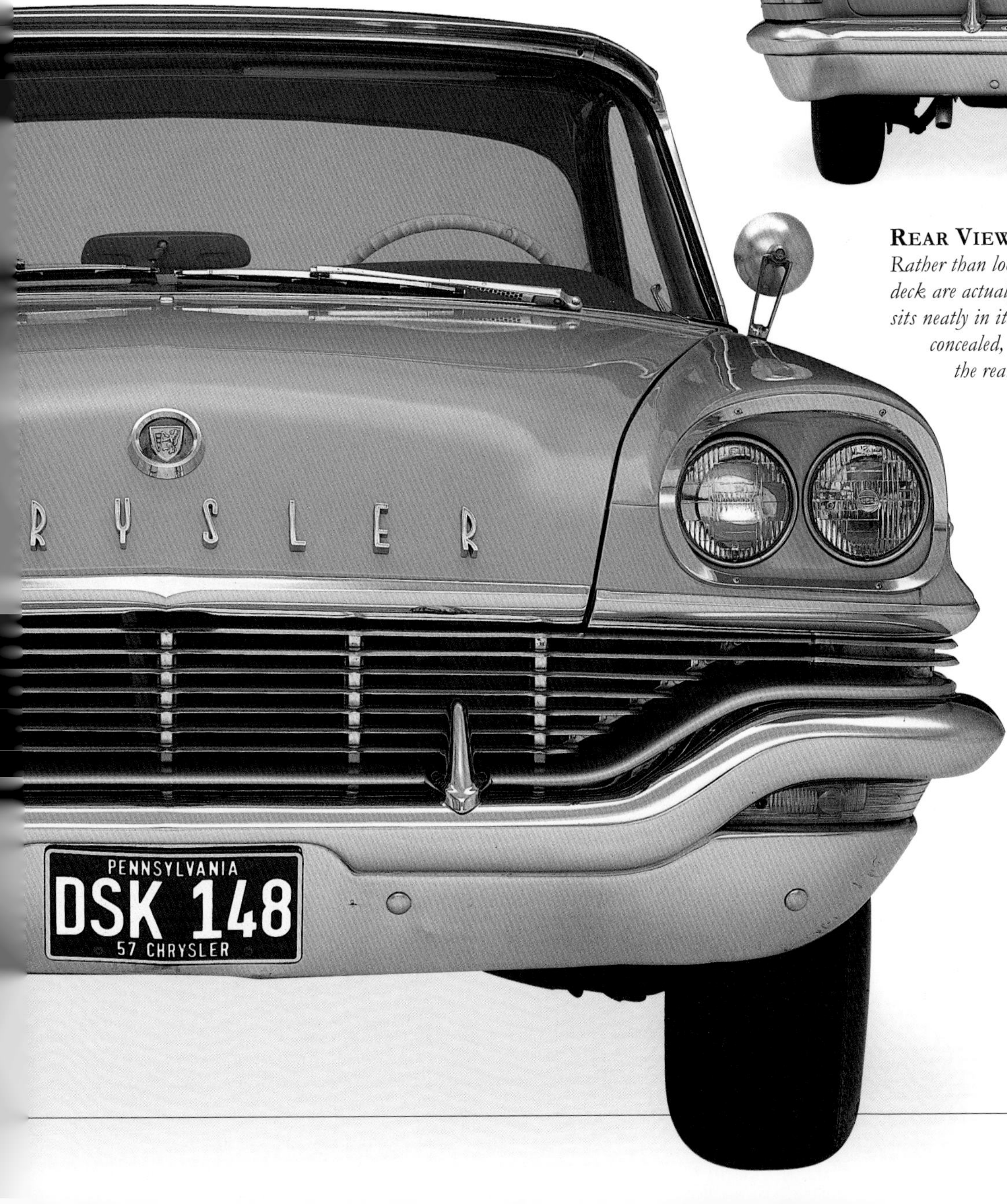

SPECIFICATIONS

MODEL 1957 Chrysler New Yorker
PRODUCTION 34,620
(all body styles)
BODY STYLE Four-door,
six-seater hardtop.
CONSTRUCTION Monocoque.
ENGINE 392cid V8.
POWER OUTPUT 325 bhp.
TRANSMISSION Three-speed
TorqueFlite automatic.
SUSPENSION *Front:* A-arms and
longitudinal torsion bar;
Rear: semi-elliptic leaf springs.
BRAKES Front and rear drums.
MAXIMUM SPEED 115 mph
(185 km/h)
0–60 MPH (0–96 KM/H) 12.3 sec
A.F.C. 13 mpg (4.6 km/l)

PENNSYLVANIA
DSK 148
57 CHRYSLER

1958 BUICK
Limited Riviera

1942 LIMITED BADGE,
USED AGAIN IN 1958

WHEN YOUR FORTUNES are flagging, you pour on the chrome. As blubbery barges go, the '58 Limited has to be one of the gaudiest. Spanning 19 ft (5.78 m) and tipping the scales at two tons, the Limited is empirical proof that 1958 was not Buick's happiest year. Despite all that twinkling kitsch and the reincarnated Limited badge, the bulbous Buick bombed. For a start, GM's Dynaflow transmission was not up to Hydra-Matic standards, and the brakes were not always trustworthy. Furthermore, in what was a recession year for the industry, the Limited had been priced into Cadillac territory – $33 more than the Series 62. Total production for the Limited in 1958 was a very limited 7,436 units. By the late Fifties, Detroit had lost its way, and the '58 Limited was on the road to nowhere.

ENGINE
The Valve-in-Head B12000 engine kicked out 300 horses, with a 364 cubic inch displacement. These specifications were respectable enough on paper, but on the road the Limited was too heavy to be anything other than sluggish.

FENDER
ORNAMENTS
MAY LOOK
ABSURD BUT
WERE USEFUL
IN PARKING
THE BUICK'S
HUGE GIRTH

— CHROME CRAZY —

THE 1950s WAS THE DECADE OF consumerism. A confident post-war America saw manufacturers developing new products each year, producing goods with limited lifespans and creating a "fad culture"; new materials were being developed and marketed to a "must have" public. Chromium was one example. The metal with a shiny coating swept the nation and, apart from adorning cars and motorcycles, could be found on the surfaces of products as diverse as food mixers and radios, refrigerators and wall clocks. It really was the ultimate, all-purpose, star-spangled metal.

A CHROME
FOOD MIXER
FROM THE
1950s

CHROME
KITCHEN
FURNITURE
WAS ALL THE
RAGE IN THE
FIFTIES

Brighten your Home
with *Virtue*
GAY, NEW *FESTIVAL* PATTERN

REAR DESIGN
The Buick's butt was a confused jumble of bosomy curves, slanting fins, and horizontal flashings. The trunk itself was big enough to house a football team.

WINDSHIELD
The large windshield was served by wide-angle wipers and an automatic windshield washer.

SPECIFICATIONS

MODEL 1958 Buick Limited Riviera Series 700

PRODUCTION 7,436 (all body styles)

BODY STYLE Two- and four-door, six-seater hardtops, two-door convertible.

CONSTRUCTION Steel monocoque.

ENGINE 364cid V8.

POWER OUTPUT 300 bhp.

TRANSMISSION Flight-Pitch Dynaflow automatic.

SUSPENSION *Front:* coil springs with A-arms; *Rear:* live axle with coil springs. Optional air suspension.

BRAKES Front and rear drums.

MAXIMUM SPEED 110 mph (177 km/h)

0–60 MPH (0–96 KM/H) 9.5 sec

A.F.C. 13 mpg (4.6 km/l)

1958 BUICK LIMITED RIVIERA

Buick's answer to an aircraft carrier was a riot of ornamentation that went on for half a block. At rest, the Limited looked like it needed a fifth wheel to support that weighty rear overhang. Air-Poise suspension was an extra-cost option that used pressurized air bladders for a supposedly smooth hydraulic ride. The system was, however, a nightmare to service and literally let itself down.

TRIMMINGS
Interiors were trimmed in gray cloth and vinyl or Cordaveen. Seat cushions had Double-Depth foam rubber.

GRILLE
The "Fashion-Aire Dynastar" grille consisted of no fewer than 160 chrome squares, each with four polished facets to give some serious sparkle.

INTERIOR
Power steering and brakes were essential and came as standard. Other standard equipment included an electric clock, cigarette lighters, and electric windows.

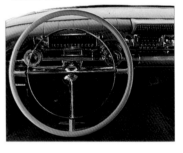

DECORATION
Unique to the Limited were 15 utterly pointless chrome slashes down both rear fenders.

1958 EDSEL
Bermuda

TRANSPORTATION FOR THE LARGEST OF FAMILIES

WITHOUT THAT INFAMOUS GRILLE, the Bermuda wouldn't have been a bad old barge. The rest looked pretty safe and suburban, and even those faddish rear lights weren't that offensive. At $3,155 it was the top Edsel wagon, wooing the public with more mock wood than Disneyland. But Ford had oversold the Edsel big time, and every model suffered guilt by association. Initial sales in 1957 were nothing like the predicted 200,000 but weren't disastrous either. The Bermudas, though, found just 2,235 buyers and were discontinued after only one year. By 1958, people no longer believed the hype, and Edsel sales evaporated; the company ceased trading in November 1959. Everybody knew that the '58 recession killed the Edsel, but at Ford major players in the project were cruelly demoted or fired.

EDSEL MASCOT
The Edsel name was chosen from 6,000 possibilities, including Mongoose, Turcotinga, and Utopian Turtletop.

INTERIOR
Never one of Edsel's strongest selling points, the Teletouch gear selector was operated by push buttons on the steering wheel. It was gimmicky and unreliable.

ENGINE
"They're the industry's newest – and the best," cried the advertising. Edsel engines were strong 361 or 410cid V8s, with the station wagons usually powered by the smaller unit.

E400 ON VALVE COVERS INDICATES AMOUNT OF TORQUE

TELETOUCH BUTTON SENT A SIGNAL TO THE CAR'S "PRECISION BRAIN"

FORD WHEELBASE
Edsel wagons were based on the 116 in (295 cm) Ford station wagon platform.

1958 EDSEL BERMUDA

Looking back, one wonders how one of the most powerful corporations in the world could possibly have signed off on such a stylistic debacle. '58 Edsels weren't just ugly, they were appallingly weird. The Bermuda's side view is innocuous enough and no worse than many half-timbered shopping center wagons of the period. Note how the roof is slightly kinked to give the huge panel extra rigidity.

SPECIFICATIONS

MODEL 1958 Edsel Bermuda
PRODUCTION 1,456 (six-seater Bermudas)
BODY STYLE Four-door, six-seater station wagon.
CONSTRUCTION Steel body and chassis.
ENGINE 361cid, V8.
POWER OUTPUT 303 bhp.
TRANSMISSION Three-speed manual with optional overdrive, optional three-speed automatic with or without Teletouch control.
SUSPENSION *Front:* independent coil springs; *Rear:* leaf springs with live axle.
BRAKES Front and rear drums.
MAXIMUM SPEED 108 mph (174 km/h)
0–60 MPH (0–96 км/н) 10.2 sec
A.F.C. 15 mpg (5.3 km/l)

LIGHTS
Zany boomerang rear clusters contained turn signal, stop, and reverse lights.

FRONT VIEW
Grille was so prominent that it required separate flanking bumpers.

INTERIOR
All wagons had four armrests, two coathooks, dome lights, and vinyl white headlining.

COLOR
This Bermuda is painted in Spring Green, but buyers had a choice of 161 different color combinations.

1958 LINCOLN
Capri

A RANGE OF ALL-NEW LINCOLNS WERE BROUGHT
OUT IN 1958 TO CHALLENGE CADILLAC

IN POSSIBLY ONE OF the most outrageous half-truths ever written, Lincoln copywriters insisted that the '58 Capri was "impressive without being ostentatious" and had a "tasteful, classic elegance." In reality, it was a stylistic nightmare, two-and-a-half tons of massive bumpers, sculpted wheel arches, and weirdly canted headlights. What's more, in the jumbo 430cid Continental V8 it had the largest engine available in an American production car at the time.

This visual anarchy and the '58 recession meant that sales halved from the previous year, and Ford realized that the Capri was as badly timed as the Edsel. Even so, the luxury Lincoln had one solid advantage: it was quick *and* it handled. One magazine said, "it's doubtful if any big car could stick any tighter in the corners or handle any better at high speed," a homily helped by the unitary body, rear coil springs, and potent new brakes. The '58 Capri was one of the last driveaway dinosaurs. The door was closing on an era of kitsch.

UNITARY BODY
In '58, Lincoln switched to a unitary body, eliminating a chassis frame for the first time in 10 years. Suspension, drivetrain, and engine units were fastened to the body structure to minimize weight and offer a smooth ride. However, prototypes flexed so badly that all sorts of stiffening reinforcement were added, negating any weight savings.

STYLING
The Capri used every stylistic trick that Motown had ever learned, but only desperate men would put fins on the rear bumper.

ENGINE
The big new 430cid V8 engine walloped out 375 horses, giving a power output second only to the Chrysler 300D. Lowered final drive ratios failed even to pay lipservice to fuel economy, with the Capri returning a groan-inspiring 10 mpg (3.5 km/l) around town.

INTERIOR
For a price just short of $5,000, standard features included electric windows with childproof controls, a six-way Power Seat, a padded instrument panel, and five ashtrays, each with its own lighter. Seat belts and leather trim were optional.

SUSPENSION
This was the first year that Lincolns had coil springs for rear suspension.

1958 LINCOLN CAPRI
Lincoln's dramatic restyle of '58 was not one of their happiest. The frivolous fins of '57 were trimmed down, but the sculpted bumpers and scalloped fenders were still a mess. Ford's brief for the '58 Lincolns was to out-glitz Cadillac in every area, but somehow they didn't quite get it right. Instead, the Lincoln made the Caddy Eldorado look downright divine.

INTERIOR
The largest passenger car of the year, the Capri could accommodate six or even seven people, riding on an enormous, elongated 131 in (3.33 m) wheelbase.

FINS
By '58 the size of fins was falling, partly due to fashion, and also to reduce the risk of injuring pedestrians in road accidents.

WINDSCREEN
Tinted glass was a $50 option, along with translucent sun visors at $27.

SPECIFICATIONS
MODEL 1958 Lincoln Capri
PRODUCTION 6,859
BODY STYLE Four-door, six-seater sedan.
CONSTRUCTION Steel unitary body.
ENGINE 430cid V8.
POWER OUTPUT 375 bhp.
TRANSMISSION Three-speed Turbodrive automatic.
SUSPENSION Front and rear coil springs.
BRAKES Front and rear drums.
MAXIMUM SPEED 115 mph (185 km/h)
0–60 MPH (0–96 KM/H) 9 sec
A.F.C. 14 mpg (5 km/l)

TIRE SIZE
9x14 tires couldn't cope with the Lincoln's prodigious weight. Cost-cutting and an obsession with a soft ride meant that most cars of the period wallowed around on potentially lethal undersized rubber.

1958 PACKARD
Hawk

DISTINCTIVE, BIZARRE, AND VERY un-American, the '58 Hawk was a pastiche of European styling cues. Which is why there were no quad headlights, no athletic profile, and no glinting chromium dentures on the grille. Inspired by the likes of Ferrari and Mercedes, it boasted tan pleated-leather hide, white-on-black instruments, Jaguaresque fender vents, a turned metal dashboard, gulping hood air-scoop, and a broad fiberglass shovel-nostril that could have been lifted off a Maserati. And it was supercharged.

But Packard's desperate attempt to distance itself from traditional Detroit iron failed. At $4,000, the Hawk was overpriced, underrefined, and overdecorated. Packard had merged with Studebaker back in 1954, and although it was initially a successful alliance, problems with suppliers and another buyout in 1956 basically sealed the company's fate. Only 588 Hawks were built, with the very last Packard rolling off the South Bend, Indiana, line on July 13, 1958. Today the Hawk stands as a quaint curiosity, a last-ditch attempt to preserve the Packard pedigree. It remains one of the most fiercely desired of the final Packards.

SALES LITERATURE HERALDED THE ARRIVAL OF "A DISTINCTIVE, NEW, FULL-POWERED SPORTS-STYLED CAR"

EURO STYLING
The door mirror was designed to replicate the knock-off hub spinners of wire wheels on European sports cars, but it looked out of place with the Hawk's discreet styling.

REAR VIEW
Despite its European airs, no American car could escape the vogue for fins, and this car has two beauties. Nobody was too sure about the spare wheel impression on the trunk, though, which was likened to a toilet seat.

TWIN EXHAUSTS
Standard on the Hawk, but fishtail embellishers were an optional accessory.

ENGINE
Flight-O-Matic automatic transmission and a hefty, supercharged 289cid V8 came standard, hurling out 275 horses; 0–60 mph (96 km/h) took just under eight seconds. The Hawk's blower was a belt-driven McCulloch supercharger.

"SUPERCHARGED "GO" AT THE TIP OF YOUR TOE," READ THE BROCHURE

1958 PACKARD HAWK

Uniquely, the Hawk had exterior vinyl armrests running along the side windows and a refreshing lack of chrome gaudiness on the flanks. The roof line and halo roof band are aeronautical, the belt line is tense and urgent, and the whole plot stood on 14-inch wheels to make it look lower and meaner.

AIR VENTS

Front fender vents were shamelessly culled from British Mark IX and XK Jaguars.

STEERING

Power steering was a $70 factory option.

FRONT ASPECT

The Hawk was one of the few Packards that dared to sport single headlights and, along with that softly shaped front bumper and mailbox air intake, looked nothing like contemporary Americana.

— SPECIFICATIONS —

MODEL 1958 Packard Hawk
PRODUCTION 588
BODY STYLE Two-door, four-seater coupe.
CONSTRUCTION Steel body and chassis.
ENGINE 289cid V8.
POWER OUTPUT 275 bhp.
TRANSMISSION Three-speed Flight-O-Matic automatic, optional overdrive.
SUSPENSION *Front:* independent coil springs; *Rear:* leaf springs.
BRAKES Front and rear drums.
MAXIMUM SPEED 125 mph (201 km/h)
0–60 MPH (0–96 KM/H) 8 sec
A.F.C. 15 mpg (5.3 km/l)

INTERIOR

To stress the Hawk's supposed sporting bloodline, the interior was clad in soft hide with sports-car instrumentation. In addition, you could specify a raft of convenience options that included power windows and air-conditioning.

1958 RAMBLER
Ambassador

WHILE THE GOVERNMENT WAS telling consumers "You auto buy now," American Motors boss George Romney was telling the President that "Consumers are rebelling against the size, horsepower, and excessive styling of the American automobile." Romney's Ramblers were the only industry success story for a recession-racked 1958 when, for the first time ever, more cars were imported than exported. The Ambassador was Rambler's economy flagship, and road testers liked the speed, room, luxury, thrift, and high resale value. Also, it was reasonably priced, had a safety package option, "deep-dip" rustproofing, and a thoroughly modern monocoque shell. But buyers weren't buying. Motorists may have wanted economy and engineering integrity, but cars still had to be cool. The sensible Ambassador was an ugly, slab-sided machine for middle-aged squares.

THIS IS A DOUBLE-SAFE SINGLE UNIT BODY
BUILT WITH AN ADVANCED METHOD OF BODY CONSTRUCTION IN WHICH THE BODY AND FRAME ARE COMBINED INTO A SINGLE ALL-WELDED STRUCTURAL UNIT
PIONEERED AND BUILT EXCLUSIVELY BY
AMERICAN MOTORS CORP.
DETROIT   MICHIGAN

WHAT, NO CHASSIS?
Chassis-less body construction was a Nash/AMC tradition also used by many European nameplates, namely Jaguar. Few American manufacturers were interested in following suit. Despite modest dimensions, the Ambassador was accommodating; it had a very high roof line and could just about carry six passengers.

9,000 ELECTRIC WELDS REPLACED CONVENTIONAL BOLTS AND REDUCED IN-CAR RATTLES AND SQUEAKS

INTERIOR
The custom steering wheel was an option, along with power steering at $89.50. Flash-O-Matic automatic transmission could be column-operated or controlled by push buttons on the dashboard. The Weather-Eye heater, another option, was thought to be one of the most efficient in the industry.

1958 RAMBLER AMBASSADOR

AMC stylist Ed Anderson did a good job with the '58 models, cleverly reskinning '56 and '57s with longer hoods, different grilles, and taillights. But with modest tail fins and a plain rump, the Ambassador was no matinee idol and looked more like a taxi than an upscale sedan. The six cars in the range included three station wagons.

ENGINE

The cast-iron 327cid V8 motor gave 270 bhp and, despite a one-barrel carb, could reach 60 mph (96 km/h) in 10 seconds. The same engine had powered the '57 Rambler Rebel.

SPECIFICATIONS

MODEL 1958 Rambler Ambassador

PRODUCTION 14,570 (all body styles)

BODY STYLE Four-door, six-seater sedan.

CONSTRUCTION Steel monocoque body.

ENGINE 327cid V8.

POWER OUTPUT 270 bhp.

TRANSMISSION Three-speed manual with optional overdrive, optional three-speed Flash-O-Matic automatic.

SUSPENSION *Front:* independent coil springs; *Rear:* coil with optional air springs.

BRAKES Front and rear drums.

MAXIMUM SPEED 105 mph (169 km/h)

0–60 MPH (0–96 KM/H) 10 sec

A.F.C. 18 mpg (6.4 km/l)

MODEST FINS

Sales literature championed the "sensible fin height" as an aid to safer driving by not obstructing rear vision.

SUSPENSION

Rear air suspension was an optional extra, but few buyers ordered it. Just as well, because reliability problems caused the industry to drop the whole concept soon after.

ORNAMENTATION

The sweepspear was one of the Ambassador's few concessions to ornamentation, and helped to break up an otherwise solid flank.

1959 CADILLAC
Eldorado

STAMP
CELEBRATES
THE CADILLAC'S
MOST OUTSTANDING FEATURE

THE '59 CADILLAC ISN'T SO MUCH a car as a cathedral– a gothic monument to America's glory years. Overlong, overlow, and overstyled, it stands as the final flourish of the Fifties. We might marvel at its way-out space-age styling, those bizarre fins, and that profligate 390 cubic inch V8, but the most telling thing about the '59 is its sheer in-yer-face arrogance. Back in the Fifties, the United States was the most powerful nation on earth. With money to burn, military might, arrow-straight freeways, and Marilyn Monroe, America really thought it could reach out and touch the Moon. But when the '59 Caddy appeared, that nationalistic high was ebbing away. The Russians had launched Sputnik, Castro was getting chummy with Khrushchev, and there were race riots at home. A decade of glitz, glamour, and prosperity was coming to an end. America would never be the same again, and neither would her Cadillacs.

ENGINE
Base engine on the '59 was a five-bearing 390cid V8 with hydraulic lifters and high compression heads. Breathing through a Carter four-barrel, it developed 325 bhp, but with the Eldorado V8 and three Rochester two-barrels the '59 could muster an extra 20 bhp.

INTERIOR
Standard lavish fare on the '59 Convertible – power brakes, power steering, auto transmission, power windows, two-speed windshield wipers, and a two-way power seat.

CADILLAC COUPE DE VILLE
The de Ville lineup was two sedans and a coupe, trimmed like the Series 6200 with the same standards plus electric windows and power seats. Sticker prices were $5,498 (Sedan) and $5,252 (Coupe

AUTRONIC EYE
Automatic headlight-dipping came courtesy of the optional Autronic Eye, which could sense the lights of oncoming cars. At just $55, futuristic technology had never been so accessible.

UP-TO-DATE FEATURES
Options were amazingly modern, with air suspension, cruise control, remote trunk lock, and bucket seats.

STAR QUALITY
Test drivers praised the 1959's handling, ride, and superb power steering. Performance was sensational, delivered in utter silence with honeylike smoothness.

TRUNK
The massive trunk has enough room for a small golf tournament.

SPECIFICATIONS

MODEL 1959 Cadillac Eldorado
PRODUCTION 11,130
BODY STYLE Two-door, six-seater convertible.
CONSTRUCTION Steel body, X-frame chassis.
ENGINE 390cid V8.
POWER OUTPUT 325–345 bhp.
TRANSMISSION Three-speed Hydra-Matic automatic.
SUSPENSION All-round coil springs with optional Freon-12 gas suspension.
BRAKES Front and rear hydraulic power-assisted drums.
MAXIMUM SPEED 115 mph (185 km/h)
0–60 MPH (0–96 KM/H) 10.3 sec
A.F.C. 12.1 mpg (4.3 km/l)

1959 CADILLAC ELDORADO

Detroit's dream-makers produced visions of the future, and the '59 was the most florid of all. For one hysterical model year it was the preeminent American automobile, and at close to $6,000 you really had to have some serious juice to own one. 11,130 Series 62 convertibles were built in '59 and cost $5,455. Quality was patchy though, with too many rattles and a distinctly un-Cadillac propensity for rust. Even so, enthusiasts rank the '59 as King of the Caddies.

MORTGAGE MODEL
The rare Biarritz Convertible had a sticker price of $7,401, the cost of an extremely substantial house.

ULTIMATE FIN FASHION
The wackiest fins of any car ever, the '59s were elbow high. Cadillac's finny trademark was an aviation cliché, calculated to lend lifeless steel the allure of speed, modernity, and escape.

CONTROVERSIAL FINS, KNOWN AS "ZAP", WERE LATER RIDICULED

1959 DODGE
Custom Royal Lancer

TWO-DOOR CUSTOM ROYAL HARDTOP
STICKERED AT $3,151 IN '59

LICKING ITS WOUNDS FROM the '58 recession, Detroit came up with more metal, muscle, and magnificence than ever before. As always, Chrysler's offerings were the gaudiest, and the '59 Custom Royal had fins and finery to spare. And boy, could it go. Engine options went all the way up to a 383cid D500 motor with twin Carter four-barrels that heaved out a whopping 345 bhp. "Level Flight" Torsion-Aire suspension was a $127 extra that "lets you corner without side sway, stop without brake dive." There was no doubt that the copywriters were having a ball.

With a Forward Look profile, chromed eyebrows, four enormous taillights set in yet more chrome, and topped by towering duotone fins, the Custom Royal was a stylistic shambles. The brochure has a mailman beaming approvingly at the riotous '59 Custom with a catchline that runs, "reflects your taste for finer things." Complete garbage maybe, but that's the way they sold cars in '59.

LANCER BADGE
The Lancer name actually referred to an upscale trim level that was standard on all hardtops and convertibles. The Custom Royal was Dodge's top offering.

FORWARD LOOK POLICY
In 1957 Chrysler introduced a new type of styling to its whole range. Cars should be longer, sleeker, and have exuberant tail fins. It was a resounding success until about 1960, when poor quality control – due in part to overwhelming demand – saw a dramatic decline in sales.

INTERIOR
The cabin had plenty of toys, including an "Indi-Color" speedometer that changed color as speed increased, variable-speed windshield wipers, padded dash, automatic headlight dimming, and swiveling seats in Jaquard fabric and vinyl.

PUSH-BUTTON THREE-SPEED
TORQUEFLITE TRANSMISSION
COST A PRINCELY $227

CHASSIS
The ladder chassis was substantial but orthodox, and springing was by ball joints and torsion bars, with optional Level-Flight suspension.

ENGINE
The 361cid Super Ramfire V8 in this Custom Royal pushed out 305 bhp but paled beside the D500 performance option. Its heavy-duty shocks, revised coil springs, and torsion bars gave what *Motor Trend* magazine called "close liaison with the road." D500s were at the top of their class for performance and handling.

WEIRD TOOTHPASTE-CAP PROTUBERANCES HOUSED THE PARKING LIGHTS

THE DODGE'S FINS WERE ACTUALLY SET ON TOP OF THE REAR THREE-QUARTER PANELS AND ACCENTUATED BY SEPARATE COLORS

THIS ROYAL LANCER HAS AN OPTIONAL TRUNK LIGHT

FIN FUNK
Despite the raucous rear end, the Custom Royal's fins were less exaggerated than most. The '59 Cadillac and Chevy Impala had much wilder rear-fin styling.

THIS CAR IS FITTED WITH OPTIONAL LANCER HUBCAPS

THE ROYAL WAS LONGER, LOWER, AND WIDER THAN ANY PREVIOUS DODGE

SPECIFICATIONS

MODEL 1959 Dodge Custom Royal Lancer
PRODUCTION 11,297
BODY STYLE Two- or four-door, six-seater hardtop.
CONSTRUCTION Steel body and chassis.
ENGINE 230cid six, 326cid, 361cid, 383cid V8s.
POWER OUTPUT 138–345 bhp.
TRANSMISSION Three-speed manual with overdrive, optional three-speed TorqueFlite automatic.
SUSPENSION *Front:* torsion bars; *Rear:* leaf springs.
BRAKES Front and rear drums.
MAXIMUM SPEED 90–120 mph (145–193 km/h)
0–60 MPH (0–96 KM/H) 8–14 sec
A.F.C. 12–17 mpg (4.2–6 km/l)

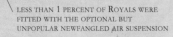

LESS THAN 1 PERCENT OF ROYALS WERE FITTED WITH THE OPTIONAL BUT UNPOPULAR NEWFANGLED AIR SUSPENSION

THE RISE AND FALL OF THE GREAT AMERICAN FIN

This baby can flick its tail at anything on the road!

THE '57 DESOTO FIREFLITE'S FINNY REAR

WORLD WAR II GAVE AMERICA its fins, and it was an airplane that did it – the Lockheed P-38. In 1941 Harley Earl and his coterie from the GM design staff visited the Selfridge Field Air Force base near Detroit. Sworn to secrecy, they were allowed to view the P-38 only

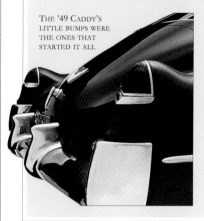

THE '49 CADDY'S LITTLE BUMPS WERE THE ONES THAT STARTED IT ALL

from a distance, but were rapt by its pointed nose, contoured streamlining, greenhouse cockpit, and twin tail booms.

Obsessed with this brave new styling metaphor, Earl grafted a dorsal fin onto the prototype '48 Cadillac. But when he presented his new motif to senior GM executives, it bombed. Earl's confidence was shaken and

he stormed back to the studio, railing "take that goddam fin off, nobody wants it." The designer refused and Earl nearly fired him. Three days later, Earl returned, saying "that fin's okay, let's keep it on." A good move, as 1949 was one of Cadillac's best-ever sales years.

Earl couldn't possibly have foreseen the fad he was starting What was little more than a jumped-up taillight progressively mushroomed to shoulder height. After Cadillac, Oldsmobile followed in '49, Buick in '52, Chrysler in '55, Hudson, Studebaker, and Nash in '56, and conservative old Uncle Henr held out until 1957. But by '59 the fin had become so grotesqu that the Chevrolet Impala's razorlike rear looked sharp enough

1959 DODGE
Custom Royal Lancer

IMPOSING BACKSIDE
Vestigial rear window pillars are so thin that the roof seems to float above the body. Combined with the high trunk line and low roof line, it makes for a chunky rear view.

OPTIONAL TWIN ANTENNAE WITH RADIO COST $14

THE RATIO OF GLASS TO SHEET METAL IS NEARLY ONE-TO-ONE AND GIVES THE COCKPIT AN AIRY FEEL.

R·2885

NY EMPIRE STATE 60

o draw blood. Satirists laid into the fin
with vicious glee. John Keats, in his
book *The Insolent Chariots*, likened the
American car to an overweight concubine.
"With all the subtlety of a madam affecting
a lorgnette, she put tail fins on her
overblown bustle and spouted
wavering antennae from each fin."

Surprisingly, Virgil Exner, Chrysler's design guru, bravely
attempted to argue that fins had a practical advantage. Using
a scale model of a DeSoto in a wind tunnel, he claimed that
roadholding was improved and steering corrections in strong

BELIEVE IT OR NOT, THE FINS ON THE '60 CHEVY IMPALA WERE ACTUALLY TONED DOWN FROM '59

crosswinds reduced by up to 20 percent. But in reality it was
impossible to argue with conviction that this absurd stylistic
excess had a serious function. After fins had shrunk in the early
Sixties, no one reported worse handling or steering vagaries.

The fin was really the first of a cornucopia of visual
novelties that gave consumers a reason for changing their cars
every year. Cynically, the industry knew that these appalling
appendages were just a tool to hasten the process of dynamic
obsolescence, but a gullible public identified the fin with
luxury and prestige, taking it as the punctuation mark of a
well-styled car. It is endlessly fascinating to think that such
a simple styling device managed so completely to entrance
an entire decade of American car buyers.

THE EXPERIMENTAL CADILLAC CYCLONE TOOK THE FIN MOTIF TO NEW EXTREMES

FADDISH FRONT
The front end was the auto industry's idea of high style in '59.
Quad headlights had ridiculous hooded chrome eyebrows, and
the grille was outrageously overwrought. Such ostentation was
merely a crutch for
hobbling from one
expensive restyle
to the next.

WINDSHIELD IS SOLEX
TINTED, AN $18
OPTIONAL EXTRA

VARIABLE-SPEED WINDSHIELD
WIPERS AND WASHERS COST
$18.25 EXTRA BACK IN '59

THE ABSURD
OVER-CHROMED
OVERRIDERS HOLD
PARKING LIGHTS

R·2885

NY EMPIRE STATE 60

1959 EDSEL
Corsair

STEERING WHEEL LOGO

BY 1959 AMERICA HAD LOST her confidence; the economy nose-dived, Russia was first in space, there were race riots in Little Rock, and Ford was counting the cost of its disastrous Edsel project – close to 400 million dollars. "The Edsel look is here to stay" brayed the ads, but the bold new vertical grille had become a country-wide joke. Sales didn't just die, they never took off, and those who had been rash enough to buy hid their chromium follies in suburban garages. Eisenhower's mantra of materialism was over, and buyers wanted to know more about economical compacts like the Nash Rambler, Studebaker Lark, and novel VW Beetle. Throw in a confusing 18-model lineup, poor build quality, and disenchanted dealers, and "The Newest Thing on Wheels" never stood a chance. Now famous as a powerful symbol of failure, the Edsel stands as a sad memorial to the foolishness of consumer culture in Fifties America.

REAR LIGHTS
Tail and backup lights were shared with the '58 Continental to save on tooling costs.

1959 EDSEL CORSAIR CONVERTIBLE

By 1959, the Corsair had become just a restyled Ranger, based on the Ford Fairlane. Corsairs had bigger motors and more standard equipment. But even a sticker price of $3,000 for the convertible didn't help sales, which were a miserable model year total of 45,000. Ford was desperate and tried to sell it as "A new kind of car that makes sense."

DECORATION
The dominating chrome and white sweepspear that runs the entire length of the car makes the rear deck look heavy.

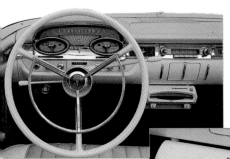

INTERIOR
The dashboard was cleaned up for 1959, and the unreliable Teletouch transmission deleted in favor of a Mile-O-Matic two-speed with column shift. The eight-tube push-button radio was available at $64.95.

IN-CAR VINYL
This charming Philips record player is an optional accessory fitted in the early 1960s.

MIRROR
The hooded chrome door mirror was remote-controlled, an extremely rare option.

"GUARD RAIL" FRAME DESIGN WITH FULL-LENGTH SIDE RAILS

BALL JOINT FRONT SUSPENSION

CHASSIS
The substantial steel girder chassis incorporated full-length side rails and five cross-members. It was hauled along by either an Edsel Express 332cid V8 producing 225 bhp or a Super Express 361cid V8 developing 303 bhp. 77 percent of all 1959 Edsels were powered by V8s, with the Economy Six making up the numbers.

SPECIFICATIONS
MODEL 1959 Edsel Corsair Convertible
PRODUCTION 1,343
BODY STYLE Two-door, five-seater convertible.
CONSTRUCTION Steel body and chassis.
ENGINE 332cid, 361cid V8s.
POWER OUTPUT 225–303 bhp.
TRANSMISSION Three-speed manual with optional overdrive, optional two- or three-speed Mile-O-Matic automatic.
SUSPENSION *Front:* independent with coil springs; *Rear:* leaf springs with live axle.
BRAKES Front and rear drums.
MAXIMUM SPEED 95–105 mph (153–169 km/h)
0–60 MPH (0–96 KM/H) 11–16 sec
A.F.C. 15 mpg (5.3 km/l)

COLOR
Petal Yellow was one of 17 possible exterior colors.

FRONT VIEW
Roy Brown, the Edsel's designer, claimed that "The front theme of our newest car combines nostalgia with modern vertical thrust." Other pundits compared it to a horse collar, a man sucking a lemon, or even a toilet seat.

19 NEBRASKA 60
35-110
THE BEEF STATE

1959 FORD
Fairlane 500 Skyliner

THE '59 SKYLINER WAS 3 IN (7½ CM)
SHORTER THAN THE '57–'58 MODELS

FORD RAISED THE ROOF in '57 with its glitziest range ever, and the "Retrac" was a party piece. The world's only mass-produced retractable hardtop debuted at the New York Show of '56, and the first production version was presented to a bemused President Eisenhower in '57. The Skyliner's balletic routine was the most talked-about gadget for years and filled Ford showrooms with thousands of gawking customers.

Surprisingly reliable and actuated by a single switch, the Retrac's roof had 610 ft (185 m) of wiring, three drive motors, and a feast of electrical hardware. But showmanship apart, the Skyliner was pricey and had precious little trunk space or leg room. By '59 the novelty had worn off, and division chief Robert McNamara's desire to end expensive "gimmick engineering" led to the wackiest car ever to come out of Dearborn being axed in 1960.

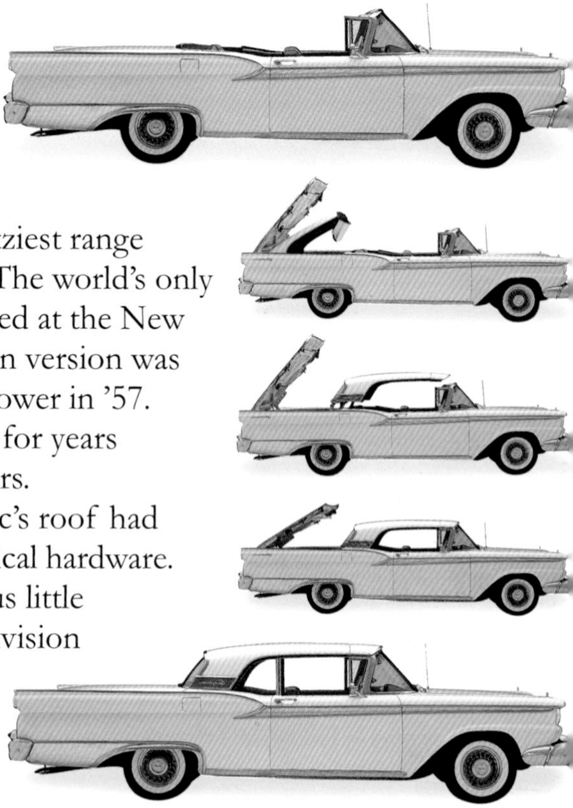

ROOF SEQUENCE

A switch on the steering column started three motors that opened the rear deck. Another motor unlocked the top, and yet another motor hoisted the roof and sent it back to the open trunk space. A separate mechanism then lowered the rear deck back into place. It all took just one minute but had to be done with the gear shift in "Park" and the engine running.

ENGINE

The Skyliner's standard power was a 292cid V8, but this model contains the top-spec Thunderbird 352cid Special V8 with 300 bhp.

REAR STYLING

Fins were down for '59, but missile-shaped pressings on the higher rear fenders were a neat touch to hide all that moving metalwork.

1959 FORD FAIRLANE 500 GALAXIE SKYLINER RETRACTABLE

The Skyliner lived for three years but was never a volume seller. Buyers may have thought it neat, but they were justifiably anxious about the roof mechanism's reliability. Just under 21,000 were sold in '57, less than 15,000 in '58, and a miserly 12,915 found buyers in '59. At two tons and $3,138, it was the heaviest, priciest, and least practical Ford in the range.

INTERIOR

Available options included power windows, tinted glass, a four-way power seat, and Polar-Aire air-conditioning. The $19 Lifeguard safety package included a padded instrument panel and sun visor.

The new **FORD SKYLINER** world's only Hide-Away Hardtop

SKYLINER COSTS

Ford spent $18 million testing the Skyliner's roof. Ironically, the Retrac's biggest fault wasn't electrical problems but body rust.

— SPECIFICATIONS —

MODEL 1959 Ford Fairlane 500 Galaxie Skyliner Retractable

PRODUCTION 12,915

BODY STYLE Two-door hardtop with retractable roof.

CONSTRUCTION Steel body and chassis.

ENGINE 272cid, 292cid, 312cid, 352cid V8s.

POWER OUTPUT 190–300 bhp.

TRANSMISSION Three-speed manual, optional three-speed Cruise-O-Matic automatic.

SUSPENSION *Front:* coil springs; *Rear:* leaf springs.

BRAKES Front and rear drums.

MAXIMUM SPEED 105 mph (169 km/h)

0–60 MPH (0–96 KM/H) 10.6 sec

A.F.C. 15.3 mpg (5.4 km/l)

MANUAL OPERATION

If the power failed, there was a manual procedure for getting the roof down, but it was rarely needed.

FUEL TANK

This was located behind the rear seat, not for safety but because there was nowhere else to put it.

1959 PLYMOUTH
Fury

Fury
A BOLD AND BRASSY NAME FOR
PLYMOUTH'S KITSCH CLASSIC

AMAZINGLY, THE '59 FURY was aimed squarely at middle-class, middle-income America. Amazingly, because it was as loud as Little Richard and as sexy as Jayne Mansfield. One of the most stylistically adventurous cars on the road, the futuristic Fury was pure "Forward Look." Plymouth's ads bellowed that it was "three full years" ahead of its time, and the '59 model was the most strident of the lot. That razor-edged profile made Plymouth a nameplate to kill for, especially if it was the top-of-the-line Sport Fury, which came with a personalized aluminum plaque that read "Made Expressly For."

Sales of Plymouth's suburban trinket boomed in '59, with 89,114 Furys helping Plymouth rank third in the industry and celebrate the company's 11-millionth vehicle. With serious power and looks to stop a speeding train, the Fury wowed God-fearing America. But that rakish impudence couldn't last, and by '61 the Fury's fins were tragically trimmed. In the annals of kitsch, this one goes down as a real honey.

HEAVY-METAL VILLAIN
Stephen King's 1983 black comedy *Christine* used a '58 Fury as a demonic monster that suffocates its victims and eludes destruction by magically reconstituting itself. On screen, the Fury certainly looks like one of the baddest cars on the block.

ENGINE
The 318cid V8 pushed out just 230 horses, but Chrysler was starting to beat the performance drum as hard as it could. Top speed hit three figures, and acceleration was also brisk. The sheer bulk of the car plus those skinny tires must have made things a touch scary at the limit.

INTERIOR
Inside was comic-book spaceship, with push buttons galore. Swiveling front seats on Sport Furys were aimed at portlier buyers. The unlovely padded steering wheel was a $12 option.

REAR SPORT DECK
The optional trunk-lid appliqué spare tire cover was meant to make the car upscale, but it looked more like a trash-can lid.

STAR STATUS
The '59 Fury is rightly regarded as one of Virgil Exner's all-time masterpieces.

FINS

Everyone had fins back in 1959, but the Fury's showed real class.

TASTEFUL FLAIR

Is that slogan tongue-in-cheek? Plymouth sold the Fury's bold lines as the perfect example of taste and discrimination. It could only happen in '59.

GOOD TASTE IS NEVER EXTREME

HEADLIGHTS

40 optional electronic dipping for the headlights relieved the driver of yet one more little hardship.

LUXURY OPTIONS

Optional extras ranged from power brakes and the Golden Commando V8 to two-tone paint and contoured floormats.

1959 PLMOUTH FURY

Chrysler design chief Virgil Exner liked to see classic lines bolted onto modern cars, and the trunk-lid spare tire cover on the Fury is one example of this. The profile of this two-door hardtop shows off the Fury's fine proportions. The shape is dartlike, with a tense urgency of line. The sloping cockpit and tapering rear window melt deliciously into those frantic fins.

FIERCE FRONT GRILLE

Cross-slatted grille was all new for '59 and made the front end look like it could bite.

SPECIFICATIONS

MODEL 1959 Plymouth Fury

PRODUCTION 105,887 (all body styles and including Sport Furys)

BODY STYLE Two-door hardtop.

CONSTRUCTION Steel body and chassis.

ENGINE 318cid V8 (360cid V8 optional for Sport Fury).

POWER OUTPUT 230 bhp (Sport Fury 260 bhp, or 305 bhp with 360cid V8).

TRANSMISSION Three-speed manual with optional overdrive, optional three-speed TorqueFlite automatic, and PowerFlite automatic.

SUSPENSION *Front:* torsion bars; *Rear:* leaf springs.

BRAKES Front and rear drums, optional power assistance.

MAXIMUM SPEED 105–110 mph (169–177 km/h)

0–60 MPH (0–96 KM/H) 11 sec

A.F.C. 17 mpg (6 km/l)

1959 PONTIAC
Bonneville

THE BONNY WAS
MOTOR TREND'S 1959
CAR OF THE YEAR

IN THE LATE '50S, Detroit was worried. Desperately trying to offer something fresh, manufacturers decided to hit the aspirational thirty-somethings with a new package of performance, substance, and style. Pontiac's "Wide Track" Bonneville of '59 was a sensation. General Manager Bunkie Knudsen gave the line an image of youth and power, and Wide Track became all the rage. *Car Life* picked the Bonneville as its "Best Buy" and so did consumers. By 1960, soaring sales had made Pontiac the third most successful company in the industry.

The prestige Bonneville was also a dream to drive. The 389cid V8 pushed out up to 345 horses and, when the Tri-Power mill was fitted, top speeds hit 125 mph (201 km/h). At 6 ft 4 in (1.93 m) wide, the Custom two-door hardtop wouldn't fit in the car wash. But nobody cared. In 1959, America spent $300 million on chewing gum, the supermarket was its temple, and the ad jingle its national anthem. A self-obsessed utopia of comfort and convenience was about to go horribly wrong.

WILD AND WACKY
Garish three-color striped upholstery was meant to give the Bonneville a jaunty carelessness and appeal to the young at heart. Warehouse-like interior dimensions made it a true six-seater.

DOUBLE FINS
With consumers crying out for individuality, Pontiac gave the Bonneville not two fins, but four.

GRILLE
The split grille was new for '59. After reverting back to a full-length grille for just one year, it became a Pontiac trademark in the early '60s.

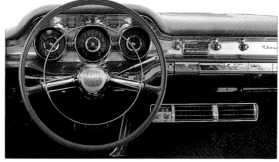

INTERIOR
The riotous interior had as much chrome as the exterior, and buyers could specify Wonderbar radio, electric antenna, tinted glass, padded dash, and tissue dispenser. The under-dash air-conditioning unit is a later, optional accessory.

1959 PONTIAC BONNEVILLE SPORT COUPE

Flushed with success, Pontiac claimed that it was the maker of "America's Number One Road Car." Ads for the Bonneville were thick with hyperbole, suggesting that "when you arrive, bask for a minute in the respectful spotlight of admiration that's always focused on this striking, tasteful car." The broad-shouldered appearance was macho, tough, and suggestive, and appealed to the public; 27,769 Sport Coupes like this were sold in 1959.

SPECIFICATIONS

MODEL 1959 Pontiac Bonneville Sport Coupe
PRODUCTION 27,769
BODY STYLE Two-door, six-seater coupe.
CONSTRUCTION Steel body and chassis.
ENGINE 389cid V8.
POWER OUTPUT 260–345 bhp.
TRANSMISSION Three-speed manual, optional four-speed Super Hydra-Matic automatic.
SUSPENSION Front and rear coil springs.
BRAKES Front and rear drums.
MAXIMUM SPEED 110–125 mph (177–201 km/h)
0–60 MPH (0–96 KM/H) 9–11.5 sec
A.F.C. 15 mpg (5.3 km/l)

CHASSIS
The chassis was known as Spread-Tread and gave much crisper cornering than was possible in previous models.

1958 BONNEVILLE
Pontiac's '58 Bonnevilles were 9 in (23 cm) shorter and 5 in (13 cm) narrower than the Wide Track '59s. The most obvious difference was in the grille, which was a one-piece affair on the '58 model. Sales literature from that year crooned that the Bonneville "sets a new pattern of dynamic luxury for those who like their motoring rare and exciting."

BRAKES
Early Bonnevilles had bad brakes, but the '59s had finned drums and 10 percent more lining area.

The Sixties

If the Fifties changed the way America looked, the Sixties changed the way Americans thought. Assassinations, demonstrations, confrontations, a youth with a conscience, and a war nobody wanted made the nation take a long hard look at itself.

FORD FALCON COMPACT

AWAY FROM THE UNREST and upheaval of the decade, America still found time to enjoy life. The economy was in rude health, average earnings were $150 a week, and attendances at amusement parks boomed. JFK promised a new order and there were new distractions like felt-tip pens, nondairy creamer, and a dance called the Twist.

And there were drugs, lots of them. A Harvard researcher called Timothy Leary dabbled with recreational pharmaceuticals and became a cult hero by appearing on stage in 1967, dressed in white with flowers in his hair. He told half a million stoned followers to "turn on to the scene, tune in to what's happening, and drop out of everything," neatly articulating the mantra of the Sixties.

Pampered, comfortable, and bored out of their brains, the college-age young represented 10 percent of the population and had the time and the power to pursue their own agendas. They rejected parental values of rising early, working hard, and saving money, and instead lashed into capitalism and the establishment. Anyone who was into change, high ideals, and a new order was determinedly pursued by hordes of wide-eyed devotees. The popularity of cult icons like Jack Kerouac, Martin Luther King Jr., and JFK soared to a new high.

Main Street America may have smiled nervously at Ken Kesey's best-selling novel, *One Flew Over the Cuckoo's Nest*, but the

THE LEGENDARY JFK
The youngest President ever elected was sworn in on January 20, 1961. Saying "the torch has been passed to a new generation of Americans," he promised strong leadership and hope for the Sixties.

	1960	1961	1962	1963	1964
AUTOMOTIVE	• **Chevrolet** trounces **Ford** in model year production • **Edsel** dropped after three disastrous years • Compact **Chevrolet** Corvair, **Ford** Falcon, **Mercury** Comet, and **Plymouth** Valiant appear • Car production double that of 1950 • Steel strike means aluminum on grilles and hubcaps gains popularity • 10 million families own cars	• **DeSoto** nameplate disappears • **Ford** and **Chevrolet** introduce new cast-iron engines • **Lincoln** introduces dazzling new Continental • **Dodge** launches compact Lancer • **Pontiac** launches Tempest, with transmission at rear to eliminate gearbox hump in interior • **Oldsmobile** introduces F-85 • Industry introduces lifetime chassis lubrication and self-adjusting brakes	• Fins and two-tone paint fade from most ranges • New class of intermediate model born in the **Chevy** Nova, **Ford** Fairlane, and **Mercury** Meteor • **Ford** and **Chrysler** offer V8s with 400 bhp • **Buick** offers new V6 • Calendar sales reach 6.8 million • Drag racing between **Ford**, **Chevrolet**, **Dodge**, **Mercury**, and **Pontiac** reaccelerates horsepower race	• New personal sports cars debut: **Buick** Riviera, **Studebaker** Avanti, and Corvette Sting Ray • **GM** introduces Tilt-Away steering wheel • **Chrysler** offers a new 50,000-mile warranty • Detroit agrees to install seat belts on '64 models • Car production hits record 7.3 million • Half the world's cars are in US	• **Ford** releases Mustang at New York World Fair; best-selling new car in history • **Studebaker** ends US production • **GM** suffers massive strike • **Pontiac** GTO debuts 1964 OLDSMOBILE STARFIRE
HISTORICAL	• John F. Kennedy announces he's running for President • JFK and Nixon hold live TV debate • Russians shoot down US spy plane • 10 blacks shot dead in worst-ever race riot in Mississippi • *Ben Hur* wins a record 10 Oscars, and Hitchcock's *Psycho* opens to great acclaim	• Kennedy sworn in as President • US breaks diplomatic ties with Cuba • Bay of Pigs • JFK sends 100 "advisers" to Vietnam • Berlin Wall goes up • Yuri Gagarin is first man in space THE TWIST	• More US aid for South Vietnam • JFK embargoes Cuban imports • John Glenn orbits the earth • Martin Luther King Jr. jailed for illegal march in Georgia • Telstar satellite beams pictures around the world • Supreme Court outlaws prayer in schools • Marilyn Monroe dies from a drug overdose • Decca record company turns down the Beatles	• Cuban missile crisis brings world to brink of nuclear war • JFK assassinated • Khrushchev warns the world that Russia has 100 megaton A-bomb • 200 arrested at Mississippi University race riot • Five US helicopters shot down in Mekong Delta • Alcatraz closes • Tennessee Williams' *Sweet Bird of Youth* premieres	• LBJ signs sweeping Civil Rights Act • US escalates action against North Vietnam • Malcolm X forms Black Nationalist Party • First flight of 2,000 mph (3,200 km/h) B-70 bomber • Sidney Poitier becomes first black actor to win an Oscar • LBJ retains Presidency • The Beatles appear on the *Ed Sullivan Show*

FAREWELL TO FINS
In the Sixties, Cadillacs shed their fins with indecent haste. Gone were the ridiculous tail feathers of the '59 (left), replaced by the clean, horizontal lines of the '65 (below).

subtext of cultural radicalism went straight over their heads. Artists like Warhol and Lichtenstein, with their Campbell's soup cans and cartoon blow-ups, may have appeared to be painting a democratic canvas, but in reality they were chipping away at establishment values. The problem was that only the radical youth could be bothered to listen.

While the old order blockaded Cuba, and sent "advisers" to Vietnam and John Glenn into orbit, the new order marched 200,000-strong to Washington to demonstrate over civil rights, listened to four mop-topped Englishmen called the Beatles, and joined Malcolm X's Black Nationalist Party. The Surgeon General blamed cigarettes for lung cancer, JFK was cruelly cut down in Dallas, and

SPACE MANIA
Ford's advertising campaign for '63 tapped into the national obsession with the space race: "A small spaceman makes big discoveries about Ford interiors."

Lyndon Johnson turned up the heat in Vietnam. America was changing, big time.

Hordes of middle-class students, who wouldn't normally have drawn a rebellious breath, were out demonstrating to save themselves, and the Vietnamese. Many of their colleges and universities were sucked into the war machine. Suddenly, sacrosanct freedoms like experimental sex, drugs, hair, music, and clothing were under attack as unpatriotic, immoral, subversive, and unhygienic. And, as always, it was capitalism that was to blame for fueling America's great engine of war.

A pall of paranoia fell over the nation. Everybody was chasing everybody else in the hit TV series *The Fugitive*, the CIA was blamed for the assassination of JFK, and bugs were found in the US Embassy in Moscow. The FBI tried not to investigate the murder of three civil rights workers in Mississippi and Malcolm X was gunned down in New York.

1965	1966	1967	1968	1969
• **Cadillacs** finally lose their tail fins • **American Motors** loses $13 million • **GM** makes $1.54 billion • Ralph Nader's *Unsafe at Any Speed* published	• **Oldsmobile** launches big new sports car, the Toronado • Seven safety items added to all new cars • LBJ signs Traffic Safety Act • **Lincoln** gets standard 462cid engine • Average big car price is $7,500, average compact is $3,100 • Extras add 40 percent to price of average sedan • Model year production romps toward nine million cars	• 17 new safety standards incorporated into all US cars; prices rise by 2 percent • **Pontiac** launches Firebird to fight Mustang and Camaro • **Cadillac** launches new Eldorado	• Model year production peaks at 8.4 million units • **Chrysler** adopts long-hood/short-trunk philosophy with restyled **Dodge** Charger • **Lincoln** launches Continental Mark III • Three-percent price hike is biggest in 10 years • **Cadillac** gets 472cid engine	• Side marker lights are new Federal safety requirement • Mustang, Camaro, and Firebird all get face-lifts

MALCOLM X

1967 CHEVROLET CAMARO RS

THE VIETNAM WAR escalates

1965	1966	1967	1968	1969
• Malcolm X shot in New York • Nixon visits USSR • New York abolishes death penalty • First US astronaut walks in space • Julie Andrews wins Oscar for *Mary Poppins*	• US troops launch 8,000-strong offensive in Vietnam; bombers strafe Hanoi • American H-bomb lost after midair crash • Ronald Reagan becomes Governor of California • Black student shot in back at University of Mississippi • Bob Dylan records his first music using electric guitar • Film actress Hedy Lamarr arrested for shoplifting	• North Vietnam rejects US offer of peace talks; UN calls for an end to the Vietnam War • 200,000 protest in New York and San Francisco against War • Muhammad Ali refuses draft • Paratroops called in to quell race riots in Detroit • Stalin's daughter defects • First heart transplant • First microwave oven on market • Rolling Stones in court on drugs charges	• LBJ sends 50,000 more troops to Vietnam • LBJ signs Civil Rights Bill • Antiwar riots in Chicago • Nixon elected President and calls for Vietnam conflict to be scaled down • Bobby Kennedy assassinated • Jackie Kennedy marries Onassis • Martin Luther King Jr. assassinated in Memphis • Dustin Hoffman stars in *The Graduate*	• Biggest antiwar demonstration of the decade is called the "Vietnam Moratorium" • 400,000 attend Woodstock Festival • Man lands on moon • Premieres of *Midnight Cowboy* and *Easy Rider*

Even Defense Secretary Robert McNamara was dubbed a "mother of invention." It took the Beatles to sum up America's malaise in one word: "Help!"

Ford and Pontiac tried to cheer things up with the new Mustang, Camaro, and Firebird, helped by miniskirts, The Monkees, *Mission Impossible*, and *The Munsters*. With more disposable income than ever before, Easy Street stretched from one side of America to the other. Four out of five households now owned a car, multicar families totaled 12 million, and between them they were consuming millions of gallons of gas a year.

The Pressure Builds

The music industry put on a happy face with songs like "Good Vibrations," "Feelin' Groovy," "California Dreaming," and "All You Need is Love." But in the background the soundtrack of protest still tinkled away with "Alice's Restaurant," Dylan's "The Times They Are A-Changin'," and the veiled satire of *Rowan & Martin's Laugh-In*. But the laughing stopped abruptly when Tricky Dick Nixon announced that he was running for President. The shocks never seemed to end.

Things came to a head in 1968. Anarchy was so near that many people genuinely felt America was about to disintegrate. Assassins took out Martin Luther King Jr. and Robert Kennedy, race riots flared everywhere, and the police quelled antiwar protests with savage and needless brutality. The hot,

MUSTANG MARRIAGE
Cars were marketed as a panacea for all ills. This 1965 Mustang ad implied that their new pony car was versatile enough to settle even domestic disputes: "The Select Shift. You get your way. She gets hers." For once it was pretty near the truth, as Mustangs appealed not only to the young beat generation but to buyers of almost every age. And having the longest options list around was a big contributing factor.

violent summer of '68 in Chicago was like a civil war. It was the catalyst America needed, and the machinery of change shifted up a gear.

Nixon began withdrawing troops from 'Nam, a fairer "lottery-style" draft system came into effect, and the US and USSR started talking to each other at the first of the Strategic Arms Limitation Talks. Neil Armstrong took those few giant steps for mankind, and the establishment shrugged its shoulders and let Woodstock happen. Public protest had succeeded, and the new order was here to stay. Peace and love to all.

Meanwhile, the auto industry was actually listening to what was going on. Manufacturers quickly purged their cars of futuristic frivolity and tail fins because they too couldn't ignore the cries of protest. The youth

A NEW BREED
Muscle cars like this '67 Camaro Z-28 answered the consumer's cri de coeur for distinction. The rock 'n' roll subculture of the Fifties had spread into a broad and profitable youth market that wanted to express its rebellious identity through its cars, and manufacturers were responding.

SPACE RACE VICTORY
In 1969, Neil Armstrong became the first man to walk on the moon, in an event watched by 100 million TV viewers around the world. His "giant leap for mankind" did much to reassure America that it was still the most powerful nation on earth, or indeed anywhere else.

ANTIWAR SENTIMENTS
In 1968, antiwar demonstrations in Chicago got out of hand, and the National Guard had to be called in. Demonstrators taunted soldiers, who reacted with shocking violence. Novelist Norman Mailer was among more than 250 arrested on that day.

market was rebelling against everything, including dinosaurs in their driveways. What they wanted were machines with charisma and optimism, like the fun-loving Volkswagen Beetle.

The Birth of Auto Individuality

First came the socially responsible compacts (the Lark, Valiant, and the Falcon), then the personality pony cars (the Barracuda, Mustang, and Camaro), followed by the rebellious muscle iron (the GTO, Trans Am, and Charger). Business was now brisk because, for once, the motor mandarins were offering excitement, low prices, and a new deal – auto individuality. Sixties Detroit was at its most imaginative and culturally receptive and, despite war, labor unrest, and domestic turmoil, production peaked in '69 at an amazing 8.4 million cars.

And in the age of the individual there was no better sales ploy than to offer an individualized car. Sixties option lists read like the Declaration of Independence. Buyers could create custom-made cars by choosing from a litany of permutations of engines, carburetors, transmissions, brakes, wheels, seats, interiors, and even color-coded side mirrors. By plugging into the culture of difference and

defiance, Detroit cynically stoked the fires of youthful rebellion. In 1966, Dodge launched its "Rebellion" promotion, featuring a woman standing beside a Charger holding a bomb behind her back. Buick advertised its Skylark GS as a muscle car "that will rattle your faith in the established order." Uncannily, during the Sixties, America's social and cultural changes were nearly always reflected in her automobiles. Both Washington and Detroit went through their own kind of revolution, but where Washington resisted caving in to the new order, Detroit embraced it like a newfound friend. To its credit, Motown gave customers what they wanted: machines with personality and distinction that were fun to drive, look at, and listen to.

But the status quo wouldn't stay stable for long. Left on its own, Detroit might well have continued selling mass-produced motoring mescaline through the next two decades without a hiccup, but it wasn't to be. Greed, Federal meddling, and the inability to create excitement in a noncreative atmosphere brought the industry to its knees. Bad news was just around the corner, and it was called the Seventies.

FLYING FALCON
1968 was one of the best years for the car industry, and auto makers spent $1.5 billion bringing in new models. This '68 Ford Falcon was one of many cars that boasted better safety features and a longer warranty.

1960 CHEVROLET
Impala

THE IMPALA DEBUTED IN 1958 AS A LIMITED EDITION, AND
WENT ON TO BECOME THE MOST POPULAR CAR IN THE 1960s

IN THE SIXTIES, unbridled consumerism began to wane. America turned away from the politics of prosperity and, in deference, Chevrolet toned down its finny Impala. The gothic cantilevered batwings of 1959 went, replaced by a much blunter rear deck. America was developing a social conscience and Fifties excess just wasn't cool anymore.

Mind you, the '60 Impala was no shrinking violet. Tired of gorging on gratuitous ornamentation, American motorists were offered a new theology – performance. Freeways were one long concrete loop, premium gas was cheap, and safety and environmentalism were a nightmare still to come. For $333, the Sports Coupe could boast a 348cid, 335 bhp Special Super Turbo-Thrust V8. The '59 Impala was riotous and the '60 stylistically muddled, but within a year the unruliness would disappear altogether. These crossover Chevrolets are landmark cars – they ushered in a new decade that would change America and Americans forever.

INTERIOR
The interior was loaded with performance metaphor: central speedometer, four gauges, and a mock sports car steering wheel with crossed flags. This Impala has power windows and dual Polaroid sun visors.

ENGINE
Two V8 engine options offered consumers seven heady levels of power, from 170 to 335 horses. Cheapskates could still specify the ancient Blue Flame Six, which wheezed out a miserly 135 bhp. Seen here is the 185 bhp, 283cid V8. Impalas could be invigorated with optional Positraction, heavy-duty springs, and power brakes.

REAR END
The '60 Impala sported much tamer Spread Wing fins that aped a seagull in flight. They were an answer to charges that the '59's uproarious rear end was downright dangerous.

SPECIFICATIONS

MODEL 1960 Chevrolet Impala Sports Coupe

PRODUCTION Not available

BODY STYLE Two-door coupe.

CONSTRUCTION Steel body, separate chassis.

ENGINE 235cid straight six; 283cid, 348cid V8s.

POWER OUTPUT 135–335 bhp (348cid turbo V8).

TRANSMISSION Three-speed manual, optional four-speed manual, two-speed Powerglide automatic, Turboglide automatic.

SUSPENSION *Front:* upper and lower A-arms, coil springs; *Rear:* coil springs with live axle.

BRAKES Front and rear drums.

MAXIMUM SPEED 90–135 mph (145–217 km/h)

0–60 MPH (0–96 КМ/Н) 9–18 sec

A.F.C. 12–16 mpg (4.2–5.7 km/l)

RACING IMPALA

The Impala impressed circuits all over the world. This 1961 model was deemed hot enough to compete with European track stars like the Jaguar Mark II, driven here by Graham Hill.

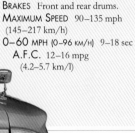

WHEELS

At $15 a set, wheel discs were a mandatory fashion accessory. Slick whitewalls were yours for just $36.

1960 CHEVROLET IMPALA SPORTS COUPE

Triple taillights and a vertically ribbed aluminum rear beauty panel helped sober up the Impala's rear end. It was still a class act and a lot glitzier than the Bel Air's plainer tail. As for the front, it was meant to be quiet and calm and a million miles from the deranged dentistry of mid-Fifties grille treatments. The jet-fighter cockpit and quarterpanel missile ornaments were eerie portents of the coming decade of military intervention.

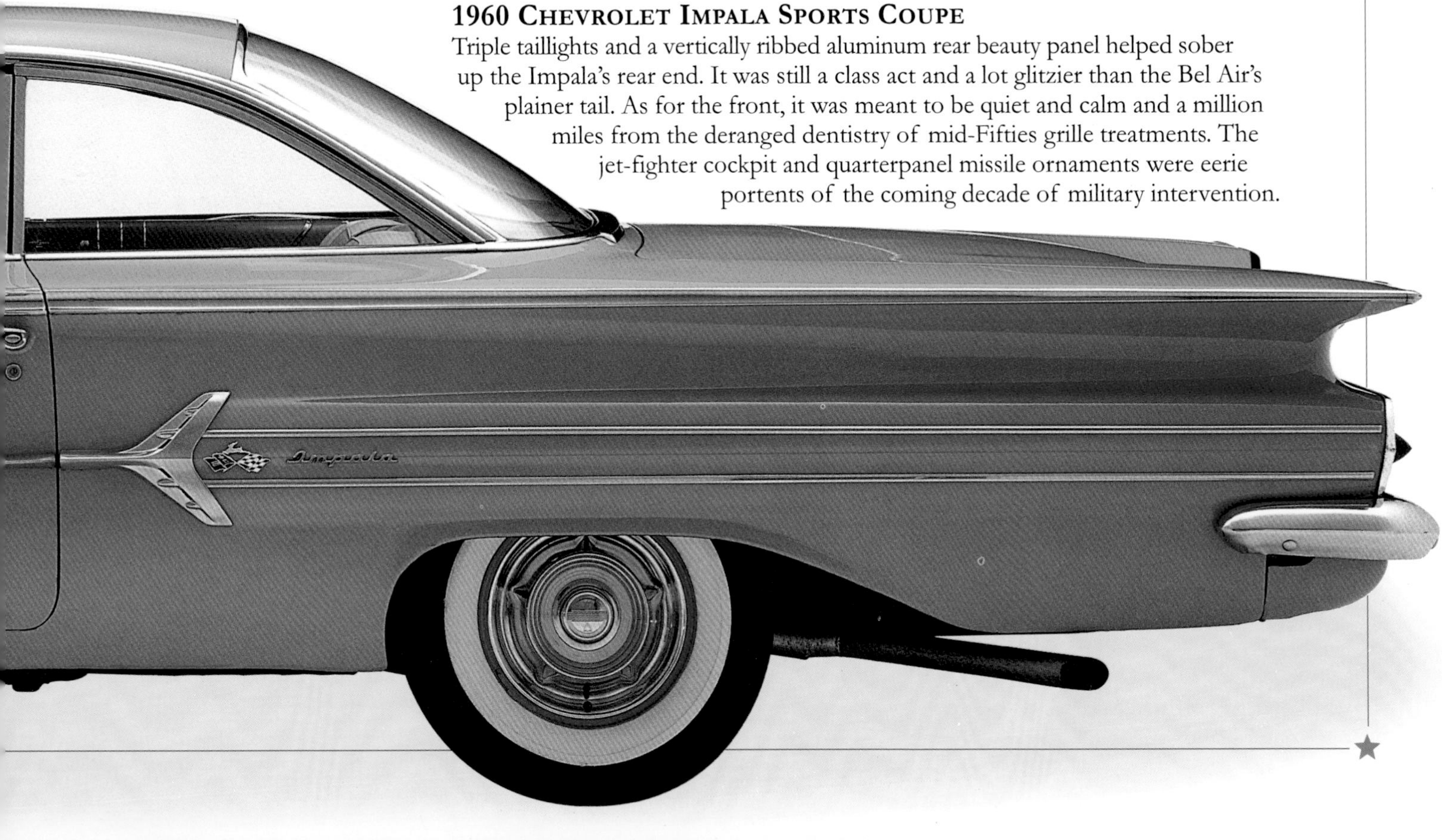

1960 CHRYSLER
300F

"RED HOT AND RAMBUNCTIOUS" is how Chrysler sold the 300F. It may be one of the strangest taglines of any American auto maker, but the 300F really was red hot and a serious flying machine that could better 140 mph (225 km/h). The rambunctious refers to the ram-air induction on the bad-boy 413cid wedge-head V8. Ram tuning had long been a way of raising torque and horsepower for drag racing, and it gave the 300F a wicked performance persona.

One of Virgil Exner's happier designs, the 300F of '60 had unibody construction, a French Pont-A-Mousson four-speed gearbox, and front seats that swiveled toward you when you opened the doors. It also boasted an electro-luminescent instrument panel and Chrysler's best styling effort since 1957. But at $5,411, it was no surprise that only 964 Coupes found buyers. Nevertheless, it bolstered Chrysler's image and taught them plenty of tuning tricks for the muscle-car wars that were revving up just around the corner.

SERIOUS COMFORT
More a coupe than a sedan, the 300F's four bucket seats were contoured in black, red, or white terra-cotta leather as here.

SWIVELING SEAT
Self-activated swiveling seats were new for 1960 and pivoted outward automatically when either door was opened. It's ironic that the burly 300F's typical owner was thought to be a flabby 40-year-old.

ENGINE
The 375 bhp 413cid V8 breathed through two Carter four-barrels with 30-inch rams and was a real gem of an engine. Chrysler carefully calculated optimum inlet manifold length and placed carburetors on the end of the tubes rather than the traditional inline, to give a steady buildup of power along the torque curve.

THIS MAGNIFICENT BLOCK SECURED THE FIRST SIX PLACES FOR 300Fs IN THE 1960 FLYING MILE COMPETITION AT DAYTONA, WITH A TOP SPEED OF 145 MPH (233 KM/H)

SOLEX TINTED GLASS WAS A $43 OPTION

WITH THE WIND[OW] ROLLED DOWN, [THE] 300F HAD A PILLARLESS LOO[K]

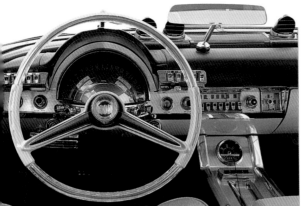

DASHBOARD

The "Astra-Dome" instrumentation was illuminated at night by electro-luminescent light, giving a soft, eerie glow that shone through the translucent markings on the gauges. It was technically very daring and boasted six different laminations of plastic, creating a rich, lustrous finish.

THE ONLY BLEMISH

The much-criticized fake spare-tire embellishment on the trunk was variously described as a toilet seat or trash-can lid. Possibly the 300F's only stylistic peccadillo, it was dropped in '61.

TACHOMETER CAME AS STANDARD

SPECIFICATIONS

MODEL 1960 Chrysler 300F
PRODUCTION 1,212 (both body styles)
BODY STYLE Two-door coupe and convertible.
CONSTRUCTION Steel unitary body.
ENGINE 413cid V8.
POWER OUTPUT 375–400 bhp.
TRANSMISSION Three-speed push-button automatic, optional four-speed manual.
SUSPENSION *Front:* torsion bars; *Rear:* leaf springs.
BRAKES Front and rear drums.
MAXIMUM SPEED 140 mph (225 km/h)
0–60 MPH (0–96 KM/H) 7.1 sec
A.F.C. 12 mpg (4.2 km/l)

HUMONGOUS TRUNK

The two-door shape meant that the rear deck was the size of Indiana, and the cavernous trunk was large enough to hold four wheels and tires.

THIS PARTICULAR MODEL HAS SURE-GRIP DIFFERENTIAL, A $52 OPTION

LENGTHY FINS

You could argue that the 300F's fins started at the front of the car and traveled along the side, building up to lethal, daggerlike points above the exquisitely sculptured taillights. Within two years fins would disappear completely on the Chrysler letter series 300.

POWER ANTENNA WAS A $43 OPTION, AND THIS CAR ALSO HAS THE GOLDEN TONE RADIO ($124) WITH REAR SEAT SPEAKER ($17)

NYLON WHITEWALLS CAME AS STANDARD

EVOLUTION OF THE CHRYSLER 300 LETTER SERIES

THE 300 SERIES started life in 1955 when Chrysler came up with the first production sedan to kick out 300 bhp. The following year it was given the designation "B," and horsepower was hiked to 340. In '57 it became the 300C, pushing out 375 horses, and by '59 the "D" was producing 380 bhp. The only 300 without a letter was the '63, which would have read as a rather confusing 300I. Otherwise, the series followed in alphabetical order, the distinguished line culminating in the 360 bhp 300L of 1965.

ADVERTISING FOR THE 300F CALLED IT "THE SIXTH OF A FAMOUS FAMILY" AND "LEADER OF THE CLAN"

1955

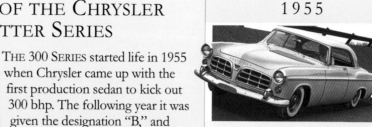

AMERICA'S ORIGINAL muscle machine debuted as the C300, an image car to lock horns with the Corvette and T-Bird. Chrysler couldn't afford a two-seater, so instead stuffed everything it could into a New Yorker body. With a special Hemi and twin WCFB carbs, it was the fastest production car in the world and became known as "the car that swept Daytona."

KEY FEATURES
- Hand-built cars
- Oversize exhaust and solid valve lifters
- Only available in black, red, or white
- Base price of $4,055
- Options list runs to only 10 features

1956

THE 300B WAS THE first of the letter cars that gave buyers a choice of eng and transmission options. The base 354cid kicked out 340 horses, but m year a 355 bhp motor was offered, a with three different transmissions. T 300B, not Chevy's fuelie 283, was the first American engine to offer a genu one horsepower per cubic inch.

KEY DEVELOPMENTS
- Revised rear end with new bumper and taillights
- Two-speed PowerFlite, TorqueFlite, an three-speed manual offered from mid-y
- Base price of $4,312
- Air-conditioning, record player, and clo set in steering wheel become options

1960 CHRYSLER 300F

BADGE
The brazen red, white, and blue 300F badge on the rear wing left nobody in any doubt that this was really a thunderbolt in drag.

SHARP END
The 300F's razor-sharp rear fins were cited by Ralph Nader in his book *Unsafe at Any Speed* as "potentially lethal." In 1963, a motorcyclist hit the rear bumper of a 300F at speed and was impaled on the fin.

AIR-CONDITIONING COST A HEFTY $510 EXTRA

AUTOMATIC TRANSMISSION WAS ACTUATED BY PUSH-BUTTONS ON THE DASH

QUESTIONABLE REAR DECK TREATMENT WAS KNOWN AS "FLIGHT-SWEEP" AND WAS ALSO AVAILABLE ON OTHER CHRYSLERS

LSU CENTENNIAL
83 138
19 LOUISIANA 60

Chrysler

1960 CHRYSLER 300F

1957	1958	1961	1965

THE THIRD LETTER CAR in the 300 series
was confusingly known as the 300C,
confusing since the '55 had been tagged
the C300. But that was where the
similarity ended. Blessed with Virgil
Exner's elegant rear finnery, it had quad
headlights, a big trapezoidal grille, a
convertible option, and a howling all-
out maximum of 150 mph (241 km/h).

KEY DEVELOPMENTS
• Silentfan drive
• Stiffer torsion bars
• Optional high-lift cams boost
  horsepower to 390
• Base price $4,929
• Now available in five exterior colors

THE 300D WASN'T that different from
the "C." With a simpler grille and
slightly changed rear lights, it pushed
out 380 horsepower and came with fuel
injection as a $400 option. Power
brakes were now standard, and the
Hemi mill was gently reworked. At
Bonneville, a 300D set a new speed
record of 156 mph (251 km/h).

KEY DEVELOPMENTS
• Compression and horsepower up
• New valve timing, pistons, and cam
• Electrojector fuel injection is first use of
  a computer in a Chrysler product; only
  16 cars fitted with fuel injection
• Last year of Firepower Hemi engine

THE 300G LOOKED much like the 300F,
but the much-lambasted toilet seat was
dropped from the rear deck, and the
front end wore Chrysler's new slanted
headlights. This would be the last year of
Exner's fins. 1,617 "G"s left showrooms
in 1961, by which time prices, swollen by
a handful of options, were homing in on
a very considerable $7,000.

KEY DEVELOPMENTS
• Standard ram manifolding
• Short-ram high-output engine available
• Power windows, cruise control, and
  undercoating standard
• 15-inch wheels now fitted

THE ELEVENTH AND LAST year of the
letter series, the 300L rode on racing
tires and shocks with a 413cid lump.
Four-speed manual stick shift was a
no-cost option and, in common with
other '65 Chryslers, it retained unibody
construction. But the 300L was not as
quick as its forebears and is the least
special of Chrysler's limited editions.

KEY DEVELOPMENTS
• Longer wheelbase
• New corporate C-body
• Last year for 413cid engine
• Column lever replaces push buttons
  on TorqueFlite
• Bigger drum brakes

POWER AND BEAUTY

The 300F was one of America's most
powerful cars, and a tuned version recorded
a one-way run of an amazing 189 mph
(304 km/h) on the Bonneville salt flats.
But despite the prodigious
performance, it was
deliberately understated
compared with many
contemporary Detroit
offerings.

THE PHRASE "BEAUTIFUL BRUTES" WAS
COINED TO DESCRIBE THE 300 SERIES

SIDE MIRROR
WAS REMOTE
CONTROLLED

FRONT TORSION BAR
SUSPENSION AND
EXTRA-STRENGTH
LEAF SPRINGS
MEANT THE 300F
HANDLED WELL

1962 FORD
Falcon

INTERIOR
The austere interior could be upgraded with an $87 Deluxe trim package, which became the Deluxe model in its own right from 1962 on. A padded dash and visors cost an extra $16, and front safety belts $21. Transmission choices were standard column-shift three-speed synchro manual or two-speed Ford-O-Matic automatic.

THE FALCON, WITH ITS SIMPLE, ULTRACONSERVATIVE STYLING, WAS DUBBED BY FORD "THE EASIEST CAR IN THE WORLD TO OWN"

FORD CHIEF EXECUTIVE Robert McNamara had a soft spot for the Volkswagen Beetle and wanted Dearborn to turn out a small compact of its own. Obsessed with gas mileage and economy, McNamara wanted a four-cylinder, since it was $13.50 cheaper to make, but was persuaded that a six-cylinder would sell better. On March 19, 1958, Ford approved its small-car program and the Falcon, the first of the American compacts, was launched in 1960.

The press was unimpressed, calling it a modern version of the Tin Lizzy. One auto writer said of McNamara: "He wears granny glasses and has put out a granny car." But cash-strapped consumers liked the new-sized Ford, and the Falcon won over 435,000 sales in its first year. The ultimate throwaway car, the Falcon may have been mechanically uninteresting and conventional in looks, but it was roomy, smooth-riding, and delivered an astonishing 30 mpg (10.6 km/l).

NEW BARGAIN COMPACT
Ford introduced "a wonderful world of savings in the new-sized Ford Falcon." Base Falcons stickered at just $1,974 in 1960.

GROWING SERIES
The Falcon line gradually expanded to station wagons, a neat-looking pickup, the Falcon Sedan Delivery, the Econoline Van range, and the sporty Futura coupe. The Futura Sprint, convertible or hardtop, came with a zesty 260cid V8.

"BIG-CAR" ENGINE
The Falcon's standard mill was a 144cid six, which the ads boasted was a "brand-new powerplant specifically designed to power the Falcon over America's hills and highways with big-car performance and safety."

FRONT GRILLE
The aluminum-stamped radiator grille changed every year. This "electric shaver" convex shape with vertical bars denotes a '62 Falcon.

SLIM DIMENSIONS
Prototypes had to be considerably widened and lengthened after Henry Ford himself complained they were too narrow.

1962 FORD FALCON
Half-a-hood shorter than full-size Fords, the slab-sided two- or four-door Falcon could comfortably seat six. Its styling was as simple as its engineering, with roly-poly rounded edges, creased body sides, and big, circular taillights. The Falcon series just about made it to the end of the decade; it was superseded in 1970 by the compact Maverick – based on the Falcon's chassis – and then by the even tinier and thriftier Pinto lines.

SPECIFICATIONS
MODEL 1962 Ford Falcon
PRODUCTION 396,129
BODY STYLE Two- or four-door hardtops, station wagons, and convertible.
CONSTRUCTION All-steel unitary construction.
ENGINE 144cid, 170cid sixes, 260cid V8.
POWER OUTPUT 85–174 bhp.
TRANSMISSION Three-speed column-shift synchro manual, optional two-speed Ford-O-Matic automatic.
SUSPENSION *Front:* coil springs; *Rear:* leaf springs.
BRAKES Front and rear drums.
MAXIMUM SPEED 90–110 mph (145–177 km/h)
0–60 MPH (0–96 KM/H) 12–18 sec
A.F.C. 25–30 mpg (8.8–10.6 km/l)

ROOF STYLING
Mid-'62 two- and four-door Falcons had a T-Bird-style roof line.

ROOMY INSIDE
Ford's marketing department boasted that the Falcon offered "honest-to-goodness six-passenger comfort – plenty of room for six and their luggage!" For once the hype was true and the interior did actually have room for occupants over 6 ft (1.8 m) tall.

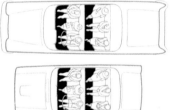

1962 FORD
Galaxie 500XL Sunliner

*500 DESIGNATION STOOD FOR
THE INDY 500-MILE RACES*

IN '62, FORD WAS SELLING its range as "America's liveliest, most carefree cars." And leading the lively look was the bright-as-a-button new Galaxie. This was General Manager Lee Iacocca's third year at the helm and he was pitching for the young-guy market with speed and muscle. Clean cut, sleek, and low, the Galaxie range was just what the boys wanted and it drove Ford into a new era. The new-for-'62 500XL was a real piece, with bucket seats, floor shift, a machine-turned instrument panel, and the option of a brutish 406cid V8. XL stood for "extra lively," making the 500 one of the first cars to kick off Ford's new Total Performance sales campaign.

The 500XL Sunliner Convertible was billed as a sporty ragtop and cost an eminently reasonable $3,350. Engines were mighty, rising from 292 through 390 to 406cid V8s, with a Borg-Warner stick shift four-speed option. Ford learned an important lesson from this car. Those big, in-your-face engines clothed in large, luxurious bodies would become seriously hip.

INTERIOR
The interior was plush and palatial, with Mylar-trimmed, deep-pleated buckets flanking the center console. Seats could be adjusted four ways manually and six ways electronically. The dashboard was padded, and front seat belts were an option.

MIRROR-LIGH
*The spotlight-mirror was a facto
option; on a clear da
the light could en
a beam ½ m
(800 meter
ahea*

SALES BROCHURE
"This year, more than ever before, Galaxie styling is the envy of the industry." Subjective sales literature maybe, but Ford's restyled Galaxies were a real success, and the new XL series offered peak performance in addition to the top trim level of the 500.

Galaxie 500/XL sunliner

STYLISH CHROM
*The arrow-straig
side flash is a f
cry from the flor
sweepspears that adorn
most Fifties model.*

HIDDEN FILLER
The fuel filler-cap lurks behind this hinged section of the anodized beauty panel. The panel itself highlights the car's width.

LIGHTS
Large, round, rear-light cluster aped the T-Bird and appeared on the Falcon as well as the Fairlane, also debuting in 1962.

ENGINE
Stock Galaxies lumbered around with a 223cid six or 292cid V8. The 500XL could choose from a range of Thunderbird V8s that included the 390cid Special, as here, and a 405 bhp 406cid V8 with triple Holley carbs, which could be ordered for $379.

SPECIFICATIONS

MODEL 1962 Ford Galaxie 500XL Sunliner Convertible
PRODUCTION 13,183
BODY STYLE Two-door convertible.
CONSTRUCTION Steel body and chassis.
ENGINE 292cid, 352cid, 390cid, 406cid V8s.
POWER OUTPUT 170–405 bhp.
TRANSMISSION Three-speed Cruise-O-Matic automatic, optional four-speed manual.
SUSPENSION *Front:* coil springs; *Rear:* leaf springs.
BRAKES Front and rear drums.
MAXIMUM SPEED 108–140 mph (174–225 km/h)
0–60 MPH (0–96 KM/H) 7.6–14.2 sec
A.F.C. 16–18 mpg (5.7–6.4 km/l)

1962 FORD GALAXIE 500XL SUNLINER
The slab-sided Galaxie body was completely new for '62 and would set something of a styling trend for larger cars. Lines may have been flat and unadorned, but buyers could choose from 13 colors and 21 jaunty two-tones. The hardtop version of the 500XL Sunliner was the Club Victoria, $250 cheaper than the convertible and twice as popular, with 28,000 manufactured in '62.

HEAVY-RIBBED FLOOR

WIDE-CONTOURED FRAME WITH DOUBLE-CHANNEL SIDE RAILS

TOP UP
Unlike this example, the rarest Sunliners have a wind-cheating Starlift hardtop, which was not on the options list.

BODY INSULATION
The Galaxie had an especially quiet ride because it was soundproofed at various points. Sound-absorbent mastic was applied to the inside surfaces of the doors, hood, trunk lid, fenders, and quarter panels, and thick fiberglass "blankets" insulated the roof.

1963 FORD
Thunderbird

THUNDERBIRDS
ARE GO

IT WAS NO ACCIDENT THAT THE third-generation T-Bird looked like it was fired from a rocket silo. Designer Bill Boyer wanted the new prodigy to have "an aircraft and missilelike shape," a subtext that wasn't lost on an American public vexed by the Cuban crisis and Khrushchev's declaration of an increase in Soviet military spending.

The Sports Roadster model was the finest incarnation of the 1961–63 Thunderbird. With Kelsey-Hayes wire wheels and a two-seater fiberglass tonneau, it was one of the most glamorous cars on the block and one of the most exclusive. Virile, vast, and expensive, the Big Bird showed that Detroit still wasn't disposed to make smaller, cheaper cars. GM even impudently asserted that "a good used car is the only answer to America's need for cheap transportation." And building cars that looked and went like ballistic missiles was far more interesting and profitable.

INTERIOR
Aircraft imagery in the controls is obvious. The interior was designed around a prominent center console that split the cabin into two separate cockpits, delineating positions of driver and passenger. T-Bird drivers weren't that young, and a Swing-Away steering wheel *(left)* aided access for the more corpulent driver.

STANDARD POWER
STEERING NEEDED
JUST THREE-AND-A-
HALF TURNS LOCK-
TO-LOCK

CONSTRUCTION WAS DUAL-UNITIZED, WITH
SEPARATE FRONT AND REAR SECTIONS
WELDED TOGETHER AT THE COWL

ROOF FUN
With the top down, the streamlined tonneau made the Sports Roadster sleek enough to echo the '55 two-seater Thunderbird.

TINTED GLASS, POWER SEATS AND
WINDOWS, AND AM/FM RADIO
WERE THE MOST POPULAR OPTIONS

ENGINE
The M Series 390cid V8 was an option that could crack 60 mph (96 km/h) in eight seconds and run all the way to 120 mph (193 km/h). It had three Holley two-barrels and five main bearings. The biggest unit offered was the 427cid V8 with 425 bhp.

THUNDERBIRD LANDAU
New for this model year was the chic Landau with a black or white vinyl top, designed to look like a leather-padded carriage top of yore. The roof was decorated in classic style, with chrome Landau irons on the sides. Leather upholstery was a plush extra at $106.

INTERIOR DESIGNER ART QUERFIELD SPENT MORE TIME ON THE T-BIRD'S INTERIOR THAN ON ANY OTHER CAR IN HIS 40 YEARS AT FORD

SPECIFICATIONS

MODEL 1963 Ford Thunderbird Sports Roadster
PRODUCTION 455
BODY STYLE Two-door, two-/four-seater convertible.
CONSTRUCTION Steel body and chassis.
ENGINE 390cid V8.
POWER OUTPUT 330–340 bhp.
TRANSMISSION Three-speed Cruise-O-Matic automatic.
SUSPENSION *Front:* upper and lower A-arms and coil springs; *Rear:* leaf springs with live axle.
BRAKES Front and rear drums.
MAXIMUM SPEED 116–125 mph (187–201 km/h)
0–60 MPH (0–96 KM/H) 9.7–12.4 sec
A.F.C. 11–20 mpg (3.9–7.1 km/l)

T-BIRDS WERE FINISHED IN 18 SINGLE SHADES OR 24 TWO-TONE COMBINATIONS

OVERHEAD
The Sports Roadster could also be a full four-seater. Trouble was, there was no space in the trunk for the tonneau, so it had to stay at home. *Motor Trend* magazine said: "Ford's plush style-setter has plenty of faults but it's still the classic example of the prestige car."

THREE SETS OF FIVE CAST-CHROME SLASH MARKS UNMISTAKABLY SUGGEST TOTAL POWER

LESSER T-BIRDS COULD OPT FOR THE ROADSTER'S WIRE WHEELS AT $343

1963 FORD THUNDERBIRD

EVOLUTION OF THE FORD THUNDERBIRD

THE BEACH BOYS were in good company as they sang the T-Bird's praises. Along with the Mustang and Vette, the Thunderbird has a special place in the American psyche. Purists maintain that proper T-Birds flew only between '55 and '66, but after a few inferior models in the '70s and '80s, the latest incarnation is actually quite a graceful car and still true to its original concept. Sadly, the '97 T-Bird marks the end of a remarkable 43-year run, with production scheduled to come to a close.

1955

FORD TOOK JUST 20 months to come up with an answer to Chevy's creaking Corvette, and didn't they do well? The 1955 to 1957 model years saw 40,000 of the original Thunderbirds leaving showrooms. While not a huge figure by Detroit's standards, this was a massive total for a new and unknown market for the American sports car.

KEY FEATURES
- First T-Bird rolls off the line on September 9, 1954
- Introduced on "T-Day" (October 22, 1954) to triumphant accolades
- Startlingly low price of $2,695
- 4,000 orders taken on first day of sale

1959

SWAPPING TWO SEATS for four in 1958 showed the powerful influence of Ford's accountants. In a search for greater sales volume, the Thunderbird nameplate was re-marketed to lose its youthful verve and become a prestige cruiser. Now, for the first time, T-Birds offered room for four, and the entire family could join the party.

KEY DEVELOPMENTS
- Ads sell T-Bird as "America's Most Becoming Car"
- 430cid Thunderbird Special V8 available
- New radical fan and revised rear suspension
- T-Bird finishes second in '59 Daytona

1964

WHILE THE THIRD-generation model (1961–63) was warmly received and sold well, the fourth generation from '64 saw the Thunderbird acquiring a middle-age spread. The subtle curves disappeared, replaced by a riot of pla and angles. With the car now weighi nearly two tons, things had gotten rat flabby. No prizes for charisma here.

KEY DEVELOPMENTS
- Complete restyle with longer hood and shorter roof
- Sports Roadster model dropped
- Five new rear axle options
- *Car and Driver* magazine lambastes T-Bird for "ego gratification"

1963 FORD
Thunderbird

WITH THE HOOD DOWN, THE BIG BIRD WAS ONE OF THE MOST ATTRACTIVE AND STIFFEST CONVERTIBLES FORD HAD EVER MADE. THE HEAVY UNITARY-CONSTRUCTION BODY ALLOWED PRECIOUS FEW SHAKES, RATTLES, AND ROLLS

REAR OVERHANG WAS PRODIGIOUS, BUT PARKING COULD BE MASTERED BY USING THE REAR FIN AS A MARKER

REAR VIEW

Ford cleaned up the rear of it prestige offering after the demise o the '58 to '60 Squarebird. Light were a simple rounded cluster, an the bumper was of the straigh and plain school of desig

LARGE TONNEAU PANEL CAME OFF EASILY BUT REQUIRED TWO PEOPLE TO HANDLE IT

19 SCENIC 68
2513
NEW HAMPSHIRE

1966

...TH A SHARPER FRONT, egg-crate ...le, and full-width taillights, the ...looked even neater; underneath ...glitter, things were basically the ...ne. A Town Hardtop and Town ...ndau were added to the range. *Car* ...é called the '66 T-Bird a "flying ...pet on autopilot" and marveled ...ts speed, silence, and refinement.

...Y DEVELOPMENTS
• ...5 bhp 428cid V8 available
• ...rices reduced for '66
• ...ush Landau is best-selling T-Bird ...r '66
• ...st year of convertibles

1970

1970

FORD'S ANSWER TO JAGUAR, the fifth-generation T-Bird from 1967 now had four doors and a tin top. Enthusiasts wailed that the most prized and individual of automobiles had turned into a truncated Galaxie, with all the trimmings. These Thunderbirds may have been groaning with every option available, but they lacked personality.

KEY DEVELOPMENTS
• New front end styling and reworked taillights
• Longer, lower, and wider
• New suspension and radial tires give "uncanny" control
• T-Bird gains 0.7 percent of total new car market

1978

1978 SAW FEW CHANGES from the '77 downsized model and, despite the car's economical pretensions, sales were a healthy 352,000 units. To add kudos to its now-emasculated Bird, Ford added a Diamond Jubilee model, calling it the "most exclusive Thunderbird you can buy." In reality the T-Bird was a pale facsimile, but the public didn't care.

KEY DEVELOPMENTS
• 351cid V8 tweaked for more performance
• Fuel consumption averages 15.1 mpg (5.3 km/l)
• Lighter power steering pump and better torque converter
• New Sports Decor option package at $466

1994

AFTER A FEW STYLE revisions in the '80s, which culminated in the classy 1989 rear-drive personal coupe that won *Motor Trend*'s Car of the Year, the revamped 1994 Thunderbird continued the fine return to form. It was now regarded as a world-class model and seen as a genuine contender with the established luxury German marques.

KEY DEVELOPMENTS
• Front and rear ends get smoother treatment
• Restyled "organic" interior with analogue gauges
• Dual airbags now standard
• Base model now stickers at $16,830

DIVINE DESIGN
Sales literature suggested that the T-Bird was the result of the combined efforts of Ford and God.

FRONT VIEW
The front bears an uncanny resemblance to the British Ford Corsair. This link is neither surprising nor coincidental, since the Corsair was also made by Uncle Henry.

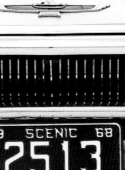

...D STYLING CREASE ...FROM FENDER ...OOR AND IS ...MODEL'S LEAST ...OMING FEATURE

LONG-LIVED V8 GAVE 12 PERCENT MORE TORQUE THAN PREVIOUS MODEL

19 SCENIC 68
2513
NEW HAMPSHIRE

1963 STUDEBAKER
Avanti

AVANTI IS THE ITALIAN WORD FOR FORWARD

INTERIOR
The Avanti's dashboard is a stud[y]
in simplicity, with Mercedes-type
gauges and very little chrome
extravagance. The center consol[e]
would look more at home in a
small aircraft. Standard equipme[nt]
included internal trunk and hoo[d]
releases and vinyl bucket seats.

THE AVANTI WAS A BIG deal for Studebaker and the first all-new body style since 1953. The last car design of the legendary Raymond Loewy, it rode on a shortened Lark chassis with a stock Studey 289cid V8. The Avanti's striking simplicity of shape was just one of Loewy's celebrated confections. From his voguish Coca-Cola dispenser to the chaste Lucky Strike cigarette pack, Loewy's creations were instant classics, and the brilliant Avanti was a humdinger.

Studebaker's prodigy was fairly audacious too, with a fiberglass body, anti-sway bars, optional Paxton supercharger, and wind-cheating aerodynamics. Dealers, however, could not meet the huge wave of orders and this, combined with other niggles like flexing of the fiberglass shell, resulted in impatient buyers defecting to the Corvette camp. Fewer than 4,650 Avantis were made, and production ceased in December 1963, the Avanti concept being sold to a couple of Studebaker dealers. They went on to form the Avanti Motor Corporation, which successfully churned out Avantis well into the Eighties.

BODY STYLING
*The slippery shape was
not wind-tunnel tested but
a piece of guesswork by Loewy.
His calculations were right on the mark: in 1962 an Avanti
R3 broke 29 Bonneville speed records, traveling faster than
a standard American car had ever done before.*

ENGINE
*The 289cid was the best Studebaker
V8 ever made, developing 240 bhp in
standard R1 tune. Supercharged R2
and R3 boasted 290 and 335 bhp
respectively, while the experimental
fuel-injected R5 produced a
howling 575 bhp.*

1963 STUDEBAKER AVANTI

More European than American, the Avanti had a long neck, razor-edged front fenders, and no grille. Early sketches show Loewy's inspiration, with telltale annotations scribbled on the paper that read "like Jaguar, Ferrari, Aston Martin, Mercedes." Lead time for the show Avanti was a hair-raising 13 months, with a full-scale clay model fashioned in only 40 days. Production estimates were as optimistic as 1,000 a month, but in the whole of 1964 Studebaker managed to churn out only 800 Avantis.

REAR VIEW
Hardly dated at all, the rear view is clean, uncluttered, and very modern. Note the ageless rear light treatment.

FRONT VIEW
Unmistakable from any angle, early '63 Avantis had round headlights, but most later '64 models sported square ones.

SPECIFICATIONS

MODEL 1963 Studebaker Avanti
PRODUCTION 3,834
BODY STYLE Two-door, four-seater coupe.
CONSTRUCTION Fiberglass body, steel chassis.
ENGINE 289cid, 304cid V8s.
POWER OUTPUT 240–575 bhp (304cid R5 V8 fuel-injected).
TRANSMISSION Three-speed manual, optional Power-Shift automatic.
SUSPENSION *Front:* upper and lower A-arms, coil springs; *Rear:* leaf springs.
BRAKES Front discs, rear drums.
MAXIMUM SPEED 120 mph (193 km/h)
0–60 MPH (0–96 KM/H) 7.5 sec
A.F.C. 17 mpg (6 km/l)

1964 BUICK
Riviera

BUICK'S '63 RIV WAS HAILED
AS A CONTEMPORARY CLASSIC

IN '58, SO THE STORY GOES, GM's design supremo Bill Mitchell was entranced by a Rolls-Royce he saw hissing past a London hotel. "What we want," said Mitchell, "is a cross between a Ferrari and a Rolls." By August 1960, he'd turned his vision into a full-size clay mock-up.

One of the world's most handsome cars, the original '63 Riviera was GM's attempt at a "Great New American Classic Car." And it worked. The elegant Riv was a clever amalgam of razor edges and chaste curves, embellished by just the right amount of chrome. Beneath the exquisite lines was a cross-member frame, a 401cid V8, power brakes, and a two-speed Turbine Drive tranny. In the interests of exclusivity, Buick agreed that only 40,000 would be made each year. With ravishing looks, prodigious performance, and the classiest image in town, the Riv ranks as one of Detroit's finest confections.

INTERIOR
The sumptuous Riv was a full four-seater, with the rear seat divided to look like buckets. The dominant V-shaped center console mushroomed from between the front seats to blend into the dashboard. The car's interior has a European ambience uncharacteristic for the period.

DIMENSIONS
Relatively compact, the Riviera was considerably shorter and lighter than other big Buicks.

CONWAY TWITTY
The crooner of tunes like "It's Only Make Believe" owned the '64 Riv featured on these pages. Aimed at GM's most affluent customers, the Riviera soon became the American Jaguar.

ENGINE
'64s had a 425cid Wildcat V8 that could be tickled up to 360 horses courtesy of dual four-barrels. *Car Life* magazine tested a '64 Riv with the Wildcat and stomped to 60 mph (96 km/h) in a scintillating 7.7 seconds. Buick sold the tooling for the old 401 to Rover, which used it to great success in its Range Rover.

SMART FRONT
The purposeful W-section front could have come straight out of an Italian styling house.

TRUNK SPACE
The substantial trunk could take two sets of golf clubs with ease, testimony to the leisure lifestyle of the average Riviera owner.

1964 BUICK RIVIERA

The Riv was America's answer to the Bentley Continental, and pandered to Ivy League America's obsession with aristocratic European thoroughbreds like Aston Martin, Maserati, and Jaguar. The grille was inspired by the Ferrari 250GT, and the hard-edged fender line predated the angular Rolls-Royce Silver Shadow by three years. The rear view was a study in simplicity, with an unembellished trunk and delicate rear lights.

DECORATION
Ineffectual side scoops weren't there to cool the rear brakes; they are the Riviera's only concession to vanity and disappeared in '65.

TRUNK LID
One optional extra was a remote-controlled trunk lid, which was pretty neat for '64.

BUICK

AMERICA'S DAIRYLAND
TWITTY
JAN WISCONSIN → 85

SPECIFICATIONS

MODEL 1964 Buick Riviera
PRODUCTION 37,958
BODY STYLE Two-door hardtop coupe.
CONSTRUCTION Steel body and chassis.
ENGINE 425cid V8.
POWER OUTPUT 340–360 bhp.
TRANSMISSION Two- or three-speed automatic.
SUSPENSION Front and rear coil springs.
BRAKES Front and rear drums.
MAXIMUM SPEED 120–125 mph (193–201 km/h)
0–60 MPH (0–96 KM/H) 8 sec
A.F.C. 12–16 mpg (4.2–5.7 km/l)

AMERICA'S DAIRYLAND
TWITTY
JAN WISCONSIN → 85

HEADLIGHTS
'63 and '64 Rivs have classic exposed double headlights. For reasons best known to themselves, Buick gave '65 cars headlights that were hidden behind electrically operated, clamshell doors.

1964 LINCOLN
Continental

CONTINENTAL ORNAMENT
WAS A MARK OF ESTEEM

THERE'S AN UNSETTLING irony in the fact that John F. Kennedy was shot in a '61 Lincoln Continental. Like him, the revamped '61 Continental had a new integrity. Substantial and innovative, it was bristling with new ideas and survived for nine years without major change. The car fit for presidents was elegant, restrained, and classically sculptured, perfect for Camelot's new dynasty of liberalism. Ironic, too, that JFK rather liked the Lincoln – he often used a stock White House Continental for non-official business.

Nearly $7,000 bought one of the most influential and best-built American cars of the Sixties. It carried a two-year, 24,000-mile warranty, every engine was bench-tested, and each car given a 200-category shakedown. Ivy League America approved, and production doubled in the first year. Even the Industrial Design Institute was impressed, awarding its coveted bronze medal for "an outstanding contribution of simplicity and design elegance."

PRESIDENTIAL WHEELS

THE DARK BLUE 1961 Continental phaeton, watched by the world in Dallas, was on loan to the White House from Ford's Special Vehicles Division for $500 a year. It had rear seats that could be raised or lowered automatically, two-way radio telephone, and thick steel-plating along the front and rear side rails. After the November 1963 assassination, it was still kept in harness, serving both the Johnson and Nixon administrations. Later fitted with a permanent solid roof, it was eventually retired to the Henry Ford Museum in Dearborn, where it still resides.

JFK IN THE PRESIDENTIAL CONTINENTAL ON THE DAY OF HIS ASSASSINATION IN DALLAS

ENGINE
Power was supplied by a huge 430cid V8 that generated 320 bhp. Each engine was tested at near maximum revs for three hours and then stripped down for inspection. Many mechanical parts were sealed for life.

MASSIVE WINDSHIELD GAVE EXCELLENT ALL-AROUND VISION

GAUGES SHOWING FUEL SUPPLY, OIL PRESSURE, WATER TEMPERATURE, AND BATTERY CHARGE WERE NEW FOR '64

INTERIOR
Every Continental had power steering and windows, walnut cappings, a padded dashboard, lush carpets, and vacuum-powered door locks as standard. The locks operated automatically as soon as the car started to move.

SUSPENSION DAMPING WAS CONSIDERED THE BEST ON ANY CAR

TO SPREAD COSTS, THE CONTINENTAL SHARED SOME OF ITS FACTORY TOOLING WITH THE '61 THUNDERBIRD

LINEAR PROFILE
Apart from the gentle dip in the waistline at the back of the rear doors, the roof and fender lines form two uninterrupted, almost parallel lines.

STATE-OF-THE-ART TOP
Eleven relays and a maze of linkages made the Continental's top disappear neatly into the trunk. The electric systems were completely sealed and never needed maintenance.

CONVERTIBLE RARITIES
Ragtop Continentals were really "convertible sedans" with standard power tops. The '64 ragtops were stickered at only $646 more than the four-door sedans, yet they remain much rarer models: only about 10 percent of all '61–'67 Lincolns produced were convertibles.

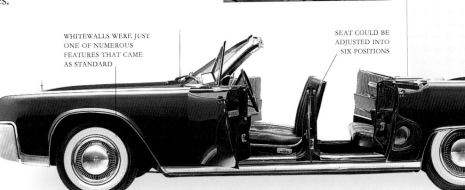

─ SPECIFICATIONS ─
MODEL 1964 Lincoln Continental Convertible
PRODUCTION 3,328
BODY STYLE Four-door, five-seater convertible.
CONSTRUCTION Steel body and chassis.
ENGINE 430cid V8.
POWER OUTPUT 320 bhp.
TRANSMISSION Three-speed Turbo-Drive automatic.
SUSPENSION *Front:* control arms and coil springs; *Rear:* leaf springs with live axle.
BRAKES Front and rear drums.
MAXIMUM SPEED 115 mph (185 km/h)
0–60 MPH (0–96 KM/H) 11 sec
A.F.C. 14 mpg (5 km/l)

EASY ACCESS
The "suicide" rear-hinged doors hark back to classic prewar coachbuilding. On older Continental Convertibles, opening all four doors at once can actually bend the floor and chassis.

WHITEWALLS WERE JUST ONE OF NUMEROUS FEATURES THAT CAME AS STANDARD

SEAT COULD BE ADJUSTED INTO SIX POSITIONS

ALONG WITH THE TOP, THE SIDE GLASS AND WINDOW FRAMES ALSO DISAPPEARED FROM VIEW AT THE TOUCH OF A BUTTON

EVOLUTION OF THE LINCOLN CONTINENTAL

THE REVOLUTIONARY Continental of 1961 ranks as one of Detroit's greatest achievements. Chiseled good looks, enviably precise tolerances, and an exclusive bloodline made it the most desirable Lincoln since the prewar K-Series. Sixties Continentals were the preeminent American luxury car and had an aura of distinction that stood out from the garish autos of the Fifties. Today it stands as evidence that, when they tried, Detroit could match the best in the world.

1940

1940 WAS THE FIRST YEAR of the Continental, a European shape based on the Lincoln Zephyr. With both coupe and convertible retailing at just under $3,000, the nation sighed in admiration at Ford's new dreamboat. By 1941 the Continental became a model in its own right. One of America's most prestigious brands had been born.

KEY FEATURES
- First cars powered by Lincoln's unreliable L-head V12
- Push-button exterior door handles in '41
- New 305cid V12 in '42, along with face-lift that gives Continental longer, higher wings, and new nose
- Headlights now flanked by parking lights

1956

OFFERED ONLY AS a two-door model with a stratospheric price tag of $10,000, nobody expected the Mark II of 1956 to sell seriously. The comely Continental was a flagship car intended to bless other Ford products with a halo of association. And it worked. In its day the Mark II was distinguished, beautiful, and made by Uncle Henry.

KEY DEVELOPMENTS
- Launched at the 1955 Paris Auto Show to universal acclaim
- Special Continental Division created to market the Mark II
- All options standard except air-conditioning
- Only 2,994 sold

1961

LINCOLN BUILT YET another landmark car with the '61 Mark III. Bold, stylish, and influential, it scooped every award going. Bristling with quality and oozing class, the Camelot Continental set new standards of US automobile engineering integrity. Lincoln wisely kept the classic shape current, with only gentle styling changes up until 1969.

KEY DEVELOPMENTS
- Automatic transmission, radio, power brakes, steering, and windows all standard
- Mild styling tweaks until major face-lift in '65, but retains basic '61 shape
- '66 sees taillights no longer wrapping around bumper
- Gentle redesign in '68, with new hood

1964 LINCOLN
Continental

IN '61, LINCOLN WAS THE ONLY MANUFACTURER TO OFFER A FOUR-DOOR CONVERTIBLE

LEAST POPULAR OPTION IN '64 WAS THE ADJUSTABLE STEERING WHEEL

QUALITY NOT QUANTITY
The '61 restyle reflected the new philosophy that big was not necessarily better. The previous Conti was a leviathan, but not so the '61. Lincoln historian James Wagner described the '61 Continental as "more like a Mercedes-Benz than a product of General Motors."

1972

LONGER, LOWER, wider, and heavier than the Mark III Continental, the Mark IV, from '70 on, still had the same sharp shape. It was based on the T-Bird and that big 460cid lived up front, albeit detuned to a paltry 200 bhp because of emission controls. In spite of the energy crisis, it sold even better than the Mark III, averaging 50,000 to 60,000 each year.

KEY DEVELOPMENTS
• New crisscross pattern grille
• New roof design with oblong opera window
• Increased leg and shoulder room for rear-seat passengers
• Cartier electric clock as standard

1984

A MARK VII COUPE joined the mid-sized Continental for '84, both with all-disc brakes and two industry firsts: gas-pressurized shock absorbers and self-sealing tires. There was also a Mark VII LSC with a performance package. The Mark VII was a credible alternative to the Cadillac Seville and Eldorado, and the LSC in particular was a very quick car.

KEY DEVELOPMENTS
• Auto-leveling electronic air suspension standard in '84
• Two-door coupe joins lineup in '84
• LSC gains high output V8 for '85
• ABS standard in '86
• 302cid V8 gets sequential fuel injection in '86

1988

THE ALL-NEW CONTINENTAL for '88 was the first Lincoln with front-wheel drive and a six-cylinder mill. Weight was down but length was up. The only available engine was the 232cid V6 with four-speed overdrive automatic, not really powerful enough for such a big old tank. Computer-controlled suspension adjusted for changes in the road.

KEY DEVELOPMENTS
• Increased interior and trunk space
• Now a genuine six-seater
• Electronic dash attracts criticism and is revised in '89
• His and her airbags for '89
• Dual exhausts for '89

1995

AFTER A MODERATE restyle in '94, '95 saw a major overhaul. Aside from the exterior design changes and a new 260 bhp V8, a dazzling array of high-tech features included the ability to program ride, transmission, handling, and interior setup to suit each individual driver. This was truly a car to take Lincoln into the 21st century.

KEY DEVELOPMENTS
• New unibody design
• New 32-valve InTech™ V8 is first Ford block to be placed in transverse mounting position
• New nonsynchro four-speed automatic gearbox allows quicker shifting
• 100,000 mile (161,000 km) tune-up interval

COMPETITION BEATER
Low, wide, and mighty, the '60s Continental was considered the epitome of good taste and discrimination, and a patriotic alternative to the less sophisticated and poorly built Jaguar Mark 10 sedan.

TINTED GLASS WAS A $53 OPTIONAL EXTRA

EVEN IN '64 YOU COULD HAVE CRUISE CONTROL, FOR A MERE $96 EXTRA

HEADLIGHTS COULD SENSE ONCOMING TRAFFIC AND DIM AUTOMATICALLY

NEW YORK
KTS 340
LINCOLN

1964 OLDSMOBILE
Starfire

'64 OLDSMOBILES WERE MARKETED WITH THE SLOGAN, "WHERE THE ACTION IS"

IN 1964, LBJ SIGNED A tax-cut bill, *Peyton Place* was a TV hit, and Coca-Cola launched a new single-calorie soda called Tab. While America was on a roll, the auto industry was busy telling customers that bucket seats and center consoles would enrich their lives. Oldsmobile trumpeted that its sporty Starfire Coupe offered "high adventure that starts right here!" Lame copy aside, the Starfire was quick, with Olds' most powerful lump, a 394cid V8 that could knock on the door of 120 mph (193 km/h). A terrifying thirst for gas didn't deter buyers, especially since these were big, softly sprung mile-eaters, groaning with convenience options. Elegant and unadorned, the Starfire was one of a new breed of suburban starlets designed to make the American middle classes look as confident as they felt. And it worked.

CONVERTIBLE OPTION
The Starfire was easy on the hands, with power everything. Detroit knew that the "little woman" was becoming increasingly important in buying decisions and started to pitch their products at the shopping mall. Early Starfires were available only in convertible form and came with a special engine and deluxe interior.

ENGINE
Standard on the Starfire Coupe and Convertible was the mighty cast-iron block 394cid V8 with Rochester four-barrel carb, which churned out a hefty 345 bhp. Performance on original '61 models was positively exhilarating, but three years down the line the effect of all those sybaritic creature comforts and added weight meant that the Starfire wasn't that quick, and speed figures ended up this side of ordinary.

WEIGHT
The Starfire was no featherweight; all those luxury add-ons pushed the curb weight to nearly two tons.

TILT STEERING WAS AN OPTION AT $43

INTERIOR
Oldsmobile gave the Starfire plenty of creature comforts. Standard kit included Hydra-Matic automatic transmission, bucket seats, safety padded dash, center console, tachometer, leather trim, plus power steering, brakes, and windows. The power seat could be adjusted into six positions and the Tilt-Away steering wheel into seven.

1964 OLDSMOBILE STARFIRE

Based on the body shell of the Dynamic 88, the Starfire never looked special enough to win big sales. *Motor Trend* said: "What the Starfire misses most is a distinctive exterior like the Thunderbird." Nevertheless, they did describe the 120 mph (193 km/h) oily bits as "superior and sensational." The car's simple, extruded look was typical of the period, and very few traces of jukebox styling remained by the mid-Sixties. Lines were clean and assertive, appealing to the affluent society's newfound sophistication.

ANTISPIN OPTION
Positive-traction rear axle was a factory-fitted option.

SPECIFICATIONS

MODEL 1964 Oldsmobile Starfire
PRODUCTION 25,890
BODY STYLE Two-door, five-seater coupe and convertible.
CONSTRUCTION Steel body and chassis.
ENGINE 394cid V8.
POWER OUTPUT 345 bhp.
TRANSMISSION Three-speed Hydra-Matic automatic.
SUSPENSION Front and rear coil springs.
BRAKES Front and rear drums.
MAXIMUM SPEED 120 mph (193 km/h)
0–60 MPH (0–96 KM/H) 9 sec
A.F.C. 12 mpg (4.2 km/l)

FINS
By '64, fins were getting more truncated by the day and had almost completely disappeared by '65.

HEADLIGHTS
Guide-Matic headlights automatically dimmed for oncoming cars.

OLDSMOBILE BADGE
The Starfire name originally belonged to a jet fighter, and GM sold it as a limited edition upscale personal car. Sales began to dwindle by 1965, when it was eclipsed by the Buick Riviera. By 1967, the Starfire had been replaced by the Oldsmobile Toronado.

WHEELBASE
The Starfire was based on the Dynamic 88 and shared its 123 in (312 cm) wheelbase.

1964 PLYMOUTH
Barracuda

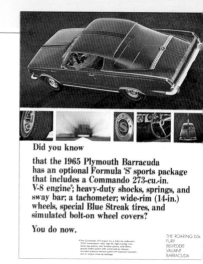

Barracuda

ROAD AND TRACK MAGAZINE SAID, "FOR SPORTS CAR PERFORMANCE AND PRACTICALITY, THE BARRACUDA IS PERFECT"

THE BIG THREE WEREN'T slow to cash in on the Sixties' youth boom. Ford couldn't keep its Mustang project secret, and the Chrysler Corporation desperately wanted a piece of the action. To get the drop on Uncle Henry, the company had to work fast. It took its existing compact, the Plymouth Valiant, prettied up the front end, added a dramatic wraparound rear window, and called it the Barracuda. It hit the showroom carpets in April 1964, two weeks before the Mustang.

A disarming amalgam of performance, poise, and refinement, Plymouth had achieved a miracle on the scale of loaves and fishes: it made the Barracuda fast, yet handle crisply and ride smoothly. The 273cid V8 made the car quicker than a Mustang, faster still if the new owner had specified the Formula S package. But that bizarre rear window dated fiercely, and Mustangs outsold Barracudas 10-to-one. Plymouth believed the long-hood/short-trunk "pony" formula wouldn't captivate consumers like a swooping, sporty fastback. Half a million Mustang buyers told them they'd backed the wrong horse.

Did you know

that the 1965 Plymouth Barracuda has an optional Formula 'S' sports package that includes a Commando 273-cu.-in. V-8 engine'; heavy-duty shocks, springs, and sway bar; a tachometer; wide-rim (14-in.) wheels, special Blue Streak tires, and simulated bolt-on wheel covers?

You do now.

THE ROARING '65s
FURY
BELVEDERE
VALIANT
BARRACUDA

THE FORMULA S OPTION
Despite the fact that the Formula offered a V8 block plus race trimmings, this was still rather tame by Plymouth standards. The '61 Fury, for example, had a 318cid unit that pushed out 230 bhp.

BARRACUDA EXTRAS
Options were not as extensive as on the Mustang, but you could still add air-conditioning, TorqueFlite automatic transmission, and sport wheel covers with chrome lugs to the Barracuda's $2,500 base price.

ENGINE
The 'Cuda's base engine was a 170cid slant six. Other mills were the 225cid six and two-barrel 273cid V8. Optional was Chrysler's new Hurst-linkage manual transmission along with new Sure-Grip differential.

THIS IS THE 225CID STRAIGHT-SIX BLOCK THAT PRODUCED 145 BHP

OPTIONAL POWER STEERING MEANT THAT LOCK-TO-LOCK WAS ONLY THREE-AND-A-HALF TURNS

ACRES OF GLASS

The fastback glass wrapped down to the rear fender line and was developed by the Pittsburgh Plate Glass Company; it was the largest use of glass in any production car to date. As a result, visibility was epic and earned the Barracuda top marks for safety.

POWER BRAKES WERE STANDARD, WITH BIG DRUMS FRONT AND REAR

BUMPER GUARDS WERE AN $11.45 OPTION

INSTRUMENT CLUSTER COATED IN EYE-EASE PAINT TO REDUCE GLARE

INTERIOR

The greenhouse interior got hot on sunny days but was well detailed and enormously practical. Standard fare were bucket seats and bucket-shaped rear bench seat.

TRUNK SPACE

The rear seats folded forward to produce an astronomical cargo area that measured 7 ft (2.14 m) long.

BUCKET SEAT COULD BE ADJUSTED INTO SIX POSITIONS

DASHBOARD

Instruments were matte silver with circular chrome bezels. The padded dash was a $16.35 extra, as was a woodgrain steering wheel, which the brochure insisted "gave you the feel of a racing car."

SPECIFICATIONS

MODEL 1964 Plymouth Barracuda
PRODUCTION 23,443
BODY STYLE Two-door fastback.
CONSTRUCTION Steel body and chassis.
ENGINE 170cid, 225cid sixes, 273cid V8.
POWER OUTPUT 101–235 bhp.
TRANSMISSION Three-speed manual, optional four-speed manual, and three-speed TorqueFlite automatic.
SUSPENSION *Front:* torsion bar; *Rear:* leaf springs.
BRAKES Front and rear drums, optional front discs.
MAXIMUM SPEED 100–110 mph (161–177 km/h)
0–60 MPH (0–96 KM/H) 8–13 sec
A.F.C. 16–22 mpg (5.7–7.8 km/l)

IN '67 A CONVERTIBLE WAS ADDED WITH POWER TOP AND REAL GLASS WINDOW

ONE OPTIONAL EXTRA WAS UNDERCOATING, A WISE INVESTMENT AT $15.70

THE FIRST BARRACUDAS WERE ACTUALLY QUITE GENTEEL

MUSCLE AND PONY MANIA

BY THE EARLY SIXTIES, buyers were bored with overchromed barges, gas was cheap, and the economy was thumping. Two types of badly needed automotive narcotic were about to emerge – the pony car and the muscle car. The first real muscle cars were the '62 Plymouths and Dodges, with their wedge-head V8s, but the machine that really defined the breed was John DeLorean's hip '64 Pontiac GTO. Stripped to the bone, it was a street-legal screamer with blistering straight-line heave, and sales went absolutely ballistic.

Ford got in on the act with its hot Fairlane and Shelby Mustang, Oldsmobile placed a

EARLY MUSTANG PROTOTYPE WAS A PROMISE OF PERFORMANCE TO COME

PRESENTING THE *Mustang* by Ford Engineers and Stylists

performance package in the F-85 and called it the 4-4-2, and Chrysler followed by stuffing Hemi engines into everything it could. The muscle car was hot news on the street because it promised not only horsepower, but individuality, too. With a landslide of performance options, auto makers let buyers kid themselves that their cars were almost custom-made. One ad for the Dodge Challenger boasted, "This is a car you buy when you decide you don't want to be like everyone else."

Plymouth was too late with the '64 Barracuda to cash in on the muscle-car mania, but by '68 things were really cooking with special performance packages and a monster 440cid mill

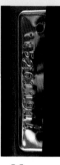

1964 PLYMOUTH
Barracuda

THE BARRACUDA WAS A PLYMOUTH VALIANT FROM THE ROOF LINE DOWN AND SHARED ITS POWER AND SUSPENSION

VEHICLE NUMBER
This was located on a plate on the front left doorpost and became visible when the door was opened.

YOUTH MARKET
Based on the mass-market, best-selling Valiant, the Barracuda was aimed at a completely new market: rich young things with a desire to look cool.

P L Y M O U T H

19 400TH ANNIVERSARY 65
1W166142
FLORIDA

a year later. By 1970 it had launched the Rapid Transit System and shortened the name of its pony prodigy to the tough-sounding 'Cuda. From then on, every manufacturer worth a damn was following Chrysler's example and rolling out muscle metal like it was the elixir of youth.

In '65, there was another automotive revolution in the Ford Mustang. A tamer form of rebellion, Ford's pony car had performance, handling, style, and youthful optimism. Built from off-the-shelf Falcon and Fairlane components with every option possible, Ford's new form of auto opium could be made all things to all men, or indeed women. It was a stomping success and sold a whopping 417,000 in its launch year. Despite churning out a frenetic 1,740 cars a day, Mustang demand always ran way ahead of supply.

Then with GM's '67 Firebird and Camaro came a rash of pony-car imitators, Mustang clones with similarly long hoods and gaping mouths. But Detroit could never leave well alone, and both the pony car and the muscle car grew

THE '64 OLDSMOBILE 4-4-2 CUTLASS WAS SWIFT BUT NOT TRIM

BY '67, THE BARRACUDA HAD A STING IN ITS TAIL

gradually longer, fatter, and slower. By '71, both the Barracuda and the Mustang had ballooned in proportions, and sales gradually evaporated. Ironically, both the pony and muscle car had lost their *raison d'être* – they no longer showed individuality. Come 1972, the social tenor of America had matured, and Detroit quietly drew the curtain on two of its most imaginative motoring genres.

OBSCENELY QUICK '70 HEMI 'CUDA OFFERED LEGALIZED MISCHIEF

BOLD STYLING

Compared with the Mustang, the Barracuda's front was busy, cluttered, and lacked symmetry, but it was a brave and bold design. Had the Mustang not been launched in the same month, things might have been very different.

PRISMATIC DAY-AND-NIGHT MIRROR COULD BE ADJUSTED TO DEFLECT ANNOYING HEADLIGHT GLARE AT NIGHT

INTERIOR COLORS AVAILABLE WERE GOLD, BLUE, BLACK, OR THIS ATTRACTIVE RED

REMOTE-CONTROLLED SIDE MIRROR WAS A $12 CONVENIENCE OPTION

1965 CHRYSLER
300L

CONVERTIBLE FORM
A mere 440 two-door convertibles were produced, as well as 2,405 hardtops. Competition was particularly stiff in '65 and the 300L had to fight hard against the Oldsmobile Starfire, the agonizingly pretty Buick Riviera, and the market leader, Ford's flashy Thunderbird.

CHRYSLER

THE FAMOUS 300 NAMEPLATE THAT HAD FIRST
MADE ITS MARK IN THE LATE FIFTIES WAS NOW IN ITS FINAL YEAR

BACK IN '55, CHRYSLER debuted its mighty 300 "Letter Car." The most powerful automobile of the year, the 300C kicked off a new genre of Gentleman's Hot-Rod that was to last for more than a decade. Chrysler cleverly flagged annual model changes with letters, running from the 300B in 1956 all the way through – except for the letter I – to this 300L in 1965.

And '65 was the swan-song year for the Letter Series specialty car. The 300L sat on high-performance rubber and suspension and was powered by a high-output 413cid 360 bhp mill breathing through a four-barrel Carter carb. By the mid-Sixties, though, the game had changed and Chrysler was pumping its money into muscle-car iron like the Charger and GTX, an area of the market where business was brisk. The 300L was the last survivor of an era when the Madison Avenue advertising men were still trying to persuade us that an automobile as long as a freight train could also be a sports car.

SUSPENSION
Torsion-bar front suspension gave uncanny poise and accuracy to such a big car.

TRIMMINGS
Red or black leather could be specified for the last word in luxury.

HEADLIGHTS
These live behind a horizontally etched glass panel.

REAR AXLE
Rear axles could be fitted with positive traction at extra cost.

HIDDEN FILLER
Concealed fuel filler was topped by a badge confirming that this was a 300L.

BODY
300Ls had unibody construction, with the front subframe bolted rather than welded onto the main structure. Noise, vibration, and harshness were greatly reduced.

ALASKA 66
98506
1867 NORTH TO THE FUTURE 1967

INTERIOR
Front buckets plus a center console were standard on the L, as was column instead of push-button automatic gear shift. The rear seat was molded to look like buckets but could accommodate three people.

1965 CHRYSLER 300L
Styling of the 300L was by Elwood Engle, who had replaced Virgil Exner as Chrysler's chief of design and had worked on the Lincolnesque '64 Imperial. Although Chrysler's advertising claimed that this was "The Most Beautiful Chrysler Ever Built," the "Crisp, Clean, Custom" look of '63–'64 had ballooned.

LUMINOUS LETTERING
The letter L in the center of the grille lit up with the headlights.

ENGINE
The non-Hemi V8 was tough and reliable and gave the 300L very respectable performance figures. The L was quick, agile, and one of the smoothest-riding Letter Series cars made, with 45 bhp more than the standard 300's unit.

SPECIFICATIONS
MODEL 1965 Chrysler 300L
PRODUCTION 2,845
BODY STYLE Two-door hardtop and convertible.
CONSTRUCTION Steel unitary body.
ENGINE 413cid V8.
POWER OUTPUT 360 bhp.
TRANSMISSION Three-speed automatic, optional four-speed manual.
SUSPENSION *Front:* torsion bar; *Rear:* leaf springs.
BRAKES Front and rear drums.
MAXIMUM SPEED 110 mph (177 km/h)
0–60 MPH (0–96 KM/H) 8.8 sec
A.F.C. 12–14 mpg (4.2–5 km/l)

LABELING
The letter L in the center of the grille was one of only a few places on the car where it could be distinguished from a standard 300.

1965 FORD
Mustang

THE MUSTANG
WAS THE FIRST "PONY" CAR

"A POOR MAN'S THUNDERBIRD for the working girl," the Mustang was compact, modern, young, and affordable. For a fraction of what the Edsel debacle cost, Ford Vice-President Lee Iacocca's offering captured the hearts and minds of a generation of American youth.

Based on the humble Ford Falcon, the Mustang was technically unremarkable but had square-jawed looks and carefree classlessness. Within two years of its '64 debut, one million had left showrooms.

But from a peak of 600,000 sold in 1966, sales evaporated to 150,000 by 1970. Heavier, longer, wider, and slower, the sleek horse had become a fat pig. As Iacocca later remarked, "our customers abandoned us, because we'd abandoned their car."

RACING MUSTANGS
Crisp handling and compact dimensions led to the Mustang becoming one of the first American cars to enjoy competition success on European racetracks.

INTERIOR
The base price was $2,372, but buyers ordered an average of $1,000 worth of the 70 option available. Interior trim could be personalized with a myriad of decor option packs, and extras such as full-length center console and retractable seat belts jazzed up the basic model.

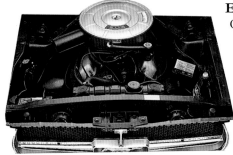

ENGINE
Original '64 engines were the 170cid six and 260cid V8. 1965 saw a 200cid six and 289cid Challenger V8 take over as base engines, with optional 225 bhp four-barrel Challenger and 271 bhp High Performance units. About 73 percent of Mustangs were fitted with the brilliant 289, which was a light, efficient, and gutsy engine.

COLOR CHOICE
Honey Gold was one of 15 exterior colors on offer to Mustang buyers.

BRAKES
Power front disc brakes were a shrewd option on V8s and cost $58.

THE LEGENDARY 289
The 289cid Challenger V8 came into service in the Autumn of '64 and would remain part of the Mustang stable until it was dropped in performance-oriented 1969.

1965 FORD MUSTANG HARDTOP COUPE

The Mustang's styling was the work of Joe Oros, David Ash, and Gale Halderman. The basic long-hood/short-trunk formula was pioneered on the Mustang and became known as the "pony car" look, carrying on into the early '70s. When the Mustang debuted in April 1964, it was offered in two body styles: hardtop coupe and convertible. A few months later, the official 1965 range contained another model in a 2+2 fastback coupe. The hardtop coupe, also known as the notchback, was by far the most popular model throughout the Mustang's lifespan.

REAR STYLING
The notchback rear aspect has classically perfect proportions. The simple bumper and overriders are positively chaste compared with earlier Detroit confections.

SPECIFICATIONS

MODEL 1965 Ford Mustang
PRODUCTION 559,451
BODY STYLE Two-door, four-seater coupe, fastback, and convertible.
CONSTRUCTION Steel unitary body.
ENGINE 200cid six, 289cid V8.
POWER OUTPUT 120–271 bhp.
TRANSMISSION Three-speed manual, optional four-speed manual, and two-speed Cruise-O-Matic automatic.
SUSPENSION *Front:* coil springs; *Rear:* leaf springs with live axle.
BRAKES Front and rear drums; optional front discs
MAXIMUM SPEED 110–123 mph (177–198 km/h)
0–60 MPH (0–96 KM/H) 7.6–9 sec
A.F.C. 17 mpg (6 km/l)

USEFUL EXTRA
The $42 optional Equa-Lock limited slip differential helped keep rear wheels from burning rubber.

1966 CHEVROLET
Corvair Monza

Corvair

ANOTHER DESIGN TRIUMPH FROM
BILL MITCHELL'S GM STUDIO

INTERIOR
The all-vinyl interior was very
European, with bucket seats and
telescopic steering column. The
restrained steering wheel and
deep-set instruments could have
come straight out of a BMW.

BY 1960, SALES OF DINOSAURS were down, small-car
imports were up, and Detroit finally listened to a market
screaming for economy compacts. Then along came
Chevrolet's adventurous answer to the Volkswagen Beetle, the pretty, rear-
engined Corvair, which sold for half the price of a Ford Thunderbird.

But problems soon arose. GM's draconian cost-cutting meant that a crucial
$15 suspension stabilizing bar was omitted, and early Corvairs handled like pigs.
The suspension was redesigned in '65, but it was
too late. Bad news also came in the form of
Ralph Nader's book *Unsafe at Any Speed*,
which lambasted the Corvair. The new
Ford Mustang, which had become *the*
hot compact, didn't help either. By 1969,
it was all over for the Corvair. GM's stab
at downsizing had been a disaster.

MONZA MANIA
The early Corvair Monzas, with deluxe
trim and automatic transmission, were
a big hit. This 1961 example was one
of over 143,000 sold that year, over
half of the grand total.

ENGINE
Corvairs had alloy, air-cooled,
horizontal sixes. The base unit was a 164cid with
four Rochester carbs developing 140 bhp. The
hot turbocharged motors could push out 180 bhp.

140 REPRESENTED
POWER OUTPUT

END OF THE LINE
By the end of '68, sales of the handsome
Monza coupe were down to just 6,800 units and
GM decided to pull the plug in May '69.
Those who had bought a '69 Corvair were
given a certificate worth $150
off any other '69–'70
Chevrolet.

WHEELS
*Wire wheel covers were a
pricey $59 option on the
Monza. White sidewalls
could be ordered for an
extra $29.*

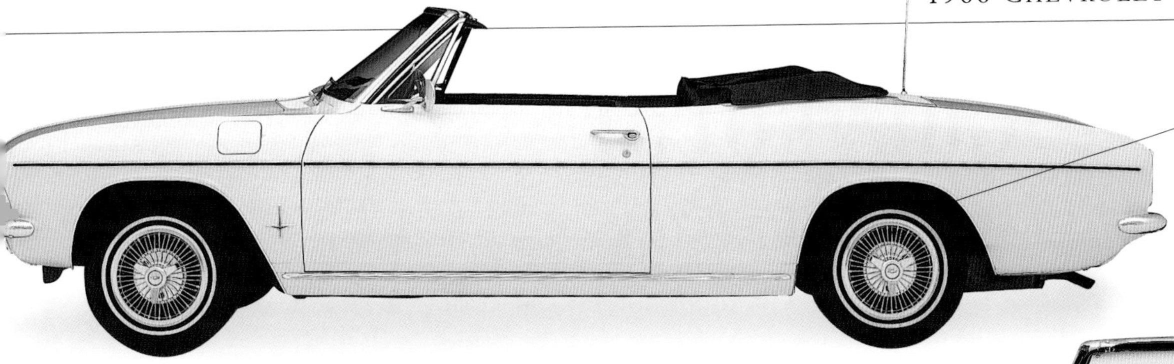

SUSPENSION
*The post-'65 Corvair
had Corvette-type fully
independent rear suspension
via upper and lower control
arms and coil springs.*

WINDOWS
*Side windows were made
of specially curved glass.*

HOOD
*Most tops
were manually
operated and
stowed behind
a fabric tonneau,
but this model
has the $54
power top option.*

1966 CHEVROLET CORVAIR MONZA CONVERTIBLE
After very few styling changes for the first five years, the
new body design for '65 had a heavy Italian influence with
smooth-flowing, rounded lines that impressed
the automotive press. *Car and Driver* called it
"the best of established foreign and domestic
coachwork." The new longer, wider, and lower
Corvair initially sold well but floundered
from '66 on, in the face of the rival
Mustang and Nader's damning book.

SPECIFICATIONS

MODEL 1966 Chevrolet
Corvair Monza
PRODUCTION 60,447 (1966,
Monza only)
BODY STYLE Two- and four-door,
four-seater coupe and convertible.
CONSTRUCTION Steel unitary body.
ENGINE 164cid flat sixes.
POWER OUTPUT 95–140 bhp.
TRANSMISSION Three-speed
manual, optional four-speed
manual, and two-speed
Powerglide automatic.
SUSPENSION Front and rear
coil springs.
BRAKES Front and rear drums.
MAXIMUM SPEED 105–120 mph
(169–193 km/h)
0–60 MPH (0–96 KM/H) 11–15.2 sec
A.F.C. 20 mpg (7 km/l)

1966 CHEVROLET
Corvette Sting Ray

1966 PRODUCED THE
HIGHEST SALES OF
THIS VETTE SERIES

THE ORIGINAL STING RAY Corvette ('63 to '67) is the most collectible of them all. With roots going back to the Sting Ray Special Racer and experimental XP720, production cars had a luscious fastback profile, split rear window, hidden headlights, and doors cut into the roof.

Underneath the body there was a new ladder-type frame, independent rear suspension with double-jointed driveshafts and, for the first time, a power steering option. Output ranged from 300 to 425 brake, with the big-block 427cid L88 pushing out a howling 530. The public went wild, and the Sting Ray's reception in '63 caused as many ripples as the Jag XKE. In 1965, four-wheel discs became available, along with side-mounted exhausts. Among the fastest Vettes of all, hot 427s could run the quarter mile in 13.6 seconds and top a genuine 150 mph (241 km/h). Now highly prized, a fuel-injected, disc-brake '65 or big-block 427 will prove a highly entertaining and lucrative investment.

1963 SPLIT-SCREEN COUPE
Bill Mitchell, GM's head of styling, loved the Vette's split rear window, but humorless critics and the automotive press said that it was "dumb and blocked rear vision." Sadly, by 1964, it was history.

ENGINE
The 327cid Turbo-Fire cast-iron block V8 was the Vette's base power plant, producing 300 brake through a single four-barrel Holley carb. Three-speed manual transmission was standard, with optional two-speed automatic available at $195 and three types of four-speed manual shift also offered.

LOGO
Sting Ray nomenclature was introduced in 1963 and became a synonym for American racing pedigree.

INTERIOR
Buyers could specify leather seats, tinted glass, headrests, shoulder harness, teak steering wheel, telescopic steering column, and air-conditioning, a very rare option on the convertible. Tachometer, seat belts, and electric clock came as standard equipment.

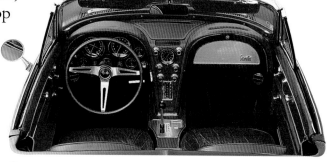

BRAKES
Optional four-wheel discs were unreliable, and it took Chevrolet 17 years to redesign them.

FRONT VIEW

Hidden headlights, large hood bulge, and muscular wheel-arch lines give the Vette a mean look.

INTERIOR OPTIONS

Telescopic steering column and genuine teak steering wheel were options for '65 and '66.

SPECIFICATIONS

MODEL 1966 Chevrolet Corvette Sting Ray

PRODUCTION 27,720

BODY STYLE Two-door, two-seater coupe and convertible.

CONSTRUCTION Ladder frame with fiberglass body.

ENGINE 327cid, 427cid V8s.

POWER OUTPUT 300–425 bhp.

TRANSMISSION Three-speed manual, optional four-speed manual, and two-speed Powerglide automatic.

SUSPENSION *Front:* coil springs; *Rear:* independent.

BRAKES Front and rear drums, optional front and rear discs.

MAXIMUM SPEED 118–150 mph (190–241 km/h)

0–60 MPH (0–96 KM/H) 4.7–8 sec

A.F.C. 10–17 mpg (3.5–6 km/l)

1966 CHEVROLET CORVETTE STING RAY

The '66 Sting Ray Roadster listed at $4,084 and weighed as much as a Camaro. Some 17,762 rolled off the St. Louis line in the '66 model year, almost double the number of Fastback Coupes. This was the penultimate year of the Sting Ray; 1968 saw the restyled Corvette introduced without the Sting Ray name. It reappeared in '69 as the Stingray (one word).

HARDTOP OPTION

Convertibles were offered with a beautiful, snug-fitting, detachable hardtop from 1964, rather than the soft top as here.

ENGINE

The fuel injection option ended in '65 because of high cost.

PERFORMANCE REAR

Positive Traction rear axle could be ordered for an extra $42.

1966 PONTIAC
GTO

GTO STOOD FOR GRAN TURISMO OMOLOGATO AND WAS POACHED FROM FERRARI

"THE GREAT ONE" was Pontiac's answer to a youth market with attitude and disposable cash. Detroit exploited a generation's rebellion by creating cars with machismo to burn. In 1964, John DeLorean, Pontiac's chief engineer, shoehorned the division's biggest V8 into the timid little Tempest compact with electrifying results. He then beefed up the brakes and suspension, threw in three two-barrel carbs and a floor shift, and garnished the result with a name that belonged to a Ferrari. In 1966 it became a model in its own right, and Detroit's first "muscle car" had been born. Pundits reckon the flowing lines of these second-generation GTOs make them the best-looking of all. Engines were energetic performers too, with a standard 335 bhp 389cid V8 that could be specified in 360 bhp high-output tune. But by '67 GTO sales had tailed off by 15 percent, depressed by a burgeoning social conscience and Federal meddling. The performance era was about to be legislated into the history books.

INTERIOR
GTOs were equipped to the same high standard as the Pontiac Tempest Le Mans. Items included ashtray lights, cigarette lighter, carpeting, and a power top for convertibles. Air-conditioning and power steering could be ordered at $343 and $95 respectively.

ENGINE
The base 335 bhp 389cid block had a high-output Tri-Power big brother that pushed out 360 bhp for an extra $116. The range was expanded in '67 to include an economy 255 bhp 400cid V8 and a Ram-Air 400cid mill that also developed 360 bhp, but at higher revs per minute.

BIG BLOCK
Pontiac was the first mainstream manufacturer to combine big-cube power with a light body. In tests, a '66 Convertible hit 60 mph (96 km/h) in 6.8 seconds.

TURN SIGNALS
Turn signals in the grille were meant to mimic European-style driving lights.

HEADLIGHTS
The stacked headlights were new for Pontiacs in '65 and were retained on GTOs until the end of the decade.

SPECIFICATIONS

MODEL 1966 Pontiac GTO Convertible
PRODUCTION 96,946 (all body styles)
BODY STYLE Two-door, five-seater hardtop, coupe, and convertible.
CONSTRUCTION Steel unitary body.
ENGINE 389cid V8s.
POWER OUTPUT 335–360 bhp.
TRANSMISSION Three-speed manual, optional four-speed manual, and three-speed Hydra-Matic automatic.
SUSPENSION Front and rear coil springs.
BRAKES Front and rear drums, optional discs.
MAXIMUM SPEED 125 mph (201 km/h)
0–60 MPH (0–96 KM/H) 6.6–9.5 sec
A.F.C. 15 mpg (5.3 km/l)

1966 PONTIAC GTO CONVERTIBLE

John DeLorean's idea of placing a high-spec engine in the standard Tempest body paved the way for a whole new genre and gave Pontiac immediate success in '64. Had Ford not chosen to release the Mustang in the same year, the GTO would have been the star of '64, and even more sales would have been secured. As it was, sales peaked in '66 with almost 100,000 GTOs going to power-hungry young drivers whose average age was 25. The Convertible was the most aesthetically pleasing of the range.

PERFORMANCE REAR
The GTO came with heavy-duty shocks and springs as standard, along with a stabilizer bar.

LENGTH
It might look long, but the GTO was actually 15 in (38 cm) shorter than Pontiac's largest models.

1967 FORD
Shelby Mustang GT500

GT500 NAME WAS ARBITRARY AND DID NOT REFER TO POWER

LOOKING BACK FROM OUR ERA of weedy political correctness, it's amazing to remember a time when you could buy this sort of stomach-churning horsepower straight from the showroom floor. What's more, if you couldn't afford to buy it, you could borrow it for the weekend from your local Hertz rent-a-car. The fact is that the American public loved the grunt, the image, and the Carroll Shelby Cobra connection. Ford's advertising slogan went straight to the point – Shelby Mustangs were "*The* Road Cars." With 289 and 428cid V8s, they were blisteringly quick, kings of both street and strip. By '67 they were civilized, too, with options like factory air and power steering, as well as lots of gauges, a wood-rim Shelby wheel, and that all-important 140 mph (225 km/h) speedo. The little Pony Mustang had grown into a thundering stallion.

WOOD-RIM STEERING WHEEL

DASHBOARD
The special Shelby steering wheel was standard, along with Stewart-Warner oil and amp gauges and a tachometer red-lining at 8,000 rpm. Two interior colors were available – parchment and black.

CHUNKY FRONT
'67 Shelbys had a larger hood scoop than previous models, plus a custom-built fiberglass front to complement the stock Mustang's new longer hood.

— CARROLL SHELBY —

CARROLL SHELBY, the most charismatic ex-chicken farmer you could ever meet, smiled when he told me the Hertz story. "We delivered the first batch of black-and-gold cars to Hertz the day before a hailstorm. The cars had racing brakes that really needed carefully warming up. When the ice storm hit, dozens were totaled. My reputation with Hertz went down the tubes big time." But the Hertz connection was good for the Shelby, and there are tales of people renting 350s and 500s for the weekend and bringing them back with bald tires and evidence of racing numbers on the doors. There was even one case of somebody lifting a 289 Hi-Po out of a Hertz Shelby and substituting the stock 289 from his aunt's notchback, hoping no one would notice.

CARROLL SHELBY RECEIVES HIS TROPHY FOR WINNING THE RIVERSIDE GRAND PRIX IN 1960

INTERIOR DECOR WAS BRUSHED ALUMINUM WITH MOLDED DOOR PANELS AND DOOR LIGHTS

G.T. 500

SHELBY'S SPRINGING WAS SIMILAR TO THE MUSTANG WITH FRONT SWAY BAR, STIFF SPRINGS, AND GABRIEL SHOCKS

ENGINE
The GT500 had the 428 Police Interceptor unit with two Holley four-barrel carbs. Oval, finned aluminum open-element air cleaner and cast-aluminum valve covers were unique to the big-block Shelby.

SHELBY PLATE
Carroll Shelby gave the early Mustangs his special treatment in a dedicated factory in Los Angeles. Later cars were built in Ionia, Michigan.

INTERIOR
All GT350s and 500s boasted the standard and very practical Mustang fold-down rear seat along with Shelby's own padded roll bar. Shelbys came in fastback only; there were no notchbacks and convertibles were only available from '68 on.

SCOOPS ACTED AS INTERIOR AIR EXTRACTORS

REAR DECK IS MADE OF FIBERGLASS TO SAVE WEIGHT

SPECIFICATIONS
MODEL 1967 Ford Shelby Cobra Mustang GT500
PRODUCTION 2,048
BODY STYLE Two-door, four-seater coupe.
CONSTRUCTION Steel unitary body.
ENGINE 428cid V8.
POWER OUTPUT 360 bhp.
TRANSMISSION Four-speed manual, three-speed automatic.
SUSPENSION *Front:* coil springs; *Rear:* leaf springs.
BRAKES Front discs, rear drums.
MAXIMUM SPEED 132 mph (212 km/h)
0–60 MPH (0–96 KM/H) 6.8 sec
A.F.C. 13 mpg (4.6 km/l)

POPULAR CHOICE
Shelbys were a big hit in '67, with 1,175 350s and 2,048 500s sold. Prices were also about 15 percent cheaper than in '66.

WHEELS ARE OPTIONAL KELSEY-HAYES MAGSTARS

EVOLUTION OF THE FORD MUSTANG

NO OTHER CAR HIT its target like the Mustang. Aimed at the 18–24 market, it was charismatic, youthful, and cheap; mass-produced individuality had never looked so good. With their litany of options, Mustangs could be everything from a secretary's economy compact to a street racer's howling banshee. Iacocca's prodigy may have spawned the Firebird and the Camaro, but its legacy is far greater than that. Thirty-odd years later, America still loves the galloping pony.

1962

THE MUSTANG'S ANTECEDENTS go back to the Project T5 styling study created in 1962 by engineer Herb Misch and design chief Eugene Bordinat. Meant to take on British Triumphs and MGs, it had independent springing, a tubular frame, integral roll bar, and a 60-degree 1927 cc V4 engine.

KEY FEATURES
- Ford backs sporty, compact Project T5
- Mustang styling exercises approved in just 21 days
- Target market is youth
- Prototype debuts in time for US Grand Prix at Watkins Glen

1964

LAUNCHED IN APRIL 1964, the Mustang was such a colossal hit that production at the Dearborn factory couldn't cope and spilled over to the Ford plant in San Jose, California. By the end of the year the Pony had notched up 263,000 sales and the full calendar year production total for '65 of 418,000 units was an industry record.

KEY DEVELOPMENTS
- Early cars have 260cid V8s
- First batch has nonadjustable passenger seats
- Base price is an amazing $2,368
- Lee Iacocca makes the front cover of *Time* magazine

1969

THE MUSTANG QUICKLY put on weight and, far from being a compact, had grown into a luxury Grand Tourer. Mi you, power was up, too, with screamer like the Mach One and whopping Boss 429. Moving away from the pony-car philosophy wasn't one of Ford's best ideas, and '69 model year output fell to 190,727 units, down from 300,000.

KEY DEVELOPMENTS
- New sports roof fastback body style
- New ultra-high performance models Boss 302 and Boss 429
- Luxury Grandee model launched
- 81.5 percent of all '69 'Stangs have a V8

1967 FORD *Shelby Mustang GT500*

FOR THE SHELBY, THE MUSTANG'S REAR LIGHTS WERE REPLACED WITH THE '65 T-BIRD'S SEQUENTIAL LIGHTS

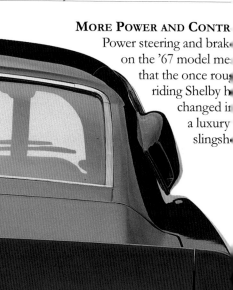

SHELBY G.T. 500

19 GEORGIA STATE 67
USA 716
SHELBY

MORE POWER AND CONTR
Power steering and brak on the '67 model me that the once rou riding Shelby h changed in a luxury slingsh

1971

THE MUSTANGS OF '71 grew in every dimension except for height. Heavier, wider, and more bloated than its lithe predecessors, the Mustang lost its way, and sales plummeted to nearly a third of '65–'66 numbers. Everybody knew that this wasn't the way to go, but over the following three years things would get even worse.

KEY DEVELOPMENTS
• Boss 302 and 489 dropped in favor of Boss 351
• Standard base engine now a 250cid six

1974

APOLOGETICALLY BILLED AS "the right car at the right time," the Mustang II wasn't worthy of bearing the hallowed name. With parts borrowed from the subcompact Pinto, it was a knee-jerk reaction to the Arab oil embargo. Still, for all its ordinariness, sales were strong, with 385,000 Mustang IIs finding buyers in the first year.

KEY DEVELOPMENTS
• New body designed by Ghia
• Now billed as a "luxury subcompact"
• Pared down four-model line-up
• Base engine is asthmatic 140cid four
• Mach One gets 171cid V6

1979

THE FIFTH-GENERATION Mustangs were clean, taut, and crisply styled. On the down side, handling wasn't great, interior space was limited, and build quality couldn't match the Japanese. The Iran–Iraq war meant that performance was out and economy was in, but the desire for power would soon return, and the Mustang would rise again.

KEY DEVELOPMENTS
• New color-keyed urethane bumpers
• Heavy aerodynamic influence
• Wicked 302cid V8 option
• Cobra option has 2.3 turbo four

1993

1993 MUSTANGS WERE among the most civilized and refined of the breed. The 5-liter V8 was considered quick enough to make a highway patrol car, and the limited edition Mustang Cobra included GT40 heads and roller rockers. This incarnation kept the customers satisfied until the splendid all-new Mustang arrived on the scene in 1995.

KEY DEVELOPMENTS
• Three body styles available in LX 5.0 guise
• Base models run on 88 bhp four
• Driver's airbag standard
• GT Mustangs push out 225 bhp

FORCED CHANGES
The standard center-grille high-beam headlights were forced to the sides in some states because of Federal legislation.

AT THE END OF '67, CARS WERE RENAMED SHELBY COBRAS, BUT FORD STILL HANDLED ALL PROMOTION AND ADVERTISING

SHELBY BODIES WERE NEW FOR '67, WITH A SHARKLIKE FRONT GRILLE AND UPDATED HOOD WITH RAM-AIR OPENINGS

428CID V8 STARTED LIFE IN THE ORIGINAL AC COBRA

RACING-STYLE LOCK PINS WERE STANDARD ON THE HOOD

APRIL GEORGIA STATE 1967
USA 716
SHELBY

1967 OLDSMOBILE
Toronado

NARROW GRILLE WAS A TORO STYLING TRADEMARK

THE FIRST BIG FRONT-DRIVING LAND YACHT since the Cord 810 of the Thirties, the Toronado was an automotive milestone and the most desirable Olds ever. With a 425cid V8 and unique chain-and-sprocket-drive automatic transmission, it had big-car power and outstanding road manners, and it could crack 135 mph (217 km/h). Initial sales weren't great, with sober buyers plumping for the more conventional Riviera, but by '71 the Riviera's design had lost its way. Then the Toronado really came into its own, selling up to 50,000 a year until the mid-Seventies. From then on, however, the more glamorous Cadillac Eldorado, also with front drive, outsold both the Riviera and the Toronado. Built on an exclusive slow-moving assembly line, Toronados had few faults, which was remarkable for such a technically audacious car. Even so, the press carped about the poor rear visibility, lousy gas mileage, and voracious appetite for front tires. But time heals all wounds, and these days there's no greater collector's car bargain than a '66–'67 Toronado.

NOVEL FRONTAL STYLE
The concealed headlights and horizontal bar grille were genuinely innovative but would disappear in '68 for a heavier and less attractive front-end treatment. The Toronado's design arose in a free-expression competition organized by Olds in 1962. It became the marque's top model to date, and the equivalent of the Buick Riviera.

TOP-FLIGHT CREDENTIALS
The Toronado was brisk, poised, and accurate. Understeer and front-wheel scrabble were kept to a minimum, and the car handled like a compact. Acceleration was in the Jaguar sedan league, and flat out it could chew the tail feathers of a Hi-Po Mustang.

ENGINE
The torque converter was mounted behind the 425cid V8, and the gearbox under the left cylinder bank, with both connected by chain and sprocket. Hailed as unbreakable, this arrangement enabled the engine to be placed directly over the front wheels, resulting in near-perfect weight distribution.

FROM 1972 ON, TORONADOS WERE BUILT EXCLUSIVELY IN LANSING

THE TORONADO NAME CAME FROM A 1963 CHEVROLET SHOW CAR AND HAS NO KNOWN MEANING

INTERIOR

Standard equipment included Turbo Hydra-Matic tranny, power steering and brakes, Strato-bench front seat, de luxe armrests, rear cigarette lighters, foam seat cushions, a special chrome molding package, and interiors in vinyl, leather, or cloth.

THE TORONADO WAS MEANT TO COMBINE TRADITIONAL BIG-CAR POWER WITH OUTSTANDING HANDLING AND TRACTION

HIGH ENGINE TEMPERATURES AND THE HUGE ROCHESTER 4GC FOUR-BARREL CARB CAUSED MANY UNDERHOOD FIRES

DOORS WERE HEAVY AND DIFFICULT TO OPEN; BUILT-IN ASSISTANCE CAME IN 1967

INDIVIDUAL STYLE

The Toro was a dream-car design. Despite sharing a basic body with other GM models like the Riviera and Eldorado, it still emerged very separate and distinctive. *Automobile Quarterly* called it "logical, imaginative, and totally unique," and *Motor Trade* nominated it Car of the Year in 1966.

SPECIFICATIONS

MODEL 1967 Oldsmobile Toronado
PRODUCTION 21,790
BODY STYLE Two-door, five-seater coupe.
CONSTRUCTION Steel body and frame.
ENGINE 425cid V8.
POWER OUTPUT 385 bhp.
TRANSMISSION Three-speed Turbo Hydra-Matic automatic.
SUSPENSION *Front:* torsion bar; *Rear:* leaf springs with solid axle.
BRAKES Front and rear drums.
MAXIMUM SPEED 135 mph (217 km/h)
0–60 MPH (0–96 KM/H) 8.5 sec
A.F.C. 11 mpg (3.9 km/l)

GM'S FRONT-DRIVE FIRST

Offered only as a hardtop coupe, the Toronado was GM's break with the past and the first commitment to front-wheel drive, which would become a corporate theology by 1980.

C-PILLARS SWEEP GENTLY DOWNWARD, WHILE ROOF FLOWS SMOOTHLY INTO RAKISH FASTBACK SHAPE

CURVED BODY IS EMPOWERED BY BOLDLY FLARED WHEEL ARCHES; UNADORNED FRONT AND REAR TUCK CLEANLY AWAY

STANDARD RUBBER WAS 8.85/15

EVOLUTION OF THE OLDSMOBILE TORONADO

ONE OF THE MOST startling designs GM has ever come up with, and the first front-wheel drive car for 30 years, the Toronado didn't stay audacious for very long. As with so many other American machines of the era, it swelled, lost its individuality, and eventually lumbered into obscurity. But those first bewitching Toronados that left the Lansing plant in Michigan are a monument to a moment in time when the US auto industry could have led the world.

1967 OLDSMOBILE TORONADO

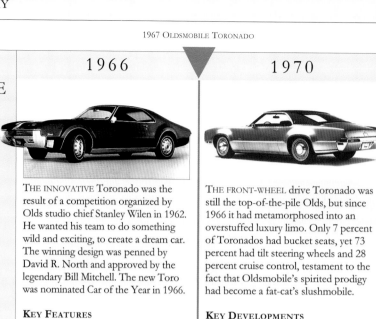

1966

THE INNOVATIVE Toronado was the result of a competition organized by Olds studio chief Stanley Wilen in 1962. He wanted his team to do something wild and exciting, to create a dream car. The winning design was penned by David R. North and approved by the legendary Bill Mitchell. The new Toro was nominated Car of the Year in 1966.

KEY FEATURES
• Unique retractable headlights
• Narrow horizontal grille
• Standard power steering and power brakes
• 425cid V8 standard
• Two trim levels – standard and de luxe
• Olds calendar year production peaks at 586,381

1970

THE FRONT-WHEEL drive Toronado was still the top-of-the-pile Olds, but since 1966 it had metamorphosed into an overstuffed luxury limo. Only 7 percent of Toronados had bucket seats, yet 73 percent had tilt steering wheels and 28 percent cruise control, testament to the fact that Oldsmobile's spirited prodigy had become a fat-cat's slushmobile.

KEY DEVELOPMENTS
• 455cid 370 bhp V8
• Turbo Hydra-Matic transmission, power steering, and power brakes standard
• Interior trims in vinyl, cloth, or leather
• Custom Toro outsells basic 10-to-1
• Sticker price $5,216

1972

BIGGER, HEAVIER, AND longer, the '72 Toro still had front-wheel drive but labored under the 1971 restyle, which made it look as if it had been squashed flat. The car was no longer sporty but pompous and plutocratic. It continued to sport the 455cid engine, but power was down to 250 bhp, and even more power emasculation was to follow.

KEY DEVELOPMENTS
• All Toronados now made exclusively in Lansing, Michigan
• Factory price $5,341
• Toronado Brougham sells 17,824
• Standard Toro sells 31,076
• 1972 is Oldsmobile's 75th year in the automobile business

1967 OLDSMOBILE
Toronado

MARQUE LEADER
The supreme Olds of the Sixties, the Toro was sophisticated both in its styling and underpinnings.

ALTHOUGH AN ENORMOUS CAR, THE TORONADO WAS A RAKISH FASTBACK

PRONOUNCED FLARED WHEEL ARCHES ARE THE FOCAL POINT OF THE TORO'S CURVED FUSELAGE

ROOF LINE TUMBLES SMOOTHLY DOWN TO REAR DECK

1977

THIS WAS A HARD YEAR. The 55 mph (88 km/h) speed limit had been around since 1974, catalytic converters were law in California, and gas had doubled in price since '72. GM offered a limited run of full-size cars with airbags, but buyers weren't interested. Cars clearly had to get smaller, but the 1977 Olds Toronado was still as big as they come.

KEY DEVELOPMENTS
• T-Top roof available
• Sledlike dimensions cause buyer resistance
• Public sees Toronado as just another socially irresponsible leviathan
• Front view panned as a return to "Detroit's worst stylistic excesses"

1979

ALTHOUGH STILL LARGE, lumbering, and none too economical, Olds' luxury coupe was now a lot smaller than the previous behemoth. The fully independent suspension gave a smooth ride but was overly soft with too much sway and bounce, and handling was no great shakes. The Toro was now a traditional and conservative prestige cruiser.

KEY DEVELOPMENTS
• 252cid V6 and 307cid V8 the best engines
• 350cid diesel engine encounters huge buyer resistance
• Fuel consumption of 15 mpg (5.3 km/l) is criticized
• Toro now very similar to Buick Riviera, which also went front-wheel drive in '79

1986

THE ALL-NEW TORO descendant, though still front-wheel drive, proved a sales debacle. Loyal Toronado buyers hated the shrunken styling, closely resembling other GM models such as the Riviera and Eldorado. The trimmed-down Toro still pitched heavily and its steering was woolly. It was marketed as a six-seater, but the back seat only had room for two.

KEY DEVELOPMENTS
• 231cid fuel-injected V6 is widely praised
• Gas mileage is up, at 20 mpg (27 km/l) average
• Trunk criticized for being too shallow
• "Bustle back" rear styling wins few friends
• Maximum horsepower a miserable 170 bhp

1991

NEW BODY PANELS in 1990 increased the car's length, in a deliberate reskin to revive flagging sales. Antilock braking, an option since 1988, became standard and a new "3800" engine, also launched in '88, added 15 bhp. In 1990 Toros gained a stronger 170 bhp V6 with electronically controlled four-speed automatic. But by 1992 Oldsmobile had dropped the car.

KEY DEVELOPMENTS
• Optional dashboard visual information center is panned by the press
• Driver's-side airbag introduced in 1990
• '90 body restyle improves looks, if not sales
• Fuel-injected V6 returns 22 mpg (7.8 km/l)
• Big recall in '92 for missing steering-rack bolts

UNFORTUNATE RESTYLE

It was a great shame that the Toronado lost its distinctive front. Bill Mitchell tried hard to defend its simplicity but lost out on the 1968 model, with its heavy rectangular grille.

STANDARD STICKER PRICE WAS $4,585; DE LUXE VERSIONS RAN TO $4,779

FRONT-WHEEL DRIVE WAS NOVEL IN 1966 BUT WOULD BECOME A COMPANY PHILOSOPHY FOR GM

1968 DODGE
Charger R/T

AN AGGRESSIVE, WARLIKE NAME FOR
THE ULTIMATE MACHOMOBILE

IN 1967, LYNDON JOHNSON was carpet-bombing Hanoi, and civil-rights unrest exploded in Detroit. Both abroad and at home, America was racked by confrontation. On the freeways, another battle was taking place – the horsepower wars of Ford, General Motors, and Chrysler.

The second-generation Dodge Charger from '68–'70 was the embodiment of aggression and marketed with bellicose abandon. Copywriters screamed that it was "American guts shaped like a Mach 2 jet on wheels." For $3,480 the Road and Track Charger came with beefed-up brakes and springs and an engine named after a gun – the Magnum 440 V8. Even the classic Coke-bottle shape had a predatorial meanness, with hooded lights and a sinister sneer. Bill Brownlie, Dodge's design chief, wanted "something extremely masculine that looked like it had been lifted off the Daytona track." One of the most handsome muscle cars of the Sixties, the Charger gave a generation of restless young Americans exactly what they wanted – a machine for waging war on the street.

— FILM CAR CHASES —

THE BADDIES GET
AIRBORNE IN *BULLITT*

IN THE 1968 THRILLER *Bullitt*, Steve McQueen tears around the Mission district of San Francisco in a dark green Mustang Fastback, chased by villains in a deadly black big-block '68 Charger R/T. Nine minutes of apocalyptic thunder and tire squeal make this the best car pursuit ever filmed, period. To take the battering from Frisco's roller-coaster streets, the Charger's suspension was modified and many parts were Magnafluxed to detect potentially fatal hairline cracks. McQueen did much of the driving himself, but the more dangerous leaps were done by stunt driver Bud Ekins. In the final scene the poor Charger was stuffed with TNT and impact detonators so it would explode in a sensational fireball when it careened into the dummy gasoline pumps. Chargers and their Challenger cousins also starred in *The Dukes of Hazzard*, *Vanishing Point*, and with Elvis Presley in *Speedway*.

THE DODGE
CHALLENGER
IN *VANISHING
POINT*

1968 DODGE CHARGER R/T

The ads called the Charger "a beautiful screamer" and were aimed at "a rugged type of individual." The profile is all-aggression, with shoulder-padded lines, mock vents on the doors, and twin exhausts that roared. Long and low with an evil brutality, the Charger was a design masterpiece that looked dramatic even when standing still. Few other American cars of the period possessed such harmony, balance, and poise.

PERFORMANCE EXTRAS
The R/T came with twin drainpipe exhausts, heavy-duty brakes, and F70x14 tires.

INSIDE STORY
Chargers were also for those who liked it "soft inside." All had a clock, heater, cigarette lighter, and illuminated ashtray as standard.

ENGINE

440cid V8s pushed out 375 bhp and could crack 60 mph (96 km/h) in under seven seconds. Ultra-potent 426cid Hemis could do it in five, courtesy of a staggering 425 bhp. The V8 engines were incredibly heavy, with the 426 weighing in at an outrageous 765 lb (347 kg).

INTERIOR

The cockpit is stark, masculine, and all-vinyl. Epic performance was read from the large tachometer and speedo, and vital functions from the temperature, oil, and voltage gauges. TorqueFlite three-speed automatic was standard.

SPECIFICATIONS

MODEL 1968 Dodge Charger R/T
PRODUCTION 96,100 (all Chargers)
BODY STYLE Two-door, four-seater fastback.
CONSTRUCTION Steel body and chassis.
ENGINE 426cid, 440cid V8s.
POWER OUTPUT 375–440 bhp.
TRANSMISSION Three-speed TorqueFlite automatic, optional four-speed manual.
SUSPENSION *Front:* torsion bars; *Rear:* leaf springs with live axle.
BRAKES Front and rear drums.
MAXIMUM SPEED 113–156 mph (182–251 km/h)
0–60 MPH (0–96 KM/H) 4.8–7 sec
A.F.C. 12–15 mpg (4.2–5.3 km/l)

MEAN GRILLE

The concealed front lights disappear under hinged covers to create a mean-looking front view.

TURN SIGNALS

Flashing turn signals facing the driver were built into the hood scoop.

POWER

The engine had buckets of stump-pulling torque that would rock the car from side to side when idle. The 426cid Hemi unit cost an eminently reasonable $605.

1968 MERCURY
Cougar

THE '67 COUGAR ALSO CAME OUT IN THIS DAN GURNEY SPECIAL-EDITION MODEL

THAT THE COUGAR WAS SUCH A RUNAWAY success is empirical proof that the mid-Sixties "pony car" market really was turbocharged. After all, this was just an upscale, stretched Mustang, and nobody thought that the Lincoln-Mercury small dealer base could cope anyway. But cope it did, selling 150,000 Cougars in its debut year of '67 and 110,000 in '68, as a performance-hungry America rushed to get a slice of Mercury's "untamed luxury."

Mercury fielded three Cougar models for '67: the base, the GT, and the XR-7. GTs had the bad-boy 390cid V8, and XR-7s the 289cid V8 with plush hide trim. The Cougar scooped *Motor Trend*'s Car of the Year award for '67 and Lincoln-Mercury boasted that it was "the best-equipped luxury sports car money can buy." Admirably plugging the gap between the Mustang and the T-Bird, the Cougar had European styling, American power, and a luxury options list as long as a Sears catalog.

INVIGORATING COUGAR
Lincoln-Mercury wanted to invigorate its image and return it to the hot-car days of the late Forties and early Fifties. The Cougar was a watershed car and revived its fortunes, blessing the rest of the range with an aura of performance and restrained luxury.

INTERIOR
All Cougars featured pony-car essentials like standard bucket seats, walnut-grain steering wheel, center console, and floor shift. Bench seats were available but seldom specified.

ENGINE
Standard fare for the '68 was the 210 bhp 302cid V8. Power could be gently upped by specifying a 230 brake version, or boosted with a variety of blocks up to the massive 335 bhp 428cid GT-E V8. Three-speed manual was standard, with four-speed manual and three-speed automatic options.

SOUPED-UP COUGAR
Cougars were converted to Group 2 configuration for Trans-American sedan racing, and included high-performance modifications, a stripped-out interior, and a four-speed Borg-Warner box.

REAR SEAT REMOVED

FRONT DISC BRAKES

SPECIFICATIONS
MODEL 1968 Mercury Cougar
PRODUCTION 113,726
BODY STYLE Two-door,
four-seater coupe.
CONSTRUCTION Steel unitary body.
ENGINE 302cid, 390cid, 428cid
V8s.
POWER OUTPUT 210–335 bhp.
TRANSMISSION Three-speed
manual, optional four-speed
manual, and three-speed
Merc-O-Matic automatic.
SUSPENSION *Front:* coil springs;
Rear: leaf springs.
BRAKES Front and rear drums;
optional front discs.
MAXIMUM SPEED 105–130 mph
(169–209 km/h)
0–60 MPH (0–96 KM/H)
17.3–10.2 sec
A.F.C. 16 mpg (5.7 km/l)

SIDE LIGHT
One of the only differences between the '67 and '68 models is the addition of this side marker light.

BRAKES
The dual hydraulic brake system allowed separate operation of front and rear brakes "for even more braking assurance." A warning light on the dashboard indicated pressure loss in either brake system.

1968 MERCURY COUGAR
With their Remington shaver grilles, concealed headlights, and blended-in bumpers, Cougars were good-looking cars. By 1972, yearly sales of the top-line XR-7 exceeded those of the cheapest Cougar, and in '74 the base model was dropped. For real performance, buyers opted for the GT-E package, with a colossal engine, twin hood scoops, steel wheels, quadruple exhausts, and heavy-duty suspension.

REAR VIEW
Sequential taillights à la T-Bird were now a standard Ford trademark, and the dual exhausts added to the aggressive rear view.

MALE MERCURY
"The relationship between a man and his car is a very special thing," opined the '67 Mercury sales brochure – no real surprise from a company that prided itself on making "the man's car."

HEADLIGHTS
The Cougar's disappearing headlights were hidden behind vacuum-powered slatted covers that opened automatically when the lights were turned on.

1969 CHEVROLET
Corvette Stingray

CHEVROLET AND CHECKERED FLAGS
REFLECT THE CAR'S RACING PEDIGREE

THE AUTOMOTIVE PRESS REALLY lashed into the '69 Shark, calling it a piece of junk, a low point in Corvette history, and the beginning of a new trend toward the image-and-gadget car. Instead of testing the Vette, *Car and Driver* magazine simply recited a litany of glitches and pronounced it "too dire to drive," sending ripples of rage through GM. To be frank, the '69 was not the best Vette ever. Styling was boisterous, trunk space vestigial, the seats had you sliding all over the place, and the general build was shoddy. Two great engines saved the day, the 327cid and three incarnations of the big-block 427. With the hottest L88 version hitting 60 mph (96 km/h) in five-and-a-half seconds and peaking at 160 mph (257 km/h), these were cars that were race-ready from the showroom floor. Despite the vitriol, the public liked their image, gadgets, and grunt, buying 38,762 of them, a production record unbroken for the next six years – empirical proof that, occasionally, car journalists do talk hot air.

ENGINE
If the stock 427 was not enough, there was always the 500 bhp ZL1, a 170 mph (274 km/h) racing option package. To discourage boy racers, no heater was installed in the ZL1; only two were ever sold to retail customers.

BIG DADDY
With the 427 unit, the Vette was the biggest, heaviest, fastest, thirstiest, cheapest, and most powerful sports car on the market.

SHARK-BASED DESIGN
GM chief Bill Mitchell was an admirer of sharks – "they are exciting to look at"– and wanted to design a car with similar lines. In 1960 a prototype car was made called the Mako Shark and the end result was the 1963 Sting Ray, reputedly Mitchell's favorite piece of work. A further prototype in 1966, the Mako Shark II, produced the 1968–72 generation of Stingray.

INTERIOR
A major drawback of the '69 was its sharply raked seats, which prevented the traditional Corvette arm-out-of-the-window pose. While the telescopic tilt column and leather trim were extras, the glove compartment had been introduced as standard in 1968.

STINGRAY BADGE
Chevy stopped calling its Vette the Sting Ray in 1968, but thought better of it in '69, reinstating the name as one word.

WHEELS
Wheel-rim width increased to 8 in (20 cm) in 1969, wide enough to support even fatter tires.

HEADLIGHTS
The '69 retained hidden headlights, but instead of being electrically operated they now worked off a vacuum to give slow but fluid illumination. In 1984 the electric system was reinstated.

SPECIFICATIONS

MODEL 1969 Chevrolet Corvette Stingray

PRODUCTION 38,762

BODY STYLE Two-seater sports and convertible

CONSTRUCTION Fiberglass, separate chassis.

ENGINE 327cid, 427cid V8s.

POWER OUTPUT 300–500 bhp.

TRANSMISSION Three-speed manual, optional four-speed manual, three-speed Turbo Hydra-Matic automatic.

SUSPENSION *Front:* upper and lower A-arms, coil springs; *Rear:* independent with transverse strut and leaf springs.

BRAKES Front and rear discs.

MAXIMUM SPEED 117–170 mph (188–274 km/h)

0–60 MPH (0–96 KM/H) 5.7–7.7 sec

A.F.C. 10 mpg (3.5 km/l)

1969 CHEVROLET CORVETTE STINGRAY

The Stingray filled its wheel wells very convincingly with an aggressive, menacing presence. Any similarity to the European sports cars that inspired the original Corvettes had by now withered away, replaced by a new, threatening personality. In the annals of motoring history, there is no car with more evil looks than this 1968–72 generation Corvette.

ROOF PANEL
Half of the '69 production were coupes with twin lift-off roof panels and a removable window – making this Stingray almost a convertible.

EXHAUST
The side-mounted exhaust system was an option only in 1969, but was withdrawn in 1970 because of excessive heat and noise.

The Seventies

Seventies America had more pressing concerns than protest. For the first time ever, the world's most affluent society was in the red. For a people weaned on plenty, the coming decade of debt would rattle America's confidence like nothing before.

CARS' LICENSE PLATES CELEBRATED AMERICA'S 200TH ANNIVERSARY

FOR AMERICANS and their cars, the Seventies were the end of an era. Popular resentment seethed on the streets. Watergate, crime, welfare dependency, and busing made many people anxious and angry. The United States, so powerful for so long, now seemed adrift, divided by race, class, sex, and war. As one pundit concisely put it: "Sometimes you get the feeling that nothing's gone right since John Kennedy died. We've had the Vietnam War, all the rioting, and now we can't even get any gas. Before America used to win everything, but now sometimes I think our sun has set."

Americans weren't worse off in the Seventies; it's just that their expectations of growing prosperity now seemed less well founded. The shining optimism of the Fifties and Sixties had waned, and nothing did more to blunt the nation's confidence than the economic malaise of '73–'74. Nixon devalued the dollar, productivity sagged, inflation and unemployment ballooned, and Uncle Sam could no longer cut it in world markets. The once mighty industrial engine had stalled, and commercial America seemed to do little more than buy and sell burgers and root-beer floats.

SLEAZE AT THE TOP
After Richard Nixon's post-Watergate resignation in 1974, no American official above the rank of dogcatcher would ever be trusted again.

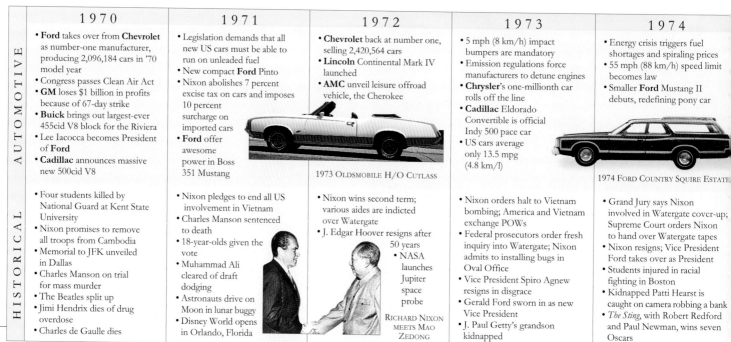

	1970	1971	1972	1973	1974
AUTOMOTIVE	• **Ford** takes over from **Chevrolet** as number-one manufacturer, producing 2,096,184 cars in '70 model year • Congress passes Clean Air Act • **GM** loses $1 billion in profits because of 67-day strike • **Buick** brings out largest-ever 455cid V8 block for the Riviera • Lee Iacocca becomes President of **Ford** • **Cadillac** announces massive new 500cid V8	• Legislation demands that all new US cars must be able to run on unleaded fuel • New compact **Ford** Pinto • Nixon abolishes 7 percent excise tax on cars and imposes 10 percent surcharge on imported cars • **Ford** offer awesome power in Boss 351 Mustang	• **Chevrolet** back at number one, selling 2,420,564 cars • **Lincoln** Continental Mark IV launched • **AMC** unveil leisure offroad vehicle, the Cherokee 1973 OLDSMOBILE H/O CUTLASS	• 5 mph (8 km/h) impact bumpers are mandatory • Emission regulations force manufacturers to detune engines • **Chrysler**'s one-millionth car rolls off the line • **Cadillac** Eldorado Convertible is official Indy 500 pace car • US cars average only 13.5 mpg (4.8 km/l)	• Energy crisis triggers fuel shortages and spiraling prices • 55 mph (88 km/h) speed limit becomes law • Smaller **Ford** Mustang II debuts, redefining pony car 1974 FORD COUNTRY SQUIRE ESTATE
HISTORICAL	• Four students killed by National Guard at Kent State University • Nixon promises to remove all troops from Cambodia • Memorial to JFK unveiled in Dallas • Charles Manson on trial for mass murder • The Beatles split up • Jimi Hendrix dies of drug overdose • Charles de Gaulle dies	• Nixon pledges to end all US involvement in Vietnam • Charles Manson sentenced to death • 18-year-olds given the vote • Muhammad Ali cleared of draft dodging • Astronauts drive on Moon in lunar buggy • Disney World opens in Orlando, Florida	• Nixon wins second term; various aides are indicted over Watergate • J. Edgar Hoover resigns after 50 years • NASA launches Jupiter space probe RICHARD NIXON MEETS MAO ZEDONG	• Nixon orders halt to Vietnam bombing; America and Vietnam exchange POWs • Federal prosecutors order fresh inquiry into Watergate; Nixon admits to installing bugs in Oval Office • Vice President Spiro Agnew resigns in disgrace • Gerald Ford sworn in as new Vice President • J. Paul Getty's grandson kidnapped	• Grand Jury says Nixon involved in Watergate cover-up; Supreme Court orders Nixon to hand over Watergate tapes • Nixon resigns; Vice President Ford takes over as President • Students injured in racial fighting in Boston • Kidnapped Patti Hearst is caught on camera robbing a bank • *The Sting*, with Robert Redford and Paul Newman, wins seven Oscars

FACT AND FICTION
Sam Peckinpah's 1972 film The Getaway *was a violent orgy of non-stop car crashes, mirroring the rising tide of crime and amorality that deeply worried Seventies America.*

SLUGGISH 'STANG
The 1973 Mustang was big, fat, and slow. Sales had been sliding since '67, and the third-generation car did nothing to stop the rot. Ford's pony car had changed, and not for the better.

But the most painful blow of all was the energy crisis. The Yom Kippur War in 1973 saw Arab nations raise oil prices by 387 percent, which, for a country like America that consumed so much of the stuff, was a nightmare best left undocumented. Gas station lines snaked into the horizon, and the last digit of license plates – odd or even – determined the days of the week you could buy gas. A blanket 55 mph (88 km/h) speed limit was a daily reminder that things were going horribly wrong. Retail prices hit the stratosphere, unemployment went off the charts, and inflation soared into double digits. A headline in the *Washington Post* articulated America's anxieties: "Things will get worse before they get worse."

While Watergate and Vietnam had shaken people's complacency, economic infirmity absolutely terrified them. The American Dream had been built on the foundations of prosperity and plenty, and without them that special vibrancy and energy that so characterized the postwar years simply evaporated. Economic progress had been America's opiate, helping to accelerate productivity, home ownership, education, and the consumer good life. And for all its vulgarity, the much-lambasted consumer culture did more than just improve the comfort of Americans.

1975	1976	1977	1978	1979
• Gas is double its 1972 price • Catalytic converters become law in California • Congress passes Energy Policy and Conservation Act • **Cadillac** offers fuel injection on 500cid V8 • **Chrysler** axes palatial Imperial • "Baby" **Cadillac** Seville appears, smallest Caddy for 50 years • Ill-fated **AMC** Pacer launched as **Chevy** Vega/**Ford** Pinto competition	• Bicentennial celebrations invigorate auto industry • **Chevrolet** launches all-new subcompact Chevette • Last **Cadillac** Eldorado Convertible rolls off the line • Sumptuous **Lincoln** Mark V debuts • **Lincoln-Mercury** introduces upgraded Capri II	• **GM** downsizes whole fleet as sop to superficial functionalism • **Ford** F-Series pickup is best-selling American vehicle • **Chevrolet** withdraws the Vega • **Buick** launches scaled-down aeroback-styled Century • **GM** pilots airbags to a less-than-enthusiastic public • **Ford** introduces new T-Bird at $2,700 less than old model	• **Ford** celebrates 75th anniversary • Third-best car sales ever recorded • Lee Iacocca fired as president of **Ford**; moves to Chrysler • Third-generation **Ford** Mustang appears • **Cadillac** includes **Oldsmobile** diesel engine option on Seville • **Buick** has turbo option • **Ford** offers Fairmont compact • **VW** first foreign manufacturer since 1930s to build cars in US	• Second energy crisis sends fuel prices through the roof • Car imports rise to 22.7 percent of US domestic car market • **Honda** opens first US plant
		SKATEBOARDING CRAZE		1979 DELOREAN
• Americans evacuate US embassy in Saigon • CIA claimed to have ordered Mafia contract to assassinate Fidel Castro • Soviet cosmonauts and American astronauts shake hands in space • Gerald Ford says he will run for President in '76, as does a former Governor of California, Ronald Reagan • Jack Nicholson stars in *One Flew Over the Cuckoo's Nest*	• One million people celebrate US bicentennial in Washington, DC • Jimmy Carter wins Democratic nomination • Gerald Ford and Jimmy Carter hold televised debate • Jimmy Carter elected President • US ambassador kidnapped and killed in Beirut • Concorde completes first commercial transatlantic supersonic flight	• Space shuttle makes maiden flight • Gary Gilmore executed • Martin Luther King Jr. awarded posthumous Medal of Freedom • New York blacked out by massive power failure, leading to looting and rioting • Roman Polanski jailed for sex with a 13-year-old • Elvis Presley dies • *Rocky* wins Oscar for best film • *Star Wars* is highest-grossing film	• US and USSR discuss a strategic arms limitation treaty (SALT) • President Carter hosts Israeli–Egyptian summit • Bugs found in US embassy in Moscow • Arkady Shavchenko, highest-ranking Soviet official at UN, defects • 900 US cultists die in mass suicide in Guyana • *Superman* draws record crowds	• Atomic leak at Three Mile Island • Brezhnev and Carter sign SALT agreement • Iranian terrorists storm US embassy in Tehran • John Wayne dies • Muhammad Ali retires

KEEPING IT BIG

Detroit kept producing vast shopping carts like the monster '73 Ford Country Squire. Although groaning under the weight of energy-absorbing bumpers, the Squire was only fitted with radial tires as an option.

FINAL FLOURISH

The 15 mpg (5.3 km/l) '75 Eldorado was Cadillac's final flourish before it succumbed to environmental pressures and fielded its compact new Seville, with a fuel-economy computer on board.

It also served to distract the nation from its social and political ills. With nothing to allay their angst, most Americans now lost faith in their institutions, politicians, security, and even their future. And the motor car, so long a barometer of America's health and a prescription for escape, was in the doldrums too. The mandarins of Motown had ignored the oil shocks and the rise of Japanese imports. The city of Detroit had deteriorated into urban anarchy and earned itself the soubriquet of "Murder City USA." The management and staff at GM's 15-story headquarters went to and fro via secured entrances and exits that side-stepped the car capital's mean streets. What was going wrong for America was going wrong for the auto industry. Within a few years Honda would open its first American car factory in Ohio, and GM would post its biggest loss in history – an astonishing $760 million. The automobile quickly became the symbol of all that was wrong with American consumerism. Pressure began to mount for the government to mandate changes in Detroit's dinosaurs. The offensive began with the Federal Clean Air Act of 1970, which demanded a 90 percent reduction in three exhaust pollutants. Then, in 1975, Congress passed the Energy Policy and Conservation Act, demanding that auto makers achieved an ambitious corporate average fuel economy of 27.5 mpg (9.7 km/l) within 10 years. Worse still, bumpers had to withstand 5 mph (8 km/h) impacts without damage, a regulatory bombshell that caused creative car design to come to a crashing halt.

The Manufacturers Respond

Safety and environmental responsibility shifted the traditional balance of power from design and styling to engineering and efficiency, the only way to meet the strictures of the gray-faced legislators. The Big Three increased their offerings in the compact and intermediate classes, and in '77 GM took the unprecedented step of downsizing its entire lineup. Americans believed that the country's problems could be solved if they consumed in a more responsible and frugal way. The square, stern lines of Seventies metal comforted them that they were doing the right thing. But it was a superficial and hollow functionalism. Cars like the

CAR KEYS AND CLUTCH

While Starsky and Hutch did battle with dark forces on the streets in their red-and-white Ford Torino, the media beamed the decay of America's social fabric straight into the nation's living rooms. But wasn't Huggy Bear one cool dude?

DISCO ESCAPISM
Behind the disco throb of Robert Stigwood's '78 Saturday Night Fever lay a subtext of aimless youth whose only escape from their daily tedium was dance. It highlighted the growing disaffection of a teen-beat generation trying to find some focus in a decade of unemployment and inflation.

NUCLEAR FALLOUT
In 1979 the Three Mile Island nuclear power plant in Pennsylvania almost went into meltdown because of gas trapped inside a crippled reactor. A combination of defective equipment and operator error rocked America's confidence in her nuclear prowess.

Mustang II, Dodge Aspen, Ford Torino, and Mercury Monterey were just pale facsimiles of the far superior imports from Germany and Japan.

For manufacturers accustomed to huge profit margins from epic cars, the anemic returns on "econoboxes" seemed paltry and quality nosedived as a result. GM had to recall 6.7 million cars for engine-mount problems, Ford Pintos exploded in a ball of flame when hit from behind, the Chevrolet Vega rusted so badly that it was nicknamed "the biodegradable car," and the gumdrop-shaped AMC Pacer had steering that would seize rock solid. Even the great white hope, General Motors' 350cid diesel,

would break its crankshaft and crack its block, and the THM 200 automatic gearbox to which it was mated was the object of more consumer complaints than any other automotive transmission in history.

The Price of Intervention

Sadly, quality wasn't the only casualty in the Seventies. American cars lost their guts, glitz, and glamour. The chromium fantasy was under siege from a hurricane of killjoy legislative interference and meddling. Detroit had no choice but to turn its back on the usual extravagance, producing instead a gaggle of dreary intermediates, compacts, and subcompacts with all the charisma of old shoes.

Detroit had been allowed to party unhindered for three decades and, left to its own devices, would have done precious little to improve exhaust emissions and fuel consumption. The massive governmental pressure of the Seventies caught car makers off guard, and their engineering couldn't cope. The Seventies were all about short-term fixes to long-term problems, which is why the new generation of clean-air cars stalled, ran roughly, and were generally second-rate. The American automobile had hit rock bottom.

1978 CAMARO Z-28
Chevrolet's second-generation Camaro was not its best incarnation. Weighing almost as much as a Caprice, it could manage only 15 mpg (5.3 km/l), rode like a tin tray full of dishes, and suffered squeaks, rattles, premature rust, and deteriorating paint.

1970 CHEVROLET
Monte Carlo

CHEVROLET ADS FOR THE MONTE CARLO PROMISED THAT "GOOD TASTE SPEAKS FOR ITSELF"

NOW THE WORLD'S LARGEST producer of motor vehicles, Chevrolet kicked off the Seventies with its Ford Thunderbird chaser, the 1970 Monte Carlo. Hailed as "action and elegance in a sporty personal luxury package," it was available only as a coupe and came with power front discs, Elm-Burl dash-panel inlays, and a choice of engines that ranged from the standard 350cid V8 to the Herculean SS 454.

At $3,123 in base form, it was cheap compared to the $5,000 needed to buy a Thunderbird. But the T-Bird had become as urbane as Dean Martin, and the Monte couldn't match the Ford's élan. Even so, despite a six-week strike that lost Chevrolet 100,000 sales, no less than 130,000 Monte Carlos found buyers. Compared to a mere 40,000 T-Birds, this made Chevy's new personal luxury confection a monster hit.

INTERIOR
The Monte Carlo's interior was Chevrolet's most luxurious for the year, but was criticized for having limited front and rear legroom. Center console and bucket seats were a $53 option, as was the special instrumentation package of tachometer, ammeter, and temperature gauge at $68.

RACE STYLING
The slippery aerodynamics and near perfect power-to-weight distribution turned the car into a fine high-performance machine.

ENGINE
The potent SS 454 option was a modest $147 and could catapult the Monte Carlo to 60 mph (96 km/h) in less than eight seconds, making it a favorite with short-track stock-car racers.

HIDDEN AERIAL
The radio aerial is hidden in the windshield.

VIA-537

RACING IMAGE
The sporty checkered flag motif didn't really reflect the Monte's market place. Owners were respectable, middle-aged types with five-bedroom houses in upscale neighborhoods.

SPECIFICATIONS

MODEL 1970 Chevrolet Monte Carlo

PRODUCTION 145,975

BODY STYLE Two-door, five-seater coupe.

CONSTRUCTION Steel body and chassis.

ENGINE 350cid, 400cid, 454cid V8s.

POWER OUTPUT 250–360 bhp.

TRANSMISSION Three-speed manual, optional two-speed Powerglide automatic, Turbo Hydra-Matic three-speed automatic.

SUSPENSION *Front:* coil springs; *Rear:* leaf springs.

BRAKES Front and rear drums.

MAXIMUM SPEED 115–132 mph (185–211 km/h)

0–60 MPH (0–96 KM/H) 8–14 sec

A.F.C. 15–20 mpg (5.3–7 km/l)

1970 CHEVROLET MONTE CARLO

The Monte Carlo used the same platform as the redesigned 1969 Pontiac Grand Prix. Stylistically, the long hood and short trunk promised performance and power. The single headlights were mounted in square-shaped housings, and the grid-textured grille was simple and unfussy. The smooth-centered wheel trims were not popular with buyers and, in '71, prettier, chromed mock-wire wheels were offered. A year later, a mild face-lift saw a wider grille and vertical parking lights placed inboard of the headlights.

REAR STABILITY
Another option available, and fitted on this car, was rear antisway bars.

VINYL OPTION
Black vinyl top was a $120 option. Buyers could also choose blue, dark gold, green, or white.

PILLAR
Prodigious rear pillar made city parking literally hit-or-miss.

WHEELBASE
The Monte Carlo was built to the smaller Chevelle's wheelbase, but was several inches longer.

1970 PLYMOUTH
'Cuda

THE 440-6 WAS A $250 'CUDA ENGINE OPTION

THE TOUGH-SOUNDING 1970s 'Cuda was one of the last flowerings of America's performance binge. Furiously fast, it was a totally new incarnation of the first '64 Barracuda and unashamedly aimed at psychopathic street-racers. Cynically, Plymouth even dubbed its belligerent model lineup "The Rapid Transit System."

The '70 Barracudas came in three styles – the 'Cuda was the performance model – and nine engine choices, topped by the outrageous 426cid Hemi. Chrysler's advertising men bellowed that the Hemi was "our angriest body wrapped around ol' King Kong hisself." But rising insurance rates and new emission standards meant that the muscle car was an endangered species. By 1973 Plymouth brochures showed a 'Cuda with a young married couple, complete with a baby in the smiling woman's arms. The party was well and truly over.

INTERIOR
'Cuda interiors were flamboyant, with body-hugging bucket seats, Hurst pistol-grip shifter, and wood-grain steering wheel. This model has the Rallye instrument cluster, with tachometer, oil pressure gauge, and 150 mph (241 km/h) speedo.

STYLING
Plymouth stylists kept the shape uncluttered, with tapered-in bumpers, concealed wipers, flush door handles, smooth overhangs, and subtly flared wheel arches.

AIR CLEANER
Unsilenced air cleaners such as this weren't allowed in California because of drive-by noise regulations.

SHAKER HOOD
The distinctive shaker hood, allowing the air cleaner space to vibrate through the top of the hood, was a standard 'Cuda feature.

COLOR CHOICE
'Cudas came in 18 strident colors, with funky names like "In Violet," "Lemon Twist," and "Vitamin C."

ENGINE
The 440cid "six-pack" Magnum motor cranked out 385 bhp and drank through three two-barrel Holley carbs, explaining the six-pack label. Base engine was a 383cid V8, which pushed out 335 horses.

1970 PLYMOUTH 'CUDA
The '70 'Cuda's crisp, taut styling is shared with the Dodge Challenger, and the classic long-hood/short-trunk design leaves you in no doubt that this is a pony car. Government legislation and hefty insurance rates ensured that this was the penultimate year of the big-engined Barracudas; after '71, the biggest block sold was a 340cid V8. By '74, total Barracudas sales for the year had slipped to just over 11,000, and it was axed before the '75 model year.

SPECIFICATIONS

MODEL 1970 Plymouth 'Cuda
PRODUCTION 19,515
BODY STYLE Two-door, four-seater coupe and convertible.
CONSTRUCTION Steel unitary body.
ENGINE 383cid, 426cid, 440cid V8s.
POWER OUTPUT 335–425 bhp.
TRANSMISSION Three-speed manual, optional four-speed manual, and three-speed TorqueFlite automatic.
SUSPENSION *Front:* torsion bars; *Rear:* leaf springs with live axle.
BRAKES Front discs, rear drums.
MAXIMUM SPEED 137–150 mph (220–241 km/h)
0–60 MPH (0–96 KM/H) 5.9–6.9 sec
A.F.C. 12–17 mpg (4.2–6 km/l)

PERFORMANCE PARTS
Super Stock springs and a heavy-duty Dana 60 rear axle were standard on all 440 'Cudas.

STRIPING
Optional inverted hockey stick graphics trumpeted engine size.

1971 BUICK
Riviera

THE '71 RIVIERA WAS A RADICAL MODEL FOR TRADITIONALLY CONSERVATIVE BUICK

THE '63 RIVIERA HAD BEEN one of Buick's best sellers, but by the late Sixties it was lagging far behind Ford's now-luxurious Thunderbird. Even so, the Riviera easily outsold its stablemate, the radical front-wheel drive Toronado, but for '71 Buick upped the stakes by unveiling a new Riviera that was a little bit special.

Handsome and dramatic, the "boat-tail," as it was nicknamed, had its stylistic roots in the split rear-window Sting Ray of '63. It was as elegant as Jackie Onassis and as hard-hitting as Muhammad Ali. Its base price was $5,251, undercutting the arch-rival T-Bird by a wide margin. Designer Bill Mitchell nominated it as his favorite car of all time and, while sales of Rivieras hardly went crazy, at last Buick had a flagship coupe that was the envy of the industry.

INTERIOR
Although the Seventies interior was plush and hedonistic, it was more than a little bit plasticky. After 1972, the rear seat could be split 60/40 – pretty neat for a coupe. The options list was infinite and you could swell the car's base

sticker price by a small fortune. Tilt steering wheel *(left)* was standard on the Riviera.

ENGINE
The Riviera came with GM's biggest mill, the mighty 455. The even hotter Gran Sport option made the huge V8 even smoother and quieter, and offered big-buck buyers a whopping 330 bhp. One reviewer said of the GS-engined car, "there's nothing better made on these shores."

SUPREME STOPPING POWER
The Riviera drew praise for its braking, helped by a Max Trac anti-skid option. The Riv could stop from 60 mph (96 km/h) in 135 ft (41 m), 40 ft (12 m) shorter than its rivals.

THIS IS THE 315 BHP ENGINE; A 330 BHP UNIT WAS AVAILABLE AT EXTRA COST

PILLARLESS STYLE
With the side windows down, Buick's bruiser was pillarless, further gracing those swooping lines.

SOFT-RAY TINTED GLASS HELPED KEEP THINGS COOL

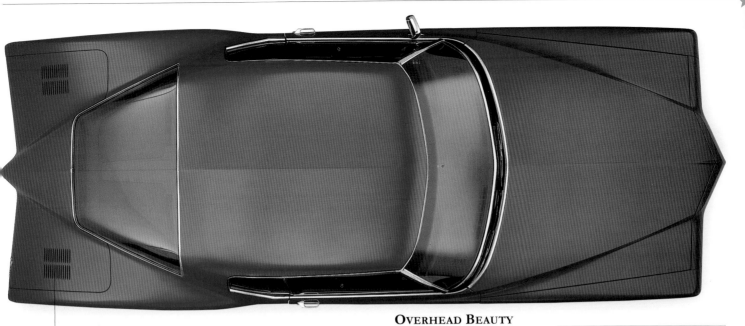

VENTS ARE PART OF THE AIR-CONDITIONING
SYSTEM AND UNIQUE TO '71 RIVIERAS

ELECTRIC TRUNK RELEASES ARE
NOT A MODERN PHENOMENON –
THEY WERE ON THE '71 RIVIERA'S
OPTIONS LIST

SEATING COULD BE
ALL-VINYL BENCH
SEATS WITH CUSTOM
TRIM OR FRONT BUCKETS

OVERHEAD BEAUTY

The Riviera's styling may
have been excessive, but it
still made a capacious five-
seater, despite the fastback
roof line and massive
rear window. The 122 in
(3.1 m) wheelbase made
the '71 boat-tail longer
than previous Rivieras.

CHUNKY REAR

The muscular rear flanks flow
into the boat-tail rear. Only a
Detroit stylist would graft a huge
chrome point to the back of a car.

WHEEL ARCHES WERE WIDE OPEN
AND WENT AGAINST THE TREND
FOR SKIRTED FENDERS

SPECIFICATIONS

MODEL 1971 Buick Riviera

PRODUCTION 33,810

BODY STYLE Two-door coupe.

CONSTRUCTION Steel body and
box-section chassis.

ENGINE 455cid V8.

POWER OUTPUT 315–330 bhp.

TRANSMISSION Three-speed Turbo
Hydra-Matic automatic.

SUSPENSION *Front:* independent
coil springs;
Rear: self-leveling pneumatic
bellows over shocks.

BRAKES Front discs, rear drums.

MAXIMUM SPEED 125 mph
(201 km/h)

0–60 MPH (0–96 KM/H) 8.4 sec

A.F.C. 12–15 mpg
(4.2–5.3 km/l)

EVOLUTION OF THE BUICK RIVIERA

THE RIVIERA TAG first appeared in 1949, when the Buick Roadmaster Riviera became the first pillarless hardtop convertible. During the Fifties, Buick spread the Riviera name all over the place, so, in 1955, for example, you could choose between a Buick Super Riviera, Roadmaster Riviera, Century Riviera, and Special Riviera. The name was so steadily misapplied that by 1971, the Riv had lost its special cachet and become just another land yacht.

1963

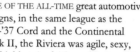

ONE OF THE ALL-TIME great automotive designs, in the same league as the '36–'37 Cord and the Continental Mark II, the Riviera was agile, sexy, and highly prized. The public loved it and it soon became the patriotic choice for Ivy League America. Even the Europeans raved. And with that 401cid V8 up front, it could even worry a Jag.

KEY FEATURES
• Standard 325 bhp 401cid V8 with optional 340 bhp 425cid V8
• Two-speed automatic transmission
• Open headlights
• Optional leather interior

1969

BY THE TIME THIS 1969 model hit the streets, the Riviera had gone through a number of rebirths. Headlights were hidden in '65, then exposed with a 1966 fastback redesign that lengthened the car, only to be hidden once more in '68. A GS (Gran Sport) option was introduced in 1965, and a larger power unit made available in 1967.

KEY DEVELOPMENTS
• Three-speed transmission from 1964
• 1966 redesign made car longer, heavier, and more curvaceous
• 1968 redesign of front view
• 360 bhp 430cid V8 unit available in 1967

1970

THE "NOW YOU SEE THEM, now you don't" headlights saga continued in this 1970 revamp; two years after they had been hidden away, out they came once more. Not that it did anything for the looks of the Riviera – the once "classic" styling had now been replaced by ugly retro design touches. A new power unit boosted output to 370 bhp.

KEY DEVELOPMENTS
• New 370 bhp 455cid V8 unit as standard
• Electronic skid-control braking system
• Now sitting on shortened Electra chassis
• All-new "E" body by Donald C. Laskey

1971 BUICK *Riviera*

VIEW FROM REARVIEW MIRROR WAS SLIGHTLY RESTRICTED

ONE-PIECE REAR WINDSHIELD CURVES DOWNWARD

DARING LINES SUCH AS THESE HAD NEVER BEFORE BEEN SEEN ON A PRODUCTION CAR

CONTROVERSIAL STYLING
The rear of the car was a Bill Mitchell "classic" that had his trademark stamped all over it, the GM supremo having also designed the rear of the '63 Sting Ray coupe. This time, however, critics were not so universal in their praise, and even Mitchell found himself having to defend the design.

LAND OF ENCHANTMENT
AMY • 589
72 NEW MEXICO USA

1977

After the "boat-tail" had been replaced by a more conventional design in 1974, there was little change until this downsizing in '77, which placed the Riviera on the same chassis as the new Electra. By this time, sales had fallen from nearly 43,000 in 1967 to 20,500, with the Riviera now regarded as just another standard luxury coupe.

KEY DEVELOPMENTS
• 1971 redesign with radical "boat-
  tail" styling, blunted slightly in 1973
• 1974 redesign is far more conventional
• 1977 model downsized
• 455cid V8 has reduced output
  of 205 bhp
• "Mac-Trac" antiwheelspin system

1979

The first front-wheel drive Buick Riviera entered the market in '79 on GM's newly downsized E-body platform. The body and mechanics were shared with the Cadillac Eldorado and Oldsmobile Toronado. Despite relatively minor styling changes from 1977, the public liked it and sales shot back up to nearly 53,000 units.

KEY DEVELOPMENTS
• Front-wheel drive
• Sporty T-type with a turbo V6 available
• Disc brakes all around
• Lightest Riviera yet

1986

Sales of the Riviera rose in 1981, then dropped back in '82. The first convertible was introduced in 1983, but poor sales saw it withdrawn after 1985. The standard Riviera had a slight frontal design change in 1984, and this was the prelude to a complete downsizing again in 1986. Hardly a successful move as sales plummeted 70 percent.

KEY DEVELOPMENTS
• Four-speed automatic gearbox
  introduced as standard in 1984
• Riviera convertible available 1983–85
• Downsized in 1986

1995

Sales hit an all-time low of just over 15,000 units in 1987, crashing to 8,625 a year later. Realizing that downsizing was probably not a good idea, Buick gave the 1989 Riviera an extra 11 in (28 cm) and a plusher ride; sales doubled. After falling sales in the early 1990s, this 1995 model harks back to the 1971–73 "boat-tail" era with its unusual yet stylish rear view.

KEY DEVELOPMENTS
• Improved V6 in 1988
• 1989 redesign lengthened the car at back
  and added more comfort and chrome
• ABS as standard in 1991
• 1995 redesign with tapered tail and regular
  V6 (205 bhp) and supercharged V6
  (225 bhp) engines

CLASSY THROUGHOUT
The lines of the boat-tail were not only beautiful at the rear, but were carried right through to the thrusting, pointed grille.

BUILT ON A REPUTATION
By 1971 the Riviera had become almost a caricature of itself, now bigger and brasher than it ever was before. It was the coupe in which to make a truly stunning entrance.

THE 455CID BLOCK COULD PUMP OUT 315 BHP AND REACH 60 (96 KM/H) IN 8.4 SECONDS

1971 CHEVROLET
Nova SS

Nova
ONE OF CHEVROLET'S SALES TRIUMPHS

THE NOVA NAME FIRST appeared in 1962 as the top-line model of Chevrolet's new Falcon-buster compact, the Chevy II. Evolving into a range in its own right, by '71 the Nova's Super Sport (SS) package was one of the smallest muscle cars ever fielded by Detroit. In an era when performance was on the wane, the diminutive banshee found plenty of friends among the budget drag-racing set. That strong 350cid V8 just happened to be a small-block Chevy, perfect for all those tweaky manifolds, carbs, headers, and distributors courtesy of a massive hop-up industry. Some pundits even went so far as hailing the Nova SS as the Seventies equivalent of the '57 Chevy.

Frisky, tough, and impudent, Chevy's giant-killer could easily double the legal limit and, with wide-profile rubber, body stripes, Strato bucket seats, and custom interior, the SS was a Nova to die for. Quick and rare, only 7,016 '71 Novas sported the magic SS badge. Performance iron died a death in '72, making these last-of-the-line '71s perfect candidates for the "Chevy Muscle Hall of Fame."

INTERIOR
Nova features included front armrests, antitheft steering wheel-column lock, and ignition key alarm system. The $328 SS package bought a sports steering wheel and special gauges, but air-conditioning and a center console were extra-cost options.

STYLING
The Nova's shell would last for 11 years and was shared with Buick, Oldsmobile, and Pontiac.

TIRES AND WHEELS
Wide-profile, bias-belted, white-lettered E70x14 tires were standard SS fare, but the handsome Sportmag five-spoke alloys were an $85 option.

PONY STYLING
Playing on the "long-hood-short-deck" phrase used so much in Sixties auto-writing, Nova ads in the Seventies ran the copyline "Long Hood, Short Price."

LIGHTS
Amber plastic lamp lenses were new for '71.

1971 CHEVROLET NOVA SS

Handsome, neat, and chaste, the Nova was a new breed of passenger car for the Seventies. Advertised as the "Not Too Small Car," it looked a lot like a scaled-down version of the Chevelle and debuted in this form in 1968 to rave reviews. Safety legislation hit Detroit hard, and the Nova was forced to carry side marker-lights, shoulder harnesses, rear window defogger, dual-circuit brakes, and impact-absorbing steering column.

BLOCK
In '71, the option of a four-cylinder block was withdrawn on the Nova. Not surprising, considering that out of 315,000 Nova sales in 1970, only 2,247 buyers chose a four.

ENGINE
The two- or four-barrel 350cid V8 ran on regular fuel and pushed out 270 ponies. At one point, Chevrolet planned to squeeze the massive 454cid V8 from the Chevelle into the Nova SS, but regrettably dropped the idea.

1971 OLDSMOBILE
4-4-2

OLDS
CHURNED
OUT 558,889
CARS IN '71

1971 WAS THE LAST OF THE 4-4-2's glory years. A performance package *par excellence*, it was GM's longest-lived muscle car, tracing its roots all the way back to the heady days of '64, when a 4-4-2 combo was made available for the Oldsmobile Cutlass F-85. Possibly some of the most refined slingshots ever to come from any GM division, 4-4-2s had looks, charisma, and brawn to spare. The 4-4-2 nomenclature stood for a four-barrel carb, four-speed manual transmission, and two exhausts. Olds cleverly raided the storeroom, using hotshot parts previously available only to police departments. The deal was cheap and the noise on the street shattering. At $3,551, the super-swift Hardtop Coupe came with a 455cid V8, Rallye suspension, Strato bucket seats, and a top whack of 120 mph (193 km/h). The 4-4-2 package might have run and run had it not hit the '71 fuel crisis head on. Which proved a shame – because it was to be a long time before power like this would be seen again.

INTERIOR
Despite the cheap-looking wood-grain-vinyl dash, the 4-4-2's cabin had a real race-car feel. Bucket seats, custom steering wheel, and Hurst Competition gearshift came as standard, but the sports console at $77 and Rallye pack with clock and tacho at $84 were extras.

ENGINE BLOCK
Oldsmobile never tired of proclaiming that its 455cid mill was the largest V8 ever placed in a production car.

FRONT REDESIGN
1971 saw a new two-piece grille with twin headlights as separate units.

SIDE LIGHTS
Huge dinner-plate side lights almost looked like front-end exhausts.

ENGINE
"Factory blueprinted to save you money," screamed the ads. The monster 455cid V8 was stock for 4-4-2s in '71, but it was its swan-song year, and power output would soon dwindle.

1971 OLDSMOBILE 4-4-2

From 1964 to '67, the 4-4-2 was simply a performance option that could be fitted into the F-85 line, but its growing popularity meant that in 1968 Olds decided to create a separate series for it in hardtop and convertible guises. Advertising literature espoused the 4-4-2's torquey credentials: "A hot new number. Police needed it, Olds built it, pursuit proved it." But despite legislation that curbed the 4-4-2's power output and led to the series being deleted after '71, the 4-4-2 had made its mark and put Oldsmobile well up there on the muscle-car map.

REAR DIFFERENTIAL
No less than eight rear-end ratios were offered, along with an optional antispin differential at $44.

REDUCED POWER
Sales literature pronounced that "4-4-2 performance is strictly top drawer," but in reality, unleaded fuel meant a performance penalty.

COLOR CHOICES
In addition to this "Viking Blue," Oldsmobile added "Bittersweet," "Lime Green," and "Saturn Gold" to its 1971 color range.

EXHAUST
Apart from the label, the twin drain-pipe exhausts were the only clue that you were trailing a wild man.

SPECIFICATIONS

MODEL 1971 Oldsmobile 4-4-2

PRODUCTION 7,589

BODY STYLE Two-door coupe and convertible.

CONSTRUCTION Steel body and chassis.

ENGINE 455cid V8.

POWER OUTPUT 340–350 bhp.

TRANSMISSION Three-speed manual, optional four-speed manual, three-speed Turbo Hydra-Matic automatic.

SUSPENSION *Front:* coil springs; *Rear:* leaf springs.

BRAKES Front discs, rear drums.

MAXIMUM SPEED 125 mph (201 km/h)

0–60 MPH (0–96 KM/H) 6.4 sec

A.F.C. 10–14 mpg (3.5–5 km/l)

1972 CHEVROLET
Camaro SS396

6,562 CAMAROS
HAD THE SS
PACKAGE IN '72

AFTER A SUCCESSFUL DEBUT in '67, the Camaro hit the deck in '72. Sluggish sales and a 174-day strike at the Lordstown, Ohio, plant meant Camaros were in short supply, and only 68,656 were produced that year. Worse still, 1,100 half-finished cars sitting on the assembly lines couldn't meet the impending '73 bumper impact laws, so GM was forced to junk the lot. There were some dark mutterings in GM boardrooms. Should the Camaro be canned?

1972 also saw the Super Sport (SS) package bow out. *Road & Track* magazine mourned its passing, hailing the SS396 as "the best car built in America in 1971." But the early Seventies were a bad trip for the automobile, and the Camaro would rise again; five years later it was selling over a quarter of a million units. This is one American icon that refuses to die.

CAMARO RACERS
NASCAR racing has always been an important showcase for manufacturers of performance iron. Chevy spent big bucks to become a performance heavyweight, and the Camaro, along with the Chevelle, was a successful racing model in the early '70s.

STYLING
The Camaro was designed using computer technology; the smooth horizontal surfaces blended together in an aerodynamically functional shape.

1972 CHEVROLET CAMARO SS396
The Camaro design survived an incredible 11 years without any serious alteration. It lured eyes and dollars away from the traditional European performance machines and became one of the most recognized American GTs of the Seventies. In addition to the SS package, Camaros could also be specified in Rally Sport (RS) and Z-28 performance guise.

WHEELS
Camaros came with five wheel-trim options.

REAR SPOILER
The SS and Z-28 packages got a rear-deck spoiler; the RS did not. The black rear panel is unique to the SS396.

GNL 158
SOUTH CAROLINA

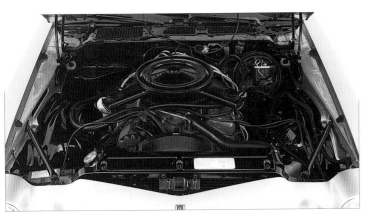

ENGINE
Camaros came with engines to suit all pockets. The entry-level V8 was just $96 more than the plodding straight six. This is the lively 396cid V8, but the legendary 454cid V8, with a mind-blowing 425 bhp, was definitely not for the fainthearted.

INTERIOR
Interior revisions for '72 were mostly confined to the door panels, which now included map bins and coin holders under the door handles. The high-back seats are a clue that this is a post-'70 model.

GOOD PRICE
Individuality and power came cheap in '72 – the SS package cost just $306 – though extras were plentiful. Under 5,000 owners chose a six compared to nearly 64,000 who opted for one of the V8 options.

COOL INTERIOR
Air-conditioning for the Camaro cost an additional $397.

EXTRA GRIP
Chevy dealers would even sell you spray-on liquid Tire Chain to improve traction on your Camaro, drag-race style.

SPECIFICATIONS

MODEL 1972 Chevrolet Camaro SS396

PRODUCTION 6,562 (SS)

BODY STYLE Two-door coupe.

CONSTRUCTION Steel body and chassis.

ENGINE 350cid, 396cid, 402cid V8s (SS).

POWER OUTPUT 240–330 bhp.

TRANSMISSION Three-speed manual, optional four-speed manual, and automatic.

SUSPENSION *Front:* coil springs; *Rear:* leaf springs.

BRAKES Front power discs and rear drums.

MAXIMUM SPEED 125 mph (201 km/h)

0–60 MPH (0–96 KM/H) 7.5 sec

A.F.C. 15 mpg (5.3 km/l)

1776 Bicentennial 1976
GNL 158
SOUTH CAROLINA

1972 LINCOLN
Continental Mark IV

INTERIOR
Standard equipment included a Cartier electric clock, wood dash, and a six-way power Twin Comfort lounge seat. Even so, it all felt a bit tacky and didn't have the uptown cachet of European imports.

THE MARK IV WAS LONGER AND WIDER THAN THE MARK III

IN 1972, $10,000 BOUGHT you TV detective Frank Cannon's corpulent Mark IV Continental, the luxury car fit to lock bumpers with Cadillac's finest. As big as they came and surprisingly fast, the all-new hunch-flanked body had a grille like the Rolls-Royce and distinctive, fake spare-wheel cover. Testers were unanimous in their praise for its power, luxury, and size, remarking that the Mark IV's hood "looks like an aircraft carrier landing-deck on final approach."

The list of luxury features was as long as a Manhattan phone directory – air-conditioning, six-by-six-way power seats, power windows, antenna, and door locks. And all standard. The air-con was about as complex and powerful as a Saturn rocket and, to please the legislators, under a hood the size of a baseball field nestled a forest of emission pipery. America may have wanted to kick the smog habit, but trim its waistline? Never.

SPACE AND COMFORT
A two-door in name, the Continental had room enough for five. The baroque interior is typical of the period, and the tiny "opera" window in the huge rear pillar became a Lincoln styling metaphor.

ENGINE
At 460cid, the Continental's V8 may have been Olympian, but it was still eclipsed by Cadillac's jumbo 500cid power plant that was around at the same time. The Mark IV block's power output for '72 was 224 bhp, a stark contrast to the 365 horses pushed out only a year before. Federal restrictions on power output had a lot to answer for.

COLOR CHOICE
The garish yellow is typical '70s, but all Mark IVs could be painted in a metallic hue for $127.

FRONT ASPECT
Shuttered headlights and heavyweight chrome bumper added to the car's presence.

───SPECIFICATIONS───

MODEL 1972 Lincoln Continental Mark IV
PRODUCTION 48,591 (1972)
BODY STYLE Two-door, five seater hardtop.
CONSTRUCTION Steel body and chassis.
ENGINE 460cid V8.
POWER OUTPUT 224 bhp.
TRANSMISSION Three-speed Select-Shift automatic.
SUSPENSION Helical coil front and rear.
BRAKES Front power discs, rear drums.
MAXIMUM SPEED 122 mph (196 km/h)
0–60 MPH (0–96 KM/H) 17.8 sec
A.F.C. 10 mpg (3.5 km/l)

1972 LINCOLN CONTINENTAL MARK IV

Rolls-Royce was mortally offended by the Continental's copy of their grille but didn't actually litigate. They wished they had because the grille went on to become a Lincoln trademark. The Mark IV offered more space for rear passengers and was the first Continental to incorporate an "opera" window into the rear pillar, albeit at a cost of $81.84.

LEATHER TRIMMINGS
Leather lounge seats were an option at $179.

REAR EXTRAS
TractionLok differential and high-ratio rear axle were both on the options list.

ROOF
The vinyl, leather-look roof was standard on all Mark IVs.

CONTINENTAL COVER
This had been a Lincoln styling trait since the early Mark Is.

TIRES
Standard rubber was 225/15 radials.

1973 PONTIAC
Trans Am

WITH THE BRAWNY TRANS AM, PONTIAC KEPT THE BRUTE-FORCE PERFORMANCE FLAG FLYING

IN THE SEVENTIES, FOR THE FIRST time in American history, the Government stepped in between the motor industry and consumers. With the 1973 oil crisis, the Big Three were ordered to tighten their belts. Automotive design came to a screaming halt, and the big-block Trans Am became the last of the really fast cars.

The muscular Firebird had been around since 1969 and, with its rounded bulges, looked as if its skin had been forced out by the strength underneath. Gas shortage or not, the public liked the 1973 Trans Am, and sales quadrupled. The 455 Super Duty V8 had a socially unacceptable horsepower of 310 and, while Pontiac bravely tried to ignore the killjoy legislation, someone remarked that their High Output 455 was the largest engine ever offered in a pony car. The game was up, and within months modifications to comply with emission regulations had brought power down to 290 bhp.

The hell-raising 455 soldiered on until 1976, and that athletic fastback body until '82. But the frenetic muscle years of 1967–73 had irretrievably passed, and those wonderful big-block banshees would never be seen again.

ELITE ENGINE
The big-block Trans Ams were Detroit's final salute to performance. The 455 Super Duty gave "the sort of acceleration that hasn't been seen in years." Reaching 60 mph (96 km/h) took under six seconds, and the engine could run all the way to 135 mph (217 km/h).

ACTION-MAN MACHINE
The Trans Am was seriously macho. *Car & Driver* called it "a hard-muscled, lightning-reflexed commando of a car."

SD ENGINE
The Super Duty V8 had cylinder heads that moved more air than Chrysler's famous Hemi. The 1973 455 SD could cover a quarter mile (0.4 km) in 13.8 seconds at 108 mph (174 km/h).

RACY FEATURES INCLUDED HOOD SCOOP AND FRONT AIR DAM, WHICH GAVE 50 LB (22.6 KG) OF DOWNFORCE AT HIGHWAY SPEEDS

SPECIFICATIONS

MODEL 1973 Pontiac Firebird
Trans Am

PRODUCTION 4,802

BODY STYLE Two-door, four-seater
fastback.

CONSTRUCTION Steel unitary body.

ENGINE 455cid V8.

POWER OUTPUT 250–300 bhp.

TRANSMISSION Four-speed manual
or three-speed Turbo Hydra-Matic
automatic.

SUSPENSION *Front:* coil springs;
Rear: leaf springs with live axle.

BRAKES Front discs, rear drums.

MAXIMUM SPEED 132 mph
(212 km/h)

0–60 MPH (0–96 KM/H) 5.4 sec

A.F.C. 17 mpg (6 km/l)

DASHBOARD

Second-edition
Trans Ams had a
standard engine-
turned dash insert,
Rally gauges, bucket
seats, and a Formula
steering wheel. The tach
was calibrated to a very
optimistic 8,000 rpm.

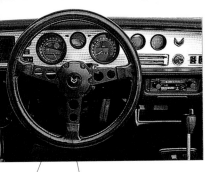

STANDARD EQUIPMENT INCLUDED
POWER STEERING, FRONT DISCS,
SAFE-T-TRACK DIFFERENTIAL,
AND DUAL EXHAUSTS

THE TRANS AM'S SPEEDO WAS
ONE OF DETROIT'S WILDEST,
MAXING AT AN UNTRUTHFUL
160 MPH (257 KM/H)

DECORATIVE DECAL

The "screaming chicken"
graphics gracing the hood
were new for 1973. Created
by stylist John Schinella, they
were a modern rendition of
the American Indian phoenix
symbol. Along with the rear-
facing "shaker" hood scoop,
the Trans Am now looked as
distinctive as it drove.

NAME IN DISPUTE

The Trans Am name was
"borrowed" from the Sports
Car Club of America, and
the SCCA threatened to sue unless
Pontiac paid a royalty of $5 per car.

ALTHOUGH BASED ON
CHEVY'S F-BODY CAMARO,
FIREBIRDS LOOKED AND
HANDLED MUCH BETTER

HONEYCOMB WHEELS, COLORED
SILVER, WERE A $36 OPTION

EVOLUTION OF THE PONTIAC FIREBIRD TRANS AM

DETROIT'S OLDEST WARRIOR, the Firebird is the only muscle car that's been in the brochures for 30 years. Based on the Camaro's F-body, the Firebird debuted in 1967, but the wild Trans Am didn't appear until '69. Surprisingly, there was little fanfare until the hot 1970 restyle. Steep insurance rates and a national shift away from performance iron didn't help sales, but in 1973, the year of the "screaming chicken" hood decal and Super Duty V8, Trans Ams left showrooms like heat-seeking missiles. Nearly killed off by GM, the T/A soldiered on into the emasculated '80s and '90s – the only affordable brute-performance car to survive recession, legislative lunacy, and every gas crisis going.

A '77 TRANS AM SETS THE PACE IN THE MOODY 1978 THRILLER *THE DRIVER*

1968

THE FIREBIRD MAY HAVE shared the Camaro's sheet metal, but mechanically they were miles apart. With five different mills, from 230 to 400cid, the Firebird was a classic example of the pony car building-block philosophy: come up with a sexy-looking machine and then hand the customer a colossal option list.

KEY FEATURES
• Introduced mid-1967
• Specially designed grille, taillights, and pleated seats
• Convertible available
• Firebird 400 has 325 bhp four-barrel powerhouse
• 82,560 sold in inaugural year

1971

THE SECOND-EDITION Trans Am had sexy curves oozing understated power. Quietly introduced in March 1969, the first Trans Am was sleek, sensual, and modern, and suited to only one body style – a quasi-fastback, which meant that the convertible was a thing of the past. The standard power unit was a potent 345 bhp Ram-Air III.

KEY DEVELOPMENTS
• Body package has rear spoiler, front-fende air extractors, and rear-facing hood scoop
• New front bumper grille molded out of Endura rubber
• Softened spring rates
• Convertible deleted

1973 PONTIAC *Trans Am*

REAR BUMPER
1973 was the "Year of the Bumper" because of Federal guidelines that rear bumpers should withstand low-speed impacts unscathed.

FLARED WHEEL ARCHES MADE THE TRANS AM LOOK EVEN TOUGHER

FOR 1973 THE FASTBACK BODYSHELL WAS GIVEN A FULL-WIDTH REAR-DECK SPOILER

BODY BY FISHER
Pontiac wanted customers to believe that Trans Am bodies were hand-built by an old-time carriage-maker.

DUAL EXHAUSTS WITH CHROME EXTENSIONS WERE STANDARD

TRANS AM

DLR 3055 D MASSACHUSETTS

1974

FOR 1974 THE TRANS AM looked even better. Styling changes included a shovel-nosed front, lower rear fender line, new grille inserts, and horizontal slotted taillights. Standard equipment was lavish, with Rally gauges, power steering, dual exhausts, and Rally II wheels. Factory price was $4,446, and 1974 model production was 10,255.

KEY DEVELOPMENTS
• Full-width rear deck-lid spoiler
• Special heavy-duty suspension
• Last year of Super Duty 455 without catalytic converter
  • Only 212 cars fitted with SD 455 and manual box

1987

THE MID-80S TRANS AM was smaller, lighter, more practical, and closer to its Camaro cousin. This year Trans Ams could have the Corvette 350cid V8, pushing out up to 225 horses, but only with automatic. Rally-tuned suspension improved the handling of V8 Birds dramatically. But even so, this was hardly the Trans Am's finest year.

KEY DEVELOPMENTS
• Four-cylinder Firebirds depart
• Nearly all engine choices shared with Camaro
• Optional 305cid V8 couldn't outrun a Toyota Supra
  • V6 version returns 7 km/l (20 mpg)

1991

AFTER A FRONT-END face-lift, the Trans Am looked a bit cluttered and gawky. In 1990 port injection went into the 305cid V8, making it marginally quicker, and in mid-1991 a convertible joined the coupe. Driver's-side airbags were now standard on all Firebirds, and dealers could install a new street-legal performance package to boost power output by up to 50 bhp.

KEY DEVELOPMENTS
• 350cid V8 returns 17 mpg (6 km/l)
• Even lower nose treatment
• Trans Am graphics appear on bottom of door
• Wide honeycomb wheels

1996

THE FOURTH-GENERATION car was a radical departure from the Eighties, with a partly composite plastic construction. Its swooping lines and raked screen echoed the Banshee concept car. Even the Europeans showed interest and, compared with sanitized Japanese sports coupes, the Firebird is still a disarming confection of American brawn.

KEY DEVELOPMENTS
• Available with V6 or V8
• Construction and safety features conform to EEC export regulations
• Handsome five-spoke alloy wheels
• Rear tea tray spoiler
• Deep cowcatcher nose

GRAPHIC APPEAL
The hood graphic actually helped sales and gave the Trans Am a unique identity.

SUPER DUTY V8 WAS AVAILABLE ONLY ON TRANS AMS AND FIREBIRD FORMULAS

EARLY SEVENTIES MODELS
From '71 to '73 the Trans Am rolled on in almost identical external guise. Underneath that vibrating scoop, power output of the 455 HO dropped to 250 bhp from the Super Duty's initial 310 horses.

DUAL BODY-COLORED MIRRORS WERE STANDARD, WITH REMOTE CONTROL ON DRIVER'S SIDE

NEW FRONT VALANCE PANEL WITH SMALL AIR DAM APPEARED IN 1973

PONTIAC

DLR **3055** D
MASSACHUSETTS

TRANS AM

1975 AMC
Pacer

THE PACER'S BODY WAS ALMOST AS WIDE AS IT WAS LONG

THE 1973 FUEL CRISIS HIT America's psyche harder than the Russians beating them into space in the Fifties. Cheap and unrestricted personal transportation had been a way of life, and then suddenly America faced the horrifying prospect of paying more than forty cents a gallon. Overnight, shares in car manufacturers became as popular as Richard Nixon.

Detroit's first response was to kill the muscle car dead. The second was to revive the "compact" and invent the "subcompact." AMC's 1975 Pacer, "the first wide small car," had the passenger compartment of a sedan, the nose of a European commuter shuttle, and no back end at all. Ironically, it wasn't even that economical, but America didn't notice because she was on a guilt trip, buying nearly 100,000 of the things in '75 alone.

PLANS DISRUPTED
Originally, AMC envisaged the Pacer to be fitted with a rotary engine that General Motors had been developing. When this was abandoned, the Pacer had to be redesigned to accommodate sixes instead.

GLASS
The Pacer had the largest glass area of any contemporary American sedan, making the $425 All Season air-conditioning option almost obligatory. Outward vision, though, was superb.

BUMPERS
Originally slated to use urethane bumpers, production Pacers were fitted with steel to save money.

WINDSHIELD
The aerodynamic windshield aided fuel economy and reduced interior noise.

HOOD
The sloping hood made for excellent driver visibility.

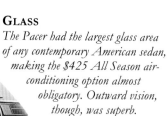

1977 AMC GREMLIN
The Gremlin was AMC's first entry into the subcompact market in 1970. Front-end, hood, and doors came from the compact Hornet. Total tooling costs were only $5 million, and an amazing 700,000 were sold.

STEERING
The Pacer's rack-and-pinion steering was one of the first available on a US car.

STYLING

Motor Trend *magazine called the Pacer's styling "the most innovative of all US small cars." Credit went to Richard Teague who also penned the '84 Jeep Cherokee.*

INTERIOR

Inside was stock Detroit, with sporty front bucket seats and cheesy polyurethane dash. But all that glass made it very hot.

1975 AMC PACER

In the mid-Seventies, the Pacer was sold as the last word; "the face of the car of the 21st century" bragged the ads. Happily, they were wrong. Pundits of the time called it a "football on wheels" and a "big frog." Surprisingly, the Pacer was never a cheap car. Add a few interior options and air-conditioning and you could easily be presenting the dealer with a check for $5,000.

INTERIOR SPACE

The Pacer had more headroom and legroom than the contemporary Chevelle or Torino and felt spacious.

── SPECIFICATIONS ──

MODEL 1975 AMC Pacer
PRODUCTION 72,158
BODY STYLE Three-door saloon.
CONSTRUCTION Steel unitary body.
ENGINE 232cid, 258cid sixes.
POWER OUTPUT 90–95 bhp.
TRANSMISSION Three-speed manual with optional overdrive, optional three-speed Torque-Command automatic.
SUSPENSION *Front:* coil springs; *Rear:* semielliptic leaf springs.
BRAKES Front discs, rear drums.
MAXIMUM SPEED 105 mph (169 km/h)
0–60 MPH (0–96 KM/H) 14 sec
A.F.C. 18–24 mpg (6.4–8.5 km/l)

1976 CADILLAC
Eldorado

THE LAST CONVERTIBLE ROLLED
OFF THE LINE ON APRIL 21 1976

BY 1976, CADILLACS HAD become so swollen that they plowed through corners, averaged 13 mpg (4.6 km/l), and were as quick off the line as an M24 tank. Despite a massive 500cid V8, output of the '76 Eldo was a lowly 190 bhp, with a glacial top speed of just 109 mph (175 km/h). Something had to change and Cadillac's response had been the '75 Seville.

But the '76 Eldo marked the end of an era for another reason – it was the last American convertible. Cadillac was the final automobile manufacturer to delete the ragtop from its model lineup and, when it made the announcement that the convertible was to be phased out at the end of '76, the market fought to buy up the last 200. People even tried to jump the line by claiming they were distantly related to Cadillac's founder. One 72-year-old man in Nebraska bought six. A grand American institution had quietly passed away.

FUNKY MIRROR
The heavy chrome adjustable door mirror was electrically operated and incorporated a thermometer that displayed the outside temperature.

HEADLIGHTS
Twilight Sentinel optio automatically turned the headlights on and off according to outside light conditions.

COLOR CHOICE
Eldos could be ordered in 21 body colors, with six convertible-top hues.

ENGINE ECONOMY
Raised compression ratios and a recalibrated carb gave the Eldo better fuel economy than might be expected from such a mammoth block.

INTERIOR
Technically advanced options were always Cadillac's forte. The Eldo was available with airbag, Dual Comfort front seats with fold-down armrests, and six-way power seat.

INTERIOR WOOD WAS CALLED "DISTRESSED PECAN GRAIN"

ALL ELDOS HAD A CATALYTIC CONVERTOR AS STANDARD

FAMILY ARMS
The Cadillac shield harks back to 1650 and the original French Cadillac family. French model names were used in '66 with the Calais and DeVille ranges.

ENGINE
Already strangled by emission pipery, the need to maximize every gallon meant that the big 500bhp V8 was embarrassingly lethargic. Even lower ratio rear axles were used to boost mileage. Hydro-Boost power brakes were needed to stop the 5,153 lb (2,337 kg) colossus.

SPECIFICATIONS

MODEL 1976 Cadillac Eldorado Convertible
PRODUCTION 14,000
BODY STYLE Two-door, six-seater convertible.
CONSTRUCTION Steel body and chassis.
ENGINE 500cid V8.
POWER OUTPUT 190 bhp.
TRANSMISSION Three-speed Hydra-Matic Turbo automatic.
SUSPENSION Front and rear independent coil springs with automatic level control.
BRAKES Four-wheel discs.
MAXIMUM SPEED 109 mph (175 km/h)
0–60 MPH (0–96 KM/H) 15.1 sec
A.F.C. 13 mpg (4.6 km/l)

1976 CADILLAC ELDORADO CONVERTIBLE
Big and slab-sided, the '76 Eldo used a front-wheel drive arrangement that had first been used on the '67 Eldorado and is still used today. The '76 Convertible had big vital statistics, measuring 225 in (5.7 m) long, 80 in (2 m) wide, and costing $10,354. Even so, such was the demand for these last convertibles that some changed hands for as much as $20,000. The last 200 off the production line were all-white, with white wheel covers.

FITTINGS
Interiors could be specified in Merlin Plaid, lush velour, Mansion Knit, or 11 types of Sierra Grain leather.

SAFETY RUBBER
These strips at the front and rear of the car were rubber crumple zones, designed to absorb impact in the event of a crash. Cadillac had some problems matching the rubber with the color on the rest of the car.

BRAKES
Eldorados had standard four-wheel discs with transistorized rear control.

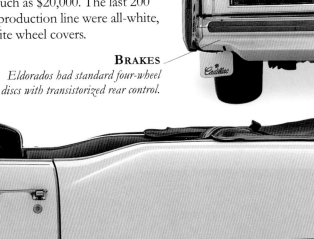

1978 CADILLAC
Seville

FORTUNE NAMED THE SEVILLE AS ONE OF US'S BEST-DESIGNED PRODUCTS

BY THE EARLY SEVENTIES, the corpulent Cadillac could average only 12 mpg (4 km/l). The energy crisis of '74 made the now-obese marque a soft target, and suddenly high-profile establishment figures were hastily trading in their "Standard of the World" gas-guzzlers for BMWs and Mercedes. A celebrated cartoon of the day showed a Caddy owner, hand over his eyes, pointing a gun at his doomed Eldorado.

The Cadillac Seville debuted in 1975. Marketed to compete with Mercedes and Jaguars, it was deliberately European in size, ride, handling, and economy. There was precious little ornamentation, and it was half a hood shorter than other Caddies. The press called it "the best Caddy for 26 years," even if it did have to suffer indignities like a diesel engine option and fuel-economy computer. A compromise car it may have been, but the downsized Caddy sold strongly from day one, and helped Cadillac weather the worst recession since 1958. For a small car, the Seville was a portent of big things to come.

AMERICA'S ENERGY CRISIS

IN MARCH 1974, AS A REPRISAL for those who had supported Israel during the Middle East war, the Organization of Petroleum Exporting Countries (OPEC) announced an oil embargo. With America soon in the grip of soaring fuel prices and frustrating lines at gas stations, President Nixon made a televised address, warning that the nation faced the worst energy crisis since World War II. The battle raged on under the Carter administration, which called for dramatic energy cuts to avert a "national catastrophe." In reaction to calls for fuel economy, GM was the first to introduce a line of diesel cars, claiming a 40 percent mileage advantage over gas-powered autos. As OPEC oil prices continued to rise, even luxury marques like Cadillac had to bow to America's new energy-conscious outlook.

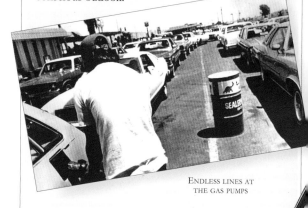

ENDLESS LINES AT THE GAS PUMPS

ENGINE
The '75 Seville's standard 350cid Oldsmobile-sourced V8 engine had electronic fuel injection, and was mounted on a steel subframe secured to the body with Isoflex damping cushions to reduce harshness and noise vibration. In 1978 came the addition of a 350cid diesel V8, which made history as the first Cadillac oil-burner.

INTERIOR
Interior trim was standard Dover cloth in seven colors, or optional Sierra Grain leather in 10 shades. A novel trip-computer option offered 11 digital displays indicating details such as fuel, inside and outside temperature, engine speed, and estimated arrival time. Standard equipment included tilt steering wheel, a fuel-monitoring system, power seats, and controlled-cycle wipers.

BODY FINISH
Bodies used Zincrometal to resist rust and were finished with a generous seven coats of paint.

BATTERY

The Seville used an innovative Delco "Freedom" battery that never needed filling.

SEVILLE SCRIPT

Other names were considered, such as Sierra, Medici, Minuet, Canterbury, Debonair, Camelot, Councillor, and Renaissance, but Seville was chosen, reinforcing the Cadillac bloodline.

SPECIFICATIONS

MODEL 1978 Cadillac Seville
PRODUCTION 56,985
BODY STYLE Four-door sedan.
CONSTRUCTION Steel unitary body.
ENGINE 350cid V8.
POWER OUTPUT 170 bhp.
TRANSMISSION Three-speed Turbo Hydra-Matic automatic.
SUSPENSION *Front:* coil springs; *Rear:* leaf springs with self-leveling ride.
BRAKES Front vented discs, rear drums.
MAXIMUM SPEED 115 mph (185 km/h)
0–60 MPH (0–96 KM/H) 11.5 sec
A.F.C. 15.5 mpg (5.5 km/l)

1978 CADILLAC SEVILLE

In 1970, Cadillac sent a questionnaire to Mercedes owners, asking them what they thought of the idea of a small Caddy. Launch price of the Seville was $13,700, $6,000 less than a comparable Mercedes, and sales of the new car rightly worried them. From May '75 to April '76, no fewer than 44,475 Sevilles were delivered, compared with 45,353 Mercedes.

REFINED REAR VIEW

The restrained rump is a far cry from the excess of full-sized Caddies, with a gently tapering rear deck, simple rear lamp and bumper treatment, hidden exhausts, and no rear overhang. Motor Trend called the Seville "delicate, bold, and pure."

RIDING IN STYLE

The Seville's plush interior reflects the tastes of 1,700 luxury-car owners who, in 1973, were invited to judge the prototype. Inside, there was a seat-belt warning that chimed rather than buzzed, since the device was meant to remind politely rather than order. Not content with such refinements, one oil sheikh cut and lengthened six Sevilles to accommodate desks, bars, and a sunroof.

FRONT VIEW

The Seville's front end is unmistakably Cadillac, with crosshatch grille and classic hood crest mascot. The computer-designed body derived from the Chevy Nova.

Future Classics

Having hit hard times, the US auto industry in the Nineties had no choice but to allow designers to build the cars of their dreams. Now there's nothing to eclipse the resurgent American car.

1987 CHEVROLET CAMARO IROC-Z CONVERTIBLE

THE WINDS OF CHANGE are howling through the corridors of Motor City. After the troughs of the '70s and '80s, the '90s mark the rebirth of the American car. Proof of Detroit innovation can be found in the latest Corvette, Camaro, Mustang, Viper, and Prowler – truly distinctive cars that promise the most exhilarating ride since the magic carpet.

Big is back, and so is horsepower. The last-of-the-line Chevy Impala SS seems a splendid reincarnation of the tire-smoking '60s screamer of the same name. And the Dodge Ram V10 is the King Kong of pickups. With the Viper's outrageous motor upfront, this was built for one purpose alone – having serious fun.

Enjoyment is back on the marketplace menu, enhanced by technology. Engines like Cadillac's 32-valve Northstar and Chrysler's 500cid V10 are epic power plants and among the best in the industry, while GM's fine electric EV1 is an instant classic and a half-billion-dollar technical *tour de force*. Motown is proving that the glory years could return, with talent to take on the best in Europe – and win.

In 10 years, auto buffs will be misty-eyed over the current Mustang and Corvette. Already the Prowler and the Viper are being feted as works of art, and the Cadillac STS is every bit as refined as a Jaguar sedan. Only the threat of the dreary "sports utility vehicle" could halt this remarkable renaissance. So come on, Detroit, keep giving us reasons to leave those stodgy imports alone.

1987 CHEVROLET CAMARO IROC-Z CONVERTIBLE
The IROC-Z Camaro boasted the Corvette's 350cid V8 with Rochester electronic fuel injection, dual exhausts, and a four-speed auto. Four-wheel discs and coil springs made it devastatingly quick, and unerringly accurate. 245 ponies meant top speed was a genuine 147 mph (237 km/h). Although dropped in 1991, the car is destined to become a collector's piece.

1990 CADILLAC ALLANTÉ
The $54,700 Pininfarina-badged Allanté was GM's priciest model ever, and the first front-drive American car with traction control. Its 200 bhp 273cid V8 gave the Mercedes-Benz SL the fright of its life. Bristling with technical innovations like sequential fuel injection, ABS, 10-way electric seats, and speed-dependent damping, the Allanté was a brave and bold step for Cadillac into the Nineties.

1992 DODGE VIPER R/T

No other car packs the sheer wallop of the Viper. A 450 bhp V10, top speed of 180 mph (290 km/h), and jackhammer acceleration make this a four-wheeled riot. Coming showroom-fresh from a mass-production car maker, the Viper makes no sense at all. Which is why it's so mischievously marvelous.

1993 FORD MUSTANG COBRA

The late-model Mustang may not look like an emergent classic, but it has always offered a large helping of serious heave. Not for nothing did all those Highway Patrol guys choose the 5-liter as a high-speed pursuit machine. That high-output 302 V8 could crack the standing quarter in 14 seconds dead and hit 60 (96 km/h) in 6.5. That's quick.

1995 BUICK RIVIERA COUPE

GM stylist Bill Porter fielded his glam, all-new Riviera in 1994. A svelte two-door five-seater, the new Riv is more than worthy of the hallowed name that's always been reserved for a very special kind of Buick. The current model, with its sloping roof line and tapering flanks, proves that Detroit has always been able to sculpt in steel.

1997 DODGE COPPERHEAD CONCEPT CAR

A Viper of a different color, the Dodge Copperhead Concept Car is a '90s Austin-Healey. Eager to trade on their street-rod heritage, Chrysler has joined in the worldwide sports-car renaissance with a bang. With coil springs, a high-output 220 bhp aluminum V6, and five-speed manual, it's anything but just a pretty face. In an engagingly humorous touch, the tires have been given a snakeskin tread.

1997 PLYMOUTH PROWLER

Chrysler's wild child, the Prowler looks drop-dead gorgeous and makes a noise like God clearing his throat. And, believe it or not, this is a production car you can buy straight off the showroom floor. Beautifully detailed, gloriously impractical, it's a complete and utter wow, and proof that once again Chrysler is pushing auto styling over the edge and back again.

INDEX

1958 EDSEL CORSAIR CONVERTIBLE

1957 FORD FAIRLANE TOWN SEDAN

1959 FORD FAIRLANE 500
GALAXIE CLUB VICTORIA

1964 OLDSMOBILE
F-85 DELUXE

1956 BUICK ROADMASTER

1957 MERCURY TURNPIKE CRUISER

ACKNOWLEDGMENTS

DORLING KINDERSLEY WOULD LIKE TO THANK
THE FOLLOWING:

Fay Singer for design assistance; Ashley Straw and Al Deane,
photographic assistants; Cricket, studio assistant; Jenny Glanville and
Kirstie Ashton Bell at Plough Studios; Cobra Studios, Manchester;
Pete Daniele and Paul Steiner for their patience and for sharing their
knowledge of American cars; Dave King (US photographer); Ken
McMahon at Pelican Graphics; Richmond Denton for the jacket
design; Terry Clarke; Barry Cunlisse of the AAC (NW); Michael
Farrington; Andy Greenfield of the Classic Corvette Club (UK); Peter
Grist of the Chrysler Corp. Club (UK); William (Bill) Greenwood of
the Cadillac Owners Club of Great Britain; Rockin' Roy Hunt; Geoff
Mitchell; DeVoe Moore, Tallahasee Car Museum, Tallahasee, Florida;
Colin Nolson; Tony Paton; Tony Powell at Powell Performance Cars;
David and Christine Smith; Dave and Rita Sword of the AAC; Marc
Tulpin (Belgian representative of the AAC); *Classic American* magazine;
Geoff Browne at *Classic Car Weekly*; Pooks motor bookshop and Cars
and Stripes for original advertising material and brochures; Philip
Blythe for supplying license plates; and Julie Rimington for compiling
the index.

DORLING KINDERSLEY WOULD LIKE TO THANK THE FOLLOWING
FOR ALLOWING THEIR CARS TO BE PHOTOGRAPHED:

Page 246 Peter Barber-Lomax; p. 250 DeVoe Moore, Tallahassee Car
Museum, Tallahassee, Florida; p. 254 The Rt. Hon. Greg Knight;
p. 258 Liam Kavanagh; p. 262 Tony Paton; p. 268 Colin Nolson;
p. 270 Nando Rossi; p. 272 John Skelton; p. 274 Alfie Orkin; p. 278
Mike and Margaret Collins; p. 280 Tallahassee Car Museum; p. 284
Dream Cars; p. 286 Dream Cars; p. 288 Steve Rogers; p. 290 Dream
Cars; p. 294 Mike and Margaret Collins; p. 296 Phil Townend; p. 298
Geoff Mitchell; p. 300 Geoff Cook; p. 302 Gavin and Robert Garrow;
p. 304 John Gardner; p. 306 Peter Morey; p. 308 Bob and Kath Silver;
p. 310 Garry Darby, American '50s Car Hire; p. 312 David Gough;
p. 316 Charles Booth; p. 318 Rockin' Roy Hunt – '50s aficionado;
p. 320 Steve Friend; p. 322 Rockin' Roy Hunt – '50s aficionado;
p. 328 Mark Surman; p. 330 Alex Greatwood; p. 334 David Stone;
p. 336 M. Fenwick; p. 338 Teddy Turner Collection; p. 342 Dream
Cars; p. 344 Tony Powell of Powell Performance Cars; p. 346 Michael
Farrington; p. 350 A & M Motors; p. 352 Maurice Harvey; p. 356
Geoff Mitchell; p. 358 Max and Beverly Floyd; p. 360 Colin Nolson;
p. 362 Benjamin Pollard of the Classic Corvette Club UK; p. 364
courtesy of Peter Rutt; p. 366 Roy Hamilton; p. 370 Barrie Cunliffe;
p. 374 Neil Crozier; p. 376 Lee Birmingham (dedicated to Bob
Richards of Newport Pagnell); p. 378 Rick and Rachel Bufton; p. 384
Alex Gunn; p. 386 Alan Tansley; p. 388 Tony Powell; p. 392 Tallahassee
Car Museum; p. 394 Cared for and cruised in by Mark Phillips; p. 396
Mike Webb; p. 398 Ian Hebditch and Jane Shepherd; p. 400 Roger
Wait; p. 404 Valerie Pratt; p. 406 Tim Buller; p. 408
William (Bill) Greenwood (COC of GB).

JACKET:
All Dorling Kindersley
photography except
front tl Quadrant Picture
Library and tr Aerospace
Publishing.

1960 FORD SUNLINER

PHOTOGRAPHIC CREDITS
l=left, r=right, t=top, c=center, a=above, b=below.
All photography by Matthew Ward except:
Andy Crawford: pp. 374–375
Dave King (London, UK): p. 237
Dave King (New York, US): pp. 250–253, 280–283, 392–393

THE PUBLISHER WOULD LIKE TO THANK THE FOLLOWING FOR
THEIR KIND PERMISSION TO REPRODUCE THE PHOTOGRAPHS:
The Advertising Archives: 233c, 318tr; **Archive Photos:** 253tl,
265br, 266bl, Reuters/Buick 391tr; **Neill Bruce:** 245tr, 326bl,
391tcr, Midland Motor Museum, Bridgnoth 277tl; The Peter Roberts
Collection c/o Neill Bruce 248cl, 249tr, 257tr, 261tcl, 277tcr, 293tcl,
348tcl, tcr, 349tl, tcr, 369tr, 390tc, 391tl, tcl, 410cr, 411tr; **Chrysler
Jeep Imports UK:** 411cr, b; The image is reproduced with kind
permission from **The Coca-Cola Company:** 236cl; **Bruce Coleman
Collection:** 378cl; "Sunbeam Mixmaster" Mixer, c.1955 United
States, chrome-plated metal, plastic, glass, **Cooper-Hewitt, National
Design Museum, Smithsonian Institution/Art Resource, NY:**
Museum Purchase through the Decorative Arts Association
Acquisition Fund 1993-150-1: photo by Dave King 300tr; **Corbis-
Bettmann:** 241tl, 244bl, 246cr, 264cr, 265cb, 346tr, 372tcr, cra, 373tcr,
404bl; **Corbis-Bettmann/UPI:** 234tr, 235b, 236bl, 238bl, 241tr,
242tr, 249tl, tcr, 252tl, 253tr, 265tl, 266tr, 277cl, 281c, 290cr, 325bl, br,
327tr, 341tcr, 344c, 360bl, 366cr, 372tcl, 380bc, 381bc, 383tr; Supplied
by **Ford Motor Company Limited:** 349tr, 369tcl; **©1978 GM Corp.:**
256tr, 257tl, 260tc, 261tl, 291cl, 292ca, 293tcr, tr, cr, 294tl, cr, 296tr,
cl, 300cr, 310cr, 315cl, 323cr, 325tl, tr, 350tl, 414bl, 415tl; **The Ronald
Grant Archives:** *The Driver* ©Twentieth Century Fox/EMI Films
Presentation 402cla, *The Getaway* ©Warner Brothers 381tl, *Tucker:
The Man and His Dream* ©Lucasfilm Ltd. 250tr, *Vanishing Point* ©Twentieth
Century Fox/Cupid Productions 374cr; **Hulton Getty:** 235cr, 264bc,
324cr, 380cr; Courtesy of **The Kobal Collection:** 245tl, 284tr, 286tr,
Bullitt ©Warner Brothers 374tr, *Christine* © Columbia 320tl, *Starsky
and Hutch* 382bl; **Ludvigsen Library:** 277tcl, 282tr, tl, 283tr, 292tc,
332tc, 333tcl, cr, 341tcl, tr, 354tr, 355tr, 362tr, 368tcl, 369tl, tcr, 372tr,
373tl, tcl, 383bl, 400c, 403tr, 410tl, 411cl, tl; **NASA:** 327tl; **National
Motor Museum, Beaulieu:** 248tc, tr, 249tcl, 265cr, 272c, 276tcr, tr,
328cl, 340tr, 358tr, 382tr, 390tl, 396tr, 403tl, N Wright 245br, 257tcr,
267br, 276tl, 280tr, 293tl, 327br, 332tr, 333tl, tcr, 340tl, tc, 341tl,
348tr, 349tcl, 355cr, 360ca, 368tcr, tr, 373tr, 380cb, 381tr, 391cl, 402tc,
tr, 403tl, tcr, 410bl; **Peter Newark's American Pictures:** 240bl, br,
244cr, 248tl, 249cr, 256tcr, 260tl, 314tr, 341cl, 354cl; **Popperfoto:**
408cra; **Pictorial Press, London:** 288tr; **Quadrant:** 252tr, 277tr,
362cl; Autocar 238tr, 239t; Auto Images 235tr; Simon Everet 260tr;
Mr Sol Feinstein 292tr; Phil Talbot 261tl, tcr, 267tr, 339tc, 390tr,
Trans-UN 403tcl; *Rex Features:* 265bl, 324bl, Jay Hirsch
242bl; SIPA *Saturday Night Fever* ©Paramount 383tl; **Phil
Talbot Car Photography:** 326cr.

NOTE
Every effort has been
made to trace the copyright
holders. Dorling Kindersley
apologizes for any unintentional
omissions and would be
pleased, in such cases, to add an
acknowledgment in future editions.